PHOENIX SQUADRON

www.rbooks.co.uk

Also by Rowland White

Vulcan 607

PHOENIX SQUADRON

HMS *Ark Royal*, Britain's last
topguns and the untold story of their
most extraordinary mission

Rowland White

BANTAM PRESS

LONDON • TORONTO • SYDNEY • AUCKLAND • JOHANNESBURG

TRANSWORLD PUBLISHERS
61–63 Uxbridge Road, London W5 5SA
A Random House Group Company
www.rbooks.co.uk

First published in Great Britain
in 2009 by Bantam Press
an imprint of Transworld Publishers

A CIP catalogue record for this book
is available from the British Library.

ISBN 9780593054505 (cased)
9780593054512 (tpb)

Addresses for Random House Group Ltd companies outside the UK
can be found at: www.randomhouse.co.uk
The Random House Group Ltd Reg. No. 954009

The Random House Group Limited supports The Forest Stewardship
Council (FSC), the leading international forest-certification organization. All our
titles that are printed on Greenpeace-approved FSC-certified paper carry the FSC logo.
Our paper procurement policy can be found at www.rbooks.co.uk/environment

Mixed Sources
Product group from well-managed
forests and other controlled sources
www.fsc.org Cert no. TT-COC-2139
© 1996 Forest Stewardship Council
FSC

Typeset in 11.5/14pt Sabon by
Falcon Oast Graphic Art Ltd.
Printed and bound in Great Britain by
CPI Mackays, Chatham, ME5 8TD

4 6 8 10 9 7 5 3

For Gardi

Contents

Author's Note   ix

Acknowledgements   xi

Maps   xviii

Section One: 1970   1

Section Two: 1971   9

Section Three: 1971   161

Section Four: 1972   197

Section Five: 1982   347

Postscript   353

Glossary   355

Bibliography   363

Appendix 1: Blackburn (Hawker Siddeley)
    Buccaneer S.2B cutaway   379

Appendix 2: McDonnell Douglas F-4K/F-4M
    Phantom II cutaway   383

Picture Acknowledgements   387

Index   389

Author's Note

Everything that follows is, to the best of my knowledge, a fair and accurate account of what happened. While I've drawn on a wide variety of different sources from home and abroad, everything included in *Phoenix Squadron* comes from them. As was the case with *Vulcan 607*, talking to such a large number of people, so many years after the event, threw up a few contradictions and anomalies. Where this occurred I have, by and large, been able to check what's been said against documentary sources. On the one or two occasions when this wasn't possible, I've tried to establish a reasonable consensus.

The presentation of the dialogue in the book needs some explanation. Where it appears in quotation marks it's either what I've been told, in interviews, was what was said by those who were there, or what's been reported in previous accounts, official, unofficial, published and unpublished. Where speech is in italics – often drawn from places like Flight Reference Cards – it represents genuine dialogue taken from another source to lend authenticity to a scene. Military operations depend on conformity and I hope it's fair to say that with crews following Standard Operational Procedures it's an accurate reflection of what was said at the time. Also in italics are characters' internal thoughts. As with direct speech, these are simply direct transcriptions of what participants told me they were thinking at the time.

I hope I've written an account that does justice to those who were there and which properly reflects the time and trouble people took to share their memories with me. Needless to say, the book's failings are my own.

R.W.
Nant-y-Feinen
September 2008

x

Acknowledgements

Phoenix Squadron could not have been written without the generous support of large numbers of people. When I first started skirting around the edges of the story, Doug Macdonald, then at the Fleet Air Arm Association, proved to be the key that unlocked the door. Doug has been tireless and inventive in his efforts to help me reach the people I needed to speak to. That he was an Observer with 892 Naval Air Squadron and aboard *Ark Royal* when the story unfolded was the stroke of good fortune upon which a project like this can depend. I'm extremely grateful to him and to his Fleet Air Arm Officers' Association colleague Paul Waterhouse. Doug steered me towards Carl Davis, Steve Park, Colin 'Boots' Walkinshaw and Mike Lucas, the aircrews who flew the mission over British Honduras. Without their willing and generous participation the book would have foundered early. I should make special mention of Mike's grace in putting up with a third interview late on a Friday night after I managed to delete his second by mistake.

Of similar importance was Rear Admiral John Roberts, *Ark*'s Captain throughout the period. John could not have been a more charming interviewee despite enduring repeated visits and endless questions. The time spent with him proved to be crucial.

As the project took root, need for information grew. John

Ford was tireless in trying to help me try to bring to life flying operations aboard *Ark Royal*. I've leant heavily on the detailed notes and careful explanation – not to mention vivid descriptions – John provided.

My contact with members of Carl Davis's Buccaneer squadron wasn't limited to the four men who flew over Belize International. I was helped by a number of others. Chief among these was Pete Lewis, who flew one of the tankers in support of the mission. Dally Mankellow and Ron Sandry – who supplied a valuable insight into the work of 809's engineering team – also willingly shared their memories.

But I didn't stop with the Buccaneers. Nick Kerr, then Boss of *Ark*'s Phantom squadron, was an early supporter of the book. Along with a wealth of material from Doug Macdonald, Nick's strong opinions and colourful recollections helped open a door on 892 NAS, a unit that was unique in British aviation history. Adding flesh to the bones were Jerry Granger-Holcombe, Nigel Charles, John Froggatt, Harry O'Grady and John Dixon. I'm thankful to them all. I was also lucky to meet Lionel Smith, who not only described the complexity of the engineering challenge presented by the Phantom, but also took the time to provide me with some of the outstanding colour photographs he took while on board *Ark Royal*.

There were two other frontline units on board *Ark Royal* at the time and Ed Featherstone and Guy Holman took the time to talk to me about life on the Sea King and Gannet squadrons respectively. Both added greatly to the big picture.

Others who were on board *Ark* in 1971–72 helped me flesh out other departments of the ship. Vice Admiral Mike Gretton, Rear Admiral Ewan Maclean and Rear Admiral Mike Simpson cast their minds back on my behalf. So too did Admiral Sir John Treacher, Admiral Sir Raymond Lygo and Rear Admiral Nick Goodhart and all provided valuable material for the book.

The story continued to grow and so too did the list of ex-naval officers I began to pester. I was fortunate that Captain

David Roome, Pete Sheppard, Mike Cunningham and Dom Malcolmson were all happy to talk.

A special mention should go to Brigadier General Dick Lord, who, despite having left the Royal Navy by the time the story in *Phoenix Squadron* begins, ended up making a hugely important contribution to the story. I took advantage of a trip to South Africa to meet Dick. It proved to be a privilege.

Although the focus of this story, the Navy were not the only branch of the British armed forces involved in the crisis of 1972. And I was greeted with similar hospitality and enthusiasm by those who, at the time, had been in the Army and Air Force. Former Grenadier Guards officers Richard Besly and Richard Corkran both had vivid memories of their time in Belize and they were of great benefit to me in trying to draw a richer picture of events. Alongside them, Robert Woodfield took time to talk to me and show me around the Grenadiers' archives. And for an RAF perspective I'm indebted to Martin Hooker, who recalled the role played by the RAF Regiment and showed me around their museum at RAF Honington, and to Glen Beavis, webmaster of www.rafregiment.net, who steered me towards a number of RAF Regiment veterans with memories of British Honduras. With respect to the flying side, I'm grateful to Simon Baldwin, who put me in touch with Terry Cairns, who steered me towards John Morgan. John provided me with a fascinating and detailed insight into life on a Canberra reconnaissance squadron and its involvement in the 1972 crisis.

Trying to capture the uncertainty and anxiety of the diplomatic story was always going to be vital. I was exceptionally lucky to be able to talk to the two men on the ground, Sir Richard Posnett, the incoming Governor of British Honduras, and John Weymes, then British Consul to Guatemala. Without them the military side of the story would have been isolated in an unsatisfactory vacuum.

There were others in Central America who brought a unique and non-British perspective to events. In Belize, I was welcomed by Ambassadors David Gibson and James Murphy.

Ambassador Murphy also generously gave me copies of his books on the history of what's currently being referred to as the 'differendum' between Belize and Guatemala. Carl and Mary Faulkner were also perfect hosts and painted a vivid picture of expatriate life in 1972 Belize City. In helping set up my trip to Belize and warning people of my impending arrival, I have to thank Lou Ann Burns of the Belize Embassy in London. Lou Ann was enthusiastic and encouraging from the moment she was unlucky enough to pick up the phone and her help ensured that my visit was worthwhile. Thanks too to Peter Eltringham, author of the *Rough Guide to Belize*, for helping point me in the right direction.

Iain Stewart, who wrote the *Rough Guide to Guatemala*, performed a similar role in Guatemala. In introducing me to Mike Shawcross, he could not have put me in the hands of a more generous, helpful or interesting guide to a fascinating country. Mike put me up in his home and, without him, I shudder to think of how pointless my days spent in Guatemala might have been. Mike introduced me to his friend Dennis Wheeler and, somehow, in the three days I was in Guatemala, got me in through the doors of the Guatemalan Ministry of Foreign Affairs, to meet Roberto Palermo, the Guatemalan government minister who had responsibility for Belize. I'm grateful to Dennis and to Señor Palermo for sharing their memories with me.

A special mention needs to go to Mario Overall of the Latin American Aviation Historical Society. Not only has Mario written extensively about the Guatemalan Air Force, but he patiently answered scores of questions and found answers where he didn't have them to hand. I leaned heavily on his deep knowledge and access. I remain amazed that Mario was able to arrange for me to meet him inside La Aurora air force base. It was the most unexpected part of my trip to Guatemala. And immensely valuable.

In trying to place the story in context I cast the net wide and there were a number of people in the United States who contributed to a story that, of course, took place in America's backyard. Chief among these was Brigadier-General Wallace Green who was kind enough to talk to me at length, despite, I suspect, wondering why I was interested in such an obscure corner of American history. In helping to illuminate other aspects of American involvement, I'm grateful to Captain Dan Pederson USN – and to the author Robert K. Wilcox for putting me in touch with him – and to Lieutenant Toby Buschmann USN. A handful of other greatly respected American writers were also generous in their support of my efforts and thanks go to Stephen Coonts, Robert F. Dorr, Dan Hagedorn and Wayne Mutza. Nor was overseas involvement limited to the US, and Heinz Forsmann was kind enough to talk to me about his time with the Marineflieger, the German Naval Air Arm.

In my efforts to gain access to the right archives and documents I was given vital assistance. At the Fleet Air Arm Museum, Catherine Cooper could not have been more supportive and helped me dig up real treasure. Dr Malcolm Llewellyn-Jones of the Navy Historical Branch tracked down some important documents and pushed through a Freedom of Information request to get them declassified for me. At the Foreign and Commonwealth Office, Matthew Forbes was kind enough to do the same thing. His efforts too revealed key pieces of information. Sebastian Cox of the Air Historical Branch also helped me track down key documents. And, in Belize, Charles Gibson allowed me to run riot in the Belize National Archive in Belmopan – and in doing so, I think, break all the normal rules. His help, too, yielded a handful of enormously important documents. Lastly, Professor Peter Hennessy helped point me in the direction of Vice Admiral Sir Louis Le Bailly. Sir Louis took the time to enlighten me on goings-on within the Chiefs of the Defence Staff Committee meetings.

The most memorable part of the research for the book was, without a shadow of doubt, a trip to Thunder City in Cape Town to fly in both a Hunter and a Buccaneer. I'm enormously grateful to their owner, Mike Beachy Head, for generously helping to make this possible, and to Ulf Spindler and to my pilot Ian Pringle for their time and effort while I was there. The experience was incredible – and invaluable in helping me gain a feel for fast jet flying.

Once again Lalla Hitchings waded through hours of arcane conversation in transcribing the interviews for the book. Without Lalla, this book simply wouldn't have seen the light of day. I'm incredibly lucky to have found such an outstanding collaborator. I was introduced to Lalla by my friend James Holland. And James too has been a source of great encouragement along the way.

My agent, Mark Lucas, while suggesting that I had 'a job on my hands', was encouraging from the outset, when the project existed as little more than an eagerness to write a book about *Ark Royal*. Showing equal faith – and in the absence of anything to go on other than my own enthusiasm, faith is what it was – was my publisher at Transworld, Bill Scott-Kerr. If Bill had any doubts he kept them to himself and gave me free rein. In Mark and Bill I'm working with a team who have the best understanding of this kind of book that any author could possibly hope for. I'm fortunate to be working with them both.

At Transworld, Bill works alongside a brilliant and dedicated group of people. As I write, the production, marketing, sales, rights and publicity teams are already swinging into action behind *Phoenix Squadron*. I'm grateful to them all for their hard work on the book's behalf. Particular mention must go to Stephen Mulcahey for designing such a striking jacket and to my copy-editor, Mark Handsley, whose careful work on the manuscript helps save me from embarrassment.

I've tried to fit writing in alongside my day job. I haven't always been successful in doing that. Most bosses would have been unable to hide their concern over such a time-consuming and distracting piece of moonlighting, but Helen Fraser, Tom Weldon and Louise Moore at Penguin could not have been more patient or understanding. Their care and thoughtfulness has been neither unnoticed nor unappreciated, even when it must have seemed to them that my focus was somewhere else entirely. Without their support it wouldn't have been possible to write the book.

If I'm honest, I can't say that my children Rory and Jemima were much help at all. Although they did remind me from time to time of what was really important. They shared that role with my wife Lucy, for whom I have to reserve my biggest thank you. I could never have done this without your selflessness and support. You kept the world away when I needed you to. I can only wonder at what you endured in doing so and marvel at your strength and kindness. You're more than I deserve. So, until next time . . .

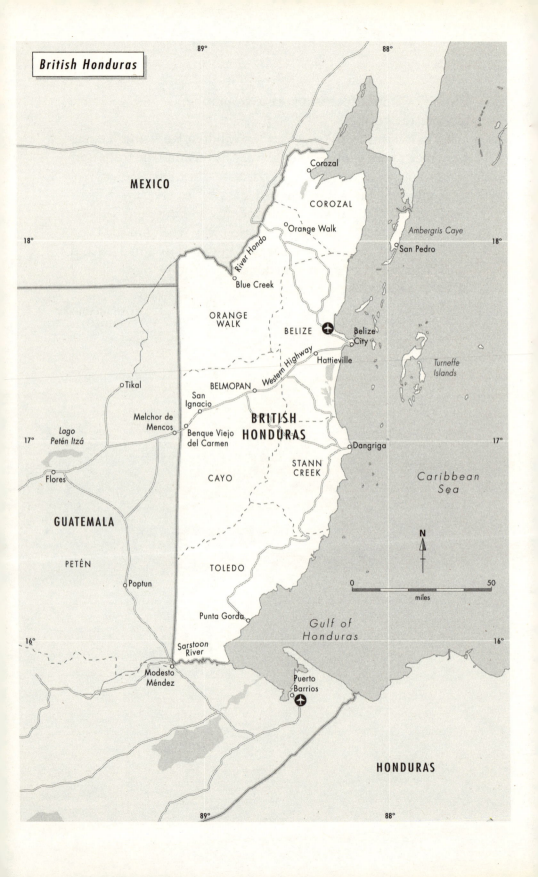

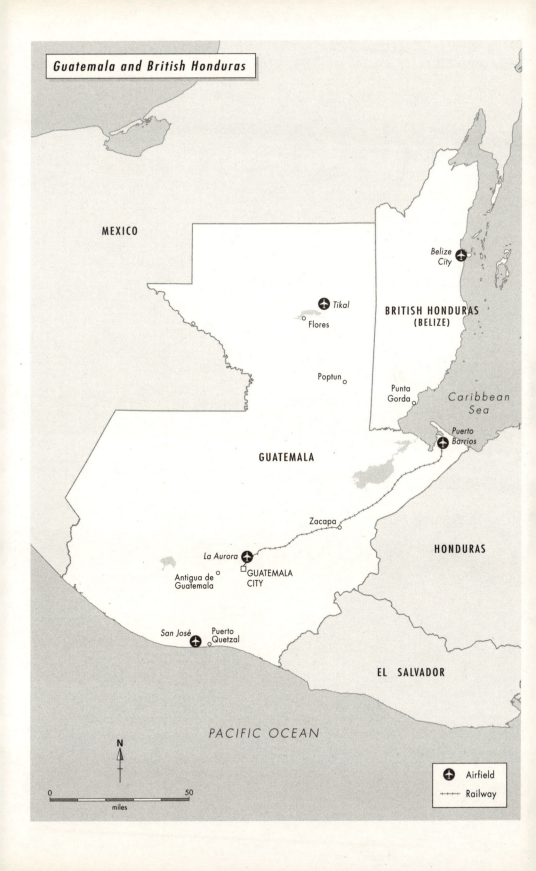

Guatemala and British Honduras

MEXICO

Belize City ✈

BRITISH HONDURAS
(BELIZE)

✈ Tikal

○ Flores

Poptun ○

Punta
Gorda ○

Caribbean
Sea

GUATEMALA

✈ Puerto
Barrios

Zacapa ○

HONDURAS

La Aurora ✈
Antigua de
Guatemala ○
□ GUATEMALA
CITY

San José ✈ ○ Puerto
Quetzal

EL SALVADOR

PACIFIC OCEAN

N

0   50
miles

✈ Airfield
+—+—+ Railway

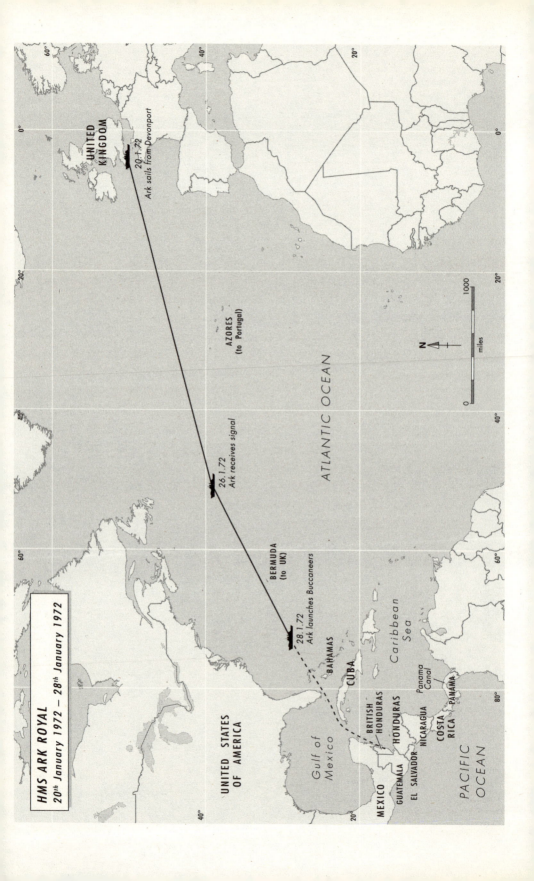

HMS ARK ROYAL
20th January 1972 – 28th January 1972

UNITED KINGDOM

20.1.72
Ark sails from Devonport

ATLANTIC OCEAN

AZORES
(to Portugal)

26.1.72
Ark receives signal

BERMUDA
(to UK)

28.1.72
Ark launches Buccaneers

UNITED STATES
OF AMERICA

Gulf of
Mexico

BAHAMAS

CUBA

Caribbean
Sea

MEXICO

GUATEMALA

EL SALVADOR

BRITISH
HONDURAS

HONDURAS

NICARAGUA

COSTA
RICA

PANAMA

Panama
Canal

PACIFIC
OCEAN

N

miles

0   1000

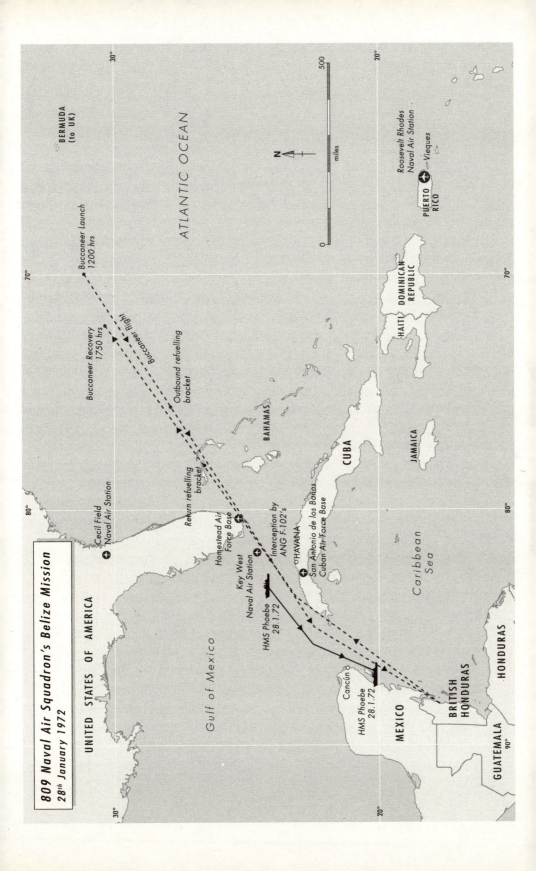

809 Naval Air Squadron's Belize Mission
28th January 1972

UNITED STATES OF AMERICA

Gulf of Mexico

Cecil Field
Naval Air Station

Homestead Air
Force Base

Key West
Naval Air Station

HMS Phoebe
28.1.72

Interception by
ANG F.102's

HAVANA

San Antonio de los Baños
Cuban Air Force Base

CUBA

Return refuelling
bracket

Outbound refuelling
bracket

Buccaneer flight

Buccaneer Recovery
1750 hrs

Buccaneer Launch
1200 hrs

ATLANTIC OCEAN

BERMUDA
(to UK)

BAHAMAS

JAMAICA

Caribbean
Sea

HMS Phoebe
28.1.72

Cancún

MEXICO

BRITISH
HONDURAS

GUATEMALA

HONDURAS

HAITI

DOMINICAN
REPUBLIC

PUERTO
RICO

Roosevelt Rhodes
Naval Air Station

Vieques

N

miles

0   500

30°

20°

30°

20°

90°

80°

70°

80°

70°

SECTION ONE

1970

The quality of your training will vary and sometimes you will be in over your head. You will miss many important family events. There will be long stretches of tedious duty aboard ship. You will fly in very bad weather and/or at night and you will be scared many times . . . And some days – where the scheduling Gods have smiled upon you – your jet will catapult into a glorious morning over a far-away sea and you will be drop-jawed that someone would pay you to do it.

From a letter to an aspiring naval aviator

Prologue

Two flaming yellow-white discs stared back like an owl's eyes in the night. As the big fighter thundered upwards into a black Mediterranean sky, the awesome power of her reheated engines lost their hypnotic grip on those watching from the ship. The overwhelming fury of the jet's catapult launch dispersed like the dense clouds of steam left in its wake, the sound reduced to a rumble on the wind. The burning reheats receded, rising and shrinking into the distance before, abruptly, they blinked off. The Phantom continued her climb away from the carrier at full military power, 11 tons of dry thrust, but from the ship she was now invisible against the ink sky. Lieutenant Commander Nick Kerr had watched her go, unable to resist the raw theatre of a night-time F-4 Phantom launch.

Pretty spectacular, he thought. It never failed to impress. Now, with his wingman away, it was his turn.

From the cockpit, Kerr looked around, keenly anticipating his own launch. It was a familiar scene, but never routine. Night-flying from an aircraft carrier was never routine. Thick veils of steam that streamed from the catapult tracks curled and danced around the flight deck. To his right was *Ark Royal*'s island, the only part of the ship that rose above the flat top of the rough steel flight deck. Her pennant number, RO9, painted black against the battleship-grey background, was visible in the metronomic red flash of Kerr's jet's navigation light. His Phantom sat taut, harnessed to the catapult shuttle, her nose reared high above the deck like a cobra ready to strike.

Around him, the catapult crew, known as Badgers because of their black and white surcoats, swarmed around the jet, leaning into the fierce wind that blew over the deck. Signalling with an illuminated glowing green marshalling baton, the yellow-jacketed Flight Deck Officer – FDO – instructed Kerr to wind the engines up to full power. With his left hand, Kerr slowly pushed the two throttle levers through the détentes into full reheat. At the back of the Phantom the twin jet pipes flared and expanded as if working out how to accommodate the massive energy generated by the reheats, burning like two furious yard-thick oxyacetylene flames. High-pressure cold water was sprayed on to the deck and the jet blast deflectors that rose vertically out of the flat deck. Without the water, both would begin to melt and blister from the fierce heat. Kerr and his Observer, Lieutenant Gerry Kinch, saw the glow from the burners in the cockpit's rear-view mirrors. Inside, the Phantom trembled like a rocket ready to rise from its launch-pad. High up in *Ark*'s bridge behind panes of thick armoured glass, faces lit like children's on bonfire night by the flare of the afterburners, those looking out over the spectacle could feel the extraordinary ferocity resonate in their chests. It was a lot worse for those outside. It was much more than noise.

The FDO, standing beyond the lethal reach of the big fighter's starboard wing, held the glowing green baton high above his head. Standby for launch. Kerr's eyes scanned the cockpit dials again, paying particularly close attention to the engine instruments to the right: rpm, temperatures and fuel flow. Nothing amiss. He switched the red nav light on the jet's spine from its intermittent flash to a steady blaze. He was ready to go. With the nav light on continuously, the FDO would bring the baton down from above his head to touch the deck – a deliberate, exaggerated action leaving no room for misunderstanding.

Then a couple of seconds of anticipation, head pressed firmly back against the ejection seat. And a mule-kick in the back as the 25-ton jet is dragged down the catapult track – 0–180 mph in a second and a half – and thrown off the edge of the deck ahead. The moment of truth for any naval aviator.

Kerr waited, his eyes fixed on the soft green light of the FDO's baton. It remained resolutely aloft. And he waited, concern creeping into his thoughts. *What the hell's going on?*

'Can you see anything?' he asked Kinch. The Observer couldn't help. There didn't appear to be anything wrong. There were none of the Badgers you might expect to be ducking underneath the jet if there were a problem with the catapult. Kerr clicked the RT transmit button on the throttle levers. On Channel 1, he asked Flying Control – Flyco – what the problem was.

'Stand by' was all he got in reply.

The posture of the FDO provided the first clue. He was standing more upright now, no longer leaning forward against a 20-knot wind over the deck. *Ark* must have lost forward speed. The FDO flicked on a second marshalling baton. Red this time. Slowly and deliberately he raised it aloft to join the green stick already above his head. *Shit.* The launch was going to be scrubbed. But now was perhaps the most dangerous time. The powerful steam catapult was primed, ready to fire Kerr's 25-ton jet off the ship's angled deck into the night. The big interceptor quivered and strained against the hold-back strop that harnessed her, the blast from her two Rolls-Royce engines in full reheat barely contained. But both the Phantom and the catapult now had to be brought back from the brink. Before throttling back, Kerr had to be 100 per cent certain that the catapult had been made safe. If the cat fired *without* the assistance of over 41,000lb of thrust delivered by the jet's twin engines – a cold shot – or if the Phantom tried to take off without the boost of the catapult, then Kerr and his Observer would be taking a swim. At best.

While the FDO held both batons high, Kerr kept the throttles forward up against the stops. Both men waited. Both needed to be certain. Then the Phantom pilot watched as one of the batons was slowly lowered. Green. The FDO kept the red one held above his head. A single red baton was Kerr's guarantee. He was clear to kill the power. But he waited a moment longer. He wanted to be more than certain. Mistakes made on the deck of a carrier are punished swiftly and cruelly. No amount of care or caution was ever too much.

He gave it another beat – the blast of the engines still broiling the water-cooled deck behind – then, satisfied it was safe, Kerr finally pulled the two throttle levers back through the détentes towards him to come off the power. As the spinning turbines spooled down, the tall hydraulic nosewheel strut contracted, lowering the jet's two-man cockpit towards the deck. And then Kerr caught his first glimpse of what lay ahead. From the waist catapult, halfway down the length of the flight deck, he could see ahead down the ship's port flank. And what he saw took his breath away.

Heeling over, nearly broached, her hull exposed and her sleek superstructure leaning away towards the waves, was the dark shape of a Soviet 'Kotlin' class guided-missile destroyer. She'd been making a nuisance of herself for days, shadowing, teasing and harassing the big carrier. But now, at night, her Captain had cut it too fine and she'd been T-boned by *Ark Royal*'s bow. Dwarfed by the Royal Navy carrier, the 3500-ton Soviet escort was being swung around, powerless at this point to save herself from the forward momentum of nearly 50,000 tons of British steel. As *Ark* shook, her engines straining at full astern in a desperate effort to save the situation, Kerr could almost feel metal scrape against metal. There was a grinding inevitability about the way the Soviet's bow jack-knifed back, the whole ship then dragged back down *Ark*'s side as the destroyer's stern was driven forward by the bigger ship. Kerr could do nothing but watch in horror at what was unfolding, his eyes fixed on the point of the collision just abaft the destroyer's sharply raked rear funnel.

Like a grappling hook, *Ark*'s great starboard anchor had torn into the superstructure of the 'Kotlin' just below the SA-N-1 Goa surface-to-air missile launcher. And into the missile magazine located immediately below it. As *Ark* and the 'Kotlin' continued their tangled dance, that magazine had become the fulcrum around which the Soviet ship was being brutally wrestled.

And it was this that most alarmed Kerr as he sat transfixed. A qualified Air Warfare Instructor – AWI – he knew that each Goa SAM was armed with a powerful high-explosive fragmentation warhead and enough rocket fuel to carry it to a height of six miles. He also knew that the Soviet destroyer's magazine contained sixteen of them. And he knew that the SA-N-1 Goa was known to be a notoriously unstable weapon. If they went up – and it would only take one of them to explode to trigger them all – then *Ark*'s bow would be vaporized. And, with it, so too would he.

From behind his oxygen mask Kerr stared wide-eyed, forgetting even to breathe, as he watched the accident unfold.

Only later, shaken by what he'd seen – and news of the loss of seven Soviet seamen – did he have time to gather his thoughts and reflect on how close he had come to an unexpected and spectacularly dramatic end. And of all the ways in which a naval aviator can meet his maker – and they are many, varied and usually violent – this was definitely not one that he'd ever considered before.

SECTION TWO

1971

I pray you tell Her Majesty from me that her money was well given for the Ark Royal, *for I think her the odd ship in the world for all conditions; and truly I think there can be no great ship make me change and go out of her.*

Lord High Admiral of England, Lord Howard of Effingham, writing to Elizabeth I's Secretary in 1587, the year before *Ark Royal* became his flagship against the Spanish Armada

Chapter 1

Captain John Roberts RN caught the little blue and yellow British Rail train from his home in Havant and made the short journey west to Plymouth. From the station, he took the short walk to Her Majesty's Dockyard, Devonport. He was looking forward to becoming acquainted with the most famous name in the Royal Navy. There was a time, many years earlier, when, as a young sub-lieutenant, he thought he would never get to see a ship bearing the name *Ark Royal*.

Roberts joined the Navy at the age of thirteen. Born in Rawalpindi, in what became Pakistan, Roberts was the son of an RAF pilot who'd flown First World War-vintage Bristol F2B fighters against Afghan tribesmen on the North-West Frontier in the 1920s. But after returning to Britain Roberts's father spent six weeks as a guest aboard a Royal Navy destroyer sailing between Gibraltar, Tangiers, Casablanca and the French Mediterranean ports. The RAF man became convinced that the Navy offered the most splendid life imaginable and put his son's name down for Dartmouth in 1938. In 1941 the young John Roberts joined the battlecruiser HMS *Renown* while she was out of action being refitted in the Rosyth dockyards. Throughout 1940 and 1941, *Renown* had served alongside the aircraft carrier HMS *Ark Royal* in the Western Mediterranean as part of Force H. And such was the bond that developed between the two ships that legend had it that if they were ever to be separated, one of them would be sunk. And sure enough, on 14 November 1941, news arrived in Rosyth that HMS *Ark*

Royal, one of the Navy's most iconic ships, had been sunk by a U-boat as she made her way back to Gibraltar. For all the distress her loss caused aboard *Renown*, Roberts, so new to the battlecruiser's Ship's Company, had never set eyes on her famous companion.

But now, thirty years later, another aircraft carrier bore her proud name – the fourth ship to do so. And the main threat to *Ark Royal*'s existence in her current incarnation had come not from German torpedoes, but from British politicians. She'd only survived by the skin of her teeth.

By 1971, Britain's withdrawal from Empire was well advanced – all but complete. What had been a post-war trickle became, during the 1960s under Harold Wilson's government, a tumble. The names of those colonies granted independence made up a long and evocative list: Barbados, Borneo, Botswana, British Guiana, the Cameroons, The Gambia, Jamaica, Malawi, the Maldives, Malta, Mauritius, Nigeria, Sierra Leone, Singapore, Somalia, Tanzania, Trinidad and Tobago, and Uganda. And it all had a bearing on defence planning.

The end of 1971, it had been decided, would mark Britain's final withdrawal from what had always been known simply as 'East of Suez'. The only exceptions – other than Hong Kong – were the British Indian Ocean Territory and Pitcairn in the Pacific, home of the descendants of the Mutiny on the *Bounty* – and, given the islands' history, there were unlikely to have been too many tears shed within the Admiralty if the politicians had washed their hands of that one too.

Ironically, though, the 1960s, as the flag came down on Britain's last substantial overseas possessions, were something of a boom time for the Fleet Air Arm. For most of the decade, five ships, *Eagle*, *Victorious*, *Hermes*, *Centaur* and *Ark Royal* herself, shared Britain's global responsibilities. Official policy was to ensure there were always two of them East of Suez. And, in order to meet that commitment, the five ships, none of them in the first flush of youth, were worked hard.

In 1961, De Havilland Sea Vixens and Supermarine Scimitars from *Victorious* and *Centaur* established air superiority over Kuwait in opposition to a rumoured Iraqi invasion. In the mid-sixties, FAA squadrons patrolled the skies over Borneo alongside the RAF and helped prevent 'confrontation' with Indonesia erupting into full-blown war. In early 1964, a potential army mutiny in Tanganyika was nipped in the bud by swift naval intervention, including a show of force from the squadron of Blackburn Buccaneers on board *Victorious*. And, from 1965, both *Ark Royal* and *Eagle* spent long periods on station off East Africa as part of the Beira Patrol, enforcing the blockade of Ian Smith's rebel Rhodesia. Throughout, FAA helicopter squadrons flying from the Commando carriers *Albion* and *Bulwark* had been in action from Dar-es-Salaam to Aden and Sarawak. As the decade drew to a close, there were very few Fleet Air Arm aviators who had failed to acquire sometimes extensive operational experience.

Despite ageing ships and increasingly outmoded aircraft the Fleet Air Arm had acquitted itself well. But in doing so it had also sown the seeds of its own destruction. With the successful transfer of colonial power to independent democratic governments around the world, the Navy's fleet carriers were deemed surplus to requirements. Any future aerial contribution to the defence of our remaining overseas responsibilities would, it was decided, be the job of the RAF. Denis Healey – Harold Wilson's Defence Secretary – had made his decision: the carriers had until the end of 1971 and no longer. Beyond that date the Royal Navy would be retiring from the business of fixed-wing flying. Newspaper recruitment ads for naval aircrew tried to look on the bright side: 'For piloting helicopters involves two forms of flying', the copywriters explained perkily. 'The conventional sort. Of getting from A to B. And hovering.'

After being ushered respectfully through the gates by the Dockyard Police, John Roberts continued on through to the centre of the dockyard. A keen sportsman, fair-haired, urbane and unflappable, Roberts cut an elegant figure as he made his way towards the ship. Her island and with it the bridge, radio masts, funnel and the towering 'bedstead' aerial of the Type 965 air defence radar were visible high above the roofs of the dockyard buildings. And she was the centre of attention. Thick cables and pipes connected her to the shore like IV lines to a patient in intensive care. With dockyard workers clambering over her, attending to her needs, the air was filled with the noise of air-hammers, rivet guns, welding torches, and the clatter of scaffolding. But even as she rested in dry-dock, away from the sea, dependent and unable to fend for herself, she was commanding. Her name was painted in red capitals against the grey hull below the quarterdeck. *Ark Royal* was awesome.

He wasn't sure what the rules were, but the police weren't around. No one was paying attention. The Captain made his way down successive flights of slippery steps descending towards the floor of the dock. *Ark Royal*'s keel rested on great wooden beams running the length of the ship. Further thick balks of timber propped between her and the walls of the dry-dock supported her, keeping her from toppling over. But Roberts saw he could get right in underneath her. There wasn't much headroom – barely more than a foot or two – but it was enough. Standing on the damp floor of the dock underneath the massive black hull of the great ship, he looked up and down her length. Her vast bulk filled his field of vision in every direction. Up close you could see the welding between the steel plates; visible evidence of the labours of the men who built her.

It had been a drawn-out affair. Her keel was laid down at the Cammel Laird shipyard in Birkenhead on 3 May 1943, a year after King George VI had approved changing her name from *Irresistible* to *Ark Royal*. But the end of the war, changing shipbuilding priorities and the need to accommodate a stream of modifications and innovations meant it was seven years to the day before she was launched. Liverpudlians had good reason to wonder which would eventually be finished first: *Ark* or their magnificent Gilbert Scott-designed cathedral. But just after noon on 3 May 1950, with the sound of a 21-gun salute still ringing in the ears of a watching crowd of nearly 50,000 people, Queen Elizabeth – later to become the Queen Mother – named her, broke a bottle of champagne over her bows and saw her slip slowly into the Mersey. Ten steel decks built above double-bottom compartments. It was another five years before *Ark* was commissioned into the Royal Navy in February 1955, the first ship in the fleet to accommodate all of the important post-war developments in naval aviation, from powerful steam catapults able to launch a new generation of faster, heavier jet aircraft to an angled flight deck that allowed them to land more safely.

John Roberts thought he'd missed his chance of ever taking command of an aircraft carrier – and that he'd therefore missed out on realizing an ambition that had taken root soon after he transferred to the Fleet Air Arm in 1945. But there was no way round it; the writing was on the wall for the Navy's carriers. On VJ Day the Royal Navy was operating fifty-nine aircraft carriers of various descriptions. A fleet of twelve in 1950 was just three-strong in 1970. By the spring of 1972, there simply weren't going to be any.

When the decision to dispose of the carriers was taken in 1966, the Navy's hopes of building a brand-new class of three 63,000-ton ships to replace the current carriers were dashed. It was a devastating blow to the Senior Service provoking the resignation of both the Navy Minister and the First Sea Lord. Since the high-water mark of the Second World War, the Navy had suffered a painful contraction. A death by a thousand cuts accompanied the Navy's journey from victory in 1945 to the humiliating 'Cod Wars' with Icelandic fishermen of the early seventies. Along the way, bases at Singapore, Bahrain, Aden and Simonstown in South Africa were all closed. In 1966, *Ark*'s days too were numbered.

But the carrier decision was made with *Ark Royal* on the cusp of a major £32 million refit. Only the potential uproar over dockyard redundancies if it was abandoned persuaded the Wilson government to see it through to its completion, due at the end of 1969. She would emerge from it a substantially new ship, capable of operating a state-of-the-art air group. While work on her had progressed, Cunard's new liner, the *QE2*, was under construction on the Clyde. By those in the know, rebuilding *Ark Royal* was felt to be the more ambitious job. Yet even the successful completion of the refit was barely going to postpone the inevitable. Unbelievably, the plan became to radically overhaul the Navy's largest warship at great expense so that she might continue to serve for just two more years until, at the end of 1971, she'd go for good along with the rest of the carriers.

But then *Ark Royal* was thrown a lifeline.

In June 1970, the British electorate voted in a new Conservative government with Ted Heath as Prime Minister. As people had been casting their votes, large numbers of British soldiers, sailors and airmen were deployed in Singapore and Malaysia to take part in Exercise BERSATU PADU. This extraordinary logistical exercise was designed to demonstrate Britain's ability to reinforce allies in the Far East after the demise of the carriers. Despite encouraging post-exercise analysis, the exercise was not an unqualified success. Among the conclusions drawn, two were very telling. Without air superiority over the reception airfields in Singapore and Malaysia the men and materiel from Britain could not have been delivered. Aircraft carriers had the ability to provide that vital initial air superiority. The other realization was that only the Australian light carrier HMAS *Melbourne*, and the McDonnell Douglas A-4G Skyhawks of her small fighter squadron VF-805, provided anything like adequate air cover for the fleet. The RAF English Electric Lightnings and Royal Australian Air Force Dassault Mirage IIIOs operating from shore bases at Butterworth and Tengah just didn't have the legs to maintain effective patrols out over the sea. The Skyhawks' ability to provide timely and valuable Close Air Support to troops on the ground was also noted.

Australian naval aviators had driven home the unique strengths of organic, carrier-based air power at an opportune time. And yet the connection between *Melbourne*'s Skyhawks and *Ark*'s reprieve was more oblique. VF-805's potent little attack jets had been ordered in 1965 to make certain that, faced with increasing instability in South-East Asia and a deteriorating situation in Vietnam, HMAS *Melbourne* had a modern, effective air group. And it was Vietnam that, rather unexpectedly, helped ensure *Ark Royal*'s survival.

US policy was to keep a minimum of three aircraft carriers off the coast of Vietnam. Guaranteeing this twenty-four hours a day, 365 days a year, without pause, placed immense pressure on the US carrier fleet and meant rotating the schedules of as many as eight carriers. Throughout the sixties, the British carriers *Eagle*, *Ark*, *Victorious*, *Centaur* and *Hermes* helped plug any gaps in America's naval presence elsewhere in South-East Asia caused by her huge commitment to Vietnam. But it wasn't just the US Navy's Pacific Fleet that carried the burden on Yankee Station. Such were the overwhelming demands of the war that Atlantic Fleet carriers also regularly deployed to the Gulf of Tonkin. And it was the potential repercussions of this on NATO's defence of Western Europe that persuaded the new British government to keep *Ark Royal*, refitted and modernized, in business. If *Ark* were to lead one of the two Carrier Groups that made up the NATO Atlantic Striking Fleet, she would relieve the strain on the hard-pressed US Navy carrier fleet. By the end of the new British government's first month, the Secretary of State for Defence, Peter Carrington, had asked the MoD for a study into the pros and cons of keeping *Ark* in service. By October the decision to run her on was made.

Standing under *Ark Royal*'s great eclipsing hull John Roberts recalled the day he was asked by the Naval Secretary to come in for a chat. Roberts had been working in the MoD as Director of Naval Air Warfare when he took the call. He presented himself the next morning at ten o'clock, was shown in and took a seat.

'John, I've been wondering what to do with you next.' The politician paused and smiled. 'I'm going to give you

Ark Royal.' It couldn't have been better news. And now here he was, standing underneath her looking up and thinking about the magnitude of what lay ahead. Displacing over 43,000 tons – over 50,000 fully fuelled, stored and carrying her aircraft on board – she was nearly 850 feet long, over 110 feet wide and from keel to funnel over 180 feet tall. Sailing her would be like laying the NatWest Tower on its side and taking it to sea. Only, *Ark Royal* was one and a half times the size of Britain's biggest skyscraper.

How on earth can I control this?, he asked himself. After the frigates and destroyers he'd previously skippered, just the thought of taking such a behemoth in and out of harbour, with sometimes less than ten feet of clearance underneath her, was daunting. Touching the bottom – and the court-martial that was bound to follow – was an ever-present danger at Devonport. And that was before he even got to open water. Once there, the task was no less intimidating. Even refitted, *Ark* was going to have to operate at her peak to keep pace with her American counterparts. To compensate for her smaller size, fewer aircraft, older machinery and less-advanced surveillance and communications systems, *Ark*, her Ship's Company and her squadrons were simply going to have to work harder to stay level. Her *people* would have to bridge the gap. And in going face to face with the Warsaw Pact in the North Atlantic with the Cold War at its height, she'd be playing a very different game to the global policing of the sixties. It was a harder, bleaker, less-forgiving undertaking. And the stakes were very high indeed. The next time the great ship put to sea she'd be under his command. He thought about the merciless task that lay ahead. And he relished it – looking forward to going to sea; and looking forward to the arrival of the squadrons. The possibility that *Ark Royal* might be called on to intervene in a colonial crisis was very far from his thoughts.

Chapter 2

John Weymes had been back in London for five years after a career with the Foreign Office had so far taken him from Panama in 1953, to Bogotá, Colombia, Berlin and Taiwan. In 1968, after three years in Whitehall, he found himself, much to his surprise, working in Harold Wilson's Private Office at Number 10 Downing Street. Now, though, his five years was up. If he was going to continue to receive government help with his children's boarding school fees, he needed another overseas appointment. He called an old friend in the personnel department.

'What have you got for me? Presumably you're looking for a job for me overseas?' There was a long pause.

'Look, John, give me a couple of weeks and I'll get back to you.' It sounded as if his friend was going to be starting from scratch. When they next discussed it, his friend was even more circumspect.

'I can't tell you yet, because it's all going through the board, but here's a hint . . .' He passed Weymes a newspaper cutting with the headline: 'GERMAN AMBASSADOR MURDERED IN GUATEMALA'.

'It sounds like Guatemala then . . .' Weymes managed, and his friend's veneer of discretion collapsed.

'Yes, it's quite a posting.' He continued enthusiastically, apparently unperturbed by the kidnap and killing of the German diplomat, explaining that Weymes would be appointed British Consul. 'You've got Spanish; you've got Latin/Central

American experience and we're hoping the board will agree and then we'll send you off.' Two weeks later it was signed off and he began to be briefed for the posting. While the way the posting to Guatemala had first been introduced had been alarming, Weymes knew from meeting British diplomats travelling to and from Guatemala via Panama that, despite dreadful internal security problems, it was a beautiful country. And yet it was difficult to entirely put aside the violence endemic in Guatemala. This was rammed home during his interview with the Foreign Office Security Department. Weymes was given three pieces of advice:

'First, don't get kidnapped. HMG does not deal with terrorists. Secondly, you're advised to buy a weapon, a gun of some sort. Practise frequently in the garden so people will hear you firing, will know that you're armed, and that you can use it. And thirdly, get a fierce dog!'

The increasing gloom Weymes felt at the prospect of what he was letting himself in for was lifted a little by the prospect of his own domestic circumstances. He would be living in the British Ambassador's Residence in Guatemala City. The house and grounds occupied a whole city block near La Torre, where city district Zone 4 meets Zone 9. Looking after him would be a staff of six or seven, including a cook, a maid, a laundry girl and a butler who doubled as a driver. There was also a swimming pool.

They were quite some digs for someone of Weymes's grade. But they too came with strings attached. The only reason Weymes, as Consul, rather than as Ambassador, would be enjoying its comforts was because there was no British Ambassador in Guatemala. There hadn't been one since 1963, when Guatemala cut formal diplomatic relations with Britain after internal self-government was granted to British Honduras. It had been a development that Guatemala regarded as completely unacceptable.

The little colony that sat on the southern Yucatán peninsula between her eastern border and the Caribbean Sea was the last remaining British mainland territory in the Americas. And

Guatemala claimed her as her own; a rogue Guatemalan province that appeared as Belice – and as part of Guatemala – on all Guatemalan maps of the region. Belice's position as her neighbour's 23rd Department was written into Guatemala's 1945 constitution, and seats, decked in Guatemala's national colours of sky blue and white, were set aside in Congress ready for Belice's return to the fold.

Belice, they declared, *es nuestra*.

Belize is ours.

Belize City was growing up fast. Colourful and elegant wooden colonial houses topped with red-brown or pale-green corrugated iron shared the streets with new buildings. The tangles of steel that emerged from reinforced-concrete pillars revealed their recent construction. Her population was 30,000 and rising and the little city needed to accommodate them. Belize City flanked the mouth of Haulover Creek, from which silty brown water pumped out to sea, where it mixed with the clear blue waters of the Caribbean. From the north side of the city, the swing bridge over the river led to the main business district, the courts, the imposing white Governor's House on Regent Street and St John's Cathedral, built with the bricks that had served as ballast in the holds of the sailing ships that shaped the country's history. Surrounded by mangrove swamps, barely rising above sea level and criss-crossed with open drainage canals, Belize City was hot, humid and colourful. Palm trees lined the seafront at St George. Bright handpainted signs decorated the walls of shops and eateries, while long, low canoes driven by small outboards buzzed in and out of the town centre. Belize City was the very epitome of a Caribbean capital. And yet she was neither the capital nor, strictly speaking, Caribbean.

Nearly 5000 miles south-west of London, British Honduras was not, even by the standards of the day, a particularly familiar corner of Empire. Roughly the same size as Wales, she had a small population of just 122,000 people, whose health and well-being had only once been of any recent concern to most Britons. In October 1961, 262 people lost their lives when Belize City was hit hard by Hurricane Hattie. A fifteen-foot tidal surge breached the sea walls and sent a five-foot-high wall of water racing through the capital 'as though there had never been land'. Such was the devastation that a decision was taken to move the capital inland to a location fifty miles away off the unpaved Western Highway. Christened Belmopan, and with a population of barely 3000, the new capital had yet to truly find her feet, despite the internal government and a number of foreign missions having relocated there. So steamy little Belize City remained the country's cultural and commercial hub, and Stanley Field, the airfield to the north of the City, the country's only international gateway.

Despite her location on the mainland of the Central American isthmus, British Honduras was in heart and soul a Caribbean country. English-speaking and comfortably multi-racial, she seemed to have little in common with Central American neighbours like Guatemala, El Salvador and Nicaragua – certainly there were few of the serious internal troubles that bedevilled them. Instead she was optimistic, a small country just beginning to appreciate the potential wealth offered by having the world's second-longest barrier reef fringing her coast. And with Britain's retreat from Empire, she was yearning to make her way in the world, independent and proud. This, though, was complicated by her history.

The first Europeans to come ashore in British Honduras in 1511 didn't fare well. Five survivors of a shipwrecked Spanish vessel were immediately sacrificed by Mayan Indians. The rest of the crew were enslaved. To some extent, the balance of that initial contact was reflected in the country's subsequent experience with the Spanish Empire. The *Conquistadores* never enjoyed the same level of dominance in the territory which became British Honduras that they did elsewhere in Latin America. Partly this was because Mayans, for all their similarly extraordinary pyramids and cities, never enjoyed the same unity and cohesion as the Aztec and Inca empires. As a result, Mayan civilization couldn't be as simply decapitated and controlled as the Incas had been with Pizarro's killing of Atahualpa. The territory's other piece of outstanding good fortune was that it did not possess gold. It was simply not worthwhile for the overstretched Spanish to occupy such financially unrewarding ground. The nearest permanent Spanish garrisons remained north of the Hondo and south of the Sarstoon, beyond the two rivers that became the borders of British Honduras. Within the boundaries of those two rivers, the Spanish limited themselves to sporadic – usually sickeningly cruel – attempts to impose themselves. Had they found the wherewithal to occupy the country, her subsequent history might have been a great deal more straightforward.

Largely abandoned by the Spanish, the coast of British Honduras became a haven for buccaneers. Many of them, as Great Britain became more powerful and influential in the Caribbean following the capture of Jamaica in 1655, were British. In 1717, Blackbeard himself spent time in the waters off the coast and even, it was said, had treasure buried on Ambergris Caye, the largest and most northerly of the pretty low-lying islands off British Honduras.

Permanent British settlements grew up along the coast as logging, rather than plundering Spanish treasure ships, became the main source of income. And yet even as these were recognized by treaties between Britain and Spain they were still subjected to regular attack by Spanish forces. The truth is that the Baymen, as the logging community focused around the mouth of the Belize River had become known, were fairly ungovernable. They were the men on the ground and they pretty much did as they pleased regardless of what Spain, Britain or anyone else told them to. And yet the British increasingly took the view that they may be an unruly mob but they're *our* unruly mob. Troops were first sent to the Baymen's defence from Jamaica in 1746. Then, in 1765, Rear Admiral Sir William Burnaby, the commander of the Royal Navy squadron in Jamaica, arrived with Captain James Cook to provide protection against Spanish attack and establish the rule of law.

Burnaby's Code addressed the issues of the day. Its rules included:

- No swearing and profane cursing. Penalty half-a-crown fine
- No theft allowed
- No enticing seamen to abandon ship
- No kidnapping, i.e. press gang methods of recruiting, except for pilots for one day only
- In an emergency the authority of the commander of a warship in the bay should take precedence

The Navy was beginning to impose some shape on the place, but ambiguity surrounding the sovereignty of the Belize River settlement continued until 1798 and the Battle of St George's Caye. Fearing attack by Spain after the outbreak of war between Britain and Spain in 1796, the Baymen appealed to the Governor of Jamaica for help. HMS *Merlin*, a sloop armed with eight 18-pounder guns, and the men of the 6th West India Regiment were sent. The Baymen too had prepared for war, knocking together seven rafts made from tree trunks, each armed with a 9-pounder gun. Then they gave them names like *Towzer*, *Tickler*, *Teazer* and *Swinger*. On 3 September, the 32-strong Spanish fleet arrived. And by the end of 10 September, it had been defeated and fled north to Caye Chapel, where the Spanish buried their dead before returning to Mexico. Spain never again threatened the Belize River settlement. In defending Belize, slaves had fought alongside freemen. And their success against overwhelming odds created a legend that endured. Celebration of the victory at St George's Caye would become a rallying point around which, nearly 200 years later, the people of British Honduras built a sense of national identity and in which they invested their hopes of independence.

In the wake of the battle, the Baymen declared that 'the tenure and possession of the country is altered. His Majesty holds it by force and it may in some degree be considered a conquered country.' But while the Union Flag flew over the settlement, the British government didn't quite see it that way. And it was to be another sixty-four years before, on 12 May 1862, the Colony of British Honduras was finally established.

Now, in 1971, Britain was as eager to grant British Honduras her independence as she had been reluctant to assume responsibility just a century earlier. But things were rarely that easy.

Chapter 3

After a career in the Colonial Service, then the Foreign and Commonwealth Office, that had taken him to Uganda, the Congo, the UN in New York and the Pacific islands, Richard Posnett was back in London, recently installed as head of the West Indies Department of the FCO. Posnett knew that decolonization in the Caribbean had a habit of being complicated. Despatched at short notice from the UN in 1969, he'd witnessed first-hand something akin to farce unfold in Anguilla when British paratroopers and London policemen had been flown in because Anguilla did *not* want to become independent alongside St Kitts. But if the pitfalls in the Caribbean were well understood, Posnett had not properly registered the potential for trouble in Central America. And British Honduras was on his watch. After taking over the West Indies department, the sandy-haired, easy-going diplomat had made it his business to visit every one of the islands that he had responsibility for. British Honduras was also on his itinerary. In three days as a guest of the popular, respected Governor, Sir John Paul, he'd met government ministers, including the Premier, George Price, and been impressed by a visit to see Mayan ruins hidden in the jungle. While he'd been there, Sir John had told him that he wanted to move on before the end of the year. The old Governor was disappointed not to have been able to shepherd British Honduras closer towards independence and, he confessed, was struggling a little with the isolation and reduced surroundings of Belmopan. Posnett returned home knowing that much of the job of recruiting a new Governor would fall to him. What he didn't realize was the seriousness of the Guatemalan claim on British Honduras, nor its inextricable relationship with any developing plans for the colony's independence. Neither had he grasped the capacity there was in Guatemala for devastating violence.

Acting on the advice of the FCO Security Officer, John Weymes arrived in Guatemala City with a bulldog called Sally. It seemed no one in Guatemala had ever seen anything like Sally before. Weymes got used to cars stopping, double-takes and alarmed expressions as he walked her along the pavements surrounding the Ambassador's Residence.

'What sort of animal is that?' people would ask. If there was a Spanish name for bulldog, Weymes didn't know it. Instead he just tried to translate directly.

'Perro de torro,' he'd tell them. She was a great comfort to him. Especially as he'd chosen to ignore the suggestion that he arm himself.

The British Consulate was in a single-storey Spanish colonial-style house built around an internal courtyard garden. Located between Avenidas 2 and 3 in Zone 1 of Guatemala City, it felt like it could be the home of a small import/export company. In contrast to where Weymes was living, it wasn't grand. Zone 1 had been devastated by an earthquake in 1917. With much of the original architecture lost, it was now an unsightly jumble of old and new. But Calle 11, the street where the British had set up shop, wasn't too bad. The pretty church at the western end of the street certainly improved the view.

Just before eleven in the morning, on 19 January 1971, Weymes left his office to go and talk to the young Vice-Consul, David Osborne. As they spoke they were suddenly stopped by the sound of gunfire. It was a familiar sound after dark, but not by day. And not so close. This was right on top of them.

'My God, that's us!' Weymes shouted. The reports from the guns were coming from the Consulate's entrance hall. Then rounds began to crack through the locked metal grille across the courtyard into Weymes's office, shattering all twelve windows. Then it stopped. Outside, their four attackers turned and walked away calmly towards a waiting red Toyota, got inside and sped off. Once they were sure it was over, Weymes and Osborne made their way outside towards the entrance of the Consulate. Weymes looked nervously through the grilled door, where he saw the dead body of the guard. He'd been shot nine times. Scattered on the floor were the brass casings from .45-calibre bullets. The terrorists had taken the dead guard's machine pistol with them as they left. The phone rang. Weymes picked it up.

'What's happened?' It was his counterpart at the nearby American Embassy, already aware there had been an incident.

'We've just been attacked and the guard's been killed. How did you know?'

'We received a warning that we were going to be attacked at 11 a.m. and we shut our doors. We had no time to warn you that the caller said that if they couldn't hit the American Embassy, they'd go to the British Consulate.'

The killing in Guatemala was out of control. But that was nothing new. When Guatemala's President, Colonel Arana Osorio, won a one-sided election in 1970 he was very clear indeed about his plans: 'I intend,' he promised, 'to pacify the country and if that means turning it into a cemetery then I shall do so.' And he'd been as good as his word. There was never any reason to doubt it. He'd shown no instinct to shy away from the use of force before. In fact, he'd earned his reputation by doing just the opposite.

Whereas British Honduras had escaped any significant lingering effects of Spanish colonial rule – simply because the Spanish had opted not to rule – Guatemala lived every day with its consequences. It had done so since the day in 1821 when the last Captain General signed the Act of Independence. Enshrined in the Act were the old colonial power structures and the supremacy of the church. The next 150 years saw power in Guatemala lurch from right-wing misrule to left-wing misrule and back again, as often as not by way of a coup. All the time it was the Guatemalan people who suffered for it. It seemed they were rarely considered except when their numbers and discontent could be exploited by an aspiring dictator to oust the dictator in power. Arana Osorio, alongside his Defence Minister, Vassaux, and the Army Chief of Staff, Kjell Laugerud, was just the latest strongman at the helm.

Arana had risen to prominence through the success of his bloody campaign against guerrillas in the Zacapa and Izabal districts in the east of Guatemala. In pursuit of victory, he'd never shown the slightest inclination towards restraint – his two nicknames, 'Jackal of the Oriente' and 'Butcher of Zacapa', were a testament to that. But his success in the countryside had driven the rebels into Guatemala City itself. And so the inhabitants of the sprawling capital had to endure the curfews, kidnappings, shootings, hijackings and bombings that defined life under Arana's State of Siege. The ravines around the city were used to dump the corpses in; a particularly gruesome haul of bodies in a cave on the side of a nearby volcano earned it the description the 'Clandestine Cemetery', while the Motagua River that ran through the city became known as the 'Arana Highway' because of the number of bodies that floated downstream.

At a loss, John Weymes compared it to the Wild West. He imagined casting a second-rate western. It was easy. Arana was the sheriff, the left-wing terrorists were the baddies, the lawmen were the security forces, right-wing death squads were the vigilantes, and the State of Siege itself represented martial law.

After the shooting at the Consulate, it was high time, Weymes thought, to pay heed to the other piece of advice he'd been given before leaving London. Through a friend who'd been a Colonel in the Guatemalan Army, Weymes acquired a .22-calibre automatic pistol and holster which he packed down his waistband. He loaded it with soft-nosed hollow-point bullets – illegal throughout much of the world because of the terrible injuries they inflict as they deform and expand on impact – and began to practise shooting in the garden.

Chapter 4

While Weymes, getting used to the new .22, fired round after round behind the high walls of the Ambassador's residence, on a remote Scottish air station on the shores of the Moray Firth 809 Naval Air Squadron were getting to know their new CO. Lieutenant Commander Carl Davis was happy to be back in Scotland at Royal Naval Air Station Lossiemouth. He had fond memories of time spent at Lossie flying Seahawks as a junior pilot – a Squadron Joe. The late fifties had been relatively care-free days – sport, a thriving social scene and flying. And, located in the lee of the Highlands, Lossie was blessed with some of the best flying weather in the UK. The place had real spirit. It had suited Davis, an ebullient, no-nonsense character, down to the ground.

As a boy growing up near Leominster, Davis had considered it a bonus that his school was perched right on the edge of the little airfield at Shobdon. After a brief career on the front line during the Second World War, Shobdon had become well-known as a glider field. Davis used to while away hours sitting on its perimeter watching the long-winged sailplanes wheel around the skies over Herefordshire. But after this kindled an interest in aviation, it took him a while to realize that flying was where his own future lay. Studying chemistry at Birmingham University bored him enough to abandon it. So too did work as a draughtsman that carried with it vague hopes that it would lead to architecture. Then a presentation by a Fleet Air Arm pilot in a local hotel captured his imagination. Flying off aircraft carriers didn't look like it would bore him at all.

Now, after a career that had taken him from his first deck landing off Malta in a Hawker Seahawk aboard *Ark Royal* to the Fleet Air Arm's first operational Buccaneer squadron flying from HMS *Victorious* in the Far East, he was back at Lossie to combine the two. He was the new Boss of 809 NAS, *Ark*'s Buccaneer strike squadron. And like his ship's new Captain, John Roberts, Davis had thought he'd missed the boat.

In 1963, Davis, who'd been expecting to leave the Navy to fly for the airlines, had a change of heart, transferring from the short-service Supplementary List to the Navy's General List. By 1970, after securing his Watchkeeping Certificate aboard HMS *Dainty* and tours as an Instructor and as CO of a training squadron, Davis was studying at Camberley in the grounds of Sandhurst doing the Army Staff Course when he took a call from the Navy Appointer.

'You'll be pleased to hear, Carl, that you're going to be the next CO of 809.' *Ark*, he was told, was going to be kept on. And then he was asked conspiratorially if he wouldn't mind keeping all this under his hat until *Ark*'s reprieve was made public. It did nothing to dampen his enthusiasm. *To run your own front-line squadron*, he supposed, *is what every aviator wants to do*. But he had simply not dared hope for it. Since the 1966 decision to scrap the carriers it had looked increasingly unlikely he would ever get the chance. Instead he'd been wondering just what a future in the Fleet Air Arm might hold.

The battle in Whitehall over the future of Britain's carrier force had been bitter and corrosive. Either the RAF got its new General Dynamics F-111 swing-wing bombers from America, or the Navy got a new generation of carriers. Winner takes all. Forced by the Treasury to fight each other for money, the argument brought out the worst instincts of both services. That the RAF, in support of its claim that it could provide shore-based air cover for the fleet, had moved Australia 300 miles to the west was well-known in naval circles. In return, FAA aircrew, offered the chance to transfer to the Air Force, had access to written notes which rehearsed reasons for not wanting to make the switch. Top of the list was that 'the smugness and inefficiency of that organization would stifle me'. Such was the enmity between the two services that only two Navy officers could be persuaded to switch their allegiance and both subsequently changed their minds. It was inter-service rivalry at its most unproductive – with temperatures running so high that neither side was able or willing to look beyond narrow party lines. And, in the end it was all for nothing. After setting the Navy and Air Force at each other's throats and scrapping the carriers, the government then cancelled its order for F-111s. It had successfully stiffed them both.

The RAF's victory in the Battle of Britain in 1940 had secured it a place in the British national psyche in much the same way that Trafalgar had for the Navy or Waterloo for the Army. And yet the RAF had, perhaps, never quite been able to shake off the siege mentality it had adopted in the 1920s when it was fighting for its continued existence as an independent service. Its insecurity was understandable. As recently as 1957, the Air Force had been faced with the disappearance of Fighter Command after a Defence White Paper announced that Britain had no further need for manned fighters and that in future the country's air defence would rely solely on guided missiles. But the history of the Fleet Air Arm had also felt like a long battle for survival.

The Admiralty were not, initially, terribly impressed by aeroplanes, as their letter to Orville and Wilbur Wright made very clear. 'They would not,' they wrote, 'be of any practical use to the naval service.' They soon changed their tune, however. On 1 July 1914, the Royal Naval Air Service was established. In 1918, it was rolled into the new Royal Air Force alongside the Royal Flying Corps, only to re-emerge as the Fleet Air Arm of the RAF in 1924 – its aircraft owned and operated by the Air Force. The Navy only won back complete control of the Fleet Air Arm in May 1939, just three months before the outbreak of the Second World War.

On 26 September 1939, 250 miles north-west of Heligoland, three Blackburn Skua IIs of 803 NAS flying from the Navy's newest aircraft carrier, HMS *Ark Royal* – the third ship to bear the name – shot down a Dornier Do18 flying boat. And by doing so claimed the first confirmed fighter kill of the war.

Six years later, on 13 August 1945, eight Supermarine Seafire IIIs of 887 NAS took off from HMS *Indefatigable* to escort an air strike against targets near Tokyo. At 0545, as the formation flew over the beach, it was pounced on by over a dozen Japanese Zero and Zeke fighters. The British pilots slammed their throttles forward to full power. Rolls-Royce Merlin engines let out a meaty, percussive roar and the Seafires turned in to engage their attackers. Soon the sky was a maelstrom of machine-gun and cannon fire, falling wreckage, flames, curving trails of white smoke, and pilots slowly descending under parachute canopies. For the loss of one of their own, their leader, Sub-Lieutenant Freddie Hockley, the British Seafires were credited with seven kills, three probables and four damaged. It was the final dogfight of the Second World War.

First in, last out. Flying from aircraft carriers, the Fleet Air Arm had been responsible for the first and last aerial victories of that long six-year war. And, since 1945, Fleet Air Arm fighters have shot down a further twenty-four enemy aircraft. The RAF, by contrast – for all its many, and sometimes extraordinary, post-war achievements – has shot down none.

The FAA also punched above its weight when it came to the glamour and derring-do of post-war record-breaking. Since 1945, the Official World Air Speed Record had twice been claimed by ex-Royal Navy pilots.

On 25 September 1953, Lieutenant Commander Mike Lithgow RN set a new world record of 735.7 mph in a Supermarine Swift Mk 4 flying at a height of around thirty feet above the road from Azizia to Bur El Gnem, fifty miles south-west of the Libyan capital of Tripoli.

Three years later, just before midday on 10 March 1956, Lieutenant Commander Peter Twiss RN landed his silver, dart-shaped experimental jet, the Fairey Delta 2, at Boscombe

Down in Wiltshire. Twiss had just become the fastest man who'd ever lived by streaking across the skies between Ford and Chichester at an average speed of 1,132 mph. It was the first time the record had been raised above 1000 mph. The press thrilled at the news that the record had been reclaimed for Britain, while Twiss, relieved at not having let the willing little aeroplane down, recoiled at the prospect of becoming a 'sort of supersonic male Marilyn Monroe'. Twiss's fear was a legitimate one. The test pilots became national heroes who inspired a generation of British boys.

Carl Davis was no exception. While growing up he had a signed photograph of an earlier British air speed record-breaker, Group Captain 'Teddy' Donaldson. Donaldson had given it to Davis's aunt while staying at her guest house in Herne Bay and she'd sent it on to her nephew. The picture had long since been put away. Test pilots like Donaldson, Lithgow and Twiss, not to mention their contemporaries like Geoffrey de Havilland and Neville Duke, captured the imagination of the post-war British public, but it wasn't to last. The ambition and invention shown by the British aircraft industry in the fifties, showcased each year at the Farnborough Air Show, was all but strangled by the 1957 Defence White Paper. It was announced that development work on every project other than what became the English Electric Lightning was to stop. But one other jet escaped the cull, slipping through apparently unnoticed: an advanced naval strike aircraft called the Blackburn Buccaneer. And it had been designed with a very specific purpose in mind.

On 30 April 1954, the Admiralty announced that Commander Lionel 'Buster' Crabb was missing presumed dead following a diving exercise at Portsmouth. Crabb was a Second World War naval frogman – a winner of the George Medal for his bravery during counter-sabotage operations against the Italians in the Mediterranean. What, the press wondered, was a former Royal Naval Volunteer Reserve diver doing in Portsmouth harbour while the Soviet 'Sverdlov' class cruiser that had carried First Secretary Khrushchev on a state visit to the UK was berthed there? The Admiralty was quick to deny any involvement, but its fascination with and fear of the 'Sverdlovs' was well known. Fourteen of the 17,000-ton 'Sverdlovs' were built. Armed with twelve 5.9-inch guns in four triple turrets and another twelve 3.9-inch guns in six twin turrets, they posed a great threat to vital British sea lanes. And one against which the Royal Navy had no effective counter. In 1951, the Admiralty even recommissioned HMS *Vanguard*, the Navy's last battleship, before thoughts turned to the possibilities offered by a carrier-borne, low-level strike aircraft designed specifically as a 'Sverdlov killer'. And by the time Crabb's mutilated body was washed up on the south coast a year later – his throat cut by a Soviet Navy diver – Blackburn Aircraft Limited was already building a full-size mock-up of its ground-breaking new bomber in its factory in Yorkshire. The company's history of producing successful naval aircraft was a little chequered, and following the Second World War it had even been reduced to producing bread bins. But with the Buccaneer, Blackburn's designers and engineers really nailed it.

With her peculiarly voluptuous area-ruled fuselage and high T-tail, the Buccaneer looked like nothing else in the sky. But she was designed and built without compromise for one customer who knew what they wanted. It made a big difference. Bravely, at a time when flying faster than sound was *de rigueur*, no attempt was made to make her unnecessarily supersonic. As a result she could fly further, lower and, ironically, because her unusual rotating bomb bay allowed her to carry a 4000lb bomb load internally, *faster* – her rivals slowed down by the unaerodynamic warload slung under their wings. But she was, in her initial S1 form, seriously underpowered. Contemporary promotional films would admiringly describe the virtues of in-flight refuelling for extending the Buccaneer's range while failing to mention that it was practically a necessity. Fully loaded with fuel and weapons, the S1 barely had the power to get off the deck, so she was launched with half-empty tanks and topped up in the air. This was all to change with the first flight, in 1963, of the S2. Fitted with the more efficient, more powerful Rolls-Royce Spey bypass engine, the Buccaneer came of age. She was, simply, the outstanding low-level strike aircraft of the day. As if to underline the point, in 1965 a Buccaneer S2 flew home from Goose Bay, in Canada, to Lossie without refuelling. A distance of 1,950 miles. It was the first ever non-stop crossing of the Atlantic by a Fleet Air Arm aircraft and clear evidence of the new bomber's long reach. But it was in the high-speed, low-level role where she really excelled.

She was completely at home flying at 500 knots just 50 feet above the waves. She felt like she could do it all day. Rooted and utterly composed, it was like being on rails. Without the drama and discomfort of being bounced around by choppy air and gusts of wind, things happened more slowly for her crew. Given that flying a strike jet at little more than wave-top height is an inherently intense, exhausting occupation, the exceptional ability of the Buccaneer took a little of the sting out of it. In doing so, she delivered her aircrews to their targets in better shape. And *that* gave them a better chance of hitting them.

Designed from the outset as a naval jet, she suffered from none of the frailties that land-based conversions were prone to. Crews joked that the Buccs were laid down and launched rather than built, such was their structural strength. You looked at the heavy hinges of the folding wings, the solidity of the main-gear oleos or inside surfaces of the massive clamshell airbrakes that opened and closed like crocodile's jaws below the tail and you got the impression she'd been cast in a foundry.

But Blackburn had built a world-beater. And the Fleet Air Arm knew it. Buccaneer crews flew supremely confident that if they wanted to kick down your door, you weren't going to be able to stop them.

In 1963, Carl Davis had flown in the FAA's first operational Buccaneer S1 squadron as it ironed out the new jet's wrinkles. Now he was about to take command of the last, with the S2 firmly established as an outstanding, mature weapons system. Within a year, 809 would be the *only* Buccaneer squadron left in the Navy. During a two-month handover period at Lossie alongside his predecessor, Davis completed refresher courses before taking over alone. He could see he was inheriting an outfit that was in extremely good shape. He would have to hit the ground running. Fortunately, he was also inheriting a very experienced Senior Pilot, or SPLOT, who would be able to help make sure he did.

Colin Walkinshaw couldn't remember how he'd acquired the nickname 'Boots', but it had stuck. A cultured and thoughtful character, Walkinshaw had impressed all those who'd served with him. 'Boots' had joined the Navy as a General List Officer. In effect this meant he'd signed up for a full-term naval career, unlike the Supplementary List aviators who joined to fly for eight years before returning to civilian life. Walkinshaw had joined the Navy aged eighteen at his father's suggestion. He'd not even thought about the possibility of flying until, during his time at Dartmouth, he spent two weeks at RNAS Brawdy in Wales enjoying Air Experience Flights in Vampires, Piston Provosts and Balliols. He volunteered for the Fleet Air Arm on returning to Dartmouth. As a General List Officer, though, before he could begin flying training, he had to get his Watchkeeping Certificate. And in order to do so, in 1959 the Navy sent him to the Caribbean.

Serving as West Indies Guardship, HMS *Ulster* was based in Bermuda, but spent most of her time sailing further south. After the routine at Dartmouth, 'Boots' found life on board the frigate hectic as they anchored off different islands for a few days, then spent forty-eight hours at sea before stopping in a new location. In Grenada following a hurricane, *Ulster*'s Ship's Company helped repair power and water supplies and clear drainage, and worked to get hospitals back up and running. After Grenada had been helped to her feet they sailed west towards British Honduras. On this occasion, the mainland colony had escaped the winds and as a result *Ulster*'s visit was essentially social. With the frigate anchored off Belize City, the ship's officers went ashore for a party held by the Governor at

Government House. Friendly conversations over cocktails led to further invitations.

Come back to dinner.

Come and spend the day with us on Sunday.

And in passing, someone mentioned the Guatemalans.

'We have a problem with next door,' Walkinshaw was told. 'They keep on rattling their sabres at us across the border.' And he thought no more about it. He never imagined he'd have cause to.

Chapter 5

Guatemalan anger over the dispute with Britain wasn't beyond producing moments of comedy. The year before HMS *Ulster*'s stopover, the Guatemalan President, General Ydígoras Fuentes – a firebrand who'd seized power after the assassination of his predecessor and had wasted no time in then challenging the Mexican President to a pistol duel – also paid a visit. In April 1958, Ydígoras presented himself at the border crossing of Benque Viejo brandishing a copy of the Guatemalan constitution. Unsure of what was expected of him, the corporal on duty at the Benque police station phoned his superiors, who in turn sought the advice of the Governor. The Governor made it clear that the General was very welcome. But that if he wanted to be treated with the kind of pomp and ceremony a visiting head of state might expect, he should, in future, try to give more notice of his arrival. Ydígoras returned immediately to Guatemala with his constitution.

And in January 1962, Francisco Sagastume, a political opponent of Ydígoras, slipped into British Honduras with his twenty-strong army. On arrival at Pueblo Viejo, five miles past the border, Sagastume burnt photographs of the Queen and Duke of Edinburgh and declared that liberation was at hand before borrowing a truck from local policemen – who seemed eager to get him on his way – and moving on east to Punta Gorda, the largest town in the southern Toledo District of British Honduras. Three miles from their goal they ran out of petrol and were rounded up by police backed by a handful of troops from the Royal Hampshire Regiment.

Both episodes were well-received in Guatemala – and Sagastume's excursion became the defining moment of his life. But while neither was more than a stunt, both provided evidence that Guatemala's wounded pride and resentment over British Honduras were still close to the surface.

The collapse of the Spanish empire in Central America left in its wake several unresolved territorial issues. The most peculiar of these was British Honduras. Since 1483, when the Pope had – with hindsight rather expansively – granted Spain all of Central America, the Spanish had never physically occupied the territory of British Honduras. So in 1821, when newly independent countries and federations unyoked themselves from Spain, she was an anomaly. As she had never been settled by anyone but the British, there were doubts as to whether she was even in Spain's gift.

A simple treaty, signed by Britain and Guatemala in April 1859, sought to settle things. Article 1 of the treaty agreed the boundaries between Guatemala and British Honduras. But it was Article 7 that became the foundation of the dispute that followed. And all it said was, after confirming 'the limits of the two countries being now clearly defined', that both parties would give their 'best efforts' to establishing, by road or river, 'the easiest communications' between the capital of Guatemala and the Atlantic Coast near Belize City. That's it.

The treaty was ratified in September of the same year. But Article 7 became the pretext for all subsequent Guatemalan claims.

By the 1930s, after the discovery of oil in Mexico and Venezuela, the failure of 'best efforts' to bear fruit led to calls for the 1859 treaty to be thrown out. Guatemala renewed her claim on the southern half of British Honduras and, in 1948, Britain was forced to despatch the cruiser HMS *Sheffield* when intelligence reached London that she planned to act on it.

Past ambiguities had hardened into bitter conviction. In Guatemala, opinion over British Honduras became an article of faith – a historical kick in the face that needed to be made right. And nowhere is wounded pride more dangerous than Latin America. Simmering border tensions and territorial disputes always had the potential to tip into war.

In July 1969, after riots at World Cup qualifiers, expulsions of migrant workers and a breaking off of diplomatic relations, the Salvadorean army invaded its neighbour Honduras (not British Honduras) in what's subsequently been known as the 'Football War'. The hundred-hour conflict saw the last ever dogfights between Second World War-vintage' fighters, when Honduran Air Force Vought F-4U Corsairs tangled with El Salvadorean North American F-51 Mustangs in the skies over the border. During the war, a Salvadorean Mustang was impounded at Guatemala's La Aurora Air Force base after making an emergency landing. It was a further reminder that the use of force came easily in Central America.

By 1971, it was clear to John Weymes in Guatemala City and Sir John Paul in British Honduras that the Guatemalans were no less willing to use their own Air Force to make a point. When Fuerza Aerea Guatemalteca (FAG) F-51s machine-gunned and sank four Salvadorean fishing boats, one crew member was killed, several were wounded and another was listed as missing – his body never found. The Guatemalan Army was quick to explain:

We are in a state of siege and having had information that an invasion of Guatemala was being prepared the Guatemalan Air Force was ordered to patrol the coasts of the Pacific, discovering today at 1525 hours in territorial waters more than fifteen vessels without a flag which were within Guatemalan waters less than a mile from the coast of 'Las Lisas' with the evident intention of disembarking. They were warned to identify themselves which they did not do whereupon the Guatemalan Air Force proceeded to do its duty, opening fire as any other nation would have done in defence of its sovereignty.

And the Salvadoreans were supposed to be allies.

In his new office in Belmopan, reading the Guatemalan statement in a telegram from the Foreign Office, Sir John couldn't help but highlight that last line and scribble a question mark in the margin. The Guatemalan generals were paranoid. Seeing threats real and imagined in every shadow and round every corner they were, by their own admission, inclined to shoot first and ask questions later.

When the Guatemalan Ambassador to the UN was asked about British Honduras and replied that his country 'would deal with the problem the way matters have always been dealt with in Central America', his answer dripped with malevolence. And it provided neither the British Governor nor Weymes with much cause for comfort. And then, in February 1971, a squadron of seven FAG F-51D Mustangs of the Escuadrón de Caza took off from La Aurora airbase south of Guatemala City. Taking their lead from the Squadron Commander, Major Francisco Consenza, the American-built piston-engined fighters climbed and turned to the north-west and set course for a remote airstrip carved out of the dense jungles of El Petén at Tikal Archaeological Park. It was an exotic location for a military deployment. Tikal was the site of some of perhaps the most spectacular Mayan ruins ever discovered.

Until the strip had been built in 1951 the difficult overland journey to Tikal had taken days. Tikal's inaccessibility was one reason why the treasures there had remained unexplored for so long, despite explorers hearing tantalizing rumours of 'a living ancient city, the white towers of which could still be seen above the treetops in the middle of the tropical jungle'. Tikal was awe-inspiring. Limestone stepped pyramids rising steeply hundreds of feet into the air were just the most eye-catching feature of the largest Classic Maya city in Central America. Abandoned by the Maya in the tenth century, it had been over-taken by the rainforest in the centuries that had followed. But with the building of the strip, the trickle of archaeologists that followed the first formal expedition in 1848 turned into a large-scale excavation that began in 1956. By 1971, the archaeologists had released from the grip of the jungle much of a site estimated to cover 23 square miles.

Two days before the Mustangs arrived, a pair of Douglas C-47s of the Escuadrón de Transporte carrying tents, supplies, spares and ammunition flew in. Operación TIKAL, as it was known to the FAG, was designed to test the fighter squadron's ability to operate effectively from the unpaved strip – away from the facilities at La Aurora. It wasn't easy. The officers and men lived under canvas in the rainforest for nearly a month, training with Mk 81 125kg iron bombs, 5-inch rockets and BLU-32B napalm canisters for attacks against ground targets. Each Mustang also carried six .5-inch machine guns mounted inside the wings.

Crucial to the FAG's choice of the airstrip for the exercise was its location. Tikal was only thirty-one miles from the border with British Honduras.

Chapter 6

As her bows rose and fell through the Atlantic rollers, John Roberts stood on *Ark Royal*'s bridge looking down through thick armoured glass at carefully arranged aircraft spotted around the flight deck. Each aircraft type, and there were five aboard *Ark*, was completely distinctive. But you'd be hard-pushed to describe them as a good-looking collection. Handsome possibly, purposeful probably, and certainly an acquired taste, there was a case to be made for them being the most ungainly-looking collection of aeroplanes ever assembled on one ship's deck. There was none of the clean-lined elegance of earlier generations of FAA aircraft, fondly remembered fighters like the Seafire, Sea Fury, Sea Hornet and Seahawk. When the first McDonnell-Douglas F-4 Phantoms were delivered to the Royal Navy, one admiral was sufficiently alarmed to ask whether it had been delivered upside down. The big interceptor's awkward accumulation of mismatched angles, edges and curves had already earned it the nickname 'Double Ugly' from its American pilots. It was also an American who described the Buccaneer as 'the world's ugliest aircraft, from every ugly angle'. The Fairey Gannet AEW3 was simply as awkward-looking as her name suggested – and that was *before* they bolted a large, disfiguring search radar beneath her tall, piscine fuselage. With her wings folded up like origami, the Gannet didn't look like she could possibly ever fly. The Westland Sea King HAS1 was the fourth – and newest – member of *Ark*'s frontline. The Sea King at least looked like a

44

helicopter. But it wasn't just about looks. The Phantom, Buccaneer, Gannet and Sea King – along with the two old Wessex helicopters of the Search and Rescue Flight – were the most capable and complete air group that the Royal Navy had ever assembled. After being forced to take second-best for most of its existence, the FAA had, as the curtain came down, got itself ahead of the curve. And carrying them all through the long swells was *Ark Royal* herself. She now had the biggest deck ever seen on a British aircraft carrier – extended in almost every direction during her long refit. One new 200-foot steam catapult had been fitted along the angled flight deck – the waist cat. The 154-foot bow cat had been completely reconditioned. Projecting forwards from each of them were *Ark*'s now increasingly familiar bridle catchers – fitted to prevent the thick steel cable that attached the aircraft to the catapult shuttle from falling into the sea after each launch. Completing the comprehensive reworking of *Ark*'s flying facilities were, jutting out from the bridge to port, a long extension sideways to Flyco which now offered panoramic views forward and aft, chocks in the deck tailored to fit the undercarriage of the Phantoms and Buccaneers, and the brand-new direct-acting arresting gear that had been vital to coping with the higher landing speeds and weights of the F-4s. *Ark Royal* had been well and truly 'Phantomized'. With her squadrons embarked, she was the most powerful surface ship the Royal Navy has ever put to sea. Before or since.

As the *Ark Royal* steamed west, her role within and value to NATO's Atlantic Striking Fleet now clear, her sister-ship, HMS *Eagle*, had begun her long goodbye, a final Far East cruise before Britain shut up shop East of Suez. *Eagle* was to be paid off on her return. The relationship between the ships was always an unequal one, but the rivalry that existed between the two 'Audacious' class carriers was particularly strongly felt aboard *Eagle*. *Ark* had always enjoyed the greater recognition and affection, her name deeply ingrained in public consciousness. It was all in that name, *Ark Royal*, first coined after Sir Walter Raleigh sold the 692-ton, 100-foot long *Ark Raleigh* to the Crown and renamed her. There had been two others since, including the famous Second World War carrier. The present *Ark* was the fourth. And her Battle Honours said it all:

Armada 1588
Cádiz 1596
Dardanelles 1915
Norway 1940
Spartivento 1940
Mediterranean 1940–41
Bismarck 1941
Malta Convoys 1941

Eagle couldn't compete. A proud name and a proud ship, she shared honours for the Mediterranean and Malta Convoys campaigns of the Second World War. On there too, though, was Lowestoft, the less than evocative setting of a battle fought in 1665.

John Roberts was taking his ship to AFWR – the US Navy's Atlantic Fleet Weapons Ranges off Puerto Rico. It was the first time a British carrier had been given the opportunity to take advantage of the vast, state-of-the-art training facilities there. It was a chance for *Ark Royal* and her air group to try to put it all together – to make sure that they were pitch-perfect and fully worked up in every department. The Americans called it OPREDEX – Operational Readiness Exercise. And each one of *Ark*'s four squadrons needed to measure up. Without the F-4s and Gannets *Ark* was vulnerable from the air, without the anti-submarine Sea Kings she was exposed from the deep, and without the Buccaneers she was pointless. As useful, as one well-worn phrase goes, as a self-licking ice cream. John Roberts had to be able to deliver all of these capabilities on demand, without pause or demur. AFWR would help make sure he could, as well as exposing any weaknesses. Gaining access to the US Navy ranges had been hard fought for by Roberts's immediate superior, Flag Officer Carriers and

Amphibious Ships – FOCAS – Admiral John Treacher. The Admiral's own combat experience flying Supermarine Seafire FR47s during the Korean War had left him in no doubt about the value of the realistic training the US ranges could provide.

The aircrews took advantage of what was on offer. And they pushed themselves hard. Always inherently dangerous, the job of a naval aviator offered no quarter in peace or war. A single, momentary error of judgement could have fatal consequences.

Chapter 7

Phantom 007 swooped down from her target's starboard quarter – unloading, diving from height to build up speed. The key to flying and fighting the McDonnell-Douglas F-4 Phantom II was speed. Keep it high and you were always in with a chance. Lose energy, get too slow, and you'd get tagged. And that was just what Lieutenant Nigel 'Toobs' Charles and his Observer, Lieutenant Commander Dougal Macdonald, knew was about to happen to their opponents.

The two jets were carving up one of the US Navy's 'Warming Areas', large boxes of sky off Florida's Atlantic coast, cleared of civil traffic. Before closing for the dogfight, the Observers had each practised BVR – Beyond Visual Range – intercepts using the Phantom's powerful AN/AWG-11 pulse-Doppler radar. Now, though, it was fully developed ACM – Air Combat Manouevring – each pilot looking to get close enough to their opponent to claim a guns kill. In this, 21-year-old 'Toobs' Charles excelled. Charles made a virtue of being an uncomplicated character. 'I ain't very bright,' he'd tell people, 'but I can't half lift things.' A fierce loose forward on the rugby pitch, he took the same marauding approach to dogfighting. In the Observer's seat was 892 Naval Air Squadron's Air Warfare Instructor, Dougal Macdonald, a Scot with his own reputation for hard-nosed belligerence in the air. They were, as Dave Hill and Jerry Granger-Holcombe – the crew of the other Phantom, 001 – were about to discover, a formidable partnership.

Easy meat, thought Macdonald, as Charles pulled back on the stick, hauling the jet's nose up, power from the two reheated Rolls-Royce Speys driving her into a tight starboard turn in search of a tracking solution on the other jet. In the back, Macdonald was pushed back into his seat by the mounting 'g'. He tensed his calf, thigh and stomach muscles to try to force the blood out of them – keeping it from draining away from his brain – and stop himself blacking out. An inflatable g-suit – speed jeans – around his waist and legs inflated under g-loading, like the cuffs used to check a patient's blood pressure, to help his own efforts. As Charles pulled, 007's nose raised level with the horizon and the 'g' piled on. Their bodies grew heavier – twice their normal weight at 2g. As they pulled 5g in search of a firing angle, each man weighed upwards of 60 stone. Any movement demanded huge physical effort. You could hear stilted breathing and involuntary grunts over the intercom.

Charles and Macdonald were closing in, barely 250 yards behind, the white underside of the other Phantom exposed and vulnerable. In 001 Hill was trying to throw them off, raising the nose, pulling into a turn to kill the angle. Trouble was he'd lost energy. His speed was down low, less than 300 knots, and the big interceptor didn't like that at all. She was deep into the buffet.

As the aircrew grow in weight under 'g' so too does the airframe. And so, therefore, does the lift needed from the wings to keep it in the air. Pulling 4g, a Phantom doesn't weigh 25 tons – it weighs 100. Get this equation wrong and your multi-million pound Mach 2 all-weather wonder jet will fall out of the sky as surely as a sack of spuds dropped from a bridge.

Charles was ready to call 'Fox three. Knock it off.' Tell them they'd been nailed. When to his astonishment, the other Phantom suddenly appeared to be pointing straight at him.

'Shit, how did he do that?' a shocked Charles asked Macdonald. But Hill had lost control of his aircraft. Without the air speed to cope with his efforts to haul her out of the sights of their attacker, the F-4, always a pig at high angles of attack, just pitched up and let go, the airflow over her wings no longer fast or smooth enough to keep her flying. 001 was falling.

'Dougal,' Charles shouted, 'he's in a spin!'

Macdonald glanced at the altimeter: 8000 feet. Too low. In the intensity of the dogfight they'd bust through the briefed hard-deck of 10,000 feet. Dave Hill didn't have the altitude to recover from a spin.

'They'd better get out quickly,' said Macdonald over the intercom as he watched the stricken jet tumble past their port side. And he pressed the RT button to transmit.

Inside 001, Jerry Granger-Holcombe knew it was over.

'I'm going,' he told Hill, his hands already on the yellow and black ejection seat handle between his legs.

'Eject! Eject! Eject!' shouted Macdonald into the oxygen mask clamped over his face as he twisted round trying to keep a bead on the falling Phantom. Granger-Holcombe heard the urgency in the Scot's voice crackle through his helmet as he pulled the handle. Fractions of a second later, a cat's cradle of cords around his shins tightened, pulling his legs back towards his body, ensuring that when the Martin-Baker Mk H5 zero-zero ejection seat fired, he'd keep them. Then, in sequence, the canopy jettisoned and the primary cartridge fired, followed by two secondary cartridges. And within half a second of pulling the handle, Granger-Holcombe exploded out of the cockpit at a speed of 80 feet per second.

Charles, keeping a careful eye on his own speed, turned back towards 001 and saw a single parachute.

'One of them's out,' he confirmed, then watched as the falling Phantom smashed into the calm surface of the sea in an eruption of white water and steam. He'd only seen one 'chute.

'One's gone in with the aeroplane.'

Ashore at Naval Air Station Cecil Field, Lieutenant Harry O'Grady, 892 Squadron's Fighter Controller, heard it all unfold over the RT.

Macdonald's Scottish accent again cut through the static.

'Mayday! Mayday! Mayday!' he began, reporting what had

50

happened – the loss of the jet, its position, but no confirmation of whether or not both men had got out.

As Charles and Macdonald flew west, a laconic American voice crackled over the RT.

'We got a Down Bird,' it drawled.

Few flight regimes gulp fuel faster than fully developed ACM. With full reheat engaged, the Phantom burns fuel at a colossal rate. Charles was able to manage just one low, lazy circuit of the scene before they, reluctantly, had to turn for home. At Naval Air Station Cecil Field, Harry O'Grady scrambled a pair of Bell UH-1 Huey search-and-rescue helicopters. A hundred miles out to sea, at the limit of their range, each would only be able to carry a single survivor.

By the time that 'Toobs' Charles spotted Dave Hill descending under his parachute, a dinghy pack swinging below him on a long lanyard, Jerry Granger-Holcombe was already in the water. Charles had seen both 'chutes but he hadn't seen them both in the air at the same time.

Jerry Granger-Holcombe had injured his hand during the ejection and wasn't able to release himself from his parachute canopy. But he was lucky that the sea was like a millpond. With his good hand, he managed to clamber into his little one-man dinghy and collapse the 'chute. Dave Hill soon found him.

'Fancy seeing you here!' his Pilot quipped with a smile.

'Yes, nice afternoon for a swim . . .' After exchanging pleasantries the two flyers locked their dinghies together and waited to be rescued. A big four-engined Lockheed P-3 Orion droned on to the scene almost immediately to reassure them that help was indeed on it its way.

As they were flown back to Jacksonville Hospital aboard the Hueys, the crew of Granger-Holcombe's helo pointed out the sharks cruising below the surface all the way from where they'd gone down to the Florida coast. *Exciting*, he thought . . .

Harry O'Grady met the two aviators in the hospital, where celebrations for their safe recovery began with medicinal brandy. Reunited with the rest of the squadron at Cecil Field, they continued late into the night, underneath walls plastered with pin-ups and posters revealing US naval aircrews' real feelings about Ho Chi Minh. Heaped on the floor of the mess were Hill and Granger-Holcombe's two soaking-wet parachutes. As the party took hold and the beer flowed faster, Harry O'Grady's counterpart in the Cecil Field Air Control Center asked him whether the downed F-4 had been the fighter or the target.

'Target,' O'Grady told him.

'Man,' said the American, smiling and shaking his head, 'you Limeys play it for real!' And with a few Gimlets inside him – and the crew safe – O'Grady smiled proudly. But the bottom line was that 892 had still lost one of their precious F-4s. And it was a loss that the Navy's tiny Phantom fleet could ill afford.

On 6 December 1959, the prototype McDonnell-Douglas Phantom, the YF4H-1, took off from Edwards Air Force Base, California, on Operation TOP FLIGHT. At a height of 50,000 feet, the pilot, Commander Lawrence Flint, levelled off, opened the throttles of the two General-Electric J-79 turbojet engines and accelerated to over Mach 2. Then he pulled back on the stick and the big jet soared into the vertical, trading speed for height. He carried on up, the sky turning dark blue-black, the curve of the earth visible behind him, until the engines, starved of oxygen, flamed out. Flint continued upwards, weightless as he gently coaxed the gliding jet over the top of the parabola. He'd recorded an altitude of 98,557 feet. And the world record for absolute altitude had been won back from the Soviet Union.

Following Operation TOP FLIGHT the Phantom went on to break closed-circuit records around courses laid out across the Mojave desert, set a new record for transcontinental flight between Los Angeles and New York of 2 hours, 48 minutes, set an average speed of 902.769 mph flying at barely 150 feet across the White Sands Missile Range in New Mexico, break every time-to-height record in existence – and, in the process, top 100,000 feet. And, in November 1961, Operation SKY-BURNER finally wrested the World Absolute Speed Record away from Britain's Peter Twiss by recording a mean speed over two runs of 1,606.3 mph, a whisker short of Mach 2.6, or over two and a half times the speed of sound.

The US Navy's new interceptor, the McDonnell-Douglas F-4 Phantom II was proving to be a genuinely astonishing aeroplane. That, of course, was before the British – unable to resist the temptation to take something apart and try to put it back together again – got their hands on it. In the summer of 1964, the F-4 was ordered for the Fleet Air Arm, but in order for it to be able to operate safely from the smaller decks of British carriers, a few alterations needed to be made, the most significant of which was the replacement of the US aircraft's J-79 engines with reheated Rolls-Royce Speys. These, in combination with an extended nosewheel undercarriage leg, would provide the Royal Navy's Phantom, the F-4K, with the necessary power and lift to launch safely from shorter British catapults. On paper it looked like a winning combination, providing greater overall performance and better fuel economy. In practice, the extra drag created by fitting the big British engines negated the hoped-for benefits. And yet, as disappointing as this was, once the teething problems with the new Rolls-Royce turbofans were sorted out, it was far from disastrous. The Phantom was just too strong a design. Operationally, the differences in performance were marginal – and did nothing to dent the effectiveness of the Phantom's weapons system. An advanced pulse-Doppler radar, able to pick out targets against clutter from the sea's surface, married with four medium-range AIM-7 Sparrow radar-guided missiles and four heat-seeking AIM-9 Sidewinders, meant that when they were delivered in 1967 the Fleet Air Arm's Phantoms were, by a long chalk, the most capable fighters in service in Britain. They soon had a chance to remind people of that when, just a few months after 892 NAS – destined to be the Fleet Air Arm's only front-line Phantom unit – was recommissioned at the end of 1968, they set a record of their own. Competing in the *Daily Mail*

Transatlantic Race, Lieutenant Commander Brian Davies, the squadron Boss, and his Senior Observer, Lieutenant Commander Pete Goddard, set a fastest time between New York and London of 4 hours, 46 minutes. Such a leap in performance and capability had needed some careful preparation.

An exchange programme between the Royal Navy and US Navy had existed for many years. But from 1964 onwards, in advance of the Phantom's introduction into Royal Navy service, small numbers of experienced FAA Pilots and Observers were sent to Naval Air Station Miramar in California, where they flew as instructors on VF-121, the US Navy Fleet's Replacement Air Group, or RAG. At 'Fightertown, USA', the Brits helped train rookie crews in the rudiments of flying and fighting the F-4 before these students were posted to front-line squadrons. At the end of their tours, the British exchange crews were able to bring home great experience of the Phantom and its systems, but the relationship was a reciprocal one. The presence of British instructors on VF-121 made available a handful more US Navy aircrews to the front-line fighting in Vietnam – a war that by the end of the decade had sucked in over half a million US troops. A war that was not going well.

And there were some who feared that American involvement in Guatemala was heading in the same direction. 'The war in Guatemala has already begun,' wrote one commentator, 'and to date thousands of Guatemalans have been killed as well as several North Americans, among them the US Ambassador and two military attachés.' Ironically, it was hard experience and lessons learnt from Vietnam that were helping to fuel the conflict in Guatemala. Between 1961 and 1967, the number of graduates from the Jungle Training course at the US Army's School of the Americas at Fort Gulick in the Panama Canal Zone jumped from 1700 to nearly 10,000. Along with their own soldiers, US instructors also taught ever-rising numbers of students from throughout Latin America in counter-insurgency. In Panama, Guatemalan soldiers were trained in a range of skills that included small-group patrolling, jungle survival, camouflage, booby-traps, interrogation and psychological operations. Guatemalan troops took what they'd learnt home and used it to devastating effect on both left-wing guerrillas and the civilian population accused of harbouring them. All in all, America's record in Guatemala provided little cause for celebration. In 1954, CIA pilots flying a shambolic collection of old Republic P-47 Thunderbolts, supported by a US naval blockade, overthrew Guatemala's elected President, Jacobo Arbenz. The coup was ordered after Arbenz instigated land reforms that threatened the Guatemalan holdings of America's United Fruit Company. On the Board of the UFC was Allen Dulles, the CIA's new Director. The messy CIA operation that overthrew Arbenz seemed always perched on the cusp of failure, but its eventual success was the catalyst for the coups, dictatorships, terrorism and counter-insurgency wars that had stalked Guatemala ever since.

The School of the Americas counter-insurgency course was developed by US Special Forces in reaction to Castro's seizure of power in Cuba. And Cuba loomed large in the thinking of both the American and the Guatemalan governments. From September 1960, two secret Guatemalan military bases, code-named JMTrax and JMMadd, provided a home for Brigade 2506 – the force of Cubans in exile being trained by the CIA for the Bay of Pigs invasion. A failure to destroy Castro's air force on the ground on the first day led to the decimation of Brigade 2506's limited air support by Cuban Lockheed T-33s and old British piston-engined Hawker Sea Fury FB11s. Of the ground force put ashore on Cuba's south coast, 114 were killed and 1189 captured. In a doomed effort to preserve a degree of deniability, the US had been half-hearted in its support of the Cuban exiles. America hadn't played to her strengths and as a result she'd been humiliated. But it was relatively easy to shrug off the failure of a poorly equipped, American-sponsored exile air force. Of far greater emerging concern was the worryingly poor performance of *American* pilots on the other side of the world. US Navy pilots in Vietnam were struggling to gain the upper hand against the enemy. And, by the end of the sixties, concern about their poor performance had become so acute that addressing the situation became a priority for US admirals. And in the effort to turn things round, the small British contingent at Miramar would play an important part.

Chapter 8

Alongside its Phantom squadron, Miramar was home to VF-124, its equivalent Crusader RAG. And it was Vought F-8 Crusader jockeys who walked into the bar at Happy Hour with the biggest swagger. The single-seat F-8s were *real* pilots' jets, known to their pilots as 'The Last of the Gunfighters'. Relatively small and agile, armed with machine guns and short-range missiles, they were out-and-out dogfighters. The Phantom, by contrast, was huge, carried a crew of two and wasn't even equipped with a gun, relying instead on guided missiles alone. For all its record-breaking, the Navy never expected their new interceptor to get tangled up in the messy business of dogfighting. It was supposed to be beyond all that. And Miramar's F-8 pilots had become bored of ambushing them. Screaming into someone's six o'clock only to provoke a gentle 2g turn in response – where was the fun in that? They'd almost started to ignore the Phantoms until one of them stumbled on to the tail of an F-4 being flown by a Royal Navy Air Warfare Instructor called Geoff Hunt. And *he* wasn't having any of it.

In response to the indignity of discovering an F-8 on his tail, Hunt slammed the Phantom's engines through the gate to engage full afterburner and pulled into a screaming turn towards the attacking F-8. And then the two jets fought until their fuel was gone. The Crusader pilot landed with eyes like dinner plates.

Only the best were selected to go on the Royal Navy's Air

Warfare Instructors' Course. And for most students it was the most demanding, most rewarding flying that they would ever enjoy. Ground theory at HMS *Excellent*, the Naval Gunnery School in Portsmouth, was followed by three months' intensive flying with 764 NAS at Lossiemouth. Flying three, four and sometimes five sorties a day in the squadron's Hunters, students would learn about every aspect of modern tactics and weaponry, from ACM and developing spatial awareness leading divisional attacks of four aircraft, to delivering nuclear weapons. Sandwiched around the flying they were given lessons on how to brief and debrief a sortie, and taught about teaching. Because when they were posted to their next squadrons, it would be as the squadron AWI – the resident expert: 764 instructed its students to join their squadrons and share what they'd learnt, spreading that expertise throughout the whole front line. And they'd been doing it since 1959. Through the instructors on exchange at Miramar, the AWIs' methods made their way into perhaps the most well-known programme in the history of naval aviation: Topgun.

The Brits at Miramar did their best to fit in. They gave themselves US-style call signs. But rather than the Vipers and Mavericks that seemed to prevail, they came up with Alien, Dogbreath, Cholmondley and Spastic. When Lieutenant Dick Lord RN arrived at Miramar in 1966 he called himself Brit One – because he was South African and because he liked the idea of his American wingman having to call himself Brit 2. Lord was staggered by the size of the operation the US Navy had there. Sitting on the hard-standing were more aircraft than made up the entire Fleet Air Arm. His own squadron, VF-121, had over eighty. And it was in the unit's sheer size – the volume of people involved – that Lord, a single-minded and talented fighter pilot, quickly realized that a problem lay. As he passed around the debriefing cubicles that surrounded the main room he listened in. No one teaching tactics was more revered than those pilots who'd killed MiGs in Vietnam.

'All right kid, you fly like this,' Lord heard them say, 'because this is how I flew in Vietnam. And if you don't, they're going to bust your ass!' Then in the next cubicle he'd hear something completely different.

'All right kid, you fly like *this*, because that's how *I* flew in Vietnam. And, if you don't, they're going to bust your ass!' There was no clear, consistent message. He could only imagine how it must scramble the brains of eager-to-impress young students.

For the debriefing following his first sortie as an instructor, Lord asked for coloured chalk. On the AWI Course at Lossie, after every engagement he scribbled down headings, speeds, who did what, when, where errors were made. Then, in the debrief after the sortie, he could re-create the fight on the blackboard, pick it apart in detail and learn from it. It took the ego and subjectivity out of it – stopped a debrief just becoming a pissing contest. Now using the same techniques at Miramar he pointed out his students' errors and explained how and where he'd gained an advantage. And soon he found that his debriefs were starting to get crowded. Dan McIntyre, Boss of the air-to-air section of VF-121, noticed it too and asked him to write a revised ACM syllabus for the whole squadron and tour the West Coast bases lecturing US Navy attack pilots on ACM.

Lord threw himself into it and, in early 1968, was slipped a dusty file marked 'Top Secret: For US Eyes Only' containing USAF Major John Boyd's work on energy manoeuvrability. Shot through with mathematical formulae as it was, he could see why the report had been gathering dust. But Lord stuck with it and realized it was gold dust. Boyd had used graphs to illustrate the performance envelopes of different fighters. By overlaying one graph with another, Boyd's work could show you exactly where your own aircraft's advantage lay. And exactly where your weaknesses were to be found. Lord added it to his teaching, amused that he was now lecturing on something he wasn't even allowed to have read.

As the war in Vietnam deepened, sucking in men and materiel in ever greater quantities, alarm was growing among US admirals about the performance of the Navy's fighters – and especially about its new 'hot ship', the F-4 Phantom. By the end of the sixties, the F-4 had only accounted for thirteen MiGs. The older, simpler, gun-armed F-8 Crusader had eighteen. More worryingly, the overall American kill ratio against the MiGs was stubbornly refusing to rise much above 2:1. Just two small, cheap enemy jets for every multimillion-dollar American fighter. Throughout the Second World War and Korea the ratio had been closer to 10:1. Something had clearly gone wrong.

In the summer of 1968, Dick Lord left Miramar to become the Royal Navy's pre-eminent weapons and tactics instructor, the Air Warfare Instructor of 764 NAS itself. But his legacy at Miramar was there for all to see in the standardization, organization and rigour of the new VF-121 tactics course. A couple of months after Lord returned to the UK, one of his fellow instructors, Lieutenant Commander Dan Pederson USN, the squadron's Operations Officer, became the first CO of the Navy Fighter Weapons School. NFWS was soon dubbed 'Topgun'. Its role, like 764, was to take the best crews in the fleet and, for a month, give them intense and comprehensive tuition in aerial combat before sending them back to share that knowledge in squadron Ready Rooms throughout the Navy. Topgun wasn't consciously modelled on the Royal Navy's Air Warfare Instructors' Course, but the similarities were pronounced, and Pederson was quick to acknowledge Lord's contribution – he'd attended some of the Fleet Air Arm pilot's lectures himself. Dick Lord's work at the VF-121 Tactics Group was the foundation on which Pederson and the original eight Topgun instructors built their course. One of the eight, John Nash, maintained that the month-long course was 'nothing more than an extended course of the RAG tactics syllabus'. And, of course, Lord had written that syllabus.

In 1970, a Phantom launched from the deck of the USS *Constellation* shot down a MiG-21 with an AIM-9 Sidewinder missile. It was the first MiG shot down by the US Navy in nearly two years of war. The pilot's name was Lieutenant Jerry Beaulier. And he was a graduate of the first class ever to pass through Topgun.

Dick Lord's parting gift to Miramar was a typed fourteen-page document he called 'Flying and Fighting the Phantom'. It was a distillation of all he'd learnt about the jet in his time in the tactics group. Copies were handed to every single VF-121 student on his arrival at Miramar. It was also sent to McDonnell-Douglas, the Phantom's manufacturer. They were sufficiently impressed to quote from it on the opening page of the F-4's operating manual, known as NATOPS:

> To be successful in the fighter business the aircrew must, first and foremost, have a thorough background in fighter tactics. They must acquire an excellent knowledge of all their equipment. Then they must approach the problem with a spirit of aggression, and with utter confidence.

It sat alongside just one other quotation. And that was from Manfred von Richthofen, the Red Baron: the most famous fighter pilot who's ever lived.

Dougal Macdonald was Dick Lord's last ever student at 764 NAS. Not everyone coped with either the physical or the psychological stresses of the AWI Course. Over three months, students spent a *lot* of time pulling 'g' and flying straight at the ground – and that was never a game for the faint-hearted. And in being an Observer rather than a Pilot going through the Air Warfare Instructors' Course, Macdonald was a rarity. As a Looker he had no direct control over the aircraft, but, in having responsibility for navigation and operating the weapons system, he controlled nearly everything else. Without him, the guy in the front seat could fly fast and make a lot of noise, but he couldn't fight a war. It was a lesson that old-school fighter jocks were still getting to grips with. A fighter with a two-man crew was more capable than a single-seater. The workload was shared; you had an extra pair of eyes.

Dick Lord took the young Observer under his wing, flying as Pilot on most of Macdonald's sorties himself. He was determined that Macdonald was going to get through. His first impression of any young aircrew he met came from the look in their eyes. Macdonald was tough and eager, his eyes were alive with the spark Lord was looking for. Much more than the Pilots, Lord knew, the Lookers were completely outside their comfort zone at 764. But Macdonald thrived during his time at Lossie.

And, as a result, 892 had lost one of its Phantoms, hounded out of the sky by Macdonald and his Pilot. In his small cabin back aboard *Ark Royal*, the squadron Boss, Nick Kerr, was relieved to hear that Hill and Granger-Holcombe had got out safely. And he looked forward without any enthusiasm whatsoever to a lot of bloody paperwork and the board of inquiry that would follow their ejection.

Chapter 9

Carl Davis, the Boss of *Ark*'s Buccaneer squadron, wasn't too distracted by the loss of 892's Phantom. Nick Kerr's crew were safe after all. He was more irritated that, along with Kerr, he'd been made to stay aboard the ship glad-handing local dignitaries, rather than disembark with the rest of 809 alongside the Phantoms to Naval Air Station Cecil Field.

In any case, as a naval aviator you *had* to be fatalistic. There was barely an officer in any of the fixed-wing squadrons who hadn't had first-hand experience of tragedy. When he was CO of a Hunter training squadron Davis had watched helpless as a student inexplicably flew straight into the sea. The Senior Observer – SOBS – of 809 had survived an ejection from a Buccaneer after a mid-air collision. Another squadron pilot, Pete Lewis, had broken both legs and been extremely lucky to survive following a low-level ejection. The picture was the same on the Phantom squadron. The Gannets too. Guy Holman, CO of 849 'B' flight, *Ark Royal*'s Airborne Early Warning unit, had watched as a 500lb bomb, dropped by a Sea Vixen, exploded the moment it left the aircraft. All that followed the blast was falling wreckage and an empty parachute. He'd seen a Gannet flip over on final approach and kill its pilot. And he'd been Flight Deck Officer when a good friend seemed have landed on safely, only for his arrestor hook to be ripped out of the back of the Gannet when the wire, stuck like a jammed inertia reel seat belt, failed to run out. The broken Gannet's momentum took it over the front of the deck and into the sea.

The Observers got out. But Holman had to watch as his friend, the Gannet sinking in the wake of the ship, tried three times to escape, each time getting trapped as the cockpit canopy ran forward and back on its runners. He never made it out.

Even the Sea King helicopter squadron had an Observer whose back had been so damaged during an ejection that the medics banned him from ejection seats, restricting him to flying helicopters instead – a couple of inches shorter than he'd been while flying fast jets.

There was no escaping it. The FAA's accident statistics in the sixties were horrifying – worse than the fatality rates for the German F-104 Starfighters, and they had earned the unenviable sobriquet of 'The Widowmaker'. But the journalist who first unearthed this fact was quickly persuaded not to run with it. It was not, he was told, in any way a good news story about the bravery of 'Our Boys'.

While sitting in his cabin late one night, Dick Lord learnt of the avoidable death of a young pilot he'd once instructed. The news so upset him that he pulled out a sheet of paper and started writing down in pencil the names of all the men he'd known who'd been killed in the seven years he'd at that point served in the Fleet Air Arm. There were seventy-five of them. *It's slaughter*, he thought to himself as he looked up and down the columns of names of those who'd been lost.

But you had to push it to the back of your mind. Accidents were a fact of life. Naval aviators just had to clear out their locker, drink to their fallen comrades in the wardroom. And sing. Sing at the top of their lungs.

> *All the birds of the air fell a-sighing and a-sobbing*
> *When they heard of the death of Poor Cock Robin*
> *When they heard of the death of Poor Cock Robin*

Beyond letting it all out on the night, they could *only* be unsentimental about it. Friends and colleagues were lost, but the squadrons had to carry on.

Now, six months into the job, Carl Davis had the measure

of his: 809 had been a well-worked-up, well-sorted outfit when he'd assumed command. In many ways the onus had been on him to be up to speed. But he felt like he was on top of things. And it was good to be back aboard *Ark Royal* again. When he made his way up to Flyco after arriving on *Ark* for the first time since his days flying Seahawks in the fifties, he'd been greeted by Commander (Air) – or Wings as he was universally known – with a hard punch on the chest. Davis reckoned that probably meant his arrival was regarded as good news. Wings met bad news and difficult decisions with an announcement that he was 'just off aft for a shit'. John Roberts was more conventionally welcoming. Davis, a talented batsman, had played cricket with the Captain in the Highland League when they were both up at Lossie together. As a result Davis knew him well and had great confidence in him. He also knew that despite his Captain's placid demeanour Roberts was exacting in what he expected of those serving under him and could make his displeasure felt. Davis himself had been on the wrong end of a fierce tongue-lashing from Roberts after leading a division of Seahawks too low over South Wales.

Davis also had his own top team lined up. He flew with the squadron's SOBS, Steve Park. Meticulous on detail and dedicated, the little Scot got mercilessly ribbed by the rest of the squadron for not speaking the Queen's English. At least, though, he'd managed to shake off the nickname 'Jock'. Then there was Neil 'Carbo' Maclean, the squadron's AWI – as competitive in the air as he was on the squash court. Lieutenant Ian Frenz joined in June as the new squadron Qualified Flying Instructor, or QFI, responsible for keeping everyone's flying skills up to scratch. And there was 'Boots' Walkinshaw, SPLOT, 809's Senior Pilot, and his smart, likeable young Observer, Mike Lucas. At 6 foot 4 inches, Lucas could barely fold himself into the back of a Buccaneer, but he brought with him valuable experience from a tour on 803 Squadron, the Fleet Air Arm's weapons trials squadron. Each of the four pilots led a division of four Buccs. And on that first visit to the US Atlantic Fleet Weapons

Range it was 809's divisional leaders who led the charge.

OPREDEX culminated in the launch of ten Buccaneers for a co-ordinated strike with the Americans against the little island of Argos, south-west of Bermuda. Flown in complete radar and radio silence from launch to recovery, the Buccaneer Observers relied on old-fashioned standards of navigation, dead-reckoning and plotting to guide their Pilots there and safely back to *Ark* – 'Mother'.

The squadron prided themselves – indeed their survival depended – on flying too low and too fast to be found and stopped. They took it too extremes – at 30 feet over a smooth sea, with the pilot maintaining forward pressure on the stick to keep her level, an attacking Buccaneer left a visible wake on the surface. The realistic conditions provided by AFWR gave them a chance to demonstrate that their way of flying worked. Reconnaissance photographs taken by Mike Lucas and 'Boots' Walkinshaw as they flew low over buildings on Vieques Island – AFWR's main live bombing range – suggested that the top team were not lacking in either skill or nerve. They'd cleared the ridge where the buildings were located all right. But the pictures showed they were flying *lower* than the tops of the telegraph poles that supplied them.

While the Buccaneers had done their thing, fully armed Phantoms had maintained Combat Air Patrols (CAP) between midday and midnight, sharing responsibility for 24-hour defence with fighter squadrons from an American CVA – the military abbreviation used to describe a strike carrier. On the single occasion they were called on to engage a target, they destroyed an incoming drone with a direct hit from an AIM-9D Sidewinder heat-seeking missile. In the anti-submarine exercises, 824's Westland Sea King HAS1s had shown a capability only dreamed of by US helicopter crews flying more basic, ageing Sikorsky SH-3As. Rear Admiral Treacher had sent *Ark* to the Caribbean to show she could live with the Americans. She'd done so convincingly. But the British and Americans weren't the only ones training for war.

*

As he raised the undercarriage, adjusted the throttle and trimmed his Mustang, FAG-381, in the climb, Major Francisco Consenza was pleased to be saying goodbye to the jungles of El Petén. He set a course to the south-west. Operación TIKAL was over. His relief didn't last long, though. Climbing through 3000 feet over Lake Petén Itzá, the fighter's big Packard-Merlin engine suffered a catastrophic failure, shaking the whole airframe so violently that Consenza had trouble even checking his instruments. With the engine gone, he opened the canopy and rolled the Mustang on to its back. Releasing the harness, he dropped out of the inverted fighter and parachuted to safety. As the F-51s from the rest of his squadron circled above, Consenza was picked up by a nearby Guatemalan Army recon platoon. Ready to fight another day.

For all its public commitment to finding a negotiated settlement to the dispute over British Honduras, Guatemala was going to great lengths to make sure that the squadrons of Fuerza Aerea Guatemalteca were trained and prepared for a military alternative. And it had been doing so for some time.

In late 1970, a two-seat FAG Lockheed T-33 jet flew a reconnaissance sortie over the colony. After several photo runs over the bulk-storage facilities south of the capital, the pilot climbed to medium altitude to fly over Belize City itself. In the back seat, the second crewman snapped away, the pictures showing the town's distinctive shape, built up on lobes of land projecting into the sea, either side of the mouth of the river.

The T-33 overflight was followed a month later by a low pass over Punta Gorda on the southern coast of British Honduras by one of the Mustangs of Major Consenza's Escuadrón de Caza. Observers in the little town made a note of the F-51's new camouflage scheme. The squadron's aircraft had all just received an effective new paint-job in muddy shades of green and brown. In contrast to the natural metal finish it replaced, it made the fighter incredibly difficult to spot against the ground below. All in the FAG knew it as the 'pre-invasion scheme'.

And British Honduras had no air defences of any kind. Then

in the summer of 1971 the balance of power shifted even more firmly in Guatemala's favour when eight Cessna A-37B Dragonflies were delivered to the FAG at La Aurora airbase. These rugged little jets, able to carry their own weight in bombs and rockets, were a formidable addition to the Guatemalan arsenal. Developed specifically for the Close Air Support and counter-insurgency mission, the 'Alphas', as they were known by the FAG, suited their requirements down to the ground. Indeed, they could have been designed especially for them. The new ground attack jets had proved so effective in Vietnam during project COMBAT DRAGON, their evaluation by the 604th Air Commando Squadron, that the USAF went on to order nearly 600 of them. And in Guatemala they were joining an air force whose pilots had real combat experience gained supporting ground troops in the ongoing counter-insurgency war against Fuergas Armadas Rebeldes – FAR – guerrillas.

While FAG fighter-bombers had shown they could fly over the towns and cities of British Honduras with impunity, their C-47 transports also strayed into the colony's airspace while rehearsing paratroop drops. On occasions the big twin-engined troop carriers circled menacingly over the little border town of Benque Viejo, while the soldiers they'd disgorged floated to the ground near Melchor de Mencos on the Guatemalan side of the border. It was intimidating stuff. No more so than when 154 paratroops poured out of six of the FAG's C-47s in a single drop. And they had the capacity for even bigger drops. The lightly armed British infantry company at Airport Camp was just 180-strong.

But it wasn't this, the biggest of the Guatemalan para drops, that should have given cause for the most alarm. It was another, smaller drop of just forty-eight paratroops, at Puerto Modesto Méndez, a couple of miles from the farthest, most south-western tip of British Honduras – nearly 150 miles away from the British garrison at Belize City. Its significance went unremarked and would only later become clear.

*

In mid-August, Major Richard Corkran's twelve-strong advance party flew to Washington on an RAF Vickers VC10, changing planes before flying on to Miami for the night. The next morning they took their seats aboard a propeller-driven Lockheed Electra for the last leg of the journey – a three-hour flight to Belize City.

After being commissioned into the Grenadier Guards in 1956, Corkran had spent much of his time in Africa on secondment first to the King's African Rifles and then, after Kenya's independence, the Kenya Rifles, helping train the new republic's own army. When he'd discovered that 2nd Battalion Grenadier Guards were taking over as Caribbean Guard Battalion, he made sure the scheduled unit rotation would allow him to deploy to British Honduras with his Inkerman Company before he left for his new posting. For six months away, after taking over from S Company Scots Guards, he'd be in sole charge of his soldiers. *Away from some of the bureaucracy*, he thought, *independence!* He hoped time away might also give him a chance to study for his Open University science degree.

The rest of the Company, flown in aboard a chartered Lloyd International Bristol Britannia airliner on 23 August, had less cerebral activity in mind. British Honduras was an adventure playground offering mountains, jungles and rivers, and, out on the Cayes, skindiving, sea-fishing and – if anyone managed to get the Scots Guards' speedboat, *Gobby Jock*, working – water-skiing too.

BH, as the Company quickly took to calling their new home, was also a haven for exotic wildlife. Large birds of prey seemed to maintain a constant vigil over the airfield, wheeling in the thermals rising from the hot concrete. In the rivers were manatees and caymans, their long thin snouts lined top and bottom with rows of sharp teeth. And the jungles were teeming with exotic fauna too, from the stunning red macaw to all manner of beasts real and imagined, including jaguars, the powerful leopard-like big cats native to the region. There was soon speculation about a one-eyed man-eating jaguar hunting near Airport Camp. But even while they were safely in camp, there were still venomous snakes, scorpions and spiders – including jumping spiders and black widows – to occupy the young Guardsmen's thoughts. When they weren't thinking about the heat, that is. By day and night, the low-lying land around Belize City was stiflingly hot and humid.

Corkran was lucky. The Guardsmen slept in barrack rooms cooled only by overhead fans. And in the Officers' Mess he had one of the few rooms with air-conditioning. His three Platoon Commanders, 2nd Lieutenants Sir Jamie Hervey-Bruce, 'Killer' Cartwright and John Hawkesworth, had first dibs on the others. All of them still had to contend with the mosquitos.

Corkran had been well briefed on the border dispute with Guatemala before leaving the Guards barracks at Caterham in Surrey. The possibility of Guatemalan aggression was, he understood, not thought to be high. But there had been scares before. And he didn't know if the Guatemalans knew just how short of air defence he was. *Just don't know what the silly buggers are going to do next*, he thought. And he couldn't help but rehearse worst-case scenarios in his mind.

Stanley Field Airport felt exposed. Just 16 feet above sea level, the short 5000-foot runway was the only asphalted strip in the country. Beyond the boundaries of the airfield, tangled green forest and swamp and the thick looping bends of the Belize River to the south-east protected it at ground level. But there was no elevation in any direction, nothing to complicate an attack from the air.

Looking out across the site, the single windsock flapping gently to the west of the whitewashed International Terminal, Corkran knew they were vulnerable. If the Guatemalans were to have a go, he reflected, *we've got a load of trouble*.

Chapter 10

In a week at sea, the 2700 people on board *Ark* consumed 12 tons of potatoes, 24,000 eggs, 200 gallons of ice cream, 4 tons of bread, 7 tons of meat and 40,000 cans of beer. Her eight Admiralty three-drum boilers and Parsons geared turbines could generate 152,000 shaft horse power. As *Ark Royal* steamed home to Devonport from Puerto Rico through the North Atlantic swell at an average of 19–20 knots, she was burning nearly 700 tons of furnace fuel oil – FFO – a day. Without replenishment of food and fuel *Ark* and her crew would soon be running on empty. And Replenishment at Sea – or RAS – was done while on the move.

Ark was accompanied wherever she went by one or two Royal Fleet Auxiliaries – naval support ships crewed by civilians and funded by the MoD. Barely forty-eight hours would pass before *Ark* manoeuvred alongside her attendant RFA and the two ships steamed alongside each other separated by little more than thirty yards of turbulent water. Gun lines fired across from the RFA were gathered aboard *Ark* and used to set up transfer rigs and hoses between the two ships. A successful and safe RAS depended on very precise navigation, as any small error in course or speed carried a real danger of collision. But as conscious as John Roberts was about the risk of damage to the Navy's most important ship, it wasn't the reason he invariably took the helm during an RAS. It was, instead, simply that he enjoyed it. He *loved* driving the ship.

While the ship herself relied on the fuel brought across

during Replenishments at Sea, of equal importance was the emotional well-being of those on board. And while the food and beer winched across from the RFA played a vital part in that, what really lit up the Ship's Company was the arrival of the mail. And the only flying that took place during the week-long Atlantic crossing was the launch of one of 824's Sea Kings as *Ark* passed the Azores. *Ark*'s mail would be at Lajes airport waiting to be ferried back to the ship. It was one of the rare occasions that chopper crews earned anything but good-natured abuse from the carrier's 'Heavies' – her two fixed-wing fast-jet squadrons. Most of the time, the jet jockeys looked down their noses at them. *Angry palm trees* they called the Sea Kings, flown by *chopper pukes*. The younger helicopter crews gave as good as they got. In return they regarded the fixed-wing crews as dinosaurs. *Old gits*. And there was some merit in the argument. There were no new fixed-wing Pilots and Observers coming through the Fleet Air Arm aircrew-training pipeline. The fast-jet crews had all been round the block. As the pool of RN fixed-wing crews began to dry up, some were already coming back for second tours on the Phantoms and Buccaneers. Some of the Sea King aircrew were barely into their twenties.

For the squadron Bosses like Carl Davis and Nick Kerr a long sea passage offered a chance to catch up on admin. But junior aviators – the Squadron Joes – found they had a little more time on their hands – even after the 'Morning Prayers', each unit's daily meeting and the lectures that followed. There was always a handful of pit rats who would use the time to catch up on sleep in their bunks; others would read or listen to music on portable record-players squeezed into the crevices in the pipework that ran through all of the cabins. Down in the depth of the ship's stern, over the constant hum of the air-conditioning fans and the throb of the engines, there'd be sounds like Tamla Motown, the Stones' new LP, *Sticky Fingers*, the Moody Blues or Iron Butterfly playing in the aircrew cabins. It was fine in calm seas, but when the going was rough, the music would speed up and slow down as *Ark*'s stern rose and fell sometimes thirty or forty feet, pushing pilots into their bunks and the needle into the grooves of the vinyl. And then there was the Wardroom – the ship's Officers' Mess – buried deep on Six Deck, immediately beneath one of *Ark*'s air weapons magazines.

In the evenings the Wardroom filled with officers in Red Sea Rig – open-necked white shirts, epaulettes and cummerbunds – for drinks before dinner. Under a low ceiling laced with pipes, pre-dinner drinks were consumed in a fug of tobacco smoke from naval issue Blueliner cigarettes, pipes and cheroots. The big air-conditioning unit that thrummed away in the corner had its work cut out. Wine was served with dinner and then, with no flying the next day, there were port and post-dinner drinks and thick cigars brought back from Puerto Rico.

Drinks after dinner were spoofed for, rounds of duty-free liqueurs leading, inevitably, to an outbreak of shirt pockets getting ripped off. Just because it was annoying – and funny. It paid to be on your guard. The squadron Bosses remained slightly aloof from it all, but Carl Davis enjoyed watching his own crews talk and bond with the other squadrons. *Don't they all play nicely*, he caught himself thinking. The rivalry was healthy, but so too were the friendships – and that understanding could pay dividends in the air. Nick Kerr also appreciated the value of the air group's hi-jinks. As a young officer he'd broken his own ankle in an out-of-control Wardroom bundle known as 'High Cockalorum'. Now he had his own squadron he knew anyone getting carried away would usually be smuggled out and put to bed by their colleagues before they could embarrass themselves or do any real damage. It would have been nice, it occurred to him, if someone, all those years back, had thought to try to rein him in. He also knew that as a young tyro he probably wouldn't have responded kindly to their efforts.

As Captain of the ship, John Roberts was not a member of *Ark Royal*'s Wardroom. Instead it was policed by the ship's Commander, and President of the Wardroom, Willie Gueterbock. The Commander could be fierce, but he was a clever, extremely able Executive Officer – an aircraft carrier's Second in Command couldn't afford to be anything but. For all his strengths, though, from the point of view of the squadrons Gueterbock was still a Fishhead, very definitely not an aviator. And he was a Salthorse – a non-specialist – sometimes ill at ease with the sight and sound of the high-spirited air group letting their hair down. The rest of the Navy had their own term of endearment for the fly boys: WAFUs – Wet and Fucking Useless. The expression is likely to have crossed the Commander's mind as the mood became more raucous, Carl Davis – who had to concede it was a little like watching sixth-formers let off the leash – tried gently to help the straight-backed Commander get used to the idea of his men letting off steam. 'Come on, sir,' he explained, 'these chaps have been on watch for a fortnight.'

'But what happens if we're called to action stations?'

'You've got to be realistic about this!' Davis told him with a grin. Late on a Sunday night and halfway across the Atlantic, it seemed unlikely. But you could never be sure.

At 0645 the next morning, a pair of Soviet Tu-95 Bears flew low over *Ark Royal* from the north before circling the ship at 1000 feet. Fifteen minutes later, the Russian pilots increased the power of their Kuznetsov NK-12 engines and the two giant metallic reconnaissance bombers loped away, climbing to the south – to Guinea in West Africa or Cuba to the south-west – their heavy-bladed contra-rotating propellers leaving a sound in the air like tearing calico.

The Bears were a sharp reminder that *Ark* would soon be heading up through the Greenland–Iceland–UK gap towards the North Cape, the hunting ground of the Soviet Northern Fleet. And that, as gathering tensions in Central America would soon prove, the mid-Atlantic offered no certain guarantee of a quiet life.

At Airport Camp, Major Richard Corkran worked alongside a small permanent HQ of just eight officers. Including in their numbers a Stores Officer, Medical Officer, Signals Officer, Local Intelligence Officer and REME Warrant Officer looking after the transport, they were responsible for maintaining the outpost's administration and infrastructure. A month after he'd arrived in country, Corkran was pleased to welcome their new CO, Garrison Commander British Honduras – GCBH – Colonel John Shipster. Shipster was nearing the end of a remarkable army career. A veteran of the fierce fighting in Burma – where he'd been awarded the DSO – the hell of Kohima and then the Korean War, Shipster had also seen subsequent service in British Guiana and on attachment to the US Army in Vietnam. As well as having proved himself an extraordinarily brave soldier, Shipster was also proud of his inclusion in the *Guinness Book of Records*. He held the world record for dropping an egg from the greatest height without breaking it – a feat he'd achieved with the help of a US Army helicopter. In BH, a garrison without helicopters, it was his wider experience and judgement as a soldier that would prove more valuable.

In London, as Shipster was briefed both by his predecessor and by Corkran, numbered copies of a green file classified 'Secret – UK Eyes Only' circulated round Whitehall. The document, prepared by the Joint Intelligence Committee (A), was titled 'Belize (British Honduras): The Threat from Guatemala'. The eighteen-page report reinforced Corkran's assessment from in country: 'The Belizean security forces are not capable of defending the country against armed aggression. Guatemalan forces,' it concluded, 'would be able to occupy essential points in Belize in a matter of hours . . . Little or no tactical warning of an attack by Guatemala can be expected.' Offering a straw to clutch at, the JIC suggested there would probably be 'indicators' that something was in the air. So all the British planned to do was make sure they kept their ears to the ground and try to respond to the first signs of trouble. Copies of JIC(A)(71) 35 were despatched to the Garrison HQ at Airport Camp, the British Governor in Belmopan and John Weymes at the British Consulate in Guatemala City.

*

British Honduras was just one of the potential flashpoints the military Chiefs of Staff needed to consider. At their weekly committee meetings, the Navy was well represented. As they took their seats in Room 5301 of the Ministry of Defence Main Building, as well as Admiral Sir Michael Pollock, the First Sea Lord, at the head of the table and chairing the meeting was the waspish Admiral of the Fleet, Sir Peter Hill-Norton, the Chief of the Defence Staff. Both men were former Captains of *Ark Royal*. As they worked their way through an agenda containing over 150 items, they briefly acknowledged that they'd taken note of the JIC report. But there were more pressing concerns and plenty of them. While the Chiefs' preoccupation was with NATO and the deteriorating situation in Northern Ireland, they also needed to bolster the defence of RAF Salalah in Oman, settle on how military responsibility for the New Hebrides in the South Pacific would be shared with the French, and provide for the evacuation of 600 British Nationals from South Vietnam. The possibility of *Ark Royal* supporting Britain's withdrawal from Malta in March 1972 was raised too, but her declared readiness to NATO was considered too important for her to be spared. And *Eagle*, by then, would be on her way to the breaker's yard following her final Far East cruise. With *Eagle*'s return and the withdrawal from East of Suez and a narrower focus on NATO, the admirals, generals and air marshals imagined life might become a little more straightforward. It would prove to be a vain hope.

At three o'clock in the morning, less than a week after the Bears overflew *Ark Royal*, an explosion tore through the police barracks in Benque Viejo, British Honduras, the little town on the border with Guatemala. Investigators sent from Belize City quickly determined that a high-powered hand grenade had been thrown through the glass louvres of the window. And soon a house-to-house search for further arms and explosives was underway. Police believed they were looking for a package of six grenades brought in from Guatemala with sabotage in mind. Amid excitable headlines in Belize City announcing 'SPECIAL FORCES "INVADE" BENQUE VIEJO', a Guatemalan man, Azilcar Acevado Castellanos – a member of the Rural Guard of the Petén – was arrested and detained as the newspapers stoked the flames. He was, wrote *The Reporter*, a 'Guatemalan Agent'. While in Guatemala itself, *La Nación* printed claims that Acevado had been tortured with electric shocks.

As the celebrations for 10 September – Battle of St George's Caye Day and the national day of British Honduras – drew nearer, it seemed the atmosphere in both countries was becoming more febrile – more expectant. From the Consulate on Calle 11, John Weymes reported strong rumours that the day would bring an announcement from George Price, Premier of the British Honduras government, about the colony's independence. Weymes knew that every word of the speech Price delivered to the crowds on the 10th would be scrutinized carefully by both government officials and the press in Guatemala City. And in Belize City itself people were restless too, hungry for positive news about their country's future. Behind the scenes, George Price was pushing hard to ensure he could deliver it. He'd made a formal request to secure agreement from the Queen to change the name of British Honduras to Belize. Rather than independence, on 10 September, Price wanted to announce the birth of Belize. But given the delicacy of the relationship, Weymes was sure that even this minor step would inflame the Guatemalans and be interpreted as a move towards independence. With this fear in mind, the Foreign Office, in responding to Price's request, suggested granting permission to change the name to Belize would be impossible because the Queen – who'd actually been happy to grant permission in 1966 when it was first requested – was 'on holiday'.

As he fought to prevent any change to the status quo that might unsettle the Guatemalan government, Weymes received new intelligence from Colonel Connolly, the US Military

Attaché. Military activity in El Petén was to be stepped up. Connolly had been told by the Army Chief of Staff, Kjell Laugerud, that the paratroop company at Poptun barracks was being reinforced, while a fleet of brownwater boats were carrying Marines to patrol the rivers. There was a further possibility of another paratroop company also being deployed.

In explaining the troop movements, Laugerud claimed that the terrorists, their operations disrupted and beaten back in the City, were leaving for the outlying rural departments to regroup. And that the Army were going after them.

Weymes signalled British Honduras Garrison HQ to warn them of increased military activity on the border with British Honduras. And yet for all that it provided the justification for General Laugerud's troop redeployment, there was very little evidence that the terrorists had left the capital for El Petén at all – the murders, bombings and kidnappings in Guatemala City continued without pause.

At Airport Camp, Richard Corkran absorbed the news. It came on top of the unexpected arrival of a large contingent of Fuerza Aerea Guatemalteca officers at Belize Airport. The FAG men's unannounced visit was brief and they were soon in the air again, heading back to La Aurora. The soldiers of 3 Section, 12 Platoon, on standby at the airport, joked about having frightened them off. *Obviously terrified at the warlike appearance of the airport's defenders*, they reckoned. If FAG planners had been at all uncertain about the strength of British anti-aircraft defences, they now *knew* how flimsy they were.

Chapter 11

Many of the place names in British Honduras provided intriguing clues as to how they came about. Never Delay sits just upstream of the Belize River from Meditation. Trousers Down was felt to be an occasion worth marking for posterity. Double Head Cabbage, Cool Shade and Young Girl all seem straightforward if, especially in the case of the first, unlikely inspirations. Good Living Camp has become Over the Top Camp less than ten miles down the road. And Go to Hell makes its feelings clear. None of them though reveal a more interesting history than Hattieville, the name of the town ten miles or so along the Western Highway from Belize City.

At around 2 a.m. during the night of 30 October 1961, Hurricane Hattie, a Category 5 storm, hit British Honduras. Throughout the night, screaming winds reaching 200 mph assaulted the little country as the huge churning vortex bull-dozed her way to the south-west, cutting a path of destruction seventy-five miles wide. As dawn broke, up to twenty 12-foot tidal waves, towed along in Hattie's wake, hammered through the narrow streets of Belize City leaving heavy debris and thick mud clogging the capital's streets. As the tides receded, the population began to count the cost. Effective precautions kept casualties to a minimum, but hundreds of people still lost their lives. And the population of Belize City was shell-shocked by the devastation. The two days that followed saw desperate looting of shops, businesses and damaged homes. Refugees were provided with temporary shelter inland from the capital.

Some never left and the little town of Hattieville was born, a permanent reminder of the threat to British Honduras from the ocean to the east.

And now it looked like it was going to happen all over again. The US Coast Guard had picked up a developing tropical depression in the Atlantic. The storm's latitude, longitude, windspeed, and speed and direction of travel were recorded and distributed throughout the Caribbean, while all the time the depression grew in size, power and speed. On 7 September 1971, Garrison HQ learnt that Hurricane Edith was on her way. And that she was expected to make landfall in British Honduras in less than three days.

Regular updates on Edith's progress only confirmed her inexorable progress towards Belize City. Windspeeds of 160 mph were recorded and, on 9 September, a Red One Hurricane Warning was announced. Edith was now only a day away.

Corkran's Guardsmen swung into action to help prepare BH for the storm's arrival. Caches of ration packs were stashed in various locations, and emergency bowsers filled with potable water. Motor transport was lashed down and the outboard engines of the Company's handful of assault boats were checked. Then roof-retaining hurricane wire was anchored around the semi-cylindrical corrugated-iron roofs of the Airport Camp dining hall and NAAFI buildings. As a final precaution, the Officers' Mess croquet hoops were pulled up and secured after an observant corporal spotted they were still in harm's way.

As the winds grew stronger, crowds of civilians waiting hopefully outside the gates of the camp began to grow. And yet, with early celebrations for Battle of St George's Caye Day already in full swing, not to mention final preparations for the much-anticipated day itself, the Red One Warning hadn't yet been passed on to the civilian population by George Price's government.

'Edith,' remarked Corkran's 2iC drily, 'is obviously just an imperialist plot conjured up with the sole intention of disrupting Independence Day celebrations.'

On the night of the 9th, Edith continued west across Nicaragua, killing nearly a hundred people and causing widespread flash-flooding. Fuelled by the warm Caribbean Sea, Edith once again picked up the ferocity she'd lost over land. Crossing 87 degrees West and 16 degrees South, she prowled north-west across the Gulf of Honduras at 120 mph. Straight for Belize City.

A Red One Hurricane Warning was finally announced to the public on Radio Belize just before eleven o'clock in the morning of 10 September. But it had very little effect on the progress of National Day celebrations. Premier Price was determined to have his say.

Bespectacled and wearing his trademark white guayabera, a loose-fitting Mexican-style shirt, George Price, the neat, ascetic Premier of British Honduras, spoke, his gentle, measured tones amplified by the Tannoy. Every year Memorial Park played host to the celebrations. On the waterfront, and flanked by streets lined with white-painted wooden colonial houses, it provided the perfect setting. The gathered crowds looked up at a stage decked with red, white and blue bunting and hung on Price's every word. Against a clear sky and the low shape of Hunter's Caye a couple of miles out to sea behind him, the Premier revealed his hand.

'We see the year Nineteen Hundred and Seventy-Two' – he paused – 'as the year our government shall most likely fulfil the mandate to lead Belize to sovereign independence.' And the waiting crowds clapped and cheered. In reply, Sir John Paul seemed to endorse Price's ambitions. 'Your reward,' concluded the Governor, 'is and will be the pride of citizenship in the new Belize under God, united, sovereign and independent.' The Governor did not, of course, mention dates, promises or deadlines. But his omissions were not what would be remembered or reported by those desperate for independence. Or, equally, by those who had sworn to prevent it at any cost.

At seven o'clock that evening, a Red Two Hurricane Warning was announced ordering everyone into designated hurricane shelters housed in the capital's strongest buildings, like the cinema or the Palotti Convent – where the nuns refused entry to the girls of the Bamboo Bay Night Club, their souls, perhaps, deemed already lost. And at four o'clock the next morning, with Hurricane Edith just forty miles off the coast of BH, the interference with the Signals Detachment's radios became so bad that, to all intents and purposes, communications between British Honduras and the rest of the world were lost

While the population of British Honduras bunkered down, bracing itself for the fury of the hurricane, in Guatemala City, the President, Carlos Osorio Arana, considered the text of the speeches from British Honduras with his guest, General Fidel Sánchez, the President of El Salvador. It was difficult not to regard the timing of Sánchez's two-day state visit as significant. The stance taken by the Salvadorean government on the dispute over British Honduras was well-known and was reflected by the comments of a former Foreign Secretary, Dr Guillermo Trabanino, now conducting his own investigation into the Guatemalan claim. Trabanino was quite clear.

'Belice,' he argued, 'belongs to Guatemala and it is the responsibility of all of Central America to struggle for its immediate restoration.' El Salvador was taking that responsibility more seriously than most. Just how seriously would soon become apparent.

Locked inside the Palotti Convent, while incongruously cheerful music played throughout the night on Radio Belize, a lance-corporal had stayed up until 4 a.m. sampling brandy distilled by the Mother Superior. It would have been rude – possibly a sin – to have refused. Two hours later it was time to venture outside. When the doors and shutters of the hurricane shelters were first opened at dawn on 11 September, the concerned inhabitants were greeted with clear blue skies. At the last possible moment Edith turned north, sparing BH from the destruction she subsequently unleashed on Texas, where 100 people were killed and 6000 made homeless.

Blessed with a lucky, unexpected escape, the country now had a chance to reflect on what had been said by George Price in Memorial Park the previous day. 'Belizeans,' he said, 'have waited with utmost patience for independence.' Price knew he must not disappoint them.

It sounded reassuring. But it needed to be, since many in British Honduras feared that they were going to be sold down the river. In 1965 Guatemala, Britain and the British Honduras government agreed to seek American mediation in search of a resolution. Three years later, the US Ambassador, Bethuel M. Webster, presented his draft treaty. And it led to rioting in the streets of Belize City.

In trying to balance America's regional and global interests Webster had utterly ignored the wishes of British Honduras herself. While granting her nominal independence, his draft treaty effectively handed over control of her foreign policy and defence to Guatemala. The proposals were further tainted by a suspicion in Belmopan that the US had her own agenda. It was reported that Ydígoras Fuentes, the ex-Guatemalan President, had admitted that the quid pro quo for his country's support of the CIA's Bay of Pigs adventure was US pressure for an outcome in British Honduras that was favourable to Guatemala. Not surprisingly, Webster's proposals were rejected out of hand.

But from this point on, British Honduras, squeezed between Guatemala's agitation, Britain's desire to pull out and US realpolitik, felt she could trust no one. It was the first time that concern about Britain's commitment to the future security and independence of Belize had bubbled to the surface. And once doubt took root, it needed very little further sustenance. While Britain hedged and stalled over the possibility of providing an independent Belize with a security guarantee – as she had other former colonies like Brunei, Fiji and Mauritius – it became even easier to question her resolve to act in the colony's best interests rather than her own. George Price *had* to be sceptical. It felt as if he and his government were the only ones fighting their corner.

In Guatemala, the way forward was equally opaque. September the 10th hadn't actually brought an announcement of independence. Instead it had brought something more difficult and unsettling – the suggestion that independence was just around the corner. It was a situation that needed Arana, his Foreign Minister, Dr Herrera, and the generals to fill in the gaps and make assumptions.

Following the speeches, it seemed 1972 was going to be the year Britain and the British Honduras government expected to see independence. If Guatemala were to act on her claim, she would have to do so before then. Bullying a small, newly independent neighbour would be regarded very differently by world opinion from taking a brave stand against a big, well-armed colonial power from the other side of the globe. On top of this consideration, the Americans were pulling the plug on the FAG's hard-worked F-51D Mustangs. By the end of 1972, US Military Assistance Program plans forecast that only two would remain serviceable. And the deployment of paratroops to El Petén had already been announced and reasons for it given, which could obscure any further mobilization – or, at least, plausibly explain it. In the end, it all boiled down to how much Belice really mattered to Guatemala. Guatemalan commentators had been contemptuous enough of Venezuela's inability to extract territorial concessions when British Guiana was granted independence in 1966: the pressure on Arana to roll the dice before a final opportunity to do so disappeared for good was quite real.

In the Ministry of Defence in London, British military planners had concluded that, if Arana gave in to temptation, British Honduras would be militarily extremely difficult to retake. But that trying to do so, in an essentially post-colonial world, was likely to be politically unacceptable too.

If the Guatemalan army rolled over the border, Belizeans would, in all probability, have simply to be abandoned to their fate.

Chapter 12

As British Honduras settled down after the hurricane scare, over 5000 miles away Captain John Roberts faced weather of a different kind. He was taking *Ark Royal* north towards the Soviets' backyard.

Roberts knew the cold high latitudes well. During the war he'd served on board HMS *Serapis*, a 1700-ton 'S' class destroyer escorting the punishing Arctic Convoys to Polyarnyy at the mouth of the Kola estuary. In the winter of 1944, *Serapis* was given the task of carrying a Norwegian army captain and twelve soldiers all the way up the estuary to Murmansk.

The passage had been brutal. The captain, after leaving his ship's open bridge, had to be literally chipped out of clothes cased in a two-inch-thick layer of ice. And Roberts himself witnessed the loss of HMS *Mahratta*, with just twelve survivors, to the U-boat pack that dogged their progress. But *Serapis* got through.

The Norwegians were concerned that as the Russians advanced west they would try to annexe territory. This small contingent was to accompany the Red Army with a Norwegian flag and, when the time came, plant the flag to say this far and no further. Their mission seemed barely more manageable when, after *Serapis* had berthed, a Russian official came aboard, wearing four fur coats, accepted the offer of a whisky, followed it with four more, embraced the Norwegian army captain in a friendly bear hug, then fell off the gangplank into the harbour.

Nor was it the first time that a British fleet carrier bearing the name *Ark Royal* had been seen off the coast of Norway. In the opening months of the Second World War, the third ship to bear the name – carrying a barely adequate air group of Fairey Swordfish biplanes and Blackburn Skua fighter/dive bombers – covered the British withdrawal from Narvik in north Norway. As she did so, an appreciation of the potential of naval air power was in its infancy. The Admiralty's battleship mentality had deep roots, but by 1940, even though the Fleet Air Arm was flying aeroplanes that reflected its years of neglect, it was becoming abundantly clear where the future lay.

Now, thirty years later, John Roberts was, when it boiled down to it, performing a similar job to the one he had helped that small platoon of Norwegian soldiers perform – restraining the Soviet Union. But on board his ship *Ark Royal*, alongside the American carriers USS *Independence* and USS *Intrepid*, he would be doing so with rather more firepower at his disposal.

Ark's 'big guns', the fourteen Blackburn Buccaneers of 809 NAS, embarked the day before the Gannets and Phantoms. One by one, the jets loomed out of the overcast sky before slamming on to the back of *Ark*'s dark steel deck in a collision of noise and sparks. As their hooks let go of the thick arrestor wires, each Buccaneer rocked back on her main wheels, before taxiing forward under the direction of one of the Manglers – the inevitable nickname bestowed on the Aircraft Handlers by aircrew. As one jet rolled forward, her wings folding upwards like a closing hardback book, the next Buccaneer in the circuit was already turning on to finals – the last leg of the landing pattern.

Being careful not to catch the yellow and black ejector seat handles with his feet, 809's Senior Observer, Steve Park, climbed out of the rear cockpit on to the Buccaneer's air intake and down the crew ladder to the flight deck and into the wind streaming down the centreline. His face was scored with the outline of the oxygen mask he'd been wearing during the short flight from Lossie. He felt the gentle rise and fall of the ship under his feet and inhaled the familiar smell of hot WD40, sprayed into the Bucc's engines as they unspooled to protect them from salt. *Beautiful*, he thought, *like baking bread*.

'Welcome aboard, sir.' He was greeted by the weathered faces of the Flight Deck Engineers, already busily securing the big, grey jet to the deck. As they lashed it down with chains attached to the undercarriage oleos and fixed red protective struts to the folded wings, Park and Carl Davis, leaning backwards into the wind to steady themselves, made their way aft to the sanctuary of the island.

'Look, Steve,' Davis told the Scottish Looker when they first flew together, 'I don't like Observers who talk too much. And if you do I shall pull my plug out!' Park just laughed and kept his contributions to a minimum. 'Well done, Boss' was about the extent of it. Humouring the CO was part and parcel of any Senior Observer's job. And he knew that, whatever he might say in jest, Davis, an ex-single-seater pilot, was a convert to the very real benefits of having a second crewman and fully realized the value of his Observer's contribution. Over the next couple of weeks Davis knew that his success in the air would, to a very large extent, be dependent on Park's skill, experience and attention to detail. It was true for every other Pilot in the squadron.

Exercise ROYAL KNIGHT would test *Ark*'s core capabilities – Fleet Air Defence, Airborne Early Warning, Anti-Submarine Warfare and Strike. And throughout, the ship herself had to deliver. Should anything prevent her from operating aircraft then she was a lame duck doing little more than cruising the fjords. Boilers, gearboxes, generators, condensers, catapults, arresting gear and countless other systems all had to be kept serviceable. ROYAL KNIGHT was designed to test the NATO Atlantic Striking Fleet's ability to respond to a Soviet attack against the Northern Flank. The strategy, known as Flexible Response, was outlined in a 1969 study commissioned by the NATO Secretary General and it called on *Ark Royal* and the other strike carriers to go on the offensive. First, as the Red Army mobilized, the NATO Striking Fleet would deploy beyond the GIUK gap in an effort to deter any threatened aggression. And, if deterrence failed, it would contain a Soviet invasion of Norway and prevent the Northern Fleet from breaking out from Murmansk round the North Cape into the Atlantic using all the means at its disposal. Planners believed that keeping the Warsaw Pact pinned down, fighting a three-month defensive battle, would lead either to its defeat or to the opening of a massive new front across the plains of Central Europe. Deterrence, then, was definitely the preferred option. And responsibility for that lay with the Buccaneers – the dark-grey bombers with the squadron's phoenix-and-flames motif painted on the tail. They were *Ark Royal*'s long reach.

Deep in the recesses of the old carrier's machinery spaces was a unique compartment shielded with thick lead, protected behind an airlock and monitored by geiger counters. Requiring secret access codes for entry, the Nuclear Bomb Room housed *Ark*'s magazine of WE.177A nuclear rounds. Introduced in 1969 to replace the old first-generation Red Beard 2000lb 'Special Weapon', the small size of the new 600lb bomb belied its devastating potential. The WE.177s had a boosted fission warhead codenamed KATIE A with a selectable yield of either 10 kilotons or half a kiloton which could be used, with minor modifications performed on board by *Ark*'s own 'bombheads', as either anti-submarine depth-charges or for surface attack. And, for use by *Ark Royal*, the Navy retained twenty of them. Each of the Buccaneers could carry a pair of the white-painted weapons in the bomb bay.

But only 809's divisional leaders were nuclear crews. Just four senior pairs, including Carl Davis and Steve Park, and 'Boots' Walkinshaw and Mike Lucas, planned and trained for the nuclear role. And they did so religiously.

The Strike Planning Room was located on Seven Victor – Seven Deck near the ship's stern – opposite *Ark Royal*'s church. And, unlike the church, a special pass was required to access it. Inside were chart tables and filing cabinets containing 'Secret – UK Eyes Only' and 'Limited Distribution' red-sleeved files listed only as bland strings of letters and numbers: NWSC/BU2/600/R.N. or SD 110B-0102-1.

With no flying programmed for the following day, Mike Lucas decided to take advantage of a spare couple of hours to bring himself up to date. Each crew maintained two or three files depending on which part of the world *Ark* was in. Prepared by RAF planners at Strike Command in High Wycombe, the routes, despite using old base photographs, were updated with the latest intelligence – new radars, new SAM sites, unusual troop deployments. Using nothing more advanced than a pencil and ruler, Lucas plotted a route around the radii of known threats, making a note of significant ground features that might allow him to constantly confirm his bomber's progress *en route* to the target. While *Ark*'s position changed relative to 809's nuclear targets, Lucas's point of entry 'over the beach' remained constant. The young Observer knew only the targets allocated to him and his Pilot, 'Boots' Walkinshaw. Of the rest of the nuclear crews, only Carl Davis knew them all. His squadron's task was the destruction of high-value targets along the fringes of the Baltic – Poland was on the list. The submarine facility in Estonia too. And, given where *Ark* was heading on Exercise ROYAL KNIGHT, it was a safe bet that one of those folders contained the name of Severomorsk, about twenty miles north-east of Murmansk on the Kola Peninsula.

If NATO's Flexible Response plan failed in its aim of deterrence, then Severomorsk, the home of the Soviet Navy's immensely powerful Northern Fleet, was going to be top of the list. With unrestricted access to the open ocean not enjoyed by the Baltic or Black Sea fleets, the Northern Fleet had become the focus of Soviet naval expansion. And it represented a huge concentration of military power: 17,000-ton 'Moskva' class guided-missile cruisers carrying eighteen Kamov KA-25 Hormone helicopters, 'Kresta' and updated 'Sverdlov' class cruisers armed with anti-ship missiles and heavy guns, 'Kotlin' and 'Kashin' class guided-missile destroyers, and numerous frigates and heavily armed fast patrol boats carrying cruise missiles. But most of all there were the submarines.

Severomorsk was home to the world's largest fleet of nuclear submarines. These attack boats and Boomers – the ballistic missile boats – posed what was perceived to be the greatest threat there was to the survival of the Western Alliance. At the end of 1970, British Intelligence estimated the Soviet submarine force at nearly 400 boats, of which eighty-nine were believed to be nuclear-powered. For the men, ships and aircraft of the Atlantic Striking Fleet, Severomorsk was Nemesis.

Chapter 13

Battleship *Potemkin* was immortalized by Eisenstein's 1925 silent cinematic masterpiece, but the history of the Russian and Soviet Navy had not been a particularly glorious one. After the humiliation of the Russian fleet at the hands of the Japanese in 1904–5, its Soviet successor had been so ineffectual in both world wars that it was *Potemkin*'s talismanic significance to the Russian revolution, rather than any military accomplishment, that was remembered. Stalin had pushed hard for a substantial ocean-going fleet of cruisers, battleships and even aircraft carriers, but his energetic plans had died in 1953 along with the old tyrant himself. Nikita Khrushchev had been firm in his view that large warships were only good for ferrying admirals around. And Admiral Sergei Gorshkov, on being appointed Commander-in-Chief of the Soviet Navy in 1956, found his first job was dismantling substantial parts of Stalin's embryonic fleet. Then Khrushchev was forced to revise his opinion, embarrassed by the Soviet Navy's inability to influence events during both the Suez Crisis in 1956 and the Cuban Missile Crisis six years later.

In 1963, Gorshkov ordered what remained of Stalin's fleet to sea. Four years later, during the 1967 Arab–Israeli wars, the Soviet Mediterranean Fleet was made up of around seventy warships, submarines and support ships. And by 1970, the Soviets undertook OKEAN 70, the largest global naval exercise in history. Over 200 ships and submarines, supported by Soviet Navy long-range bombers, carried out simultaneous manoeuvres in the Atlantic, Mediterranean, Indian Ocean and Pacific, coordinated from Naval HQ in Moscow. 'The Soviet Navy,' Gorshkov claimed, 'has been transformed into an important strategic force.' An opponent could no longer assume they had mastery of the oceans. Gorshkov had achieved a stunning and alarming turnaround that put at serious risk NATO's ability to keep open sea lanes vital to the survival of Western Europe.

As *Ark* prepared to sail north to take part in exercise ROYAL KNIGHT, her Officer of the Watch spotted two 'Kashin' class 4500-ton guided-missile destroyers dead ahead, ten miles east of the Shetlands. Each was armed with anti-aircraft missiles, dual-purpose guns, five torpedo tubes and four SS-N-2 Styx anti-ship cruise missiles.

Seeing the enemy up close wasn't something Commander John Ford had done for a while. But although he'd not been on the front line since the sixties, he had experience in spades. After flying combat missions at Suez during Operation MUSKETEER, he'd gone on to command a training squadron and gained a first-class Air Warfare Instructor's qualification before tours as Appointer for aircrew then as Wings at RNAS Yeovilton, where he was head of the Air Department and responsible for all Flying Ops. Now he was Wings aboard *Ark Royal* and responsible for the safe operation of a new generation of jets bigger, heavier, faster than anything he'd flown off the deck of a carrier. Although 100 recent hours flying Phantoms from shore bases helped improve his appreciation of the challenges involved, it was still a daunting prospect. A compact, precise man, he'd been given just a few months to prepare for a job that was intimidatingly complex. Even with the experience of Pete Marshall as Lieutenant Commander Flying, or 'Little F', as his number two in Flyco, the new Commander (Air) knew it would be a little while before he felt entirely at ease.

As *Ark* headed north, Wings couldn't help but feel a knot of anxiety in his stomach. It came, he realized, with the job.

Already there'd been a few gentle reminders of how fine the margins were. An 824 NAS Sea King had ditched after losing an engine. Although, in a remarkable piece of flying – and completely ignoring the rules laid down in the Standard Operational Procedures – the same helicopter's pilot had managed to take off from the water and bring his aircraft home to 'Mother' on a single engine. A Phantom had burst a tyre on landing and another of the 892 Squadron interceptors had suffered a radio failure during a night-time catapult launch. It was Wings who had to decide what should and shouldn't be done in the interests of both safety *and* maintaining flying operations. Wings who, if he didn't like the look of a jet's final approach, had the last word on whether to order a wave-off and send her crew round for another try. And now there *was* a problem. Of the four arrestor wires that normally stretched across the flight deck to snare the trailing hooks of returning aircraft, three had been chopped away with axes after failing. That left only a single wire – 1 Wire. But reports reaching Flyco suggested that even that had failed. Worse, there was a Buccaneer still airborne. It was low on fuel and the carrier was non-diversion flying. That meant that 'Boots' Walkinshaw and Mike Lucas had nowhere else to go. As the engineers worked to rectify the fault with the single remaining wire, Wings considered what to tell the Buccaneer crew. Even assuming the engineers were successful, he knew that telling a pilot the ship was down to one wire could be sufficiently unsettling to wreck any chance he had of recovering safely aboard. Wings opted not to take the risk. He knew landing on a pitching carrier deck was no walk in the park at the best of times.

During the Second World War, aircraft carrier operations were made manageable by the relatively low performance of the embarked aircraft. It sometimes seemed as if the old Swordfishes might struggle to even catch up with a steaming carrier before they plonked on the deck. Cheap, easy-to-produce piston-engined aeroplanes could be guided to the deck by a Landing Safety Officer or Batsman with little danger of him being overwhelmed by split-second decisions. Using what looked like a table-tennis bat in each hand, the Batsman gave instructions to pilots as they flew down the glidepath on finals to the back of the carrier's deck. But as aircraft performance improved it was clear, even by the war's end, that the existing system of recovering aircraft was reaching its limits. Assuming that went without a hitch, they then *had* to catch one of a row of arrestor wires or sail on forward into the steel wire crash barrier that was rigged the full width of the deck, dividing the deck in two. The back of the deck was for landing, the front for parked aircraft. Hitting the barrier invariably damaged the aircraft and could kill the pilot. And as many as one in fifty landings ended with an aircraft careering into the barrier.

But in the early 1950s, the naval section of the Ministry of Supply came up with the solutions. Led by Captain Dennis Cambell from grand offices in Thames House in London, a small team of engineers and scientists considered ways round the limitations that the existing technologies imposed. Cambell, who'd flown off the third *Ark Royal* during the war, shared in the development of the angled deck, which, by offsetting the runway at up to 11 degrees from the centreline of the carrier's deck, alleviated the need for the crash barrier. With their direction of travel now taking them across the centreline and off towards the port edge of the deck, recovering aircraft that missed the arrestor wires were free to simply accelerate and go around again. It was simple and effective and, at a stroke, one in fifty became one in 200.

Another former Fleet Air Arm fighter pilot worked on Cambell's staff. While flying Hellcats in the Far East during the last year of the war, Lieutenant Commander Nick Goodhart had been appalled that the process of deck landing was killing more men than the enemy. *We must do something better*, he thought, *deck landing's just too difficult*. And while working at Thames House he had an idea he thought might just work. To prove it, though, he needed the model of HMS *Illustrious* that decorated Captain Cambell's office, a torch, a mirror and the assistance of Miss Montgomery, his boss's secretary. Goodhart set up the demonstration. He placed the torch on the side of the model carrier's deck pointing forwards and Miss Montgomery's powder compact amidships, its mirror facing backwards. He moved both around until, standing bolt upright behind *Illustrious*, Miss Montgomery could see the torch's reflection in the middle of the mirror. Then Goodhart asked the obliging secretary to walk towards the back of the carrier, making sure to keep the light of the torch in the centre of the mirror at all times. As she approached the round-down above the ship's stern her knees bent lower and lower and her head dropped until at last her chin came to rest gently on the back of the deck. On a full-size carrier, a mirror sight placed next to the arrestor wires could bring a returning strike fighter into land in the right spot as surely as it had Miss Montgomery's chin.

The US Navy was quick to realize the potential of both innovations and it was the Navy's enthusiasm for them that ensured their survival and widespread adoption. The angled deck and the Deck Landing Mirror System – developed to become the projector sight – stood the test of time. Both now had their part to play.

But it wasn't just modifications to the ship that made it possible for Walkinshaw and Lucas to recover safely on board. For all the Buccaneer's renowned solidity and structural strength, the cleverness and subtlety of her aerodynamic design were at least as important to her success as a normal bomber. For such a large, heavy aeroplane, the Buccaneer had small wings – it was the main reason for her smoothness in the thick, turbulent air down low. Carrier landings, though, required the opposite: big wings, high lift and low speed. The solution Blackburn developed doubled the lift from the Buccaneer's small wing and reduced take-off and landing speeds by 25 knots, a huge margin. They managed it through a system called Boundary Layer Control. By bleeding hot, high-pressure air from the engines and blowing it through a series of tiny slits spread across the whole width of the wing's leading edge, they could guarantee a smooth flow of air over the wing as the aircraft reduced speed to land.

Blackburn's engineers were *fooling* the wing into thinking it was flying faster than it was.

As speed reduces, so does the lift produced by a wing. In order to produce the same amount of lift at low speed as at high speed, a wing's angle of attack needs to increase, presenting more of its underside towards the direction of travel – the reason that as airliners come in to land they look tail-heavy, their noses pointing in the air. But this only works up to a point. Increase the angle of attack too much and the smooth flow of air over the top of the wing starts to break up. At that point the wing stops flying – stops producing lift – and the aeroplane stalls and literally falls out of the sky as if it were a dropped anvil.

It was the Boundary Layer Control that kept this disastrous state of affairs at bay. And from the back seat, Mike Lucas glanced over Walkinshaw's shoulder to the top right of the Pilot's cockpit coaming – an almost subconscious check on the two dials measuring the pressure of the blowing system.

From Flyco, Wings instructed the Flight Deck party to be ready to raise the crash barrier. In the event of a failure of either all four wires or an aircraft's arrestor hook, the crash barrier, stretched across the deck between the two raised yellow and black arms beyond 4 Wire, was the only way of bringing one of the 'Heavies' back on board.

'Four greens,' reported Walkinshaw as he flew the downwind leg of his landing circuit, his undercarriage and arrestor hook safely locked down, with full flaps, airbrake and the BLC bleeding hot air over the wings.

Wings caught a glimpse of her as she flew past, his eyes otherwise glued to the Flight Deck party working furiously on 1 Wire at the stern of the ship. Then, just as it looked as if raising the barrier was unavoidable, the engineers scurried to the sides of the flight deck, pausing only to offer a clear, deliberate thumbs up to Flyco: 1 Wire was up and running.

Walkinshaw, unaware of the drama on board, gently rolled

the Buccaneer on to finals. With his gloved right hand holding the stick and the other gripping the two throttle levers to the left of his ejection seat, he levelled the wing on the centreline. The 17-ton bomber settled on to a 4-degree glideslope, closing towards the deck at no more than a knot either side of the datum speed of 137 knots. In the back, Observer Mike Lucas, his seat above, behind and slightly to the right of his Pilot, looked over Walkinshaw's shoulder. From three-quarters of a mile out, *Ark*, streaming thick black smoke above and trailing a foaming white wake behind her, looked tiny.

With nearly 500 deck landings under his belt, the picture through the metal frame and armoured glass of the cockpit ahead of him was reassuringly familiar. He was on the meat-ball – the single white light of the projector sight shining reassuringly level with a horizontal row of green lights, to confirm that he was descending along the glidepath. Too low and he'd see only red, but maintaining this picture and keeping her on the centreline the hook should snare the 3 Wire – third from the back of the deck and the only wire any self-respecting naval aviator is happy with. On a platform at the edge of the deck, alongside the projector sight itself, Lieutenant Commander Charles Hussey, the LSO – Landing Safety Officer – monitored Walkinshaw's approach.

On the roger, centreline, Hussey confirmed. 'Boots' was on the glidepath and on the centreline. He just needed to keep her there.

From looking isolated and small, over the last couple of hundred yards of the Buccaneer's descent *Ark Royal* suddenly loomed large, filling the crew's peripheral vision. In this instant the forces involved in bringing nearly 20 tons of kinetic energy from over 130 knots to a halt in less than 600 feet became overwhelmingly apparent.

But experience told Walkinshaw he had judged it right. Behind his Pilot, Lucas looked down at the deck as the jet passed over the round-down then slammed aboard. As the heavy hydraulics of the main gear absorbed and contained

the bomber's violent descent, Walkinshaw kept the power on –
insurance against missing a wire – and braced himself against
the fierce deceleration that would follow. But it never came.

Bolter! Bolter! Bolter!, called Hussey from the LSO platform
as the Buccaneer accelerated towards the front of the ship, her
hook scraping impotently along the flightdeck in a rooster tail
of orange sparks. As she reached the edge of the angled deck,
the main gear oleos seemed to throw her back into the air
as the wings once again took the strain. Trailing two dirty black
plumes of smoke, the big, gun-grey jet climbed away from the
carrier. Walkinshaw tried to think through what had gone wrong.
The approach had been spot on. He should have trapped. Just
occasionally the hook would hit the deck and bounce over the
wire, but it was rare. Mike Lucas, though, had been looking at
the deck as they came over the stern of the ship.

'I think,' he told his Pilot, 'there's only one wire there.' It was
news to Walkinshaw. *They should have told us*, he thought,
and jammed his thumb on the RT button to speak to Flyco.

'How many wires have you got?'

'One,' came the reply

'Which one is it?'

'Number one,' confirmed Little F.

Two, three and four are gone, Walkinshaw told himself,
furious at having been kept in the dark. Catching number one,
the wire closest to the stern, meant either sitting low on the
meatball, flying a lower, flatter approach, or coming over
the round-down and pulling back on the power in the hope of
dropping on to the wire. Neither was a particularly appealing
prospect. But they were the only two options.

'So I've got to go fishing for it then, have I?' 'Boots' confirmed, unable to disguise the anger in his voice. An
experienced, confident pilot, Walkinshaw gritted his teeth and
caught 1 Wire on his next approach. But once he was out of
the cockpit, he made a beeline for Carl Davis in the 809 Crew
Room.

'You've got to go up there and tell Flyco,' he told his
squadron Boss furiously. 'I'll do it if you don't want to, but

someone's got to. They *have* to tell us if there's only one wire.' The possibilities of what might have been raced through his mind. Davis passed it on, but Wings let it blow over. He understood that feelings ran high, but he was also confident that, along with Little F, he'd made the right decisions. And that they had, in difficult circumstances, brought 'Boots' back safely on board.

Ark Royal continued her transit north at 17 knots on a bearing of 320 degrees. A brisk 23-knot wind blew across her from the south-east. Sat untidily on black vinyl-covered benches, the squadrons were briefed on what lay ahead. Nothing was left to chance – diversions, radio frequencies, codewords and cryptography, call signs, rules of engagement, IFF modes, the chain of command and contingency plans. The Operations staff laid out the scenario. NATO's Flexible Response plan provided the template. ROYAL KNIGHT assumed a gradual escalation by enemy 'Orange' forces – no one imagined for a second that it meant anything but the Soviets – to which *Ark*, along with other 'Blue' forces, would respond with appropriate levels of force. The bleak environment of the Norwegian Sea created difficulties of its own and this was not overlooked. There were lectures on survival in a cold climate by one of the Surgeon Lieutenants, on meteorology, and on the potentially lethal hazards of icing in the low-flying Gannets.

As the centrepiece of Carrier Strike Group 2, *Ark Royal* led Task Force 401.2 and, on the eve of the exercise, her Battle Group took shape. *Ark* was joined by the American cruiser USS *Newport News*, the flagship of the Commander-in-Chief of the Atlantic Striking Fleet, Vice Admiral Vincent du Poix; by the USS *Dahlgreen*; by the Leander Class frigate HMS *Jupiter*; and by the Dutch frigates HNLMS *Noord Brabant* and HNLMS *Tjerk Hiddes*. Ahead of the British carrier, two further Task Forces formed up: TF 401.1, around the 60,000-ton US strike carrier USS *Independence*, and TF 401.8, led by the veteran anti-submarine carrier USS *Intrepid*. Her job was to provide a forward submarine screen – to sanitize the seas ahead of the strike carriers. Like *Ark*, she was armed with nuclear depth charges.

Sitting in his raised chair at the left of the bridge under a grey ceiling, perforated like a sheet of Meccano, dimmed lights illuminating crew members on watch around him, John Roberts glanced at his watch. At one minute past midnight Zulu time – GMT – ROYAL KNIGHT began. Neither he nor his ship would properly rest again until the exercise reached its conclusion. As his great ship plunged through an increasing swell, he was eager to get stuck in.

The next day *Ark Royal* crossed 66 degrees of latitude, steaming north across the Arctic Circle.

Chapter 14

John Weymes knew his phone was being tapped by the Guatemalan security services. It had its advantages. The Guatemalan reaction to George Price's hopes of swift independence for British Honduras was predictable enough. Egged on by press commentators who regarded their government's efforts to seek redress over Belice as feeble, a spokesman for the Guatemalan Ministry of Foreign Affairs announced that there would never be negotiations with Britain over the colony's future. As he made clear, Belice, belonging as she did to Guatemala, was not in Britain's gift. If this was picked up by the news wires and read in London, Weymes knew it would cause alarm. Since 1969 there had been eleven meetings between Britain and Guatemala. The future of British Honduras as an independent nation *depended* on a negotiated settlement.

It was a Saturday. And, rather than travel up to the Consulate in Zone 1 to send an encrypted signal, Weymes picked up the phone and introduced himself to the Foreign Office Duty Clerk in London. Over the crackling long-distance line he heard the tell-tale clicks of the tapping equipment. 'I've got a message for the Central American department,' he told them in an accent that was still recognizably Geordie. He outlined the contents of the Guatemalan spokesman's statement.

'I'm going to investigate further and I'll let them know.' Weymes replaced the Consulate phone in its cradle. Within an hour he had an invitation to visit the Guatemalan Foreign

Minister, Dr Herrera, at his *finca* south of the city off the road to Lago de Amatitlán. Sánchez, Weymes's contact in the Belice office of the Ministry of External Relations, was already there. Elegant and charming, Herrera reassured him that the spokesman had been speaking without authority and that both he and Sánchez had told him that his remarks had been unhelpful – and that he would not be making them again. It appeared to be a straightforward mistake.

But the Guatemalans *were* concerned about what had been said on 10 September. When Weymes visited Sánchez in his office at the Foreign Ministry the Guatemalan was studying the Governor's speech.

'I'm trying to read between the lines,' he told Weymes, before quoting from the text: ' "the new Belize under God, united, sovereign and independent". What does he mean by that?' queried Sánchez. The British Consul demurred, explaining that the speech was for local consumption. But Sánchez made it crystal-clear that he was not at all happy about the emphasis that had been placed on 1972 as a date for independence.

And when, at a party, Weymes explained to one of Herrera's predecessors as Foreign Minister the practical and constitutional obstacles that prevented any possibility of imminent independence, the Guatemalan diplomat was unimpressed. He looked Weymes straight in the eye.

'You seem,' he countered, referring to an earlier, inconvenient precedent, 'to have been able to find a short cut in the case of Bahrain . . .'

100029ZULU – ten o'clock GMT on Wednesday, 29 September. Lieutenant 'Sharkey' Ward held his gloved right hand up against the glass of the Phantom canopy to signal to the FDO. He and his Observer, Dougal Macdonald, were ready to launch. From the back of the jet, two ferocious orange incandescent spears roared from the two Rolls-Royce Speys turning water to steam, looking for all the world like they would burn through the steel flight deck, as if angry at being deflected by it. Ahead, more steam billowed out of the catapult track to the edge of the deck. Underneath him *Ark Royal* bulldozed through the water at 16 knots into a 20-knot south-easterly wind. When Ward and Macdonald were fired down the waist cat, 36 knots of the air speed Phantom 001 needed to fly would be provided by the combined efforts of 'Mother' and Mother Nature. That was *before* the steam catapult and over 41,000lb of thrust from the two reheated Speys made any contribution at all.

The 29th looked like being a busy day for 892's F-4s. Jerry Granger-Holcombe and his new Pilot, Lieutenant Commander Andy Auld, had already been scrambled at 0732 and there would be more to come.

In deciding in 1966 that the carriers were redundant, it was argued that, in future, the RAF would take responsibility for providing air defence for the fleet. And during the opening two days of ROYAL KNIGHT the Phantom FG1s of 43 Squadron based at RAF Leuchars, near St Andrews, had done just that. Flying under the control of the USS *Intrepid* as she sailed through the Iceland–Faroes gap on her way to the Norwegian Sea, the green-and-grey camouflaged RAF Phantoms had flown sorties averaging over four and a half hours each. But maintaining a Combat Air Patrol for less than a day nearly 550 miles out over the North Sea from Leuchars had needed twelve aircraft and fifty-three flying hours. Operating further from their home base than they had ever done previously demanded careful planning and coordination and to their credit they'd pulled it off successfully. But they were the only squadron in the RAF capable of mounting anything like that kind of operation. And even in succeeding to provide cover, they had revealed the difficulties in doing so. The fleet, meanwhile, was still on its way north.

British newspapers had recently highlighted the fragility of the country's air defences. Other than the Phantoms at Leuchars, there were just six squadrons of short-legged English Electric Lightnings defending the whole country. And of them

– assuming that the country could spare them – only the slightly longer-ranged F6 version, supported by in-flight refuelling from the RAF's small fleet of Handley-Page Victors, had any realistic chance of providing even inshore air defence for the fleet.

To keep a pair of Phantoms on station for six days 750 miles from Leuchars would require fourteen F-4s and a further ten Victors to refuel them. It was, as a contemporary study noted without exaggeration, 'a formidable challenge for any unit'. The Atlantic Striking Fleet was now operating over 800 miles from Leuchars.

Only the three squadrons of Phantoms aboard *Ark Royal* and *Independence* had any hope of defending the multi-national task force from air attack.

With the wind tugging at his clothes, the FDO looked over his shoulder at the Flyco ready lights, checked the catapult ready lights, anticipated the rise and fall of the ship through the swell, then, in a long sweeping arc, dropped his weather-beaten little green flag to the deck. Behind the armoured glass of the howdah, the catapult control position on the other side of the Phantom, a Petty Officer Engineer who, until now had kept his hands visible above his head, pressed the red 'Fire' button. A beat later 001 hurtled forward, from zero to 140 knots in a single second. Inside, Ward and Macdonald were pressed back hard against their ejection seats, trying to read their instruments through the blur, distortion and violence of their fierce acceleration.

They were on CAP station at 20,000 feet, eighty miles ahead of the fleet, in just over ten minutes.

Lieutenant Harry O'Grady, 892's bearded Fighter Controller, was known to all as the 'D'. O'Grady had been promoted through the ranks to become one of the Phantom squadron's most larger-than-life and well-loved characters. But once embarked O'Grady became the property of the ship not the squadron. And he inhabited the troglodyte world of the carrier's ADR – the Air Direction Room – situated underneath

the Operations Room at the bottom of the island. A 4 foot ×
3 foot opening in the deck allowed direct communication
between the two rooms. Together, the Ops Room and the ADR
processed the flow of information in and out of the ship.
Without them *Ark Royal* would be little more than a cruise
ship. By maintaining situational awareness, controlling the
tactical picture and keeping track of both friend and foe, they
provided *Ark* with her ability to fight. Bathed in soft orange
light and working to a soundtrack of one-sided radio conversations and the constant drone of the air-con, O'Grady sat at
his big radar display on a raised platform, surrounded by
clumsy grey consoles and analogue computers. Around him, in
the darkened room, blue-shirted ratings in headphones plotted
positions on a large transparent screen, marked with
concentric circles like a rifle target. The story it told could be
seen at a glance from either side. Small, multicoloured warning
lights twinkled across every surface. The morning had already
seen him scramble a Phantom from Alert 5 – five minutes'
standby to launch – but the urgency of that was long gone.
Phantom 013 and her crew were safely back aboard and now
he just had 001 – Sharkey and Dougal – flying lazy racetracks
at medium altitude, on CAP station to the north-east.

Then word arrived from a remote radar station in the north
of Norway. *Tramps incoming* was the message, delivered with
a hint of a Scandinavian accent. There were unidentified aircraft rounding the North Cape, the Norwegian controller
continued. O'Grady took down the number of contacts, range,
bearing, speed and altitude and repeated it over the RT. Then
he ordered the Combat Air Patrol to investigate.

*Zero Zero One, I've got trade for you. Three bogies,
050/140. Vector Zero Five Zero* – three unidentified aircraft,
140 miles to the north-east.

Roger, Vector Zero Five Zero. On Channel 15, inside the
cockpit of 001, Ward acknowledged the message from the 'D'.
He rolled the big interceptor's wings on to the intercept heading, then, with his left hand, pushed forward the throttles to
full military power and riding on 25,000lb of dry thrust

accelerated towards the visitors. At a closing speed of 15 miles a minute, 001 would be on top of them in less than ten. In the back seat of the Phantom, Dougal Macdonald leant forward into the radarscope, controlling the set using the control panel to the left and the antenna hand control to the right.

This is more like it, thought the Observer. Whatever happened during ROYAL KNIGHT, a threat from the north was what they were *really* there for. He set the range scale to 100 miles, each square of the 25-square grid equating to 20×20 miles. Ahead of him, in the nose of the fighter, the antenna of the powerful liquid-cooled Westinghouse radar swept the skies. From the ADR aboard *Ark*, O'Grady's voice came through the static again.

Zero Zero One, contacts are down the throat. Forty miles. Their targets were dead ahead now, just forty miles away and closing. Macdonald stared into the green background of the radar's cathode ray tube display, willing it to reveal his target's position. Then three yellowish rectangular shapes appeared at a distance of thirty miles on the nose. There they were. He pressed the transmit button with his thumb.

I've got them. Three bogies. Five degrees high at thirty miles. Judy! And with that last call Macdonald assumed control of the intercept from the 'D'.

Contact. Locked on. Fly the dot, he told Ward over the intercom, telling him to follow the display on his own radarscope.

Inbound were three Myasishchev M-4 Bison-As of the Soviet Air Force long-range bomber regiments. A contemporary of the American Boeing B-52 and similarly large, the big four-engined jet bombers – christened 'Hammer' by the Soviets – bristled with defensive armament. Between them, the formation heading towards 001 carried thirty 23mm cannon. The Phantom, flying with a big 500-gallon drop tank on its centre-line pylon, carried only a Sidewinder acquisition round – the missile's seeker head alone – and a Sparrow 'plug' in one of the semi-recessed missile stations in the jet's white-painted belly. Both were fitted to provide crews with realistic drills during Air Interception sorties. 001 was unarmed.

Right: Though first laid down in 1943, HMS *Ark Royal* did not join the fleet for another decade. During that period she became a fixture on the Merseyside skyline.

Above: *Ark Royal* emerged from a three-year refit in 1970. Substantially modernized, she was capable of operating the latest generation of naval aircraft. For the first time in its history, the Fleet Air Arm would be operating an Air Group from one of their carrier decks that was genuinely the match of anything else in the sky.

Left: The enemy. A Tupolev Tu-95 Bear bomber overflies a Sverdlov class cruiser. By 1970 the Soviet Navy had developed into an increasingly capable blue-water fleet.

Right: Outgunned by Sverdlovs, the Royal Navy turned to air power. The Blackburn NA39 Buccaneer, pictured in prototype form here at Farnborough, was designed specifically to counter the threat from the big Soviet cruisers. By 1970, in its S Mk 2 form, it had developed into one of the most capable low-level strike bombers in the world.

Left: After a career that had taken him from the Arctic Convoys during WWII to command of a squadron of Hawker Seahawk fighters, Captain John Roberts took command of *Ark Royal* on 9 March 1971.

Below: Lt Cdr Carl Davis, Boss of 809 Naval Air Squadron.

Above: Phoenix Squadron. The 809 NAS crest and battle honours.

Right: Taken aboard *Ark Royal* in early 1971, 809 pose in front of one of the squadron's Buccaneers.

Right: 892 NAS, *Ark's* fighter squadron, was commanded by Lt Cdr Nick Kerr. It was destined to be the only frontline Royal Navy unit to fly the McDonnell Douglas F-4 Phantom II.

Above: Supersonic and heavily armed with guided missiles and state-of-the-art radar, the American F-4 Phantom FG1 was the most powerful aircraft ever flown by the Fleet Air Arm.

Left: In the summer of 1971 *Ark Royal* deployed to the Western Atlantic for exercises with the US Navy. This picture of the British strike carrier in Florida gives a vivid impression of her size.

Left: While *Ark* was alongside, her squadrons disembarked to US Naval Air Station Cecil Field near Jacksonville, from where 892 honed their dogfighting skills out over the Atlantic. This rare picture shows a Royal Navy F-4 manoeuvring hard.

Above: One engagement ended in disaster when a Phantom stalled and crashed into the sea. This cartoon from the squadron Line Book shows her crew, Lt Dave Hill and Lt Jerry Granger-Holcombe, being picked up by a US Navy helicopter after their successful ejection.

While operating in the Western Atlantic, *Ark* became the first Royal Navy carrier to train with the US Navy at AFWR – the Atlantic Fleet Weapons Ranges – off Puerto Rico. This unique sequence of pictures shows one of the Phantoms firing an AIM-7 Sparrow radar-guided missile.

Above: 809 also took advantage of the opportunity to drop live ordnance. Here a Buccaneer with four live 500lb bombs under the wings taxies forwards for launch.

Under the radar. At over 500 knots and fifty feet – or lower – over the sea the Buccaneers were hard to detect and even harder to stop.

Right: Taken from a reconnaissance camera in the jet's bomb bay, this picture provides evidence of 809 flying their Buccaneers over the AFWR bombing ranges at seriously low level.

Above: 892 weren't confined to an air-to-air role. The multi-role Phantom was also a capable attack aircraft in its own right, as this picture of five jets bombed-up and ready to go testifies.

Left: One of *Ark*'s F-4s streaks in low over the range.

Left: While the Royal Navy exercised in the Caribbean, trouble was brewing in Central America where Guatemala had designs on its neighbour, British Honduras. With no air defence of any kind in country, the British had no way of stopping unwelcome overflights by Lockheed T-33 jets of the Fuerza Aerea Guatemalteca.

These reconnaissance pictures of Belize City, the British colony's commercial capital, were taken from a Guatemalan T-33 in 1970. Annotations were added by their Air Force's photographic section at La Aurora Air Force Base.

In this second picture the T-33's wingtip fuel tank is visible as the jet circles above the city.

Left: A Guatemalan pilot poses in the cockpit of his T-33.

As the seventies began, the Guatemalans mounted a number of increasingly aggressive operations including large-scale paratroop drops at the border and low-level fighter sorties along their neighbour's coastline.

Above: In early summer 1971, the Guatemalan F-51 Mustang squadron deployed to a rough jungle strip at Tikal, just a few minutes flying time from the border of British Honduras. Less than a year earlier, the unit's entire complement of aircraft had been repainted in an effective camouflage. It was known to all as the 'invasion scheme'.

Right: Our Man in Guatemala City. British Consul John Weymes returned to Central America in 1970, following an earlier posting to Panama. He quickly became aware of both the endemic political violence in Guatemala and the visceral strength of feeling over British Honduras.

At a distance of fifteen miles, Ward pulled the Phantom into a gentle turn away from the approaching Bisons before switching back and turning in to approach them from their starboard side. Throughout the manoeuvre Macdonald kept the beam from the AWG-11 radar locked on the formation. Neither he nor Ward had yet made visual contact with the Soviet bombers. Neither knew what they'd find.

As Ward rolled out of the turn, they both realized what they'd got. *Shit!* – surprised by what lay ahead, Macdonald groped for the camera – *haven't seen one of these before*. To the crew of the British fighter, this was a rare opportunity. The big Myasishchevs were a far less familiar sight than the Bears and Badgers that more often probed Western defences. And that was what was happening. The Russians weren't sightseeing. They were testing the Striking Fleet's defences; measuring the speed of their response. In turn, Phantom Observers carried bulky cameras with them to photograph the Russian bombers. Their evidence would be pored over by analysts at JARIC, the Joint Air Reconnaissance Intelligence Centre in Huntingdonshire. Each new bump and aerial recorded by the Observers on their Hasselblads added to the sum of NATO's knowledge of their opponents.

Ward tucked the Phantom alongside one of the Bisons while Macdonald took pictures. Its unpainted silver skin caught the thin sunlight. Sometimes the Soviet gunners tracked NATO fighters as they flew alongside, but on this occasion they were idle, pointing safely skyward. The Bison's long tapering wings swept back from the four Mikulin AM-3D turbojets that were buried within the wingroots near the slender fuselage. A large red star graced the tall vertical tailplane. *There's no denying*, Macdonald thought, *that it has a certain elegance.*

But it was easy to get seduced by the sight of the glinting jets. And it was certainly no game out over the remote seas beyond 70 degrees north. Nick Kerr's predecessor as 892's squadron Boss had been lucky to escape when he'd intercepted an Ilyushin Il-38 May, a propeller-engined Soviet maritime-reconnaissance aircraft. After being joined by the British Phantom, the Russian began a gentle descent down towards the North Sea. At 1000 feet, flying at barely 200 knots, the heavy Mach 2 interceptor struggled to maintain station 100 yards off the starboard quarter of the patrol plane. The Soviet pilot knew the Phantom was wallowing and gently descended towards the grey surface of the sea. Then the Il-38 banked sharply towards the British jet, trying to force an error – to trap the Phantom and tip it into the water. Accidents happened. Only a couple of years earlier up here in the same stretch of frozen ocean, another Badger buzzed a group of US Navy ships. After passing flat and low alongside the American anti-submarine carrier USS *Essex*, the silver Soviet bomber banked steeply to climb away. But her pilot misjudged it. The port wingtip caught the wavetops and the 60-ton bomber cartwheeled and exploded. None of her seven-man crew survived.

Nick Kerr was already in the air by the time 'Sharkey' Ward and Dougal Macdonald slammed back on to *Ark Royal*'s deck. Like his AWI, he too got lucky and was vectored to intercept a Tupolev Tu-95 Bear – the giant turbo-prop bomber that had become the most recognizable symbol of Soviet Cold War air power. As he and his Observer, John Ellis, kept formation, they could feel the noise and throb of the Bear's massive contra-rotating propeller blades as they churned through the air. Through black sun visors they could see crewmen of Aviatsiya Voyenno-Morskoyo Flota – the Soviet Naval Aviation Regiments – through the glass of the observation blisters ahead of the Bear's tail. Kerr knew that if things heated up they would never get this close. Ideally, he thought, you'd never see the enemy at all – and the Phantom, with its pulse-Doppler radar and medium-range radar-guided missiles, gave you that luxury. But in arguing the case for making BVR – Beyond Visual Range – interceptions he was fighting a losing battle. And he was tired of locking horns with his Senior Pilot, Dick Moody, over it. Moody was just back from Miramar and a tour with the US Navy on VF-121. He'd come back convinced of the need for VID – Visual Identification. The close ties enjoyed by the Royal Navy and their American counterparts brought many benefits to the Fleet Air Arm in terms of technology, tactics, training, and the exchange of ideas and intelligence. US experience with the Phantom was the foundation on which 892 was building. But, on VID, Kerr felt the Brits should go their own way.

In Vietnam, with each branch of the US Armed forces – Air Force, Navy, Army and Marine Corps – fielding what amounted to its own air force, combined with a lack of joined-up communication and control, the Phantom's unique outstanding BVR capability became a liability. The Raytheon AIM-7 Sparrow missile was designed for radar-guided head-on attacks from nearly fifteen miles away. When it worked you took down the enemy before he even knew you were there. But in the confusing skies above Vietnam there was an overwhelming danger of blue-on-blue attacks – attacks on your own side. As a result, US admirals had adopted the policy of VID. Until US Phantom pilots had positively visually identified their targets they were to remain weapons- tight. The British Admiralty followed the US lead.

It's bloody ridiculous, thought Kerr. And it was particularly galling because, for all his ambivalence about the RAF, he had a sneaking suspicion that, without the same depth of cross-pollination enjoyed by the Fleet Air Arm with the Americans at Miramar, it had fewer qualms about firing Sparrow from BVR and asking questions later. Given the overwhelming numbers the Warsaw Pact could put in the air – and the imminent introduction of their new Tupolev Tu-26 Backfire swing-wing, supersonic bomber into service – NATO needed to use every advantage it could lay its hands on. When it came to shooting down enemy aircraft, Kerr really felt he could do without having his hands tied. America had provided him with the most capable, lethal fighter plane in the skies and now, because of the mess in south-east Asia, he was being stopped from using it. But, for all the frustration it caused on this issue, the close relationship between the US and UK was clear for everyone to see in the North Atlantic during Exercise ROYAL KNIGHT. The situation in Central America, however, was a little more fuzzy.

Chapter 15

'Bomb, repeat bomb,' urged the American Ambassador to Guatemala over a secure line to Allen Dulles, the Director of the CIA. The 1953 coup attempt – backed by 'The Company' – had faltered. To shore it up, $150,000 of CIA cash was handed over to the US military on behalf of Nicaragua. In exchange for the money, three fully armed Second World War-vintage Republic F-47 Thunderbolts became the property of Nicaragua. But they were never actually delivered. From a US airbase on Puerto Rico the three piston-engined fighter-bombers only made it as far as Panama. Then the next morning, flown by CIA pilots, the barrel-shaped F-47s strafed trains and dropped bombs, while out of their open cockpits the Company men threw dynamite, hand grenades and even Molotov cocktails. During the CIA's raids, a British cargo ship that was tied alongside in Puerto Quetzal, Guatemala's largest Pacific Coast port, was attacked and sunk.

In America's backyard, Britain relied on American intelligence, and yet troop transport flights to British Honduras or, previously, British Guiana might be denied transit through US airports. And while in private Counsellor John Dreyfus, number two to the Ambassador at the US Embassy in Guatemala City, would tell John Weymes, 'We're glad you're in Belize. We think it's a good thing', there was, Weymes knew, absolutely no possibility of such a position being made public, without driving a stake through America's long, hard-fought relationship with Guatemala.

Since President James Monroe had, in 1823, expounded the idea that European powers should not interfere in the affairs of independent countries in the New World, it seemed the United States had been determined to fill the breach herself. And nowhere more so than Guatemala. From forcing the Napoleon-obsessive President Jorge Ubico to sever connections with the European Fascists and expel German landowners in the 1930s, to the coup that brought down Arbenz in 1953 and since, America made sure that the Guatemalan leaders knew which side their bread was buttered. And in exercising this influence, the permanent US presence in the Panama Canal Zone remained crucial.

Over the summer of 1971, other than independence and speculation over Guatemalan intentions, it was the exploration of space that seemed to dominate the pages of newspapers in British Honduras. The death of the three Russian cosmonauts aboard Soyuz 11 or the defection of Soviet rocket scientist Anatol Fedoseyev were front-page news, but most attention was lavished on the American moon landings. No aspect of the Apollo XV lunar rover mission in July went unmentioned. Even analysis of the rock samples brought back by Commander David Scott and his crew was headline news. But as unquenchable as the appetite of *The Reporter* and the *Belize Times* was for space stories, they missed the one that took place closest to home. Throughout the sixties the Apollo astronauts had been travelling to and from US bases in the Panama Canal Zone to undergo jungle survival training. During the same period, Douglas B-26K Counter Invaders of the USAF's 605th Air Commando Squadron were flying night-bombing missions against rebel targets in Guatemala. And, just a month before the crew of Apollo XV arrived at Albrook Air Force Base to head out into the jungle to sit round campfires in orange flight suits, 200 troops from the new Guatemalan Special Forces Battalion arrived in Panama.

Trained by US instructors at the School of the Americas, the Batallón de Fuerzas Especiales were parachute specialists, airborne troops who were dropped into operational areas, ready to engage the enemy, by the FAG's C-47 transports. For nearly a year, after the delivery of three surplus Bell UH-1D Huey helicopters through the US Military Aid Program, the paratroopers fought an effective Air Cavalry campaign against guerrillas in Zacapa and Izabal. Then once again they returned to their roots to become the battle-hardened heart of the Guatemalan Army's Parachute Corps at San José airbase on the Pacific Coast. They were Guatemala's most well-trained, experienced and professional troops. And during the year in which they had been blooded, they had been under the control of Colonel Carlos Osorio Arana, now President of Guatemala.

In British Honduras, the complicated relationship between all involved left the Premier, George Price, exasperated. With responsibility for his country's external affairs in Britain's hands he was unable to appeal to America directly. But that didn't mean he was completely voiceless. 'The United States,' he told one journalist, 'is not helping us enough. If Washington declared its categorical support for our independence, we would have independence tomorrow.' The State Department remained conspicuously and predictably silent. America's interest was in shoring up Arana and the generals. Support for Belize would destabilize them and jeopardize a relationship of much greater importance. And so Britain's little Central American outpost remained – caught between the devil and the deep blue sea.

And while it did remain, Britain simply had to live with the idea that one of her oldest and closest allies was ambivalent about her presence there but unwilling to help bring it to an end. Worse, though, was the unpalatable notion that American money, training and technical support made credible the threat from the little colony's only potential enemy.

Chapter 16

The story goes that during exercises with the Royal Navy, a US Navy fighter pilot, vectored to investigate an unidentified contact at 3000 feet, found himself flying alongside one of the Fleet Air Arm's Fairey Gannet AEW3s.

'What have you found up there?' his controller asked him. The American aviator paused to consider his answer, staring at the odd-looking machine as it ambled around the sky with one engine turned off. With a jet pipe sticking out of the side like the siphon of an octopus, bent wings, contra-rotating propellers and psychedelic swirling yellow and black spinner, and the swollen afterthought of a radome, attached underneath like the cap of a giant mushroom, there was no doubting its strangeness. But it was the pilot who most caught his eye. In the cockpit, high on top of the Gannet's tall fuselage, was a man who looked like Brian Blessed, wearing an old leather flying helmet, who, apparently engrossed in a book, didn't even look up.

'I, er, I think I've found God . . .' concluded the fighter pilot.

The Gannet crews were the odd ones out aboard *Ark Royal*. Flying an ageing propeller-driven fixed-wing aircraft, they enjoyed neither the powerful allure of the jet 'Heavies' nor the us-against-the-world brashness of the young Sea King squadron. But that's just the way the Boss of 849 NAS 'B' Flight, Lieutenant Commander Guy Holman, liked it. 'My brain,' he'd tell people disarmingly, 'just doesn't work quickly enough for the fast stuff.' He'd spent his entire flying career on

Gannets and he loved flying the old girl from the deck. 'Happy,' as he put it, 'to be a taxi driver.' Because the Gannet's job had everything to do with the men sitting behind him in the aircraft's fuselage, the two Observers operating the radar.

The AN/APS-20 radar carried by the Gannet was a vintage piece of kit. Developed by the US Navy under the codename 'Project CADILLAC' in the dying days of the Second World War to help protect the fleet from Japanese kamikaze attacks, it entered service in 1946. 849 NAS had first used the system when it was installed in their big radial-engined Douglas Skyraider AEW1s. Then, with minor modifications to the processing units, the radars were removed and installed in the new Gannet AEW3s. Since 1952, 849 had offered the Royal Navy a capability that was unique. They were the only Airborne Early Warning unit in the whole of the UK.

During an exercise like ROYAL KNIGHT, Guy Holman reckoned the two Observers, despite literally rubbing shoulders in the tiny blacked-out cabin, probably had the better of it. The Gannet's job was to fly between the ship and the fighter CAP carrying the AN/APS-20 high enough to see over the horizon. From a few thousand feet up, the old pulse radar could pick up threats hidden from the view of the ships' radars by the curvature of the earth and direct the Phantoms to intercept. The Gannets gave *Ark* breathing space – bought her time to defend herself and the ships around her.

But flying a square search pattern at 3000 feet on instruments for three hours in the freezing clag over the Norwegian Sea, he sometimes thought he'd be better off in the back. The trouble was that the AN/APS-20 was badly affected by ground clutter – unwanted radar reflections from the wave tops effectively masked the approach of incoming raids. To ensure a decent picture by allowing the radar to scan forwards rather than directly down, two or three thousand feet was the optimum height. And that meant flying at the icing point – the altitude where moisture in the air freezes. The cloud wasn't just an inconvenience – it had the potential to be fatal.

Undisturbed, supercooled water particles in the cloud could

maintain their liquid form below freezing until, destabilized by an aircraft passing through, they froze instantly to its leading edges. As the unfortunate aircraft flew on, triggering the freezing of further water particles, they too would build up on the layer already clinging to the wings. The accumulation could be visibly rapid. The pressure drop around the engine intake only accelerated it. And if the intake blocked, without cold air coming in in sufficient volume, the Double Mamba turbo-prop would quickly burn out. And that meant ditching. Worse, if ice formed on the wings or tail and destroyed the smooth flow of air over the wings, the Gannet would stall, which, with ice on the wings, there was no hope of recovering from. One of three things happened next. Either the aircraft mushed flat into the sea, or it rolled and entered a fatal spin into the sea, or it simply dived vertically towards the sea, probably breaking up before the impact. Gannet crews had been briefed again before heading north about the dangers of icing and their aircraft were equipped with a basic anti-icing system. It just didn't work particularly well. *Just avoid cunims like the plague* was Holman's basic rule of thumb.

Airborne for three and a half hours at a time, the Gannets of 'B' Flight maintained a constant vigil ahead of *Ark Royal*. By day and night they scanned the skies and seas for any signs of trouble. To deal with any air threat, Phantoms sat pre-flighted on the flight deck at Alert 5 ready to scramble. Already strapped into their seats, the crews only had to start the engines, cycle the hook and taxi forward on to the catapults. One rung down the readiness ladder were the crews waiting on Alert 20.

And while they, at least, got to sit in the relative comfort of the crew room, hanging around in the small hours of the morning dressed in a thick, unyielding rubber immersion suit was no one's idea of fun. In the dim red light, 809's Senior Pilot, 'Boots' Walkinshaw, tried to use time to catch up on admin. His Observer, Mike Lucas, drank coffee, chatted with the tanker crew and leaned back on the long, black vinyl benches in vain hope of some kip. The languor evaporated when SOBS came down two decks from the Ops Room, where he was the senior 809 crew member on duty. Steve Park had news.

'The Gannet's spotted a Skunk,' Park told them, using the Navy's shorthand for an unidentified ship contact, 'we're going to put you on five minutes' alert.' Lucas picked up his nav bag and followed Walkinshaw into the Line Hut next door, where the duty technicians handed the Senior Pilot the Flight Logs. Still bathed in red light to protect his night vision, 'Boots' scanned them and signed the A700 form to accept the aircraft, Buccaneer 026. Wearing their white helmets and bound with harnesses, leg restraints and their Mae West life jackets Walkinshaw and Lucas opened the steel hatch between the two funnel uptakes and left the safety of the island for a pitch-black flight deck.

Buccaneer 026 was lashed to the deck at Fly 3, thirty yards back on the starboard side. As the two men walked to the back of the ship by the light of red torches, careful to avoid tripping on the chains and tie-down lugs that threatened their progress, Lucas couldn't help but feel a twinge of apprehension, even isolation. Blacked out for fear of submarines, the flat expanse of the *Ark Royal's* deck at night, the colour of the red-painted runway markings washed grey by the dark, was not a comforting place to be. There wasn't a sane naval aviator anywhere in the world who actually enjoyed the business of operating from a carrier at night. There was satisfaction to be had from doing it well. Pleasure in recollection, perhaps. But most of all there was a feeling of relief, once you were back safely, that it was behind you.

Once strapped in, Walkinshaw and Lucas removed the safety pins from the seat-pan firing handle and from the canopy jettison handle, set the underwater escape handle to 'Underwater' and closed the canopy. If they needed to eject while still on deck, Lucas could only do so with the canopy closed. Open, he'd be killed as he was fired into the thick metal frame that, with the canopy pulled back on its runners, was directly above his head. Walkinshaw told Flyco they were ready.

Zero Two Six on alert.

Roger.

Then, still lashed to the deck, they waited, sharing small talk to keep things relaxed. It was more important than it seemed. Sitting in the cockpit at Alert 5 in the middle of an ink-black night with the tail of your aircraft hanging over the edge of a pitching deck was a disorientating, unnerving place to be.

Watching from Flyco, Steve Park knew it. He'd been completing his pre-take-off checks when, like a passenger in a carriage watching an adjacent train pull out from the station, he picked up movement in his peripheral vision – the jet next to them taxiing forward. But his brain told him that what he was watching was his own jet rolling backwards. And there was nowhere to roll to but off the side of the ship.

'Brakes! Brakes!' he shouted into the intercom to his Pilot, who reacted instantly, before they both realized, adrenalin subsiding, that it was a false alarm. But it was far from unknown for a carrier to lose aircraft over the side.

While at sea, John Roberts rarely ventured far from the bridge. While awake he was either on the bridge, in Flyco, in the chart house or, possibly, a deck below in the Ops Room. Sleep, such as it was, was snatched behind a curtain in his sea cabin immediately behind the compass platform. He was always on call and, during high-intensity operations of the kind demanded by ROYAL KNIGHT, never really switched off. If something was happening, he made sure he was present. Even if, for the launch of a solo Buccaneer to investigate a surface contact at three in the morning, that meant doing so in his dressing gown.

In the cockpit of 026, Walkinshaw and Lucas felt their seats pitch forward as the ship heeled steeply beneath them. *Ark Royal* was turning hard into wind. It was left to the last minute in order to keep the time the 43,000-ton carrier spent steaming straight into wind to a minimum. A predictable course made her too juicy a target for any enemy submarines that had slipped past the destroyer screen. Through the jet's heavy undercarriage they felt the ship throb as she turned through 130 degrees into the brisk south-easterly.

In Flyco, with Steve Park at his shoulder, Little F leant forward and spoke into his microphone.

Flight deck, Flyco. SAR clear engage.

Before any fixed-wing flying took place, the planeguard helicopter had to be launched. Now, on orders from Flyco, the grey Westland Wessex HAS1, her nose and tail striped with hi-visibility crimson, engaged her main rotor. The pilots of *Ark*'s Search and Rescue flight had been heard to bemoan their lot in the Wardroom. And with some justification. Flying planeguard *was* routine. The Wessex had to station herself a hundred yards off the port side of the ship during flying operations. As the ship moved forward at 16 knots, rather than hover the SAR helo would slowly fly from stern to bow, before leaning forward to pick up speed and looping round to begin the whole lazy circuit again.

'I'm so bored,' one of the SAR pilots joked over a beer, 'I sometimes wish they *would* ditch. It would give me something to do . . .' But not on a night like this. Not in the freezing waters of the Norwegian Sea. And it wasn't just Walkinshaw and Lucas either. He also had to think of his aircrewman, the Search and Rescue diver he carried on board who'd have to go in after them if they ditched.

The Wessex exploded into life in dangerous-looking clouds of smoke, its old Rolls-Royce Gazelle engine blasted into life by a detonating starter cartridge. The main rotor gathered speed above the old helicopter's fuselage.

Flight deck, Flyco. SAR clear take-off.

As the pilot pulled up on the collective lever with his left hand, the Wessex rose from the deck, leaned forward into wind to steady herself, then drifted left to hold station with the carrier as she steamed forward at 20 knots. The pilot pressed transmit.

Five Zero airborne, Channel 3.

With the SAR helo in position a hundred yards or so to port, Wings was ready to launch the Buccaneer into the night.

Flight deck, Little F's voice rang out again, *stand clear of intakes, jet pipes, start the Buccaneer.*

Zero Two Six – he spoke directly to Walkinshaw and Lucas – *Flyco, you are clear to start.*

*

HMS *Ocelot* had been following a Daily War Routine for the last two days. Since slipping under the waves when, just after eight o'clock in the morning on 27 September, her Captain, Lieutenant Commander Mike Logan RN, gave the order to dive, she'd not resurfaced. *Ocelot* – 295 feet long, black and with a hull resembling the shape of a Second World War U-Boat – was a 2030-ton 'Oberon' class diesel-electric submarine. Unable to stay underwater indefinitely, unlike her nuclear-powered contemporaries, she instead hovered just below the surface to recharge her batteries by 'snorting' – running her diesel engines through a snorkel to the surface. *Ocelot* had few of the creature-comforts on offer to the crews of the larger nuclear boats. Everything was cramped. Everything took a little getting used to. But Logan knew that he was driving what many believed was the best conventionally powered submarine in the world. The 'O' boats had established a peerless reputation for stealth. Running in ultra-quiet state she was harder for the Anti-Submarine Warfare specialists in the helos and destroyers to find and kill than the SSNs – the nuclear attack submarines. When it came to making a surprise attack, *Ocelot* had every advantage.

And, before dawn on 29 September, after completing a 180-degree search of the seas around him, Logan set course and speed for an attack on the USS *Intrepid*, moving north-east through the water at 180 feet beneath the surface.

Chapter 17

Lucas and Walkinshaw knew they were in good hands, although it was rare for a Buccaneer probe to be controlled at night by the Gannet. Cruising at 420 knots, the Buccaneer covered seven miles a minute. The Gannet's radar antenna rotated once every 6 seconds. But the old AN/APS-20 often only picked up the contact once in every three revolutions. When controlling intercepts it meant that in the 18 seconds that elapsed between glimpses of your contacts, fighter and target could be five or six miles closer together. The limitations of the system placed a premium on the skill of the two Observers.

At 400 feet over a dark icy sea, alone with only the muted orange glow of the cockpit lights and the background hum of the Buccaneer's systems and cooling fans, it was good to have them. Outside the cockpit there were simply no visual cues. Just depthless black.

This is Anyface to Zero Two Six. Skunk is in your twelve o'clock. Eighty miles.

A shade over ten minutes' flying time until they pulled up sharply to toss a bomb-shaped Lepus parachute flare into a ballistic arc over the contact to illuminate it and identify it.

Roger.

Updates on the position of the contact came through the static from the Gannet. While Walkinshaw kept the Buccaneer flying at 420 knots on the bearing provided by Lucas, he maintained a ceaseless watch on his instruments, scanning from one to another in sequence. The big Attitude Indicator, or AI – the artificial horizon – dominated the panel. Surrounding it were dials recording altitude, rate of climb, fuel, rpm, JPTs and heading, while running across the top was a distinctive strip display that measured speed. In the back, Lucas checked the CRT of the S band Homer. Any radar emissions from the Skunk would be picked up by the ARI 18218 Wideband Homer radar warning receiver – capable of picking up X and S band radar transmissions – and be displayed as a spoke along which the Buccaneer could fly directly to the target. And there was the radar in the nose too. Designed specifically to pick up big-ship contacts at long range, the Ferranti Blue Parrot set remained extremely effective at ranges of over 150 miles, but down low Lucas needed the Gannet to see beyond the horizon. From 400 feet he couldn't see much further than thirty miles ahead. He set the radar range scale to 1:1 million. The scope on the port side of his cockpit would display an area of up to sixty miles. As soon as the Skunk's masts and aerials rose above the horizon that protected them – like soldiers walking along a ridge on a moonlit night – he'd see them. If the Gannet had pointed them in the right direction, the enemy ship should burn brightly right in the middle of his orange-tinged display.

Zero Two Six, still in your twelve o'clock, crackled the voice of the controller in the Gannet, *forty miles*. Five minutes.

Walkinshaw began his cockpit checks.

'*Jettison selector – off.*

'*Jettison supply – both normal.*

'*Attack selector – vari-toss.*

'*Weapon selector – Bombs A.*

'*Bomb doors – closed.*'

The Lepus flare was carried on a pylon under the wing rather than in the jet's bomb bay.

A glowing radar return Skunk appeared on Lucas's CRT display. He moved cursors over the top of it and locked on. The bomber's own weapons system would now give Walkinshaw a cue when he needed to pull up to release the Lepus. With his left hand he nudged the throttles forward, increasing the speed to 490 knots over the water – the entry speed for the Lepus attack. And he scanned his instruments.

Lucas set the pre-release timer and the flare's ignition timer. The Buccaneer would release the store 7.5 seconds after Walkinshaw hauled her into the climb. Thirteen seconds later the Lepus ignition process would begin.

Ten miles.

Lucas called distances, keeping his own eye on the little air speed indicator and altimeter he had on the side panel next to his left leg. The big strike jet was in her element. Running in at low level, there's a belligerent smoothness about the Buccaneer. Utterly stable, the aircraft's impressive purpose and persistence allowed Walkinshaw to concentrate on the accuracy of his attack. He kept his eye on the weapons sight ahead of him.

Four miles.

At three miles the sight caged – the circle in the lower half rose over the pip in the middle.

Accept.

Walkinshaw pulled back hard on the control column. He and Lucas strained against the mounting 'g' as they were pushed back into their seat. Pulling through 4g, nudging 5, busy grey static began to nibble at the edges of their peripheral vision – the first physical effect of the blood being forcibly drained from their brains. Outside, angry white clouds of condensation flared in the low pressure over the tops of the wings as the powerful naval bomber pulled up into a 38-degree climb.

Now concentrating on keeping the wings level, Walkinshaw tracked the target circle as the Bucc zoomed into her climb. Any bank or yaw at this point and the flare would be thrown miles off target. As they climbed, the altimeter wound up through 1000 feet while the strip of the air speed indicator retreated to the left as the speed bled off. With a perceptible clunk the Lepus flare was jettisoned from the pylon, continuing on its way towards the sky above the Skunk.

They'd just done the easy bit.

With the Lepus gone, Walkinshaw rolled the climbing bomber through 110 degrees and pulled back on the stick loading the airframe with as many g's as she'd take without stalling. But there were no visual cues and no visible horizon. No way of getting your bearings. In conditions like this even the most natural pilot had to learn not to trust his instincts. 809's Senior Pilot was flying on instruments, overbanking into a steep turn that presented the jet's belly to the sky at just 2000 feet above the waves. Lucas was glad to be flying with a Pilot as staunch as 'Boots'. The urgent electronic tone of the ADD – the Airflow Direction Detector – sounded its warning. The speed of its beeping provided an aural indication of their high angle of attack and proximity to a stall. While Walkinshaw pulled the jet round and down he had to change switches in the cockpit, moving the Armament Selector on his port console back a notch to 'off'. He never looked up and out of the cockpit. And it was exceptionally easy to become disorientated.

Mike Lucas, monitoring the bank angle, height and speed from the back, helped guard against it as the Buccaneer arched back round and over towards the sea. As the nose dropped through the horizon, Walkinshaw centred the stick and rolled the jet back upright, levelling the wings against the AI as they escaped.

1400, 1200, 1000, 900, 800.

Lucas called the heights as the Buccaneer dived down to the relative safety of 400 feet again.

'Has it lit up?' Walkinshaw asked as Lucas craned his neck round to catch sight of the flare. Then, 4.1 seconds after the ignition sequence began, the Lepus lit up the night with the power of 4 million candles and exposed an Orange force frigate like a rabbit in the headlights.

With a nudge of rudder, Walkinshaw banked into a 45-degree turn to carve round and take a closer look.

An hour and five minutes after they were launched into the darkness they recovered safely back on board *Ark* and wasted no time in making their way to the ship's own greasy spoon on Two Deck – the Aircrew Refreshment Bar. And there, cosseted within bulkheads covered with centrefolds and pinups, they sat on stools at red formica tables tucking into bacon butties and hot coffee.

The USS *Intrepid*, CVS-11, was even older than *Ark Royal*. Commissioned in 1943, she'd made it through the war, surviving numerous efforts by Japanese kamikaze pilots to sink her. Now, nearly thirty years later, her luck was still holding. Because in the small hours of the morning on Saturday the 2nd, off the bleak, beautiful Lofoten Islands archipelago, it wasn't *Intrepid* that HMS *Ocelot* had in her sights, but the rather greater prize of the USS *Independence*. The *Indy* was a genuine supercarrier. Over 1000 feet long and displacing nearly 80,000 tons in deep load, she carried *two* squadrons of F-4 Phantoms, a squadron of Vought A-7 Corsair II attack jets, a squadron of Grumman A-6 Intruder strike bombers, North American RA-5 Vigilante reconnaissance jets, Grumman E-2 Hawkeye AEW aircraft and helicopters. But for all that fire-power, on this occasion she'd underestimated the threat to her from beneath the waves.

At 0253, Logan took his little 'O' Boat to periscope depth to take a first look at the huge silhouette of his target. Then he took her down again to a depth of 180 feet to consider his approach. At 0319 *Ocelot* again rose through the seas to periscope depth. This time Logan stayed there, bathed in the red light of the control room, his boat hanging beneath the surface just out of sight. Fifteen minutes later his attack team closed up and *Ocelot* set course and speed for her attack.

At 0400 the British submarine simulated the launch of a torpedo at the huge aircraft carrier. Then Logan ordered his helmsman to dive, turn through 180 degrees and make good their escape at a depth of 350 feet, satisfied in the knowledge that, had it been required of him, he could have just taken the big carrier out of commission. The *Independence* had been caught with her trousers down.

Tragedy had taught the Royal Navy about the risk to her carriers from submarines early in the Second World War. On

17 September 1939, while steaming in the Bristol Channel, HMS *Courageous* was hit by two torpedoes fired from a range of less than 3000 yards by the German submarine U-29. The 22,500-ton British carrier sank in less than fifteen minutes with the loss of 518 lives. And while the Royal Navy lost further carriers to attacks from U-boats, great effort was subsequently devoted to both protecting them and developing tactics to reduce their vulnerability.

And as *Ark Royal* steamed through the uninviting dark waters of the Norwegian sea, few were more aware of the threat from submarines than *Ark*'s 2nd Navigator, Lieutenant Mike Gretton. His father had made his reputation by meeting it.

During the Battle of the Atlantic, Gretton's father, Commander Peter Gretton, commanded a convoy close escort of three destroyers, a frigate, two corvettes and two rescue trawlers. On 18 May 1943, Commander Gretton was ordered to escort the thirty-eight ships of Convoy SC130 through a gap in the 33-strong U-boat line across the North Atlantic. They were sighted and attacked. And yet what might have seemed a promising engagement to Admiral Dönitz, the head of the Kriegsmarine, ended in total defeat for the U-boats. Five German submarines were sunk without the loss of a single merchant ship and Gretton, credited during the battle with a part in sinking U-381, was able to reach Londonderry in time for his marriage to Mike Gretton's mother.

Now, nearly thirty years later, from the bridge of the Navy's most valuable ship, his son took comfort from the knowledge that life could be made extremely difficult for an attacking submarine captain. *Ark Royal* and the rest of Task Force TF401.2, whether British or NATO allies, zig-zagged according to patterns that were worked out in advance and distributed to all the ships in the group. One set of zig-zags could be quickly exchanged for another. The order to assume a particular plan would be signalled along with a co-ordination time-check. From that point the whole task force moved in unison with minimal risk of collision. Along each leg of the zig-zag, individual ships performed a narrow weave. The combination of the two patterns hugely complicated the submarine's fire control solutions.

But TF401.2 could also fight back. Dönitz complained in 1943 that 'to a very great extent, the enemy aircraft brought about the failure of our U-boats'. And in 824 Naval Air Squadron's complement squadron of six Westland Sea King HAS1s, *Ark Royal* was equipped with the most advanced, capable anti-submarine helicopter in the world – and the most modern aircraft in the entire British arsenal. The Boss of the Phantom squadron, Nick Kerr, had thought for most of his career that a helicopter squadron was a waste of a carrier's deck space. But the day 824 embarked their Sea Kings was the day even he had to concede that the chopper boys had finally, as he liked to put it, 'stopped pissing about'.

Standby to mark dip. One Zero Five. Five thousand. Mark dip now! From the vibrating blacked-out coalhole of the Sea King's cabin, Lieutenant Ed Featherstone passed instructions to the helicopter's pilots. With a whine from the two Rolls-Royce Gnome turboshaft engines Sea King 54 had taken off from Fly 3 as *Ark* steamed downwind – there was little of the concern for wind over deck when it came to rotary-wing flying. Now, in the pitch dark just before one in the morning, Featherstone, the helicopter's Observer, wanted to bring the aircraft into the hover two miles behind *Ark Royal*. Before the crew of 54 flew ahead of the battle group to take up position in the forward anti-submarine screen they needed to clear the carrier's stern. This was where, masked by the noise of four screws churning 152,000 shaft horsepower into the water, a Soviet attack boat could sit undetected for hours, listening to everything that was going on.

Flying at the standard operating height of 200 feet, 54's pilot turned into wind and with smooth movements of the collective lever – the handbrake-like control to his left and cyclic stick on his right – slowed the big helo's forward speed. He pressed a button marked 'Trans Down' to engage the AFCS – the Sea King's Automatic Flight Control System. At the front of the control panel between him and the co-pilot a light blinked on. Then the helicopter took care of the rest. Flying the glidepath without further participation from the aircrew, 54 descended to 40 feet and stayed there controlled by inputs from Doppler aerials and a radio altimeter. At night, in foul weather, trusting the AFCS took more than a little faith.

Lower the body.

Established in the hover, the pilot spoke to his Observer over the intercom. Featherstone braced himself for the icy wind that would blow in briefly as the aircrewman next to him lowered the dipping sonar through the floor of the helicopter into the sea.

Ed Featherstone had teenage dreams of being an astronaut. But given the long odds against a boy from Leicester joining NASA, Featherstone, determined to fly, opted to join the Fleet Air Arm. The Navy, it seemed to him, might offer the challenge and excitement he was after. He passed his aircrew aptitude tests at Biggin Hill on the same 1969 weekend that Neil Armstrong and Buzz Aldrin walked on the moon for the first time. Two years later he was an Observer aboard the Royal Navy's brand-new Sea King helicopters.

A development of the American Sikorsky S-61, the Sea King was the Navy's first genuine airborne hunter-killer. Since the fifties, as the Fleet Air Arm had refined its anti-submarine helicopter operation, it had been hampered by the limited pay-load, short range and burden placed on the aircrew by earlier aircraft like the Whirlwind and Wessex. The Navy knew what it *wanted* to do; it just didn't have an aircraft capable of doing it. Until the arrival of the Westland Sea King.

With an endurance of over four and a half hours, the Sea King was also the fastest helicopter in the Navy, but it was in its gadgetry that it really excelled. To search for contacts under the sea, there was Plessey Type 195 dipping sonar. To gather information about the surface picture the Sea King had an EKCO AW391 radar capable of picking up the tiny return from any submarine unwise enough to raise its periscope above the surface. All of this information fed into the Fresnel lens below the big Tactical Plotting Display used by the Observer, from where, like a player in a game of three-dimensional Battleships, he controlled the fight, directing ships, aircraft and other helicopters to track or attack with torpedoes or depth bombs as the situation demanded. As they flew south-east through the night, Featherstone Blu-Tacked a clear acetate overlay to his display, ready to mark up the tactical picture with a Chinagraph pencil when they arrived on station.

Sea King 54 joined the forward screen, ahead of the three frigates that provided another layer of anti-submarine defence, half an hour after she'd clawed her way off the aft deck of *Ark Royal*. The timing of her arrival was carefully coordinated with the departure for 'Mother' of one of the three Sea Kings already there. By rippling her six aircraft, 824 could maintain cover round the clock. Illuminated in the glow of the display, surrounded by the whine of the turbines and the familiar relentless vibration in the cabin, Featherstone started looking for submarines.

Chapter 18

Ark Royal's Captain, John Roberts, wasn't the only participant in ROYAL KNIGHT who'd been to Murmansk before. The USS *Skipjack*, an American nuclear attack submarine, had been a more recent visitor. In late 1960, the *Skipjack* sneaked so far up the deep channel to the Soviet port that her Captain was able to see the pier through his periscope less than forty yards away. Before making the dangerous, clandestine journey, *Skipjack*'s officers had disconnected a tracking device to ensure that there would be no written record of their mission. Now SSN-585, as she was designated, was fighting for the Orange force. And, for 824's Sea Kings, that made her the enemy.

To kill submarines, *Ark*'s helicopters used a technique which had its roots in the 'Creeping Attack' technique devised by Captain Frederick 'Jonny' Walker RN, the most famous of all British Second World War destroyer Captains. Rather than use a single ship to find, then destroy, a U-boat, Walker would use one ship to maintain sonar contact with the submarine while another, operating in sonar silence and taking directions from its partner, launched its attacks. It made it harder for the U-boat to take evasive action – or even to know when an attack was about to begin.

As the Sea King hovered on autopilot just 40 feet above the sea, the vicious downwash from its main rotor whipped up the surface of the water. Even a smooth, inky, glassy swell was churned into an agitated white-topped confusion that threw spray high into the air. Above it, in the cabin on the Sea King,

Ed Featherstone had blocked out discrete areas on his overlay. In the centre of each was a distinctive symbol representing a ship or helicopter with responsibility for policing it. If the young Observer picked up an enemy sonar contact he called in two other Sea Kings. As the submarine, alerted by its own acoustic listening devices that it had been detected by the pings from Featherstone's Type 195 Sonar, turned and ran, Featherstone directed the second Sea King to fly ahead in the direction of its escape. As it drove out of range of Featherstone's sonar, it found itself boxed in by the echoes from the second aircraft. The two helicopters then worked in tandem like a pair of sheepdogs to trap the enemy boat, before directing the torpedo attack from a third helo. Once detected, with three Sea Kings on your tail, it was extremely difficult to get away. And, maintaining the screen round the clock throughout the entire duration of ROYAL KNIGHT, 824's Sea King crews made contact with the USS *Skipjack*, hunted her down and destroyed her. Twice.

Sea King 54 recovered on board at 0400. If Orange naval forces had been made to suffer at the hands of *Ark*'s squadrons, things were about to get much worse for them ashore. The stage on board the British strike carrier was being set for the 'Heavies'.

The next morning marked a major escalation. ROYAL KNIGHT entered a period the planners described as 'open aggression'. *Ark* and her air group assumed 'maximum posture' ready to launch an all-out attack. Twenty-four of 809's Pilots and Observers pulled on their flying suits over thick thermal underwear before negotiating their way through *Ark*'s narrow corridors and ladders to the main briefing room at the base of the carrier's island. Most of the squadron was there. Seven Buccs were flying strike missions. Five, equipped with extra fuel tanks in the bomb bay and with a single, heavy FR Mk 20 hose and drogue refuelling pod slung under the starboard wing, would be providing airborne tanker support. Working deep in the lower hangar – so dark and humid they'd christened it the Mushroom Farm – 809's Air Engineers had even managed to make two spare jets available. That was all fourteen of the squadron's Buccaneer S2s ready to go. Given an average serviceability of less than 60 per cent it was a remarkable achievement.

Over the last two days, the Buccaneers had been warming up with strikes against the jagged black mountains and sea-cliffs of the Lofoten Islands, against mainland targets and against Ramsund's naval base, the Arctic home of the Marinejeger-kommandoen, Norway's secretive maritime Special Forces unit, their equivalent of the British SBS or American Navy SEALs. At 68 degrees North and 16 degrees East, Ramsund was tucked into a fjord just twenty miles from Narvik. In the first two weeks of May 1940, nine of the third *Ark Royal*'s twenty-three Blackburn Skuas had been lost in combat over the north Norwegian port. Now her successor's air group were going to attack in strength. Only this time they actually had the kit they needed to do it.

Carl Davis, 809's pugnacious little squadron Boss, couldn't help but see the job of his Buccaneers attacking targets on the ground in the same way as he viewed sport. It was a challenge. About his team getting one over the opposition.

Don't bomb short, he urged his strike crews, *it's wasted. About as useful as a short putt.* Davis was clear that if your bomb tends towards going long you've at least got a chance of hitting the target – same as a long putt has a chance of dropping in the hole. Davis stood at the front of the briefing room. His legs apart, braced against the pitch and roll of the ship, he could feel the thrum of the engines through the soles of his flying boots. Behind him, as he spoke, was a blackboard divided into sections with yellow-painted headings like 'CREW' and 'ORDERS'. The briefing board carried all the details of the mission – from crews and their aircraft, call signs, diversions and radio frequencies to fuel calls, targeting information, and expected air and ground defences. If anyone strayed over the Soviet border across the Iron Curtain an urgent call of 'Brass Monkey! Brass Monkey!' would be made to turn the whole strike on its heels. As they'd made clear in 1953 when MiG-15 fighter jets shot down an Avro Lincoln BII of the RAF's Central Gunnery School while it flew through the Berlin Corridor on a training flight, the Soviets didn't muck about when it came to uninvited guests.

The Buccaneers were unarmed and subsonic. But Park and Lucas – not to mention their Pilots, the squadron Boss and 'Boots' Walkinshaw, the Senior Pilot – felt confident about their ability to get through. Their best defence was simply not to be discovered. A strike like this was flown in radio silence, or zip-lip. From the moment they strapped into the Cabs to the moment they folded the wings and shut down the engines after recovering on deck, not a single radio communication would leave the cockpit of any of the Buccs. Radio-silent procedures had been rehearsed and revised for every part of the mission, from a receiver flying alongside the tanker and waiting for a thumbs-up, to rocking the wings and drawing a finger across the throat to warn a wingman that his aircraft was on fire.

Pre-planned avoidance of known defences was smart. So too was steering wide of the source of any radar pulses picked up by the jet's Radar Warning Receiver. At the limits of a search radar's range, the RWR picked up the danger while still too far for the pulse to be reflected back to where it came from. If it was high, the pilot then pushed the bomber into a near-vertical dive, her descent controlled by the drag of the big airbrake, before levelling out underneath the searching enemy radar. And once there, penetrating well-defended hostile airspace, it was flying low and fast that remained a Buccaneer's best defence. 'The really low-level aircraft,' assured the notes on weapons and tactics given to all Buccaneer squadrons, 'is still virtually immune from present ground defences.' And, it stressed, '300 feet is not low.' And as well as ground defences, it also kept fighters at bay.

The thick air at low altitude was a great leveller. A Soviet MiG-21 *could* overhaul a Buccaneer at low level, but not for long and at the expense of huge fuel burn. Even hardened Lightning pilots had to concede that it was a hell of a job to bring down a Buccaneer. It was an uncomfortable feeling to be close to the ground at night, travelling at 550 mph, nudging down the nose in search of a radar lock amid the interference and ground clutter. You really needed to get down below them to look up, but that was near impossible.

Settled along long, straight-backed, brown-vinyl benches, the strike crews made notes. Some smoked. All listened intently to the Boss go through the sortie, refreshing them on the details of a mission they'd all spent time planning.

Steve Park and Mike Lucas had both prepared their routes in detail, plotting them on to a roller map, making sure that they knew where Orange force radars and anti-aircraft weapons were found, where and when they'd make landfall, and their waypoints there and back. By day they could check them off visually. At night, overland, they relied on Radar Prediction – using the Blue Parrot instead of their own eyes to pick out distinctive features that could confirm their progress.

Davis continued his briefing, the pauses in his speech filled with the sounds of the ship and the almost imperceptible throb of her engines. All present had long since tuned them out. Before coasting, each of the seven strike jets would receive a top-up from one of the tankers. After refuelling, the seven would descend to 50 feet over the sea flying at 540 knots until going 'feet dry', when they'd gain height and reduce speed to 480 knots, low, along the tops of the fjords, enjoying a measure of cover from the epic black cliffs – but not as much as they'd like. Ingressing deep within the protective cocoon of the vast sheer rock walls was usually out of the question because of the danger from electricity and telephone lines that were sometimes strung across them. But they'd all done it. Earlier in the exercise, a strike had been flown down a dead-end fjord. After the attack, the only way out was to pull up hard over the massive, unyielding rock face at the other end. It had had *633 Squadron* written all over it. Today 809 would be flying in loose battle formation – each pair watching the six o'clock of the other. They were briefed on their targets and on escape and evasion techniques by CBALS – less politely known as Seaballs – namely, Captain Robin Barber from 55 Carrier Borne Ground Liaison Section, the small army unit resident aboard *Ark*. Northern Norway was inhospitable in mid-summer. In October, with snow on the ground, it presented a more formidable challenge to anyone forced to endure it.

And remember, he finished, *if you're ambushed by a bear, run downhill. Bears can't run downhill – their front legs are shorter than their back legs.* The listening crews groaned at the familiar sign-off. But, faced with 750lb of angry brown bear, anything was worth a go.

One of the ship's Met Officers outlined the weather they could expect during every phase of the three-hour sortie: a 25-knot wind blowing from 230 degrees – the Observers would allow for that as they detailed a flight plan on their log cards; good visibility, around ten nautical miles – it made flying easier, but that also helped the Orange force defenders flying out of Andøya, Bardufoss and Bodø too. Before concluding, Davis invited questions then asked his squadron to synchronize their watches.

Ten seconds to eleven-forty. Five, four, three, two, one. Time is eleven-forty Zulu.

The ship's main broadcast hummed, then paused.

Hands to Flying Stations.

And high up in Flyco, Little F spoke into his microphone.

Aircrew, man aircraft.

The show was now being run from the large glazed extension to the bridge that projected out over the flight deck. From Flyco there was a bird's-eye view of one of the most dangerous environments on earth. Despite efforts to increase the flight deck area with each successive refit, the dangers were compounded by *Ark Royal*'s shortage of space. Launching a major strike like this required an enormous degree of planning, and hard work from the ACRO – the Aircraft Control Room Officer – in his office in the island. Using a mock-up of the flight deck and scale models of the five different aircraft types on board like chess-pieces, working it out was like trying to solve a Chinese puzzle. In order to move one aircraft from the back of the hangar to Fly 4, it might be necessary first to move five other aircraft out of the way. Every move had its repercussions. Today, as Buccaneer crews, sealed inside thick rubber immersion suits, streamed on to the flight deck carrying white Bone Dome helmets and nav bags, it was all about 809 Squadron's bombers.

In the low midday sun of the far north, underneath the huge revolving scaffolding of the ship's radars, the scene was a jumble of colour and long shadows. The flight deck itself was marked with a distinctive crimson-and-white dotted runway centreline. More red decorated the deck port aft just ahead of the round-down where a large red 'R' identified the ship as *Ark Royal*. Preparing the ship for Flying Operations, the Aircraft Handling party and Flight Deck Officers scurried around in well-rehearsed patterns, wearing weatherproof overalls covered with coloured waistcoats identifying their individual roles – red, orange, brown, green, yellow, blue and white. Dotted around were yellow-painted deck tractors and heavy cranes. And there were the aircraft themselves. Tucked alongside the island in Fly 3, their wings folded, were three Phantoms and a Gannet. All carried the bright red, white and blue roundels the Fleet Air Arm sported before the vogue for low-visibility markings took hold a decade later. The Phantoms, sporting handsome white bellies, had their tails flashed with red, around a white diamond containing the Greek letter omega to signify the anticipated run-down of the Fleet Air Arm's fixed-wing squadrons. The 849 Squadron 'B' Flight Gannet's spinner was a spiral of yellow and black. As the four blades began to wind up, biting into the air, the SAR Wessex added dayglo red/orange to the mix and sported the gold-rimmed ship's crest underneath the rotor head. In the upper hangar, kept out of the wind, were the deep-blue Sea King helicopters of 824 NAS. The identity of the white bird painted underneath the cockpits hadn't been immediately obvious to the aircrews. They decided early on that it had to be an 'Albastorkaduckatross'.

Noses all pointed forward like the weave of herringbone

cloth, twelve Buccaneers lined the back of the flight deck, the five tankers at Fly 3 on the starboard side, the seven strike jets sitting opposite them at Fly 4. The Buccs were finished in dark grey all over. White numbers and the red, white and blue roundel adorned the forward fuselage ahead of the big gulping oval-shaped air intakes rimmed in natural metal. On their tails was a red and gold phoenix rising from the flames. At rest and lashed to the deck, the bombers' wings pointed up past vertical from a hinge close to the fuselage. With space on deck and in the hangars at a premium, generations of carrier aircraft had employed variously complicated wing-fold mechanisms to save space while not flying. With her wings folded, the usually war-like Buccaneer seemed defanged, as if her hands were held together in supplication.

With the crews strapped into their cockpits, Little F gave the order to go, his voice amplified loud across the flightdeck.

Stand clear of intakes and jet pipes, start the Buccaneers.

Sitting in his high 'Father's Chair', John Roberts watched his air group prepare through thick armoured glass. On deck, the handlers hauled heavy lash-down chains through the lugs on the Buccaneers' undercarriage legs.

As ROYAL KNIGHT reached its conclusion, the Captain reflected on what had been achieved while *Ark* had been at sea. For the duration of the exercise, each page of the ship's log had needed an extra page of loose A4 sellotaped on top to record the intensity of Flying Operations. But through the remarkable efforts of all on board, *Ark Royal* and her aircraft had met every demand made of them. Sharing responsibility with VF-102 and VF-33, the two fighter squadrons on board *Independence*, 892 had kept a Phantom on Alert 5 for 155 hours and made 181 intercepts, of which twenty-three were Soviet intruders. To keep the Gannets on patrol, 849 'B' Flight's engineers had managed a complete engine change on board in just eighteen hours, a job normally scheduled to take thirty-six. And of eighty-three planned sorties, 824's Sea Kings had flown eighty-three. There hadn't been a time during the exercise when at least one of their helicopters wasn't airborne.

Ark's calm, easy-going Captain was satisfied. There'd been no drama and no crisis – just the way he liked it. A job well done. *Ark* had been on a big stage and a failure to perform would have been conspicuous to both the US and the rest of NATO. And to the Soviet Union.

Now, successfully launching and completing this strike would mark the culmination of *Ark Royal*'s contribution. There was a feeling of anticipation. Roberts gave orders to turn the great ship into wind.

Officer of the Watch, turn to the flying course. Revolutions One Two Six.

At the Compass Platform to his right, the Officer of the Watch, wearing a dark-blue sweater with gold-striped epaulettes, pulled a microphone towards his mouth and directed: *Revolutions One Two Six. Steer Two Nine Zero.* And below him, seven decks down in the forward steering position, another member of the Ship's Company turned a large wooden ship's wheel that wouldn't have looked out of place on the *Victory* and passed on the required revolutions to the Stygian world of the engine room.

Against the visceral wall of whistle and whine generated by twenty-four Rolls-Royce Spey engines winding up, the first dark-grey bomber, Buccaneer 035, beckoned forward by a marshal, eased ahead with a dab of power before gently bowing on the nosewheel oleo as the pilot tested his brakes. Then 035 turned to the left and continued, under her own power, towards the bow catapult. As she taxied forward, her wings slowly unfolded like opening petals and locked firmly into a horizontal position. Wings spread, she's ready to fly. And fight.

Behind her, 033 taxied forward against a 41-knot wind over the deck, through a heat haze from the engines and churning clouds of white steam, towards the waist cat. And twenty-five minutes after that, all fifteen jets were on their way. The aerial armada of Buccaneers, so heavy-hipped and bulging on the deck, now airborne were a different proposition. The weight at the rear, sloping forward towards the low nose, gave them momentum and purpose as they powered east towards the coast.

Three hours later, 809 Squadron recovered on board *Ark* after her crews had flown testing, low-level strike profiles against remote Norwegian targets. All their attacks were deemed to be successful, while every one of the Fleet Air Arm bombers managed to elude both the ground and air defences ranged against them. As ROYAL KNIGHT came to an end, 809 Squadron looked to be unstoppable and lethal.

Four days later, *Ark Royal* herself left a similar impression. With his squadrons disembarked to their bases ashore, John Roberts, driving the British carrier, led *Independence* and *Intrepid* through the English Channel in an awesome display of NATO naval power. And it was exhilarating. Roberts always took great pleasure from driving his ship, but this was something else. *Ark*, a Plymouth ship, was visiting Portsmouth for the first time in six years and she was late. To make up time, Roberts pushed the three huge warships south through the North Sea and down through the narrow waters past Norfolk and Kent at a hair-raising 23 knots. Roberts only discovered later how close his counterpart on board *Independence*, Captain O'Rourke, had been to baulking at barrelling through restricted, busy sea lanes with such speed and elan. As *Independence* detached from *Ark* after passing through the Straits of Dover, Roberts spoke to O'Rourke over the radio to make sure he'd enjoyed himself.

'Quite an exciting trip through the Channel . . .' He let it hang.

'My God, yes,' replied the American Captain quickly, knowing that he'd be meeting Roberts and his ship again soon in the Mediterranean.

Chapter 19

On 5 October, the day after the cessation of ROYAL KNIGHT's hostilities, the Dependent Territories Senior Appointments Board of the Foreign Office sought approval for their choice of a new Governor for British Honduras. From his office in King Charles Street, Richard Posnett, the Head of the West Indies Department, had been urging them to come to a decision for months. Sir John's term was due to come to an end by the end of the year and arrangements had to be made. Posnett had supplied the board with a job description back in June but had heard nothing more. Perhaps it was no surprise the board was struggling for candidates. 'The new Governor,' Posnett wrote, 'might look forward to the uneasy admin- istration of a territory with frustrated ministers, difficulties over internal security and . . . perhaps external difficulties also, for example on the frontier with Guatemala.' Furthermore, he told them, living conditions were 'hard and unattractive'. On the plus side, the salary on offer was £5500 and the job came with an official Austin Princess.

At Airport Camp, Major Richard Corkran had guests from the UK. A small team from HQ UK Land Forces in Wilton near Salisbury had flown in to update the MoD's contingency plans for British Honduras. After the JIC's August review of the Guatemalan threat to the colony, the MoD had ordered detailed plans to be revised. For three days the Colonel and his team braved the heat while Corkran showed them around BH.

They took notes of stores, geography and troop dispositions. And they talked to Corkran about the potential threat from Guatemala and his ability to meet it. They confided in him that their plan involved a brigade-sized reinforcement. And, although Corkran never got to see the results, they used what they'd learnt during their time with him to produce Operation OPTIC, the MoD's Joint Theatre Plan for British Honduras.

As much as a major NATO exercise like ROYAL KNIGHT highlighted the seriousness with which UK forces prepared for the threat from the Warsaw Pact, the MoD was obliged to maintain current Joint Theatre Plans for hotspots around the world. And to the chagrin of an MoD struggling to make the most of limited resources, exercises weren't confined to rehearsing the defence of Western Europe either. While Britain's overseas responsibilities remained, so did the need to plan and rehearse around the globe. In January 1970, for instance, Exercise FETTLE in the Bahamas had found evidence of Cuban paramilitary training in the Cays, emphasizing that, in the context of the Cold War, Cuba was more than just a paper tiger. The job was never finished. In November 1971, Exercise CLAY would go over the same ground as FETTLE, but planning had already begun for an exercise in the same corner of the world that would assume much greater importance: Exercise CADNAM, scheduled for February 1972 and designed to rehearse Britain's plans to reinforce British Honduras.

In clear Scottish skies, the two jets carved north-west from Lossie. Even when *Ark* was in port, the work of her squadrons was ceaseless. Left untouched, flying skills degraded fast, and so the training schedule remained intense. Carl Davis and Steve Park looked across at the needle-nosed jet on their starboard wing. Even though it was painted in shades of grey, was sporting anchors painted on the engine intakes and bore the legend 'MARINE' on the rear of the fuselage, it didn't look much like a naval jet. It could have come from a different planet to their own Buccaneer.

The Lockheed F-104 Starfighter was legendary. It was the first aircraft ever to hold simultaneous world records for speed, altitude and time to climb. Powered by a single afterburning J-79 engine that gave it an initial climb rate of 48,000 feet per minute, it was definitely a hot ship. It had even nearly killed Chuck Yeager, who ejected from a rocket-powered NF-104A while trying to go beyond 120,800 feet to set a new height record. And yet somehow the German Naval Air Arm, the Marineflieger, through a combination of bad luck and politics, had managed to wind up flying Starfighters in the same low-level anti-ship role as the Buccs. It was time, thought the British crew, to show them what they were missing.

Davis waved at the German pilot to signal that he was breaking formation, broke left and rolled into a dive to low level. Seconds later the F-104 flicked on to its side to follow, displaying its two black crosses on the short wings, framed within the day-glo orange paint of the big wingtip fuel tanks.

The Scottish Highlands north-west of Lossiemouth offered outstanding low flying. Large areas of virtually uninhabited hills and valleys meant the Fleet Air Arm's Buccaneer crews could hone their skills without restriction. And they did.

The two jets streaked along at a little over 100 feet above the heathland in a 450-knot tailchase. Their distinctive shapes flicked and rolled against the horizon as they scored through the air against the green grass slopes of the glens. In the cold winter air, clouds of condensation billowed and vanished over the Buccaneer's wings as she tightened and relaxed through the turns. In theory, the blisteringly fast Starfighter should have had no trouble at all keeping up. But it didn't quite work like that in reality. Arrowing straight and low across the Baltic was one thing, but twisting through the gusty air of the Highlands was another altogether. Unlike the gentle ballooning passengers experience on board a commercial airliner, hitting turbulence at this height and speed hammered through the airframe as an alarmingly rapid sequence of bangs. And the finely tuned, thoroughbred Starfighter, obliged to lug around heavy fuel tanks on the tips of its short, razor-thin wings, didn't like that at all.

Then sharp white vortice lines streamed off the wingtips as Davis reefed his Buccaneer into a tight 6g turn. It was believed the Bucc could take *twice* that before the bomb bay was torn out of its mounting. With the jet rolled through 90 degrees, her wings pointing straight up and down, the 809 Boss pulled hard towards the valley side he could see above him through the glass of the canopy. It was the side he couldn't see, the rising ground beneath his feet as the jet banked, that, if his turn was too timid, he'd hit. But the Starfighter just simply couldn't stay with them as they were pressed hard into their ejection seats. The German pilot was forced to unload and climb out. Davis and Park grinned. It always happened this way.

While 809 were disembarked at Lossiemouth, they were sharing hangar one with sixteen Starfighters of the German Navy's MFG-2. For six weeks, while the German squadron's own runway at Eggebek was being resurfaced, the ghostly howl of the Starfighter's engines graced the skies over Morayshire. And during that time a constant stream of buffeted, overstressed F-104s were stripped of their wingtip tanks and flown gingerly back to Germany for fatigue inspections.

But it was in the bar where the real damage was done. Fregattenkapitän Heinz Forsmann enjoyed being back at Lossie. Not only had he completed the Royal Navy's AWI Course with Dick Lord in 1968 at Lossie, but the base was also where he'd first become friends with Carl Davis, in the fifties, when they both flew Seahawks. The rivalry the squadrons enjoyed in the air was matched in the Wardroom. Forsmann and the MFG-2 pilots did their best to keep up with their hosts' capacity for alcohol, but he thought that maybe the Brits had the edge. In the end, though, it was food, not drink, that strained international relations. Two of Davis's men took exception to the voracious appetite of one of the visiting German pilots. So they emptied the ashtrays between two slices of bread, glued it all together with salad cream and let him tuck in. The result was predictably anarchic.

MFG-2 had been due to *host* a night in the Lossie

wardroom. Until just two days beforehand, a squadron member was killed when his Starfighter crashed operating out of Sardinia. This was the flipside of the coin for the German F-104 pilots. Like the Fleet Air Arm in the sixties, they'd suffered a horrific fatality rate. Forsmann had lost his best friend a year earlier. In eleven years flying Starfighters he attended twelve funerals. And helped lower six coffins into the ground.

You didn't have to scratch far below the surface of any front-line unit to reveal the pressure and strains that lay behind every game of spoof, every round of drinks or every ashtray sandwich. And *Ark*'s Sea King squadron was no exception.

Chapter 20

In January 1952, a pair of Westland Dragonflies of 705 NAS departed Gosport in appalling weather in an effort to provide assistance to the American freighter MV *Flying Enterprise*, broken-backed and adrift south-west of Ireland. The ship's plight, and particularly the bravery of her captain, Kurt Carlsen, had gripped the nation. One of the little piston-engined helicopters made it no further than Exeter airport before becoming unserviceable. The pilot of the second, Lieutenant Commander Suthers, refuelled at RNAS Culdrose on Cornwall's Lizard Peninsula, then took off in 50-knot winds in the hope that it might be possible to rescue the two men still aboard the listing, sinking *Flying Enterprise*. Suthers was only ten miles west of Land's End when he realized the Dragonfly simply had no chance of making it to the stricken ship and back and, regretfully, turned for home.

The Royal Navy's Search and Rescue squadrons had come a long way since that first brave, but hopeless, mercy mission. In 1971 they operated the Westland Wessex. An American design built under licence in Britain, the Wessex was an admirable workhorse and a massive step forward from the Whirlwinds and first-generation Dragonflies it replaced. And it was only twenty years since the Dragonfly itself had replaced the last Supermarine Sea Otter biplane flying boats. But the twin-engined Westland Sea King HAS1, introduced to service with the Navy's anti-submarine squadrons in 1969, represented a step change in what was possible.

Examples of the Sea King's extraordinary range and carrying capacity soon began to pile up. The most recent had occurred on 8 October 1971, when, while steaming between Singapore and the Philippines on her farewell cruise, *Ark*'s sister ship, HMS *Eagle*, received an SOS call from the SS *Steel Vendor*, an American merchantman that had run aground on an uncharted reef in the South China Sea. Despite filthy weather trailing three regional typhoons, two Sea Kings from 826 Naval Air Squadron were launched and managed to winch the entire forty-man crew to safety.

Just ten days later, Ed Featherstone was enjoying a rare Monday morning's leave at home at Ashton near Penzance. Then the phone rang. A crew member aboard the Norwegian bulk-carrier *Anatina* had fallen asleep with a cigarette in his hand. The 10,589-ton ship had been ravaged by explosions and fire. After an attempt by a tug to tow her to safety had failed, she was now adrift in the Atlantic without power or lighting in stormy seas 200 miles from the mainland. Reserve pumps were being used to clear rising water. Fifteen minutes after the call, Featherstone was in the 824 squadron offices at Culdrose helping plan the longest-range Search and Rescue mission ever mounted by the Navy. Featherstone's sums suggested that, despite the Force 8 winds, a Sea King could make it there and back with – *all being well* – up to three-quarters of an hour on the scene. The two helicopter crews pulled themselves into their immersion suits, signed for the air-craft and walked out into the weather to the waiting helos.

At 0920, the pair of big, dark-blue Sea Kings, call signs 50 and 51, took off and leant into the gale blowing in from the south-west, flying as low as possible to reduce the effect of the headwind. Featherstone was in 50, the lead helo, flown by 824's Boss, Lieutenant Commander Larry Hallett. Featherstone tuned the HF radio and pressed transmit. They were on their way, he told the RAF Nimrod maritime-patrol aircraft already on the scene, circling above the damaged ship. The Nimrod acknowledged the call. The *Anatina*'s cargo of titanium ore was starting to shift around her holds. She was in danger of sinking. And it was beginning to look as if even the powerful, long-range Sea Kings were going to be unable to do anything about it. Stronger than forecast headwinds and a new fix on the position of the *Anatina* from the Nimrod gave the two helos, Featherstone quickly recalculated, less than fifteen minutes on station. It wasn't enough. Featherstone broke the news to the squadron Boss.

'What!' Hallett replied. 'But you worked it all out!'

'Sorry, but we're not making as much ground into the head-wind and the ship isn't where we were originally told she was . . .' Featherstone radioed Culdrose and, between them, they hatched an ingenious new plan. Hallett banked away from the wind and turned south towards the Isles of Scilly.

While 50 and 51 made their way to the Scillies, two more Sea Kings took off from Culdrose carrying drums of Avcat and a high-pressure fuel pump slung in nets under the fuselage. Minutes after the two 824 helos landed at St Mary's airport, they were joined by Sea Kings flying in direct from Culdrose carrying fuel drums. With tanks full to bursting, Hallet nudged forward the cyclic. The heavily laden Sea King began to roll forward along the hardstanding. The forward speed would help them get airborne. As the ASI began to flick clockwise, Hallett twisted the throttle grip and pulled upon the collective. As the engine noise rose to a scream, the weight came off the tyres of the main gear and the big Navy helicopter hauled herself into the air. Alongside 51, 50 tipped forward, built up air speed, just a few feet from the ground, then climbed, the two of them fighting their way into a 50-knot wind doing its utmost to keep them from the *Anatina*.

Two hours later they found her, on her stern the words 'ANATINA, KRISTIANSAND'. Under an oppressive overcast sky, the long low Norwegian freighter was wallowing dead in the water, beam on to a punishing sea. *Anatina* was rolling heavily in the white-topped swell, her white superstructure blackened and wrecked by fire. The crew huddled on the exposed deck. His hands tight on the collective and cyclic controls of the Sea King, Hallett responded instinctively to gusts and the raking menace from *Anatina*'s derricks and masts and cranes as he tried to bring the helo in close, her nose pointing into the wind. Featherstone stood in the frame of 50's open door, directing his pilot.

Left and forward, forward one yard, steady, go, forward only.

With the cabin door and winch of the Sea King over the deck, the helicopter's cockpit projected out over the sea. Hallett could only see glimpses of the *Anatina* through the side windows. He lacked good references, making him dependent instead on accurate direction from his Observer. Flying the helicopter in these conditions was hard, tiring work.

Clad in a thick immersion suit, Petty Officer Dossett, 50's Search and Rescue diver, swung out of the cabin door attached to a wire that scarcely seemed substantial enough to support him let alone the added weight of each survivor.

'Winching down,' Featherstone relayed to the pilot. 'Aircrewman on,' he continued as Dossett made contact with the ship. On deck, the Petty Officer shouted to make himself heard over the overpowering noise of the helicopter's engines, the downwash and the storm itself. Above him, 50's anti-collision beacon shone bright red in the murk. But without a comms link to the helicopter, Dossett was going to have to winch back up to the helicopter again before Featherstone and Hallett could get to grips with the situation aboard *Anatina*.

Go forward two yards. Right five yards, Featherstone instructed, acutely aware of the ship's steel superstructure to the left of the thin-skinned Sea King. *In the strop – winching up.*

As Dossett reached the cabin door, Featherstone pulled him into the cabin.

'There's about ten guys that need to come off,' Dossett told him, 'and two bodies.'

That's news to me, thought the Observer, as he adjusted his expectations.

'We'll get the survivors off first,' Featherstone told Dossett and lowered him back down to the rolling deck. Above them, the

RAF Nimrod relayed information to and from Mountbatten, the rescue coordination centre in Plymouth, while, with Featherstone manning the winch, 50's co-pilot talked to Culdrose Ops on the helicopter's Collins 618T HF single sideband radio. Hallett, his arms and legs constantly at work, feeding small reactive inputs into the controls, kept 50 hovering while the *Anatina* slid and corkscrewed in the waves below.

Featherstone manhandled the first of the survivors in through the cabin door and out of the rescue strop, leaving the aircrewman on deck as Hallett withdrew to allow 51 to drift into position over the *Anatina* to pick up the next man. Circling away from the ship gave Hallett a chance to get the blood moving through his limbs again before once again returning to the hover. Inside 50, Featherstone strapped his new passenger into the exposed Sea King cabin. Deafeningly loud and vibrating underneath the beating main rotor, it offered little in the way of comfort, but the safety and security it represented were written all over the Norwegian sailor's face. With 50 standing off, 51 lowered their Observer, Lieutenant John Chandler, on to the deck of the freighter to join Dossett. By using the emergency radio in his lifejacket, Chandler was able to establish a live comms link between the two helicopters and the deck of the *Anatina*. Then Sea Kings 50 and 51 continued their dangerous relay until eleven crewmen had been lifted from the ship. But then there were the bodies. As the winch reached the height of the helo door, Featherstone reached for the stretcher. Then, caught in the fierce rotor downwash, the blue blanket covering one of the dead men blew away. Face down, his body was charred and blistered, all hair scorched away. After dying in the fire he'd lain dead for two days, drowned in water from the desperate efforts to extinguish the flames. Lumps of blackened flesh peeled away from the big man's head. Featherstone struggled not to gag at the stench as he hauled the heavy stretcher in through the door and tried to wedge it between the rear crew seats. Then he concentrated on bringing Dossett back on board.

And finally Hallett was able to swing the big helicopter

round, push forward on the cyclic stick and head for home. The smell was overpowering – even for the two pilots in the cockpit. With the cabin door open, Featherstone couldn't see his display to navigate them home, but the stench was unbearable. Dossett pulled the sliding door open six inches to get some air circulating and Featherstone agreed to squint. They'd already been away for four hours, airborne for most of it. And, even with a strong tailwind, it would be another hour and a half before Hallett was flying up the Helford River on his approach to Culdrose. After their epic mission – the longest helicopter search and rescue yet flown by British crews – 50 and 51's return had attracted quite a crowd.

On board *Ark Royal*, berthed in HM Naval Base in Portsmouth, John Roberts watched reports of the rescue on the evening news with pride. *Ark*'s Captain had little involvement with the squadrons when they were disembarked, but this was a golden opportunity to let them know he was watching. The next day he drafted a signal:

```
R191956ZS OCT
FM HMS ARK ROYAL
FOR CO 824 SQUADRON
LAST NIGHT'S TV APPEARANCE LOOKED GREAT
STUFF
WELL DONE
```

Within the MoD Main Building on Whitehall, the glowing reports of the operation in the national press, illustrated with photographs of helicopters with 'ROYAL NAVY' emblazoned on the side, were also noted. In signalling his congratulations to Culdrose, the First Sea Lord, Admiral Sir Michael Pollock, took time to mention how impressed he'd been with the coverage of the rescue. The Navy had been badly bruised by the loss of the debate over the future of the carriers. Too often, it seemed to them, military flying was assumed by the press, public and politicians to be the exclusive preserve of the RAF and the unique contribution of Fleet Air Arm was misunderstood and often overlooked. But in 824's epic 5½-hour mercy mission the Navy had provided a vivid reminder of what it could do. And one that might be remembered.

On 22 October, four days after Sea King 50 had completed her 430-mile mission, the Salvadorean Foreign Minister, Dr Walter Benecke, arrived in Guatemala for his first official visit. It was just over a month since his country's President had been received by General Arana and his government. Guatemalan attacks on Salvadorean trawlers notwithstanding, the two countries appeared to be finding common cause. News had yet to leak out about the substance of Arana's discussions with the Salvadoreans, but one thing was certain: when it came to using force to pursue her goals, El Salvador had recent form in the shape of her disastrous invasion of Honduras. Many commentators had already suggested that the underlying cause of the 'Football War' had been pressure from a growing population on an already crowded little country reaching breaking point. In the two years since the invasion that hadn't changed. Nor had the fact that the 122,000-strong population of British Honduras was spread out over 8900 square miles. With a population density of barely fourteen people per square mile, there was no doubt that the little colony enjoyed *Lebensraum*.

On the day that Benecke arrived in Guatemala City, the second revise of Operation OPTIC, the Joint Theatre Plan for British Honduras that Richard Corkran had helped inform, was published and circulated by the MoD's Department of Operations. And over 4000 miles from London, a mistake was about to be made, by the United States Southern Air Defense network, that threatened to jeopardize Britain's ability to act on the plan.

Chapter 21

On 26 October 1971, while *Ark*'s air group flew from their shore bases, an unidentified aircraft, call sign 'Cubana 877', announced over the radio that it was inbound to New Orleans airport with just twenty-five miles to run. There had been no flight plan, no prior knowledge of it and, crucially, no attempt to intercept or stop it. It had, without breaking sweat, breached the US Southern ADIZ – the Air Defence Interception Zone. While Cubana 877 was a civilian airliner, Air Traffic Control had only had the crew's word for it. The reaction to the arrival of the Antonov AN-24 from Cuba was predictably forceful. The press had a field day. Questions were asked in Congress. How could, people asked, mighty America be left so exposed to the threat of little Cuba to the south?

Just ninety miles separated Havana from Naval Air Station Key West. And since the 1962 Missile Crisis, there existed what amounted to a stand-off between Castro's Cuba and the US. The ICBMs may have been returned to the Soviet Union, but in their place came increased numbers of modern surface-to-air missiles and jet fighters.

In June 1962, the 32nd Guards Fighter Regiment, stationed at Kubinka near Moscow, was shipped to Cuba, where, by October, its Mach 2 MiG-21s were operational. In November that year, a pair of USAF F-104 Starfighters were intercepted and turned back. Earlier the same year, a glider-winged U-2 reconnaissance jet had already been shot down and its pilot killed. More recently, the Fuerza Aerea Revolucionaria (FAR) flexed its muscles more offensively. In May 1970, a flight of MiGs had thundered aggressively low over the Bahamas in protest at the arrest of fourteen Cuban fishermen caught in Bahamian waters. In a separate incident, the MiGs were to strafe a Bahamian patrol boat with 23mm high-explosive shells from their GSh-23 cannon. And in 1971, by the time of the arrival of Cubana 877 at New Orleans, there had already been eleven hijacking incidents involving demands to fly to Cuba. A twelfth, in which an American ticketing agent was killed, occurred just three days later.

In the early 1970s, with the Cold War dominating the Pentagon's strategic thinking, Cuba, with its close ties to the Soviets, was regarded as a clear and present danger to the US. The outlook of the Alert Detachment at Homestead Air Force Base, way down south at the tip of the Florida panhandle, reflected this.

In shelters a hundred yards from the end of the runway at Homestead, two delta-winged Convair F-102 Delta Daggers sat pre-flighted on five-minute alert. On their triangular tails was a thick horizontal blue stripe flashed with white lightning. Their canopies were propped open, Bone-Dome flying helmets rested on the edge of the jets' cockpits. Except when there were high winds, a ladder was pushed against the jet ready for the pilots to quickly man the interceptors. Hanging from the ladder was a placard that read 'HOT AIRCRAFT'. The pilots' parachutes were in the seats and switches needed for take-off already flipped. The 'Deuce', as it was affectionately known to all who flew it, was ready to go. Ahead of the ladder, next to the pointed black nose cone, behind the pitot tube, was another sign left by the armourers, listing exactly what weaponry the 'Deuce' was carrying in its weapons bays: four Hughes AIM-4 missiles, two radar-guided and two heat-seekers. Belt and braces. All the pilot had to do was strap in, crank up and taxi out.

Responsibility for keeping a pair of armed fighters on alert, twenty-four hours a day, lay with the 159th Fighter Interception Squadron of the Florida Air National Guard –

FANG. Surrounded by three full-strength USAF F-4 Phantom squadrons based at Homestead, the Daggers with their part-time pilots and engineers seemed a unique little concern. And yet they were in many ways the most important aircraft on the base. They were the ones given the task of defending America from air attack.

Pilots and aircraft rotated from Jacksonville, home of the 159th's parent unit, the 125th Fighter Interception Wing on Florida's north-east coast. And the Guard personnel, although most had full-time jobs, prided themselves on the 159th's professionalism and readiness. Despite keeping up flying hours and training at weekends and days off work they were on the front line – the ones with responsibility for policing the busiest, nerviest alert detachment in the United States. They got it all: a constant stream of giant Soviet Tupolev TU-95 Bears inbound to Cuba from across the Atlantic; drug-runners; hijacked airliners; and the Cubans. Just two years earlier Homestead had received a MiG-17 flown by a Cuban defector. Then they'd been forced to stand by as a Cuban transport air-craft sent to pick up the fighter suffered from a 'navigational error'. *En route* to Homestead, carrying hastily fitted recon-naissance equipment, the FAR overflew sensitive mainland installations like the Turkey Point nuclear power station, tak-ing pictures that would later be used for strike planning. With Homestead barely fifteen minutes' flying time from Cuban bases, this wasn't going to make the 159th's job any easier.

After the embarrassment and anxiety caused by Cubana 877 at the end of October, southern defences were bolstered over the course of the following year with three new F-102 Alert Detachments, in Arizona, in Texas and at Naval Air Station New Orleans, where the 159th took responsibility for a second Alert. With the scare in Louisiana shining a spotlight on the whole southern region, the Alert Detachment at Homestead were determined there wasn't going to be a Cubana 877 on their watch.

*

Lieutenant Commander George Dammeyer USN was pretty well-versed in the threat felt from Cuba. No one in the US military escaped it, but he also had a more personal interest in Florida's safety. Dammeyer was the son of a New York cop who'd retired to the sunshine state, but he was a long way from his old man now. A US Navy Bombardier/Navigator, or B/N, with operational tours in Vietnam under his belt, Dammeyer was enjoying an exchange posting with Carl Davis's Buccaneer squadron at Lossiemouth. Among US Navy attack pilots – who needed no encouragement to dismiss their oppo as a passenger – B/N had quickly and inevitably morphed into 'The Beanbag'. So while Dammeyer put up with the usual banter and piss-taking from 809, he didn't, at least, have to suffer *that* indignity for a while.

Dammeyer was paired up with Pete Lewis. And, initially, Lewis had delighted in scaring the shit out of his new Observer. Despite his experience flying night strikes in hostile air space from carriers on Yankee Station, Dammeyer had found the heights at which the Buccaneers routinely flew something of an eye-opener. It had taken a little getting used to, especially, per-haps, as one of Lewis's favourite tricks was to fly low and fast over the surface of the lochs – not down the open water in the middle, but tucked in close to shore near the road looking *up* at startled motorists staring wide-eyed at a 20-ton bomber, barrelling along at 450 knots, that appeared to be heading straight for them. But Dammeyer was soon embracing life at Lossie and could be relied on by friends to appear at the front door once a week, armed with a bottle, ready to watch Adam Faith in *Budgie*.

Dammeyer wasn't Carl Davis's only overseas recruit. At the same time that he arrived at Lossiemouth, 809 also welcomed the blond, elegant Lieutenant de Vasseau François Rouvillois MN. By 1971, France was the only other European country in the carrier game. Since the Dutch had decommissioned their single light fleet carrier, the Hr.Ms *Karel Doorman*, in 1968, the two 30,000-ton carriers of France's Marine Nationale, *Foch* and *Clemenceau*, were the only other carriers in Europe.

But they were the only carriers in the world to be fitted with ring mains dispensing red wine to their crews. The French, clearly, did things a little differently, however Rouvillois, a pilot with experience flying the Aéronavale's Dassault Etendard IVM attack jet, fitted into 809 quickly. But while 809 made their new pilot feel welcome in Scotland, at the other end of the country *Ark Royal*'s fighter squadron were preparing to conduct Anglo-French naval relations along more traditional lines. They were going to fight them.

The two 892 Squadron Phantoms headed out over the Channel spread out in battle formation. Distinctive in dark grey and white, the pair flew south-east, two miles apart, watching each other's six o'clocks. Both F-4 pilots engaged minimum burner eighteen miles out to kill their smoke trails. The first glimpse of the enemy might come from a flash of reflected sunlight. If you were lucky, though, from nearly twelve miles, you might spot a tell-tale puff of smoke from the Pratt and Whitney J-57 engines as the pilots from Flotille 14F, one of the Aéronavale's two fleet fighter squadrons, eased into reheat. At 30,000 feet, the important thing was not to load up in a turning match. Not unless you could drag the more nimble Vought F-8E(FN) Crusaders down below Flight Level Two Five. Up at Flight Level Three Zero, though, Dougal Macdonald knew they needed to keep their speed up and try to keep slashing past *Les Crouzes* in head-on attacks using the Sparrow missiles.

At a closing speed of over 2000 mph, around three times the speed of sound, the four fighters converged on each other. Straight down the throat with minimum displacement. Any distance at all between them, vertical or horizontal, would hand the advantage to the F-8s by giving them room to turn.

Visual, called the Phantom crews when they picked out the bogies against the background sky. Dougal Macdonald, his head up out of the radarscope now, saw the French jets as they streaked towards him, two tiny specks in the distance. The dots grew slowly for thirty seconds as the two pairs of fighters hurtled at each other, seemingly still distant, then with bewildering rapidity in the last second, as the jets closed the last two miles that separated them. But in that last second, they filled Macdonald's field of vision as they flashed past in a pale grey blur. *That* had been his opportunity to make an instant positive ID. Been and gone.

The Scot craned his neck to maintain visual contact with the F-8s. The most important thing was not to lose sight of them – and while they were behind the Phantom's three o'clock/nine o'clock, they were his responsibility. *Go gate. Extend*, he instructed his Pilot – reheat, put some distance between us and them – as he watched the F-8s break into a turn. John Froggatt pushed the two throttle levers forward with his left hand. At the back of the F-4 the two jet pipes blazed. Blue/orange shock diamonds took shape in their fiery wake.

Extending, he reported over the RT, alerting the second Phantom to their intentions.

Counter, Macdonald called over the RT. *We'll take the high one, you look after the low one.*

Still supersonic, Mach 1.2, five or six miles now separating them from their Crusader, Froggatt horsed into a tight, flat 5g turn, pulling hard as the big interceptor buffeted round at 20 units of angle of attack, kicking it round the corner with the reheat. As they hauled round, Macdonald forced his way forward against the g's pushing him back into his ejection seat. He needed to reacquire the F-8 on his radar to set up another Sparrow shot. The two fighters sliced past each other again like throwing knives.

For another five minutes the four jets carved up the skies, turning, unloading, extending, slashing, soaring and diving, each looking for the gunsight picture that would confirm a kill. And then the Crusaders disengaged. At that point the British Phantoms had them. Using full afterburner, the F-8s sucked their onboard fuel dry at an alarming rate. Hitting 'Bingo' fuel before the Phantoms and their big 500-gallon centreline drop tanks, the two French jets had to head for home. But the moment they turned tail, they presented the heat from their jet pipes to the infrared seeker heads of the F-4s' AIM-9

Sidewinder missiles. Outlast your opponent and the advantage is yours.

Fox Two.

The F-4 crews imagined their short-range missiles streaking towards the F-8s.

Splash two Crusaders.

The French pilots said goodbye and turned for home, switching immediately to the approach frequency at BAN Landivisiau, the Aéronavale's air station in Brittany.

Back on the ground at RNAS Yeovilton, Froggatt and Macdonald climbed out of the Phantom's cockpit and down to the ground. Sweating and exhilarated, they took off their helmets and ran their hands through wet, matted hair. There weren't many things that made you feel like a fighter pilot, but winning a cup final or playing lead guitar to a packed arena were probably up there. As he and Froggatt walked back to the squadron buildings, Macdonald pulled a packet of cigarettes from his flightsuit and shook one free. He lit it and pulled the smoke deep into his lungs.

While ashore in Somerset, 892 NAS took advantage of any opportunity to practise intercepts or fly Air Combat Manoeuvring against as wide a variety of opponents as possible. Winning the fight against a squadron colleague in another Phantom earned bragging rights, but the real sport was in DACT – *Dissimilar* Air Combat Training. From working out tactics against everything from low, slow, tight-turning types like the Navy's own Gannets to practising radar-guided intercepts against the Concorde prototypes conducting supersonic test flights from Filton out over the Irish Sea, 892's crews tried to ensure they were ready for any possible opponent. Fast or slow, old or new, every aircraft offered its own unique set of challenges and dangers to a fighter crew. And for all the attention paid to the threat from the Warsaw Pact, AWI Dougal Macdonald and his squadron Boss Nick Kerr both knew it was a mistake to take the next enemy for granted. It was impossible to predict what might be around the next corner. And the difficult job of trying to stay with an old, slow, but nimble propeller-engined aircraft like the Gannet in a 25-ton jet interceptor designed to fly at Mach 2 might turn out to be exactly what was required – as, much to their surprise, 892 were about to discover.

SECTION THREE

1971

O Lord God, when Thou givest to Thy servants to endeavour any great matter, grant us also to know that it is not the beginning, but the continuing of the same unto the end, until it be thoroughly finished, which yieldeth the true glory.

Sir Francis Drake's Prayer, May 1587

Chapter 22

'I wonder,' mused Richard Posnett's first Head of Department at the Foreign Office, 'if this is really the right career for you.'

'I rather agree with you!' Posnett couldn't help but respond. After the freedom of the overseas postings in Africa and the Pacific with the Colonial Office, he hadn't quite got to grips with the need for security back home. A demand to see his boss in his office on a Monday morning usually meant he'd left another confidential document in the wrong place. So when, in October 1971, he was summoned by David Scott, the Assistant Under-Secretary of State, Posnett's first thought was that he might have done something wrong.

'Would you,' Scott asked him, 'accept the governorship of British Honduras?'

The question stunned him into hesitation. Despite having written the job description and realizing that he fitted the bill, the offer still took his breath away. The selections board had actually thought Posnett was their man back in July, but had needed to wait on other decisions before confirming it. He was the ideal candidate for what they noted was a 'difficult job'.

'Do you need some time to think about it?' suggested Scott.

But even with thoughts racing through his head about the unsettling effect on his family there was never any possibility of Posnett saying no. As a young colonial administrator the position of Governor had seemed impossibly lofty. It had never even occurred to him to aspire to it. He did worry that his wife

Shirley might find any pomp and ceremony a bit of a chore, but, in the end, his main concern was going to be how they were going to get her double bass out to Central America in one piece.

Ashore, the radio crackled as a transmission arrived from *Ark Royal: Permission to proceed.* As a formality, five minutes before the big CVA slipped her lines on 29 October she signalled Flag Officer Portsmouth asking for the go-ahead. It was just one part of the complicated ritual involved in taking the great ship to sea. The whole operation was planned in minute-by-minute detail at the Leaving Harbour briefing the night before. An hour before *Ark* was due to sail, John Roberts left his main harbour cabin on Three X-Ray to return to the bridge. The journey along the narrow corridors and steep companionways up six decks and along two-thirds of the length of the ship took over five minutes. Pipes thick and thin ran along every wall and ceiling. Thick layers of cream, grey and pale-blue gloss paint that covered it all lent the old carrier's innards a veneer of freshness. There was little that suggested modernity, but it was comfortingly familiar. And, with her engines running again after the weeks in port, Roberts could feel his ship had come alive again. At one minute before eight o'clock in the morning on 29 October, *Ark Royal* singled up, loosening her grip on land to just one line. Twenty minutes later she cast off and drifted away from Pompey's middle slip jetty. With help from four tugs her bow swung round to the south. The turn complete, *Ark* headed towards the sea. She moved slowly through the shallow dredged channel past her predecessor, Nelson's flagship at Trafalgar, HMS *Victory*, now preserved in dry-dock. *Victory* still flew the White Ensign as she had since 1778, still in commission and serving as flagship of the Second Sea Lord, Commander-in-Chief, Naval Home Command. Beyond *Victory*, on the Southsea side, large crowds had gathered to wave goodbye to the 1971 Navy's most important warship. As *Ark* passed the harbour entrance, a small troop of sailors fired their rifles in a seventeen-gun salute.

Sailing into a light southerly wind, *Ark* cast off the last of the tugs at the Outer Spit buoy just after 0900. Three-quarters of an hour later she passed Nab Tower lighthouse. The three Trinity House keepers watched as the big ship slid slowly past, still reined in before she reached open water. Looking out to sea from the bridge, John Roberts gave instructions to the Officer of the Watch.

Come to course One Five Zero, revolutions Seven Six.

Beneath him, the ship and her crew got to work, taking *Ark* west of the Isle of Wight, before, safely into the Channel, they turned on to a westerly heading and steamed towards the Atlantic. As her four shafts drove her forward to over 20 knots, oily black smoke now streamed from the funnel. Ahead of her, spumey white water licked up the bow as it was pushed aside. Behind, her wake left a fading straight white scar in the swell.

Later that day, from his office in Whitehall, the Foreign Secretary, Alec Douglas-Home, wrote to Buckingham Palace seeking the Queen's formal approval of Richard Posnett's appointment as the new Governor of British Honduras. In doing so, he gave the job its full title – Governor and *Commander-in-Chief*. When Posnett landed in British Honduras, he'd assume local political control of the colony's defence.

Ark's main broadcast rang through the ship like an alarm. 'Medical Officer to Six Zulu at the rush.' The ghastly urgency in the voice was impossible to miss and the entire Ship's Company knew, as they listened, that something terrible had happened. No more than half an hour later, the speakers hummed and paused again.

'This is the Captain.' John Roberts's voice betrayed his distress. 'I very much regret to inform you that Junior Ordnance Mechanic David Taylor has been killed.' While servicing one of *Ark*'s three bomb lifts the usually careful safety precautions somehow failed him. Working at the bottom of the shaft, Taylor was crushed when the powerful upper weapons lift descended on top of him. There was nothing the ship's Medical Officer could do except confirm his death.

Three hours later, the job of flying ashore with his body fell to Ed Featherstone and his crew. A death at sea is usually followed by committal to the ocean, but, with *Ark* steaming just forty miles south of the Isles of Scilly, John Roberts was able to fly David Taylor's body home. The Captain turned his ship downwind to reduce the wind over the deck and all other activity was halted.

From Flyco, Wings watched as Taylor's body was carried out to Featherstone's waiting Sea King. He was struck by the stark contrast of the brilliance of the white ensign draped around the coffin against the dark greys of the warship and the unwelcoming sea beyond her.

Five Four, you're clear to launch, he told the Sea King crew. He watched the big dark-blue helicopter power up, lift from the deck, and turn away, climbing north-east towards Plymouth. And he hoped it wasn't a harbinger of things to come.

Please, God, he prayed silently as 54's flashing red anti-collision lights disappeared into murky skies, *let that be the only death we suffer this commission.*

While *Ark Royal*'s Ship's Company absorbed the news of their fellow crew member's tragic death, the inhabitants of Belize City woke up to a shock of their own. Splashed all over the front page of the country's only daily newspaper, the *Belize Times*, were details of the secret military pact between Guatemala and El Salvador. Quoting from the official bulletin of the CCT, the Confederation of Central American Workers, the *Times* reported that Guatemala now enjoyed El Salvador's unconditional support for any invasion and annexation of British Honduras. In return, El Salvador would have the opportunity to resettle thousands of families on the occupied territory. At a stroke, they explained, the Guatemalan generals would take what for so long they'd told their people was their

own, while El Salvador won a solution to its domestic population explosion. Win/win. The two aggressors wanted, they
concluded, 'to turn the Belizeans into the Palestinians of Latin
America'.

The announcement, released the same day, that Richard
Posnett OBE had been appointed as the colony's new Governor
made little impression. Tucked away inside the paper, details of
Posnett's CV were, unsurprisingly, lost in the reaction to the
news that British Honduras was at risk not just from one
belligerent neighbour, but from two.

Chapter 23

Five days after David Taylor's death, *Ark Royal* passed through the Straits of Gibraltar into the Mediterranean and steamed towards the scene of an earlier tragedy. On 13 November 1941, while running the U-boat gauntlet that laid siege to Malta, her predecessor, the third HMS *Ark Royal*, was struck amidships by a torpedo fired from U-81 which exploded with such force that the five Swordfish aircraft thrown into the air from her flight deck bounced three times before settling. Twenty minutes later, Captain Maund spoke over the main broadcast to his ship's 1600-strong company: 'Hands to Abandon Ship Stations.' HMS *Ark Royal*, Britain's first purpose-built aircraft carrier, was dying.

Now, thirty years later, John Roberts, who'd felt her loss so sharply while serving as a Midshipman aboard the *Renown*, commanded the ship that had inherited the name she made legend. Just after 1000, Roberts stopped his *Ark Royal's* engines over the approximate position where his ship's forerunner had been lost, to pay his respects. A short service of commemoration was held on the flight deck and a wreath was thrown into the sea. After a three-volley salute, engine revolutions were wound up to 120 and the fourth *Ark Royal* accelerated away to the east.

The Mediterranean had provided the setting for some of the Royal Navy's greatest triumphs. But it was during the Second World War, under the command of the brilliant, charismatic Admiral Andrew Browne Cunningham, known to all as ABC, that the Fleet Air Arm made its name, and in doing so showed beyond any doubt that aircraft represented the future of naval power. Cunningham was a sailor cut from the same cloth as Nelson. The aggression upon which the Royal Navy had built its reputation was instilled by men like them. 'Engage the enemy more closely!' Nelson had instructed at Trafalgar. Nearly 130 years later, Cunningham, determined not to let the army down during the evacuation of Crete, was dismissive of the generals' concerns that, in covering the withdrawal, the Navy would lose too many ships. 'It takes three years to build a ship,' he said; 'it takes three centuries to build a tradition.' That never-say-die attitude ensured that, during the 1941 operation, 16,500 soldiers were saved. In 1971, it still infused every branch of the Navy. And nowhere more than the Fleet Air Arm. If, preoccupied with the job in hand, the young aircrew had been largely unaware of and unmoved by the memorial service for the third *Ark Royal*, there was no danger of the commemoration that followed going unnoticed.

On ABC's orders, Operation JUDGEMENT was launched on the night of 11 November 1940. During the surprise attack on the Italian fleet in harbour at Taranto, twenty-one Fairey Swordfish torpedo bombers sank one battleship, badly damaged two more and crippled one of only two Italian light cruisers. The following morning the Italian admirals moved the ships that remained undamaged by the attack north, out of harm's way. In doing so they ended the threat posed to the British Mediterranean Fleet. Until that point the Italians had outnumbered Cunningham's force in every class of ship save aircraft carriers. It was a comprehensive victory at the cost of just two of the attacking FAA biplanes. Yet such was the ferocity of the anti-aircraft barrage they encountered that, when the possibility of a second strike was mooted, one of the aircrew made the point that 'they'd only asked the Light Brigade to do it once'. Fortunately aerial reconnaissance quickly showed that another attack wasn't necessary. JUDGEMENT had been a success. And it had a significance far beyond its effect on the balance of power in the Med. As

ABC was quick to recognize, the Fleet Air Arm had become the Royal Navy's 'most devastating weapon'. The raid's success also caught the eye of Admiral Yamamoto and the Operations Staff of the Imperial Japanese Navy. A Japanese naval delegation visited Taranto in May 1941, just six months before the devastating attack on the US Naval Base at Pearl Harbor in Hawaii.

Taranto Night celebrations were the highlight of the Wardroom calendar. And while there was usually a degree of distance between the fixed-wing squadrons and the helicopter crews, on board *Ark Royal*, at least, that tended to vanish on Taranto Night. *Ark*'s resident Sea King squadron, 824, had been one of the four Swordfish squadrons that had launched from the deck of HMS *Illustrious* in 1940.

Dinner ended with a toast: *To the memory of Taranto!* And as *Ark*'s aircrews honoured the victory close to where it had been won, in the Wardroom mess back at Yeovilton surviving veterans of the raid, always invited as guests of honour, joined in raising their glasses to the friends they'd lost.

Then, under the low tangled ceiling of *Ark Royal*'s Wardroom, the singing began. The air was thick with tobacco smoke. Armchairs and tables had been pushed back against the walls. And each man carried a drink in his hand as Steve Park, 809's Senior Observer, began to hammer out chords on an upright piano. The crews gathered around. They bellowed a full-throated rendition of what had become the Fleet Air Arm's anthem, 'The A25 Song', named after Accident Form A25.

> *I'll sing you a song about sailors who fly,*
> *They say in the Air Force a landing's OK,*
> *If the pilot gets out and can still walk away,*
> *But in the Fleet Air Arm the prospects are dim*
> *If the landing's piss poor and the pilot can't swim.*
>
> *Cracking show, I'm alive*
> *But I've still got to render my A25.*

I fly for a living and not just for fun,
I'm not awfully anxious to hack down the Hun,
And as for deck landings at night in the dark,
As I told Wings this morning, 'Fuck that for a lark.'

By midnight, those flying the next morning were long gone. Eight hours bottle to throttle. And the crews of *Ark*'s 'Heavies' needed the time and sleep. When the sun came up they would be pitting themselves against the best the USS *Independence* could throw at them.

Chapter 24

When the telephone rang in the small hours of the morning it was never good news. And, when John Weymes, asleep at home in the Ambassador's Residence, picked it up, it wasn't. At two o'clock in the morning he was summoned to an immediate meeting at the Guatemalan Ministry of Foreign Affairs off Avenida La Reforma, the busy north–south drag that bisected Zones 9 and 10 in the south of the city. Dr Herrera, the Guatemalan Foreign Minister, needed to see him now. The British Consul got up, dressed quickly and holstered his .22 automatic, then made his way across town from the Ambassador's Residence. When he arrived, he was asked to wait. The American Ambassador was in with Herrera. He came out shaking his head and left. Weymes was ushered through. The sophisticated Guatemalan Foreign Minister was sitting, flanked by Sánchez and surrounded by another eight or so of his senior aides and advisers. The whole set-up was designed to be intimidating – the late-night call, the mob-handed reception, the hard-set faces of those present. 'Tell me,' Herrera asked him, blunt, but civilized, 'what are British intentions in Belice?' The Guatemalans were unsettled and Weymes was careful not to inflame the already tense room.

'As you know, we have no hidden agenda. We are working towards a peaceful resolution of this dispute.' One of the ministry officials countered aggressively, accusing him and Britain of trying to pull the wool over their eyes and Weymes protested, before Herrera intervened.

'I don't think we should go down that road.' The official restrained himself. There was a pause as Herrera considered his next move.

'OK,' he told the British diplomat, 'thank you for coming down.'

What was that all about?, Weymes wondered as he left the Ministry. He headed straight for the Consulate, phoned his staff and called them in to Calle 11. Grateful for the recent delivery of new cipher machines, they signalled London to explain what had just happened. Something had the Guatemalans rattled – and worried that developments in British Honduras might leave them excluded.

James Bond was showing in Belize City. As George Lazenby starred in *On Her Majesty's Secret Service* at the Eden Cinema, speculation was already building in London over who the next Bond would be. Diary pieces soon reported that Roger Moore was 95 per cent certain to start filming *Live and Let Die* in the spring. And at Airport Camp, Lieutenant Hawkesworth, Lance Corporal Carnell and Guardsman Caldow all assigned themselves a '00' prefix. But alongside the jokes about 007 there were also suggestions that all three of them would be banged up in a Guatemalan gaol by nightfall.

Hawkesworth, the Inkerman Company's only Spanish-speaker, and his men were posing as tourists to cross over the border into Guatemala and see what they could discover. They passed through immigration early in the afternoon and were immediately greeted with a sign that greeted all visitors: *BELICE EST NUESTRA*. The soldiers travelled by bus to Flores. After a night in the Hotel El Itzá they visited the Mayan ruins at Tikal. The F-51D Mustangs of Major Constenza's Escuadrón de Caza were long gone. Hawkesworth and his men returned to BH the next day, struck by little more than the sight of local police armed with sub-machine guns. Unsurprisingly enough, forty-eight hours and a fifty-mile round-trip along one of El Petén's main roads revealed absolutely nothing of any value. But even if they'd been more persistent, they were, given how Guatemalan military plans were now evolving, looking in the wrong place.

While Hawkesworth and his secret agents travelled to Flores and back, 10 Platoon were on an expedition to Blue River Creek in the north of British Honduras. Corkran had sent them north to make contact with a Mexican Army platoon engaged on anti-guerrilla operations in the Yucatán. Mexico had long since formally relinquished a claim on the north of British Honduras, but had made it clear that, should Guatemala successfully act on her own claim, then that would change. And it was as a contingency against any possible Guatemalan hostility that Corkran had sent his Guardsmen up-country.

If Guatemala did move, the Guards Major wanted to make sure that he had a link with the Mexicans to the north. At least then one border was secure. But there was also a more alarming thought going through his head. Corkran was sure that in the event of any determined attack, the airport would fall, and with it the RAF's only means of resupply. *If we're being duffed up and beaten back*, he reasoned, *then to establish a landing zone with thousands of Guatemalans swarming about could be a bit tricky*. Open lines of communications with the Mexicans near Blue Creek might help secure a parachute drop zone in an area of relative safety. It made sense, but if that became necessary things were going to be pretty desperate.

Chapter 25

Lieutenant Toby Buschmann USN never forgot the time he saw a Buccaneer up close and personal for the first time. As Buschmann made his way up to the cockpit of his Vought A-7 Corsair II attack jet on the flight deck of the USS *Independence*, he was suddenly assaulted by the ear-splitting roar of jet engines from an unexpected direction. He spun round to see a single slate-grey Buccaneer wing flash along the length of the *Indy* from bow to stern – like a 600 mph shark's fin – very fast and very close to the port side of the big American carrier. He was standing level with the Buccaneer crew's white helmets as the Fleet Air Arm bomber powered past at 90 degrees of bank. With *Indy*'s deck at about 60 feet above the water, he made a quick mental calculation about their altitude. And about the clearance of their starboard wingtip from the waves. *No apparent fear of death*, he thought admiringly. *Very impressive!*

Ark's Buccaneer and Phantom crews had to work hard to be so. Over four days, the air groups from *Ark* and *Independence* flew against each other. The Buccaneers mounted ship strikes against the *Indy*, while *Ark*'s Phantoms defended the American carrier. And as the American F-4s of VF-102 'Diamondbacks' and VF-33 'Tarsiers' flew Combat Air Patrols, Toby Buschmann and his A-7 light attack squadron, VA-66, and the rest of *Indy*'s complement of A-6s and RA-5s, gunned for *Ark Royal*.

Within Carl Davis and Nick Kerr's squadrons there was a

quiet confidence that, pound for pound they were the best naval aviators in the world. But if they were, they had to be just to keep up. That qualification – *pound for pound* – was necessary, because inherent in it were the reasons why, flying from a smaller carrier, with fewer aircraft, they were even able to stand comparison with the overwhelming strength in depth enjoyed by the Americans. It came down to numbers.

Ark's sister ship *Eagle* was nearly gone. With her demise, 809 and 892 would become the sole expression of Fleet Air Arm fixed-wing jet air power – and the distillation of forty years of knowledge, experience and refinement. The Americans, though, still had a *fleet* of aircraft carriers they had to supply with pilots and backseaters. VF-121, the Phantom training squadron on which Dick Lord had been an instructor, alone had more fixed-wing jets than the entire Fleet Air Arm. The Pilots and Observers of 809 and 892 were older than many of the aircrew aboard the American carriers and, as the last men standing in the Fleet Air Arm, were often vastly more experienced. They had become, for all the wrong reasons, an elite of about forty men. None of them really had any excuse for *not* being more capable than the average American Squadron Joe.

'You *try* so much harder,' the CO of one of the *Indy*'s Phantom squadrons, VF-33, had said about the challenges of operating from *Ark Royal*. And Lieutenant Commander Richard Wyman was US Navy aristocracy too – an MiG killer. While flying an F-8 Crusader from the deck of the USS *Oriskany* in 1967 he'd downed a North Vietnamese MiG-17 Fresco.

One or two of *Ark*'s fighter pilots were envious of the opportunity some of their American counterparts had had to prove themselves in combat. Unshakeable self-belief and fierce competitiveness were in any fighter pilot's blood, but there *had* to be an element of doubt. A handful of *Ark Royal*'s aircrews had fired a few angry shots in hotspots around the world. On 809, Carl Davis and 'Boots' Walkinshaw, who had both flown rocket-armed Buccaneers over the Yemen, were among them.

And 892's Boss, Nick Kerr, had himself flown Close Air Support in Hawker Hunters while serving on exchange with the RAF at Khormaksar in Aden. But without the chance to put themselves to the test for real, all they could do was to carry on training and preparing for every scenario – trying to make sure there were no chinks in their armour. And flying in the most realistic exercise conditions possible, the Buccaneers kept getting through and the Phantoms kept making intercepts. *Their own experience* led them to believe there was no one better.

And after just a few months in Flyco, Wings didn't believe their confidence was misplaced. Despite flying heavy, genuinely high-performance jets – the most capable aircraft the Fleet Air Arm had ever flown – at or beyond what he sometimes considered to be reasonable limits, he thought *Ark*'s self-contained air group could lay claim to being the second-best air force in the world. Even he had to concede though that the top spot fell to the extraordinary recent record of the combat-proven Israelis.

But in the comparison with the Americans, size did matter. In January 1966, a Royal Navy Observer sailing with CTF-77, the US carrier task force off Vietnam, described the weight of air power produced by the big US CVAs as 'if not frightening, certainly astonishing'. More worryingly, he confessed that without the dedicated electronic warfare and flak suppression support available to American pilots, he didn't believe a British carrier could launch a strike against North Vietnam without the air group being 'decimated'. There was simply no way of knowing. Without an enemy to push against, there was a danger of any claim to be best sounding a bit hollow.

As a Peace Corps volunteer, Dennis Wheeler could never possibly have been drafted to fight in Vietnam. Aged twenty, while studying for an agriculture degree at the University of Wisconsin Wheeler attended a presentation on the Peace Corps and hung on every word. He was completely seduced by the excitement this new organization seemed to offer. He and his girlfriend Luisa, soon to be his wife, signed up. They were told they were going to be sent to Guatemala. Wheeler imagined South Seas islands and grass skirts, but Luisa put him straight pretty quickly.

The couple arrived in Guatemala in 1965, living and working in an Indian village, 7000 feet up in the mountains between the old colonial city of Antigua de Guatemala and the volcano-fringed Lago de Atitlán, described by Aldous Huxley as 'the most beautiful lake in the world'. Young, idealistic and living at the height of the late-sixties hippy era, Dennis and Luisa were soon helping Guatemalan families pursue a government offer of land in El Petén. With six Guatemalan families, they hoped to build a new settlement carved out of the jungle. Inaccessible except for the rough airstrips used to fly out the region's only export, chicle, the main ingredient of chewing gum, the members of the budding colony were flown in aboard FAG C-47 transports.

By the end of the decade, and now out of the Peace Corps, Dennis and Luisa wanted to farm land of their own, and persuaded two other American couples to join them on their great adventure. Together, the six set off in a rag-tag convoy of cars and trucks to go looking. By early 1971 they were in San Ignacio in British Honduras, just a few miles from the Guatemalan border. A $9000 offer for a farm south of the town looked promising before it fell through. But then someone suggested Guatemala.

Why not? they thought, and the 6×6 truck, the Land Cruiser and the Peugeot rolled into Guatemala, turning left at Flores to head south through El Petén along the new, unpaved road to Poptun, the little town that was the hub of the Guatemalan Army's counter-insurgency operations in the area. And where, at the nearby army base, the parachute battalion was being reinforced.

Chapter 26

'Your deck is a little bumpier than ours,' 'Toobs' Charles needled as he enjoyed a coffee with crews from the VF-102 'Diamondbacks' in their briefing room. Charles and his Observer, Dougal Macdonald, had trapped aboard the USS *Independence* in their Phantom two hours earlier and were getting stuck into the inevitable banter and one-upmanship that followed.

However carefully both ships prepared for it, cross-decking always threw up surprises. In 1969, a detachment of 892's F-4s had deployed aboard the USS *Saratoga* to deck-qualify before *Ark* came out of refit. They'd ended up being launched without reheat – at less than 60 per cent of their available power – carrying a light fuel load good only for about twenty-five minutes in the air. At full power, the more powerful engines of the British jets, angled more directly into the flight deck because of the extended undercarriage leg of their nosegear, had scorched and blistered the heavy steel, turning it viscid in barely fifteen seconds.

Aboard *Ark Royal*, mindful of *Ark*'s smaller deck, Wings had instructed the US Phantoms to arrive light on fuel. Tolerances on the British carrier were smaller. And coming too heavy or too fast would pull the arrestor wires out. Wings could afford to be a little more relaxed watching the *Indy*'s Grumman C-1 Trader trundle down the full length of the deck for a free take-off, unassisted by a boost from the catapult. Its twin piston engines and high wing had reminded him of old black and white footage of Jimmy Doolittle's Douglas B-25s launching from the deck of the USS *Hornet* on their retaliatory raid against Tokyo in April 1942.

But as the British crews finished their coffees and gathered their kit to return to the waiting jets, 'Toobs' Charles couldn't help but recall the first time he'd been catapulted from the deck of the *Independence* a month earlier. It had almost ended in disaster.

Nick Kerr had been due to launch first, but a problem with the jet kept him back. As he sat in his cockpit underneath the island, 'Toobs' Charles held the back of his hand up against the cockpit glass to signal to the Flight Deck Officer that he was ready to go. After the *Saratoga* experience, the Americans were worried about the British F-4Ks burning holes in *Indy*'s deck. The plan was to sit on the cat on minimum burner to preserve the deck, then push the throttles forward to full reheat as the Phantom was dragged down the catapult track.

Charles kept his left hand on the throttles in the side console. Kidskin gloves around smooth metal. With his right hand, he maintained a gentle back pressure on the stick, pulling against a clutched cable extending from the instrument panel ahead that ensured his stabilators would stay at the right angle of attack. Unlike the Buccaneer, which was launched hands off before being gathered in by the pilot, the Phantom had to be flown off the deck. The simple cable-and-clutch system stopped its pilots over-rotating and stalling in the critical split seconds after the catapult had done its work.

A couple of seconds after the FDO's flag touched the deck Charles was pinned against his seat by the acceleration down the catapult, but less violently than when taking off from *Ark*. *Indy*'s longer catapults meant the short journey to flying speed was a little less explosive. Charles fought the 'g' to push the throttles all the way forward to the stops. Thirty or forty feet from the edge of the deck, the catapult shuttle hit the stops leaving the job of driving the big jet forward to the

41,000lb of thrust being thrown out of the back of the engines.

Then, when the deck fell away from underneath the Phantom's nosewheel, the front of the jet pitched down towards the horizon. As it came off the edge of the flight deck, Charles's aircraft just dropped, nose low, flying towards the sea. Charles felt his stomach lurch as he lost height ahead of the giant carrier's bow. There was only 60 feet of air to play with. With both hands he grabbed the control column and ripped the cable through its clutch to raise the nose of the Phantom away from the water.

Now 25 tons of interceptor clawed its way forward on the cusp of a stall, practically standing on the awesome furnace generated from the two Rolls-Royce Speys. The surface of the sea boiled and steamed, blowtorched in the jetwash as the Phantom hovered forward nose high, relying on thick columns of thrust to keep her airborne. Charles willed his jet to gain air speed. In the back, his Observer's hands stayed close to the yellow and black of the ejection seat handle between his legs.

From the deck, after dropping out of sight, the dark-grey Royal Navy jet rose slowly into view as Charles wrestled his way into the sky, trailing two thick black smoketrails behind him.

They'd been lucky. As they settled into a safe speed and altitude, Charles thumbed the RT to warn the carrier ahead of Nick Kerr's launch. And inside Flyco his unfamiliar West Country accent crackled over the radio.

'You might,' he advised coolly, 'want to put a bit more trim on than that.'

Understatement and a refusal to be overly impressed with anything much were defining characteristics of military flyers throughout the world. Radio transmissions were unflustered and laconic. The story goes that an American fighter pilot, under attack in Korea and unable to escape, revealed his fear and distress over the RT. 'Shut up,' he was told, 'and die like an aviator.'

If you dwelt too long on what could go wrong you'd never

leave your cabin, let alone the deck. And, operating within margins as tight as they were aboard *Ark Royal*, the list of what could go wrong was a long one.

Dr Carl Faulkner had a very high opinion of the British military. As a young American soldier, he'd fought alongside British Artillery guns during the Korean War. Now he was in British Honduras with big dreams. Staying with his wife Mary Lynn and two daughters Daphne and Carla in the 34-room Fort George Hotel in Belize City, he loved the *Casablanca* atmosphere of the place. There were Brit anachronisms there looking to carve out a life among the embers of Empire. There were a few who were running away – men like Humphrey Bogart's Rick Blair, who'd ended up in the bar of the Fort George as a result of being 'misinformed'. And there were others like him who saw only opportunity. Faulkner himself didn't drink, but there were plenty at the Fort George who did. Gin and grand dreams – the usual colonial mix.

With a thriving dental practice back home in Memphis, Tennessee, Faulkner first travelled to British Honduras in 1965 to fish. Marlin, wahoo, even 100lb groupers were all there beyond the Cayes for the keen blue-water fisherman. But Faulkner had seen huge potential in the little colony. He'd already invested in cattle-ranching in the US, but British Honduras was practically untapped. By 1971, he'd bought 6000 acres of land at Burrell Boom, north-west of Belize City, and another 2000 near St Augustine in the south. Within Central America, British Honduras was uniquely attractive to an investor. It was English-speaking and it was governed by the rule of law. For now.

As he sat down at his desk in the new bungalow in Belmopan they were calling Government House, to write his final report, the outgoing Governor feared for the future. Sir John Paul was sad and frustrated that British Honduras seemed no closer to independence than it had been when he'd arrived five and a half years earlier. She was ready for it, of that he was in no doubt. But there was always the spectre of Guatemala to contend with. Without a solution to the dispute, he could see only three ways forward: maintenance of the status quo; increased autonomy for British Honduras stopping short of independence; or independence under the protective umbrella of a British security guarantee. The first two were muddled and satisfied no one. But it was the last and, on the surface at least, most appealing option that worried him most.

'Given the Guatemalans' remarkable propensity for fomenting chaos and anarchy in their own country,' he wrote, working on the assumption that they would actually *prefer* peace and stability, 'the effect of their conducting an organised campaign of subversion and violence in a neighbouring country in which they were anxious to promote anarchy does not bear contemplation.'

Chapter 27

In the late 1960s, the US Navy conducted a series of tests on pilots flying from their carriers. They attached sensors to monitor their vital signs – heart rate, blood pressure, skin temperature – as they flew missions over North Vietnam. The results were surprising. No part of the sortie was more stressful than returning to the pitching deck of the aircraft carrier at night. The crews could fly through sheets of flak or be snapping into split-second barrel rolls to avoid big SA-3 SAMs spearing up at them like ballistic telegraph poles, but it was just coming home that was the source of their greatest anxiety. There were good pilots who, after a night trap, weren't able to get out of the cockpit and climb down the ladder until their legs had stopped shaking.

And some pilots lost their nerve completely. Carl Davis and Nick Kerr kept a close eye on their own troops. At least once a week Davis and his Senior Pilot would go through the names of the crews on the squadron. 'How are they doing?' Davis asked 'Boots' Walkinshaw. 'Who's coming on? Who isn't?' And there was one, in the end, who didn't make the cut.

'It's time for you to move on,' Davis had told the pilot. Night qualification aboard *Ark Royal* was earned gradually. Once polished and proficient at deck landing by day, before flying in the dark pilots flew duskers. In the fading light of the early evening, they flew circuits, practising approaches and landing on the carrier with their arrestor hook up, then pouring on the power to go round again for another try. Up until this point,

Davis hadn't identified a problem. Then, scheduled at night for the first time, his pilot went sick. On another three occasions when his name appeared on the flying programme he reported unwell, until finally he made it into the cockpit. Davis was alongside him in another Buccaneer and heard him report to Flyco that his Master Reference Gyro was down. It was the last time he ever sat in the cockpit of a Buccaneer.

That night the pilot confessed to Carl Davis that he didn't think he could do it.

'Are you *sure* about that?' Davis pushed him. 'You're a very brave man to say it. Because if you are I shall recommend in five minutes that you leave the ship as soon as we can get you off. There's no place for you here. You understand that?'

'Oh yes, sir.' With John Roberts's blessing, the young aviator was off the ship the next day.

Jerry Granger-Holcombe crossed himself before every flight. And, so far, the Almighty seemed to have taken note of the Observer's appeal for safe-keeping. Despite ejecting for the second time in his career just a few months earlier, when he and Dave Hill had been hounded out of the skies off Florida, he was still in one piece. But Hill, after damaging his back in that ejection, was still off flying. Instead, Granger-Holcombe was flying with a new Pilot, Scotsman, Lieutenant Andy Auld. Ten days earlier, the two of them had successfully completed Auld's first series of duskers.

Now, though, just before 1930 on 17 November, it was dark.

From the air, at night, *Ark Royal* appears to be nothing more than a few spots of light in otherwise uniform black. It's virtually impossible to pick out her shape against the sea, horizon or sky. On some nights the moon picks out the white water of the wake streaming behind the ship.

Auld had already flown a number of approaches and go-rounds with the hook raised without giving cause for concern. If he'd been struggling, Wings and Nick Kerr, up in Flyco to keep an eye on his young Pilot, would have diverted him ashore to Malta to live and fight another day.

As the two senior men looked back over the deck towards the glidepath, the reassuring voice of the Carrier Controlled Approach Controller, transmitting from a room at the back of the island, came through the speaker.

Zero Zero Five, you are on the centreline and approaching the glideslope. Stand by to begin your descent. The deck is ready for you.

The operator of the CCA radar guided the returning Pilot to a point a mile and a half behind *Ark*'s stern. Watching the progress of Auld's F-4 on his radar display, the CCA Controller continued his talk-down, correcting any deviations.

Commence your descent now. Drifting slightly right of centreline. Come left three degrees. I see you correcting nicely. Keep it coming . . .

With his left hand gripping the throttle levers and his right hand gently coaxing the control column, Auld tried to settle into a smooth stable descent along the glidepath. With full flap, leading edge droop, and undercarriage and hook all hanging down below her, the Phantom, her nose high, dropped down through the night like a giant alien insect, all legs and antennae. In this high-lift configuration, descending at 19 units of angle of attack, with full blow over the wings from the Boundary Layer Control, the Phantom was immensely stable. Set up at 132 knots with 80 per cent power from the two Rolls-Royce engines, she just wanted to sit there.

Auld kept his eyes ahead scanning the black for the first glimpse of the carrier's lights. In his ears, the Airflow Direction Detector or ADD maintained a steady note in his headset, its tone telling him about the Phantom's all-important angle of attack. If he's too fast the tone will become an urgent high-pitched beeping. Too slow and it turns into a malevolent low pulse. Displayed on the HUD – the head-up display – projected on to glass ahead of him, there's another, visual, angle-of-attack indicator. It's the information most likely to keep them alive. Behind him, Granger-Holcombe called the speeds, allowing the Pilot to keep his eyes outside the cockpit, away from the green-lit blind-flying panel. And he listened to the sound of

Left: The view up Haulover Creek from the swing bridge in the heart of Belize City's centre.

Above: Belize International Airport was ten miles north of Belize City. Also known as Stanley Field, it provided the only paved runway in the country and was the only international port of entry.

Above: Airport Camp, to the north of the Stanley Field runway, was home to the garrison of just 300 British troops who had responsibility for the colony's defence.

Above: In 1971, the Grenadier Guards provided the resident infantry company. Armed with little more than assault rifles and a handful of heavier machine guns and anti-tank rounds, their CO, Major Richard Corkran, wasn't confident that his men could hold off a determined Guatemalan attack for long.

Above: Without helicopters, Land Rovers provided the Grenadiers with their only means of getting around the country. It meant that the colony's new capital, Belmopan, was a few hours' drive away, while Punta Gorda in the south was the best part of a day's drive away along unpaved roads.

Left: Atlantic Striking Fleet. In September 1971, *Ark Royal* sailed north towards the Arctic Circle to participate in Exercise ROYAL KNIGHT alongside the USS *Independence*. The two strike carriers were at the heart of NATO's plans to contain the powerful Soviet Northern Fleet. And for the duration of the exercise both would be pushed to the limits – especially the smaller British ship.

Above: Scramble. A Phantom launches from the waist catapult in full reheat. Not only did 892's fighters have to defend the fleet from air raids by attacking forces, they were also scrambled to intercept Soviet shadowers.

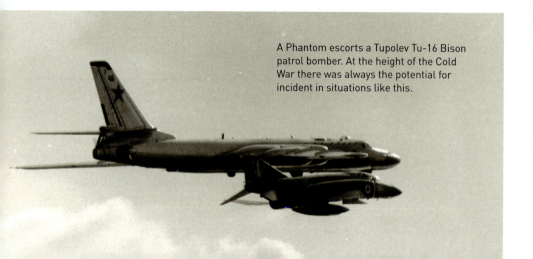

A Phantom escorts a Tupolev Tu-16 Bison patrol bomber. At the height of the Cold War there was always the potential for incident in situations like this.

Left: The view from the cockpit. During interceptions, 892's Observers always carried cameras to take pictures of their Soviet sparring partners. These would later be poured over by Photographic Interpreters in search of new intelligence.

Above: While maintaining Combat Air Patrol, 892 would have another fighter on station ahead of the fleet before its predecessor recovered to 'Mother'. This Phantom hasn't lowered the arrestor hook, which means the pilot is practising deck landing and will be flying a 'touch and go' rather than catching one of the wires stretched across the flight deck.

Above: The Fairey Gannets of 849 NAS 'B' Flight provided airborne early warning for the fleet using a radar attached beneath the fuselage. With its cranked wings, radome and contra-rotating propellors, the Gannet was one of the most distinctive shapes in the sky.

Right: This picture highlights the precision flying needed to land a fast jet on a carrier deck. Only a handful of crews were qualified to do it at night – a task which remained a challenge to even the most experienced naval aviator.

Left: A Sea King crew on deck before boarding their aircraft. Observer Lt Ed Featherstone is second from left, carrying both his Nav Bag and overlays for his radar screen.

Above: 824 Squadron's Sea King HAS1s maintained a round-the-clock anti-submarine screen around *Ark Royal*. After launching, the first task would be to check the water immediately behind the ship. A bold submarine captain could lurk there, masked by the noise of the carrier's own engines.

With HMS *Ocelot*. During Exercise ROYAL KNIGHT, this 'O' class diesel-electric submarine, operating alongside other British and American submarines, represented a formidable opponent.

Left: Throughout ROYAL KNIGHT, 809's Buccaneers launched long-range low-level strikes against strategic mainland targets. The Buccaneers' best defence was to twist low and fast through the fjords and mountains.

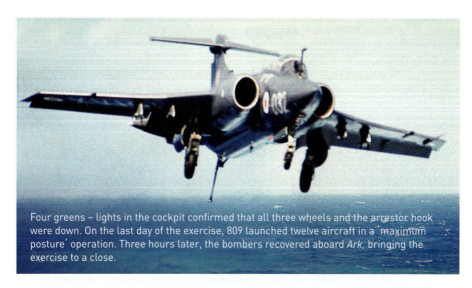

Four greens – lights in the cockpit confirmed that all three wheels and the arrestor hook were down. On the last day of the exercise, 809 launched twelve aircraft in a 'maximum posture' operation. Three hours later, the bombers recovered aboard *Ark*, bringing the exercise to a close.

Left: While disembarked at their home base of RNAS Culdrose, a pair of 824's aircraft were scrambled after a fire aboard the freighter *Anatina* left it drifting west of the Scillies. The effects of the fire are evident port of the funnel. As is the threat to the helicopter from the wallowing ship's masts.

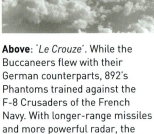

Above: *'Le Crouze'*. While the Buccaneers flew with their German counterparts, 892's Phantoms trained against the F-8 Crusaders of the French Navy. With longer-range missiles and more powerful radar, the British interceptors held a clear advantage until the distances closed.

Above: At RNAS Lossiemouth in Morayshire, *Ark*'s Buccaneer squadron were hosting a detachment of F-104 Starfighters from the German Navy. On the hard-turning low-level routes through the Scottish highlands, the razor-winged German jets couldn't live with the big British naval bombers.

Below: A page from the 892 Line Book celebrates the outcome of the ACM (Air Combat Manoeuvre) battles against the French.

Above: On the flightline at Yeovilton. As families say their farewells, 892 prepares to re-embark aboard *Ark Royal* for autumn exercises in the Mediterranean.

Right: While operating in the Mediterranean, 892's Phantoms flew off the deck of the USS *Independence*. Here one of the British jets streaks down the catapult of the American carrier past a US Navy SH-3 Sea King and the tail and folded wing of an A-7 Corsair II attack jet.

Left: Lashed down, nose and wings folded. An atmospheric shot of one of 809's Buccaneers on deck at dusk.

Left: Greeted by a long line of official dignitaries and spectators watching from the airport terminal, Sir Richard Posnett arrived in British Honduras to take over as Governor on 26 January 1972.

Below: Steaming alongside RFA *Olmeda* during a routine RAS – Replenishment at Sea – *Ark Royal* received a signal from the Admiralty ordering her to proceed with all despatch towards British Honduras on the same day as the new Governor's arrival.

Below: With British Honduras at risk of invasion from Guatemala, Captain John Roberts changed course and increased the speed to over 26 knots through heavy seas. Water rolling down the ship's flanks ripped away exposed aerials and fittings. All of which was viewed by Roberts as an acceptable price to be paid, given what was at stake.

Right: Aircraft on deck were moved to the back of the deck in an effort to protect them from the worst of the weather.

Auld's breathing, picked up over the intercom from the mic in his oxygen mask. Observers learnt to divine their Pilot's state of mind from the way they breathed. The voice of the CCA Controller crackled through his helmet.

You are now at one and a half miles. Look up for the sight.

Auld looked through the F-4's HUD for the green and white lights of the projector sight on the port side of deck.

On sight, he called. The meatball – the white light in the centre – was all he could pick out from this distance.

Roger.

The acknowledgement came from the LSO, the Landing Safety Officer. Outside, on a platform next to the gyro-stabilized Landing Sight – set up to take account of the distance between the pilot's eyeballs and the tip of the Phantom's arrestor hook – the LSO took control of Auld's approach. An experienced aviator himself, the LSO looked through a little telescope sight, keeping Auld's Phantom in the crosshairs, attuned to the slightest variation in height, drift or speed. Any deviation from Auld might result in either a bolter – a failure to catch a wire – or a wave-off, when the LSO, considering the landing too dangerous to continue, orders an abort.

The young Scottish pilot had to aim his 25-ton fighter at a section of the deck just 10 square yards in area. To do so meant flying at no more or less than a knot outside the required speed and within arc-seconds of the 4-degree glideslope. Auld kept focused on the meatball, the glowing white light of the projector sight that confirmed he was on his 4-degree glidepath,

Waiting for him on deck were the four pre-tensioned wire cables of the arrestor gear, ready to snag the hook hanging beneath his Phantom's tail, as substantial and unyielding as a piece of industrial-age ironwork.

On the roger, centreline, the LSO reassured him, his hand hovering over the wave-off button. When he drifts high or to the side, the message will change – *Slightly right, correcting to the centreline. On the roger, centreline* – the tone, if the approach is recoverable, does not.

Auld could see the deck lights now – a row crossing his path that marked the round-down and another extending forward in his direction of travel along the centreline of the angled landing area. He stayed focused on the meatball and the row of horizontal green lights on either side.

From Flyco, Nick Kerr watched Auld come in. For much of the approach the Phantom seemed almost stationary, just a small cluster of red, green and white lights hovering in the night behind the ship, slowly descending towards the horizon. Suddenly, maybe 200 yards from the flight deck, the massive white underbelly of the Phantom burst out of the night. And then, in the last seconds, things unravelled with terrifying speed.

You're low. The LSO's voice was urgent. *You're low. Power!*

Auld slammed the throttles forward. But the Phantom's Rolls-Royce Spey engines, despite a modification designed to allow carrier pilots to bring them to full power fast, still lagged behind the control inputs from the cockpit. The ADD alarm went off in their ears. In the back seat Granger-Holcombe could feel the big jet struggle to respond and the desperate demand from the LSO: *Power! Power! Power!* It was too late though. In a Phantom sitting this far back on the drag curve, low, with the engines still maybe a good second away from delivering full power, Auld and Granger-Holcombe were condemned to their fate. Granger-Holcombe instinctively reached up towards the ejection seat handle above his head.

A split second later, 25 tons of naval interceptor slammed tail first into the ramp at the back of the flight deck. In a shower of sparks and a sickening metallic screech, the main landing gear splayed out and the jet was thrown forward nose down. And, somehow, the stricken Phantom slid forward along the landing area, caught a wire and came to a halt.

'I've hit the ramp,' murmured a shocked Auld. Behind him, the force of the jet's violent vertical deceleration had kicked through Granger-Holcombe's spine and as he sat there, astonished to be on deck, he realized he was still in one piece, but that he was hurt.

Aircraft Artificer Lionel 'Smudge' Smith was working on the

Phantoms in the upper hangar, immediately below the flight deck, when he heard what sounded like a train wreck above. He felt the whole ship shudder with the force of the blow, the noise of 005's impact resonating through the steel compartments.

On deck, instead of trying to taxi to the deck park, Auld was told by Flyco to shut the jet down immediately. Bathed in the strange, artificial glow of floodlights from the island, well-drilled crash crews looking like spacemen in flame-retardant suits ran out and swarmed round the broken fighter. But *Ark Royal* – and, more particularly, the crew of Phantom 005 – had been lucky. They'd certainly been shaken by their arrival and Granger-Holcombe had taken a big hit to his back less than six months after ejecting off the coast of Florida. The two of them were taken to the sick bay to be checked by the doctor and given a brandy to calm their nerves. Over the six weeks that followed the ramp strike, Granger-Holcombe spent only another hour strapped into an ejection seat. It was January before he was back flying.

Phantom 005 herself hadn't been so fortunate. As she descended slowly into the light of the upper hangar, 892's engineers looked on. *Oh God*, thought 'Smudge' Smith, totting up the amount of work she was going to need. There was the visible damage underneath the tail where the girder-like arrestor hook had slammed into it. But the force of the impact had sent shockwaves up through the airframe and along the wing spar. The wingtips were buckled from the extremity of the shock, but most of the damage would be invisible and internal.

Between the squadron's engineers and *Ark*'s own Air Engineering department miracles were often possible. They'd milled components for supersonic jets out of blocks of solid metal on the ship's lathes. They'd had the Chief Cook bake sheets of Perspex in the ship's bread ovens to fashion new cockpit glass for a Sea King with a shattered windscreen. They'd even fixed a leaking gearbox by having the Chief Sick Bay Attendant add 1/2000th of an inch of copper plate to the offending part by running a current through a tank of copper sulphate. But the Phantom was a slightly different beast, more stressed, more sophisticated and hugely more complicated. Panel 111 on the outer wing alone had 948 screws to contend with every time you just wanted to grease the forward flap link. And on this occasion 005 was beyond them. All they could do was carry out diagnostic checks to establish the extent of the damage, look for cracks using dye penetrant spray, fold the wings and the nose, and tuck her away in the back of the hangar until she could be lightered off at Devonport.

Ark Royal was punching above her weight. But the margins were fine. The skill, ingenuity and dedication of her people kept her flying the world-class aeroplanes that guaranteed her seat at the top table. But as much as she was the apogee of British carrier air power, she was also the final throw of the dice – a rage against the dying of the light. And from time to time there were cruel reminders of it. While operating with the USS *America* in hot, windless conditions near Bermuda earlier in the year it had been painfully apparent. John Roberts was struck hard by the ease with which the US carrier had effortlessly launched a maximum posture Alpha Strike while steaming downwind. As *Ark*'s eight old Admiralty three-drum boilers struggled for nearly fifteen minutes to generate the 29 knots necessary to launch her heavily laden aircraft from *Ark*'s short catapults, Roberts could practically *feel* his American counterpart watching, thinking: *What's the matter?*

As *Ark* pushed on defiantly into the seventies, fuelled by pride and bloody-mindedness, the US shipyard at Newport News was building two huge new nuclear-powered 'Nimitz' class supercarriers with deep load displacements of over 90,000 tons each. Capable of top speeds of 33 knots, their maximum range before they needed refuelling would be in the region of one million nautical miles.

In November, a magazine called *Flight International* carried a long article titled 'From Ark to Omega', describing operations aboard Britain's last strike carrier. Tucked towards the back of the same magazine, though, was another, smaller piece with details of the launch of a space rocket from the Anglo-Australian Long Range Weapons Establishment in South Australia. And it was this piece that, ironically, some-how better reflected *Ark*'s struggle.

Built and tested for £9 million by the British Hovercraft Corporation, Black Arrow blasted off from Woomera Rocket Range at 0409 Zulu on 28 October powered by a Rolls-Royce Gamma 8 rocket engine. Ten minutes later its payload, a 150lb satellite, reached orbital speed and Britain became the sixth country to have successfully launched her own spacecraft. It remains the only wholly British satellite placed into orbit by a wholly British rocket. The name given to the little satellite was no coincidence: Prospero, after Shakespeare's magician who, in *The Tempest*, lays down his books and gives up dominion over Earth and Sky, seemed entirely appropriate.

And in British Honduras, where the *Belize Times* and *The Reporter* had been enthusiastic and exhaustive in their coverage of the space race – where Apollo XV had been front-page news and where even an unmanned mission to Mars was guaranteed column inches – Black Arrow's successful launch went unreported. As valiant an effort as it had been on a shoe-string budget, it just didn't register.

Chapter 28

A week before Christmas, a De Havilland Comet of 216 Squadron, Royal Air Force, climbed away from Belize Airport bound for Nassau in the Bahamas. On board, Sir John Paul was leaving British Honduras for the last time. As he looked out of the window at the country's distinctive coastline and Cayes, the outgoing Governor couldn't help but wonder what the future held for the little colony. He wished it well, but, of late, the noise over independence had become increasingly loud. And that meant Guatemala's reaction was correspondingly plain. The day after Sir John's departure, the *Belize Times* reported that Guatemala's President had been forced to deny that he had made any military pact with El Salvador. It was not quite as convincing a rebuttal as, perhaps, Arana had hoped it might be.

'There is no truth,' the General claimed, 'in the assertion that we are forming a pact to take over Belize.' But he was careful with his language. 'If we need to defend our rights we shall do so with our own resources . . . the media have been saying that the government of Guatemala is planning a military operation. There is no truth in this,' he asserted. The reality, though, was more straightforward: Guatemala already *had* a plan.

John Weymes had always imagined this to be the case, even if, at the same time, he'd dismissed any possible Guatemalan military plans as no more than an inevitable contingency. But he was forced to reassess his relatively generous assumptions after he spoke to a friend. The man had felt compelled to come to Weymes to share information he'd learnt the previous evening. He'd been to a dinner party where he'd sat next to a Guatemalan doctor. In conversation, the doctor – a civilian – explained that he'd recently been called to colours by the Guatemalan Army. The reason, he told Weymes's friend, had been explicitly and specifically to provide the Army with medical support for an invasion of British Honduras. Weymes had no choice but to take the intelligence at face value. He sent an immediate confidential signal to London via the Consulate's cipher machine.

Richard Posnett pulled on a coat and left his office in King Charles Street straight away. The Minister wanted to see him. Posnett walked through the arches into the grand old premises of the Foreign and Commonwealth Office's main building and was shown upstairs and ushered in to the Minister of State's office. Joseph Godber showed him a seat, then told him that the FCO had received intelligence that the Guatemalans were preparing to invade British Honduras. He seemed almost entertained by the prospect, but couldn't, he confessed, decide on his course of action.

'Shall we,' he pondered out loud, 'send a warship, or shall we send Posnett? What do you think?' For all Godber's teasing, there seemed to be some substance to what he'd said. Posnett thought quickly about the pros and cons of an early departure before answering.

'A sudden change might startle the Guatemalans and look like a panic measure,' Posnett explained. And there was another important consideration. 'An early arrival could also jeopardize our source of intelligence in Guatemala. I think I should stick to my plans.' *And still go skiing*, he thought, smiling to himself, as he left Godber's office. Posnett was looking forward to a week's holiday in the Alps before leaving for Central America, but he was satisfied that his decision was a sound one. There was still no really hard evidence of Guatemalan intentions – no smoking gun. *Godber!*, he thought, replaying the conversation, *a warship or Posnett!* But the Minister's options were shrinking.

High on Portsdown Hill, south of Waterlooville, Fort Southwick kept watch over Portsmouth Harbour. The Victorian fort had originally been ordered by Lord Palmerston, one of a series that lined the southern coast to bolster its defences against attack from the sea. In 1942, a tunnel complex over a mile long had been carved out under the old building as it became a secure home to UGHQ – the control and communication centre for Operation OVERLORD, the D-Day landings. Now it housed FOCAS, Admiral John Treacher and his staff. Every morning they would meet to note each of their ships' location and activity. All of the Navy's carriers and amphibious assault ships, *Ark Royal*, *Bulwark*, *Fearless* and *Intrepid*, had programmes stretching out into the new year. *Eagle* did not. In a month's time, Fort Southwick would give Treacher's small team a grandstand view of HMS *Eagle* coming into harbour under her own steam for the last time. Sadness and anger at the prospect of letting her go weren't far from the surface.

Dick Lord had never seen a carrier come into port from harbour side until, in late December, he stood on the northern-most mole of Durban harbour to watch HMS *Eagle* approach. The sight of her towering grey sides gracefully easing along-side, aircraft spotted on deck and men – some old friends – standing at Procedure Alpha around her perimeter, brought a lump to his throat. Since retiring from the Royal Navy imme-diately after seeing Dougal Macdonald through his AWI Course, Lord had returned to his native South Africa with thoughts of getting a job in civil aviation. But those plans were about to take a knock. He and his wife June went aboard *Eagle* that night for a cocktail party and Lord was struck immedi-ately by the familiar noises and smells that had accompanied his twelve-year career as a carrier pilot. At once he felt at home and homesick.

He returned to the harbour to watch the great ship set sail

on her final voyage, watching until she disappeared, trailing smoke behind the Bluff, the long, low hill that protected the harbour from the south. Seeing *Eagle* again had a profound effect on the former naval aviator. He realized he was kidding himself. The skill, experience and expertise the Navy had fostered in him were too precious to discard. As he drove home from the waterfront he knew deep down that he wasn't cut out to join the airlines. Within a week he'd introduced himself to the South African Air Force. And within a year he was flying Mach 2 Dassault Mirage III CZs interceptors for 2 Squadron SAAF. *Ark Royal*'s sistership had revitalized Dick Lord's future, but her own, as she steamed north towards Portsmouth, amounted to little more than razor blades.

South Africa staked a claim to possessing one of the world's oldest air forces. But Guatemala was not far behind. And on 10 December 1971 the Fuerza Aerea Guatemalteca celebrated its fiftieth anniversary. On the same day, 809 Naval Air Squadron's two senior crews took off in clear weather from RNAS Lossiemouth on one of their last training flights of the year. While the Guatemalan F-51D Mustangs and their new Cessna A-37 Alpha attack jets impressed the audience with skilful low-level displays over their La Aurora airbase, Carl Davis and Steve Park, 'Boots' Walkinshaw and Mike Lucas, flew their Buccaneers for an hour and a half across north-west Scotland. During the sortie they combined three elements: flying in battle formation, low-level navigation and air-to-air refuelling. It was a prescient selection. The four men would need to demonstrate their proficiency in all three the next time they launched from *Ark Royal* after re-embarking in January.

The Inkerman Company were also doing their best to stay sharp, and, on the day before Christmas Eve, Richard Corkran's Grenadier Guards trained for a withdrawal battle along the Western Highway between Benque Viejo and Belize City. Its speed and mobility made the manouevre one of Corkran's favourites, but he also knew it was a rehearsal for what was likely to be no more than a last-ditch effort to harass, hold up and frustrate a numerically superior enemy.

SECTION FOUR

1972

A man-o'-war is the best ambassador

Oliver Cromwell

Chapter 29

Then, on Sunday, 9 January, a few miles up the road near Dolores, a Guatemalan Army jeep was ambushed along a narrow strip of road overlooked by steep cliffs. As the jeep passed underneath them, waiting guerrillas tossed in a hand grenade. The blast killed an officer and five soldiers. And around Poptun the killing of the army patrol felt like a worrying harbinger of what might follow.

Telegram No. 7 from Harry Lewty, the British Ambassador to Costa Rica, arrived at the Foreign Office in London on Tuesday, 11 January. It contained alarming news:

```
THE COSTA RICAN FOREIGN MINISTER HAS HAD FOR
SOME TIME INFORMATION THAT GOVERNMENTS OF
GUATEMALA AND SALVADOR WERE CONTEMPLATING
INVADING BRITISH HONDURAS AND THIS WAS
CONFIRMED WHEN . . . THE GUATEMALAN MINISTER
FOR FOREIGN AFFAIRS ASKED WHAT WOULD BE
[COSTA RICA'S] ATTITUDE IF GUATEMALA AND
SALVADOR WERE TO OCCUPY BRITISH HONDURAS BY
ARMED FORCE, PERHAPS AS EARLY AS FEBRUARY OR
MARCH.
```

During a Caribbean conference in Venezuela, Dr Herrera, the Guatemalan Foreign Minister, had approached Gonzalo Facio Segreda, the Costa Rican Foreign Minister, to gauge his reaction to a military adventure. Facio rejected their suggestion out of hand, saying Costa Rica could not possibly acquiesce in the event of any invasion of British Honduras.

But Herrera was undeterred, the telegram reported. 'Failing Central American support Guatemala and El Salvador would annex British Honduras to a Federated Guatemala and El Salvador.' *Guatemala cannot*, Herrera made clear, *tolerate an independent British Honduras*. Facio immediately informed the British Ambassador in San José.

Within hours of the arrival of Telegram No. 7, in Room 5301 MoD Main Building, the British military Chiefs of Staff were discussing repercussions of this raw, new intelligence. And the Chief of the Defence Staff, Admiral of the Fleet Sir Peter Hill-Norton, instructed his Director of Operational Planning, Brigadier Mark Bond, to provide him with details of Britain's military options. While the FCO debated Britain's response with ministers, the MoD was to make sure it was ready for whatever the government might ask of the country's armed forces.

'INDEPENDENCE BID THIS YEAR', read the headline in the *Belize Times* on 14 January. Reported back to Guatemala City by the Guatemalan Consul in British Honduras, it will have done nothing to allay fears within Arana's government. In the hiatus between Sir John Paul's departure and Richard Posnett's arrival, the Premier, George Price, had spoken increasingly indiscreetly about his ambitions for an independent Belize. And if British Honduras requested independence, it was some-thing that the British had no constitutional right to deny them. Given their public and private pronouncements, Arana and the generals – if they took seriously what Price was saying – had to act or risk humiliation.

And, as the Costa Rican Foreign Minister took great care to stress in his conversation with the British Ambassador in San José, 'Guatemala has paratroops trained for a drop on Belize.'

*

While Mark Bond's Defence Operational Planning Staff – DOPS – worked on their report, the FCO alerted British diplomats throughout Central America. This flurry of signals to and fro across the Atlantic quickly yielded results. By Friday, a telegram received from the British Embassy in San Salvador made it clear that a startled El Salvador had no wish to jeopardize their relations with the UK by taking part in any action against British Honduras. This new intelligence arrived just in time to be included in Bond's note to the Chiefs of Staff.

'This information, however,' Bond pointed out, referring to the useful development from San Salvador, 'does not exclude a threat from Guatemala.' His typed nine-page document, classified 'Secret: UK Eyes Only', was with the Chiefs on the 14th.

Peter Hill-Norton was reputed to be the rudest man in the Navy. But the gimlet-eyed old Gunnery Officer was also its fiercest defender and he wasn't afraid to use his own peculiar brand of charm to win friends and influence people in pursuit of the Navy's cause. When he became First Sea Lord in 1970, he convened a meeting with all the directors of the naval departments in advance of his first Chiefs of Staff meeting.

'I want you to know,' he told the assembled captains and rear admirals in a clipped fierce bark, 'that in these meetings, if it is in the Navy's interest for me to tell a lie and you want me to tell a lie, I am perfectly happy to do it, but the one thing I insist on is that you tell me if what you're asking me to say is a lie so that I can work round it if someone starts to bone me out a bit.' He directed the final part of his manifesto to his deputy, the Vice-Chief of the Naval Staff.

'Vice-Chief, if in about six months' time the Chief of the Air Staff comes up to me and says, "First Sea Lord, I think in that meeting we had, you told us a lie", I shall turn to him and I shall say, "Yes, I did, and do you know why? It's because I think you are such a fucking little shit." '

And now, because of the untimely death of his predecessor, Hill-Norton had been elevated to Chief of the Defence Staff. In the year and a half since his announcement had left a number of his colleagues stunned, his views were no less trenchant. As Hill-Norton read through the document on British Honduras produced by the DOPS, they informed his reaction to it.

The Joint Intelligence Committee was working on an urgent revised assessment of Guatemala's military strength, but the assumptions being worked with provided more than enough food for thought. The Guatemalan Army was believed to be well-trained by Central American standards and strengthened by considerable recent operational experience against FAR guerrillas. The Air Force too – although equipped with some ageing aircraft like the F-51 Mustangs and C-47 transports – had benefited from recent counter-insurgency missions. Almost ignored was any threat from the small number of Guatemalan Navy units stationed on their Caribbean Coast. As it turned out, they were more relevant to Guatemalan thinking than might have been imagined. Furthermore, a new 45-foot armed patrol boat, the *Tecunuman* GC 651, had been delivered at the end of November. And two more were already *en route* from American shipyards.

While the MoD waited for further corroboration of the intelligence from Costa Rica, DOPS's plans considered a range of options: from a show of force to deter the threat of armed aggression, through the implementation of Operation OPTIC, to the possibility of exceeding the force strength recommended in the OPTIC 2nd Revise.

On one thing DOPS was absolutely clear: 'The existing British Army Garrison and the British Honduras security forces are not capable of defending the country against armed aggression in force. Guatemalan forces attacking in strength would be able to occupy essential points in British Honduras in a matter of hours.' And that was whether the Inkerman Coy, 2 Grenadier Guards, executed their withdrawal battle or not.

Hill-Norton didn't dwell long on whether or not the threat was credible. In the early fifties he'd served as British Naval Attaché to Argentina. He was only too well aware of the kind of strength of feeling that underpinned a situation like the one which seemed to be coming to the boil in Central America. Neither Argentina nor Guatemala wasted any time in comparing notes on their torment at the hands of the British.

But he was drawn to the mention of HMS *Ark Royal*. Both Hill-Norton and the current First Sea Lord, Admiral Sir Michael Pollock, were former Captains of *Ark*. And the old ship seemed to have a way of not letting go of people.

The DOPS plan was quick to point out that Exercise CAD-NAM – designed to rehearse elements of Operation OPTIC – was scheduled to take place throughout February and March. It meant a further 330 Grenadiers would soon deploy to the colony. Publicizing that – along with details of Exercise SUN PIRATE, a full-scale amphibious exercise due to take place in the British Virgin Islands in late February – would bring a measure of psychological pressure to bear on the Guatemalan leadership. But, short of fully implementing Operation OPTIC, DOPS considered air power the most potent way of relaying a message about British military strength and resolve. And on this front the planners had two suggestions. RAF English Electric Canberra reconnaissance aircraft could be despatched to British Honduras to provide both a visible presence and intelligence on troop movements near the border. Or they could send *Ark Royal*. By launching a number of flights over the area, she would provide the most *effective* demonstration of military power. Hill-Norton and Pollock – a less abrasive character than his boss, but no less committed to the Navy's cause – took note.

In considering their response, Hill-Norton, Pollock and their Army and Air Force counterparts, General Sir Michael Carver and Air Chief Marshal Sir Denis Spotswood, had two main considerations: speed and resources. A successful invasion of British Honduras could be carried out, British Intelligence believed, 'with little or no warning'. From the moment the order to implement OPTIC was given it was estimated that it would take over four days for the garrison to be reinforced to battalion strength. Alongside the two companies, the Joint

Theatre Plan called for two troops of SAS, a Royal Engineers Field Troop, Signals reinforcement and two Army Air Corps pilots to fly light aircraft requisitioned locally. On call in the UK would be air-portable armour, artillery, a company of Paras, helicopters, an anti-tank platoon and a team to conduct psychological Ops. If OPTIC went ahead, four RAF Buccaneers supported by six big Handley Page Victor K2 tankers would also be on standby to deploy to Palisadoes in Jamaica. Implementing OPTIC would have serious implications for Britain's other military commitments, not least Northern Ireland. And as if it weren't evident from the long list of minutes that greeted them at every committee meeting, the planners made a point of highlighting for the Chiefs the 'conditions of overstretch pertaining in the British Army at present'.

Ark Royal, Hill-Norton realized, could offer both speed and a self-contained capability that, if deployed, would keep disruption elsewhere to a minimum. It was an irony not lost on either Hill-Norton or Pollock. It had been decreed that by 1972 Britain had no further need for carrier air power outside *Ark*'s ongoing commitment to NATO. Less than a month into that new era, it seemed, *Ark Royal* might be exactly what was required. And, two days after the news from Costa Rica, British diplomats throughout Central America were informed that *Ark* would be taking part in exercises in the Caribbean area in February.

Until more news emerged from Central America, the Operational Planning Staff could only suggest that Britain kept a sharp eye out for 'indicators' of an impending attack – cancellation of domestic airline flights in preparation for a paratroop drop, for instance. It invested rather more hope in the thought that the Americans might provide some kind of unofficial warning.

After the arrival of Telegram No. 7 from San José, Weymes, the level-headed British Consul in Guatemala City, was doing what he could to establish what was going on. Part of the job of any Consul was to set up as wide a network of contacts as possible. Because of the phonetaps, talking on an open line was difficult. But relatively innocuous conversations with British expatriate farmers and archaeologists on both sides of the border might yield information about any unusual military activity in El Petén. But for more involved enquiries, Weymes tried to set up face-to-face meetings. As a Consulate rather than an Embassy, the British mission in Guatemala City came under Swiss protection. But their maintaining strict neutrality meant there was no hope of information being channelled through the Swiss. Instead, the US Embassy in Guatemala City was John Weymes's first port of call. His contacts there across the diplomatic corps, military and CIA might, he thought, help shed some light on Guatemalan intentions. He requested authority from the FCO to share the contents of Telegram No. 7 with the American Ambassador – and to stress the possible timing of an invasion.

Then, on 17 January, a telegram arrived at the FCO from the British Ambassador in Managua. The Nicaraguan President confirmed that General Arana, Guatemala's President, had already informed him personally of his intention to occupy British Honduras. And that, while privately the Nicaraguan President sympathized with the British dilemma, he would have no choice but to lend public support to a Guatemalan attack.

As a contingency, the Chiefs decided that 2 Battalion Grenadier Guards, when they flew out to British Honduras for Exercise CADNAM, were to be equipped to fight a shooting war.

And at the Guards barracks in Caterham, forty-eight hours before he left with the exercise advance party for British Honduras, Lieutenant Colonel Richard Besly, the Battalion Commander on his way out to assume command from Corkran, was told: 'You probably don't realize this, but the Foreign Office are very worried about the situation.' He was to prepare for a long deployment. But he wasn't to tell a soul.

This is pretty odd, he reflected. A thoughtful Old

Wykehamist, Besly had been out to BH in October to get a feel
for the lie of the land before CADNAM. His main concern
then was how he might best use the time in Central America to
prepare his young Guardsmen for the rigours of the fast-
deteriorating situation in Northern Ireland that they faced on
their return. That remained his overwhelming priority, but this
new development had the potential to complicate his plans
greatly. Before flying out, he knew that, whatever his orders, he
needed to bring two people in to his confidence. He told his
wife. And he told the Quartermaster. 'I don't,' Besly explained,
'want the Company coming out with their sports kit instead of
their G1098' – their equipment. The QM told the troops they
were to play it for real.

Chapter 30

Richard Corkran was in his sitting room at Airport Camp drinking whisky with the Second Secretary. Since Sir John Paul's departure, Allan Hird had been the senior British diplomat in BH. He'd been due to go out for dinner, but Corkran's whisky proved rather too good to leave. Hird phoned to make his excuses. Later in the evening there was a knock on the door.

'Excuse me, sir, is Mr Hird here?' It was one of the soldiers from the Signals detachment. When a FLASH signal came through from the Foreign Office, after connecting his earlier phone call, they'd known exactly where to find him. Hird stared at the piece of paper, then shared it with Corkran. The crucial words were: 'GUATEMALAN ATTACK MAY BE IMMINENT'. Corkran read it with disbelief.

'What do you think your lot mean by imminent? Next month, next week or tomorrow?'

After thinking for a moment, Hird replied, 'They could mean tomorrow.'

'In that case we'd better get moving.'

The two men hurried off to wake Colonel Shipster, Commander of the British Honduras Garrison HQ. Corkran worried that Shipster, the Senior Officer, would try to get involved in the operational control of the Inkerman Company. In fact, he did just the opposite. The experienced old campaigner knew the value of leaving Corkran to run his own unit. He invited the young Major to give his own orders and

Rowland White

promised that he and his small staff would do whatever they could in support. With Shipster's blessing, Corkran left to summon his orders group.

The Sea Kings of 824 NAS clattered in to rejoin *Ark Royal* in harbour. In Flyco, familiar, well-rehearsed RT exchanges filled the airwaves as the incoming pilots flew in over the cranes, wharfs, jetties and basins of HMS *Drake*, Her Majesty's Dockyard, Devonport. Each of the dark-blue helicopters flared in turn before settling on to the main undercarriage at one of the six marked landing spots on the flight deck. Below the roar of the engines and the throbbing wumph of the main rotors, a constant stream of humanity toiled up and down gangplanks to load *Ark* with stores for the voyage – the unmistakable activity of a great ship being made ready to sail. Bar the arrival of the helicopters, its rhythm had barely changed in centuries. *Ark* was fuelled to just 91 per cent to keep her draught shallow enough for her to move safely out to sea above the bottom of the channel.

An hour and a half after the last of the eight helicopters landed, John Roberts was piped on board. Already briefed in detail by *Ark*'s Operations Officer, Commander Mike Cole, about the ship's programme over the months ahead, the affable Captain was looking forward to getting out to sea again. There were exercises with the US Navy off Norfolk, Virginia, then a trip further north for a rare visit to New York, where *Ark Royal* was due to moor for a week in the Hudson River, just upstream from the *QE2* pier. Then it was on to the Atlantic Fleet Weapons Ranges again for live weapons training.

Commuting in and out from Havant, Roberts had used the time since Christmas to catch up with his paperwork. Nothing ever stood still and there were always additions and amendments to be made to even the most-established instructions. This included his Standing Orders. The Captain of every Royal Naval ship issued his own Standing Orders. John Roberts was no exception. In the case of a large ship like *Ark Royal* it could run to a hundred or so pages of typed A4. Copies were circulated to every department and officers were expected to be familiar with them. Issues dealt with ranged from religion to procedures relating to the ship's nuclear weapons. Some of the orders were Roberts's own, but many were common to every other ship in the Navy and, in some cases, to units across all three armed services. In the section relating to Security was a list of countries it was considered dangerous to have any contact with whatsoever. No dealings with any Communist country could be considered without first discussing it with *Ark Royal*'s Security Officer. Taking a business trip to Moscow, having a penfriend in Outer Mongolia or employing an au pair from Poland were all deemed to be equally worrying. But on top of the obvious list of Soviet satellite states, there was a supplementary list of countries that, while giving less cause for concern, still required members of the Ship's Company to give at least a month's prior notice to the Security Officer before visiting them. John Roberts had never given much thought to the appearance of Guatemala on that second list. But the reason for its inclusion was about to become abundantly clear to him.

As Roberts prepared to sail, the Foreign Office requested the circulation of press releases announcing that Britain was both aware of Guatemalan intentions and capable of responding. At the same time they tried to get word to General Arana through diplomatic channels. The Nicaraguan President agreed to try to make the same point to the Guatemalan President – that Britain was capable of meeting any hostile action.

When it came to their own internal security, the Guatemalan generals had demonstrated a willingness to react with force. Now the British had to make clear that, for all their obvious enthusiasm for bringing to an end their responsibility for British Honduras and their refusal to offer a defence guarantee, they were prepared to back words with action. For if the noises coming out of the Foreign Office turned out to be no more than bluster, Arana would have learnt a very valuable lesson – that the door to Belice had been left open. On the same day,

Peter Hill-Norton wrote to the Defence Secretary, Lord Carrington, with details of MoD plans, providing an account of available British military assets. And informing him that the Guards Battalion that was about to deploy on Exercise CADNAM would be equipped for war operations.

For the British Prime Minister, Edward Heath, the possibility of becoming embroiled in a conflict in Central America was particularly unwelcome. The situation in Northern Ireland was deteriorating fast. The year had begun there with an IRA bomb in a Belfast department store that had injured fifty-five women and children. And now ITN were showing footage of the Parachute Regiment's heavy-handed approach to crowd control. Rhodesia continued to be a thorn in Britain's side. The opposition was describing his Foreign Secretary as a 'doormat for a dictator', while Bishop Muzorewa predicted that the latest agreement would bring only bloodshed. And the miners were on strike. Heath was also reaching the conclusion of his long campaign to secure Britain's membership of the European Common Market. The vote in Parliament had been won before Christmas, but the week that followed the arrival of Telegram No. 7 from San José had been spent negotiating terms. Now, the day before he was due to sign the Treaty of Brussels, Heath was given a summary of the situation in British Honduras. Attached was a copy of the new Joint Intelligence Committee assessment of the threat to the colony. Little had changed. Guatemala could launch an operation against British Honduras with very little notice; she posed a threat that was potent; and the resident infantry company 'are not capable of defending the country against the expected Guatemalan aggression'. The Prime Minister's reaction to the briefing document was succinct and to the point.

'Is MoD,' he asked, 'prepared for this?'

For Dennis Wheeler and his fellow travellers, 1972 had begun promisingly. While staying in Poptun, they'd been tipped off about a small farm for sale at Ixabel, a few miles south along the road. There were a single wooden building, twenty head of cattle and a freshwater spring on the property. They fell in love with it and for $8000 they all became the new owners of Finca Ixabel. The Peugeot, the Land Cruiser and the diesel truck were parked and the three couples got to work. Quick income was the priority, so they vaccinated the cattle, built corrals and milk chutes, planted a vegetable garden and invested in poultry. And they built a small shop. Anybody, they figured, who was adventurous enough to be travelling up and down the road between Flores and Rio Dulce, was going to be curious enough to stop and visit them as they drove past. It was all the business plan they needed.

They were working hard but on their own terms, enjoying life cut off from the pressures and demands of the rat-race. But in the second half of January their idyll was suddenly disturbed. For at Finca Ixabel, half a mile from the road, their sleep was interrupted by the roar of diesel engines, shifting gear, struggling to pull heavy loads along the unpaved, heavily rutted highway. The traffic didn't let up. For night after night a constant stream of Army 6×6 trucks ferried in and out of Poptun Army base. And the six of them knew that something significant had changed.

Chapter 31

The Grenadiers' Adjutant was enjoying a long Friday afternoon lunch with the Regiment's Major General when he
received a message telling him to report to the MoD. Shaking
off the effects of the port he walked across Horse Guards to
Whitehall.

'How long,' he was asked, 'will it take you to jack up the
Battalion with anti-tank weapons and mortars and emplane?'
Before he could respond he was given his answer. 'You've got
three days . . .'

With Besly already on his way to join Corkran and the
Inkerman Coy, the MoD wanted the Grenadiers to tear up
their careful deployment plans and get out to Central America
immediately. But by the time word got to Caterham most of
the Battalion had already left for a last weekend's leave before
their planned departure in the middle of the following week.
With the help of the Thames Valley police knocking on doors
at leave addresses everyone was back at the barracks by
lunchtime on Sunday.

Over the next forty-eight hours, while their families and
loved ones tried to keep up to date with rapidly evolving plans,
the Battalion zeroed their weapons, and drew mortars,
anti-tank rounds, mines, and ammunition for their SLRs and
General Purpose Machine Guns – GPMGs – from stores. They
were fitted with gas masks and they made wills.

British Airways flight BA501 arrived in Kingston, Jamaica, just before nine o'clock on Monday evening. Richard Posnett, his wife Shirley and their baby son Jonathan went straight to their hotel. While in Jamaica, the new Governor of British Honduras had hoped it might be possible to meet SNOWI – Senior Naval Officer West Indies – Commodore David Roome, but with his two frigates, HMS *Phoebe* and HMS *Berwick*, in port in the Bahamas, it hadn't been possible for the two men to coordinate their plans. Instead Posnett looked forward to a relaxed day on the island before flying on to take up the reins in British Honduras on the 26th. But as he and Shirley enjoyed the hospitality, Posnett was unaware of just how quickly the situation there was changing. The day in Kingston would turn out to be his last quiet day for a little while.

Richard Corkran dusted down the same plans drawn up for the withdrawal battle exercise he'd staged the other side of Christmas. But before copying and distributing them he carefully amended them from 'BLANK AMMUNITION' and 'EXERCISE SECRET' to 'LIVE AMMUNITION' and 'SECRET'. Corkran's aim was less to stop a Guatemalan advance than just to try to slow it down and frustrate it as much as possible. On the ground, the road from Benque Viejo was the only option. From the border town it ran north-east to the old capital, but it offered any attacker very little room for manoeuvre. In the lush, attractive west of the country, between the little frontier town of San Ignacio and Belmopan, the road was fringed by hills and thick jungle. As it cut across the country it became flatter and more exposed beyond the new capital. Then for the last twenty-five miles to Belize City, reasonably solid ground gave way to low-lying swamp on either side of a raised highway. There was no chance of advance except along the road. But Corkran had so few men he had to make holding the airfield – keeping it open for the arrival of reinforcement by air – for as long as he could his priority.

He sent a six-man recce section out by Land-Rover to beyond the Macal River, just six or seven miles from the border. And he hoped that, if they did have news to report, they'd actually be able to communicate it. The exercise before Christmas hadn't recommended the radios to anyone. In San Ignacio, Sergeant Eddy set about trying to mine the Hawkesworth Bridge with relish using whatever explosive material he could lay his hands on. The job was made all the more sweet for knowing that it had been named after 2nd Lt Hawkesworth's ancestor, Sir Gerald Hawkesworth, a previous Governor of the colony. Any armoured column would be forced to ford the river near the low bridge instead. Sgt Eddy loosened a few screws for good measure.

East of San Ignacio, Corkran set up his anti-tank section, protected by an infantry platoon with SLRs and mortars. Other than the indirect fire of the mortars, the L6 Wombat 120mm recoilless rifles – essentially bazookas – mounted on the back of Land-Rovers were the Inkerman Company's only heavy weapons. The Wombat's big high-explosive rounds would spoil an Armoured Personnel Carrier's day, but Corkran only had twenty-six of them. He knew that some would miss and some were likely to fail. If the Guatemalans had the thirteen armoured vehicles he was expecting, it didn't leave him much leeway.

From his map-strewn wooden office at Airport Camp, Corkran asked the Signals detachment to send the only high-priority FLASH signal of his career. If he was going to make a dent in a Guatemalan advance, he was going to need more Wombat rounds, he reported back.

The rest of his men – a single platoon – were held back to defend the airfield and camp. And things felt a little shaky there too. Armed with desperately unreliable old Browning machine guns decorated with big wire concentric-circle sights, the Guardsmen might have looked menacing, but they themselves knew that they faced an uphill battle.

'If I get a Guat pilot in these sights,' one of his men told Corkran as he inspected their positions, 'he's going to die. Laughing . . .'

Backed up by a private plan to move into the jungle to

conduct guerrilla operations if they were overrun, Corkran had done what he could with the meagre resources available to him. But he had little confidence that his Grenadiers could hold the airport in the event of a determined attack from the air. When his CO, Lieutenant Colonel Richard Besly, arrived at Belize Airport that afternoon, Corkran clambered up the ramp and scrambled through the hold of the C-130 to greet him.

'The Inkerman Company is deployed to meet the threat, sir.'

Until now, the Defence Chiefs had been soft-pedalling, waiting before doing any more than despatching the rest of 2nd Battalion Grenadier Guards stored for war and bringing forward the date of their departure by a few days. But they had plans ready to go. When they met again in the MoD at 2.45 on Tuesday the 25th, much of their work relating to British Honduras was done. The plans from DOPS had been agreed on. The Defence Secretary, Lord Carrington, had been informed by telephone that the Chiefs had approved them. And, in turn, Carrington had authorized them too. The Chiefs just needed to push the button. Then, over the next thirty-six hours, a flurry of signals traffic lit the blue touchpaper.

From Tegucigalpa, the British Ambassador confirmed that President Cruz of (Spanish) Honduras was not surprised to hear of Guatemalan plans, having, the British Ambassador imagined, been alerted to them by Arana himself when the Guatemalan President tried to enlist his support for an invasion. And there was news that Mexico agreed with the British assessment and urged 'early action to restrain Guatemala by all interested parties'. Of them, Britain was at the top of the list.

Then, on 26 January, Alec Douglas-Home sent a FLASH telegram classified 'SECRET – ECLIPSE'. The US Ambassador to Nicaragua, reported the Foreign Secretary, had been so concerned about what he'd learnt of Guatemala's plans that he'd immediately passed the information on to his British counterpart without authority from Washington. Just two days earlier, Dr Herrera, in conversation with the Nicaraguan

President, had restated Guatemala's intention to invade British Honduras. As if that weren't bad enough, the news from Managua carried a real sting in the tail. The Guatemalan Foreign Minister had made it clear that *he doubted that British forces in country were capable of resisting a Guatemalan attack*, that he seemed unaware of the seriousness or implications of an invasion. And that, in Guatemala, there was an emotional attachment to the idea of armed action.

'We cannot,' wrote Douglas-Home, 'take the risk of ignoring this further indication of possible early action.'

At 7.30 the same morning, HMS *Eagle* weighed anchor off Spithead and sailed into Portsmouth harbour, streaming a 450-foot-long paying-off pennant. Secured alongside, the great ship rang off her main engines for the last time. A large white ensign flying just ahead of the flight deck round-down stood out against the grey overcast sky clamped down across the south coast. A crowd of a few thousand well-wishers, mainly the families of the men who lined the deck, braved the grim weather and drizzle to pay their last respects. She was gone before she was ready. The thick, low cloud put paid to the planned flypast by her squadrons.

From their vantage point on Portsdown Hill, John Treacher and the FOCAS staff watched her career come to a close. It seemed an unworthy end. *Centaur, Victorious, Hermes* and now *Eagle*. The carriers were on their way out, deemed surplus to requirements. In Fort Southwick, there was a pervasive mood that reflected the gloomy weather outside. Then, at lunchtime, a signal from the MoD chattered through the teleprinter. The Chiefs of Staff were deploying *Ark Royal*.

Chapter 32

Ark had crossed the Newfoundland Ridge earlier that morning. For John Roberts, the passage so far had brought to mind *The Cruel Sea*. Gales, rough seas and icy temperatures plagued *Ark Royal*'s progress. The North Atlantic in January was living up to its reputation. Every white-knuckle Replenishment at Sea with the two Royal Fleet Auxiliaries, *Regent* and *Olmeda*, which accompanied the ship carrying liquid and solid supplies, was a reminder of the critical part played by the elements in the conduct of successful naval operations.

On a vessel the size of a strike carrier, there were few opportunities for a Captain to be truly hands on. More often it was just a case of approving the actions of others. Despite his enthusiasm for driving his ship, though, he sometimes forced himself – even during the most exacting of manoeuvres – to hand her to the Commander, Willie Gueterbock, telling him, 'It's all yours, Willie, I'll be back in my day cabin if you need me.' But not this time. With *Olmeda* keeping station fifty yards to starboard, pumping FFO – furnace fuel oil – across to replenish *Ark*'s tanks, Roberts, standing on the right of the bridge, handled the ship, looking across at the oiler and down at the sea between them. As the two ships steamed along side by side at 11 knots, the water between them, where the two wakes coming off the bows met and fought for space, was a churning, turbulent channel.

Then Roberts was interrupted by his Chief Yeoman of

Signals. Unusually, he was trying to show the Captain the clipboard away from prying eyes. Roberts thanked him and read the top signal. From CINCFLEET, the Commander-in-Chief at Northwood, it ordered *Ark* to 'PROCEED WITH ALL DESPATCH TO BRITISH HONDURAS'. The Captain was immediately struck by his reaction to the words. He'd read them in *Hornblower* novels, but had never seen them for real. After nearly a year's worth of exercises, here was a real-life operational signal. And an urgent one – there's no order that comes with higher priority. 'Mr Murrell,' he asked the signalman, 'please get the Operations Officer up here.'

In his office in the Guatemalan Ministry of External Relations, Sánchez listened to John Weymes convey British fears. He was aware of the intelligence that had been coming in via Britain's embassies throughout the region but he couldn't give an official reply until he'd spoken to Herrera.

'But speaking personally,' he added, trying to reassure Weymes, 'I cannot believe these reports of an early invasion.' But the Guatemalan official, always at pains to stress the openness of his dealings with Weymes, felt obliged to mention again that not everyone in the Guatemalan government was as reasonable as he was.

'I've never denied,' he reminded Weymes, 'in fact I've warned you, that there are diehards who regard the negotiations as so unlikely of success as to be a waste of time.' And, if success meant Guatemalan control over Belizean foreign affairs and defence, then those diehards were right.

The ascendancy of the hardliners was what was feared in London. Alec Douglas-Home regarded Herrera as a 'Dove' who, he suspected, had little influence with Arana and the generals. There had been too many occasions during the negotiations over British Honduras when it was made clear, as the Foreign Secretary put it, 'that the military are the real power in the land'. The Foreign Office feared what they described as a 'mad-dog action' from Arana. And the imminent arrival of a battalion of British soldiers carried with it an inherent risk. If they were going to act, the Guatemalan 'Hawks' had a small window of opportunity. The narrower the British could make it, the greater their chances of forestalling any aggression. Now the Army, Air Force and Navy were rushing to get forces into theatre as soon as possible to shut the window completely.

At 1335PAPA, ten minutes after receiving the signal, and with his ship's FFO tanks full, Roberts veered 10 degrees off *Olmeda*'s course, before pointing *Ark* at Central America.

Port Two Zero, revolutions One Three Zero, steer Two Two Five degrees.

A further two-page signal followed from Northwood providing more details of what was required. There was intelligence suggesting an imminent invasion of British Honduras by Guatemala. The Admiralty wanted an 'air presence' over the colony. How quickly, the Chiefs wanted to know, could *Ark* provide it?

In the chart room behind the bridge, Roberts, Wings and the ship's navigators were joined by Mike Cole, up from the Operations Room. The team pored over charts laid out on the big Admiralty Research Laboratory table. British Honduras was some 2500 miles away from them. Because of the distance and urgency there were a few vital considerations: the range of the aircraft, *Ark*'s fuel burn in reaching the earliest possible launch position, the need to reduce the wind over the deck to actually prepare the aircraft, and which route to take – and the impact that would have on the speed of the ship's passage.

The choice of route offered two possibilities. The first would take them south towards the channel between Puerto Rico and the Dominican Republic. This would mean an easier rendezvous with other ships being diverted towards British Honduras as well as unrestricted airspace. But it would take longer. While the northern route was shorter, it needed overflight rights from the Americans. Wanting freedom of action, Roberts elected to go south.

Fuel was of crucial importance. In order to maintain the greatest degree of flexibility possible, *Ark Royal* was rarely allowed to let her fuel tanks drop below about 80 per cent of their maximum. But this time there was no choice. If they maintained a speed of at least 25 knots, they could cover 600 miles a day. This would bring them to the outer limits of the range of her aircraft in forty-eight hours. But running *Ark*'s old steam turbines at the 200 rpm necessary to keep up that speed would burn FFO at over double the normal rate, reducing her best range from 7000 nautical miles to a shade over 3000. To complicate this further, they'd be driving *Ark* at speeds too great for *Olmeda* to keep station. At the kind of speeds being planned, they'd be down to about 55 per cent of their fuel by Friday evening. Even operating the engines at that speed was exceptional: 220 revolutions was the maximum – anything above 180 rpm and the engine room needed time to work up to and down from them.

Revolutions Two Zero Zero, Roberts ordered.

As *Ark*, thick black smoke billowing from her funnel, left *Olmeda* trailing in her wake, a signal arrived from the Fleet Auxiliary's Captain. 'Proceed with all despatch?' it read. 'Better bring the washing machines on line.' Roberts grinned. 'Am running on washing machines,' he countered, 'holding main engines in reserve.'

The bush telegraph tended to disseminate news throughout the ship before any official announcement was made. Sitting in the 809 Crew Room at the bottom of the island on One Deck, Carl Davis had already heard someone announce confidently that all the planned exercises were off. *What the hell's all that about then?*, he thought, unsure how much credence to give it, and keen that the effort his squadron had put into working up wasn't squandered. But something definitely seemed to be up. There was that tell-tale tremble of the engines running hard. Then the ship's main broadcast hummed.

'CO 809 report to the bridge.'

Oh Christ, he thought, *what have I done wrong now?*

*

Pilot Officer Martin Hooker was in the east hangar of the RAF Regiment's HQ at Catterick working on 48 Squadron's plans to deploy to Northern Ireland. Suddenly the hatch between his office and the CO's next door flew open.

'Do you know where British Honduras is?' his squadron Boss asked. Hooker wasn't even sure he'd heard of the place let alone be able to point it out on a map.

'No, sir,' he answered.

'Neither do I. Find out where it is!' And the hatch was whipped shut again.

The Royal Air Force's own army, the RAF Regiment, was formed in 1942 specifically to provide airfield defence after Churchill had announced the previous year that 'Every airfield should be a stronghold of fighting air-groundmen . . . expected to fight and die in the defence of their airfields.' By the war's end it had acquitted itself well in every major theatre, not least Burma, where its contribution was crucial. And in the process it provided the first Allied officer into Berlin after its capture by the Soviets and earned itself a nickname: 'The Rock Apes'. It was rumoured that Goebbels had heard the legend that when the Barbary Apes left Gibraltar the British Empire would crumble, and, as a result, he planned to mount a commando raid to wipe them out. At the very least, imagined the Nazi propaganda chief, it would dent British morale. The Rock's RAF Regiment Flight was the unit entrusted with the animals' protection.

Now, 48 Squadron was the RAF Regiment's only Tiger Cat missile unit. Wire-guided and relying on a series of observation posts to provide advance warning of an attack, the Tiger Cat was, despite being new into service, a relatively limited system. Certainly less well-suited to defending an airfield than its naval equivalent, Seacat, was to defending a ship, it was none the less easily air-transportable. The big Bofors cannons and their heavy-calibre shells used by the rest of the RAF Regiment's Low-Level Air Defence squadrons would have tied up the Hercules fleet for days. And, in any case, the Tiger Cat wasn't going to be entirely without potential against the aircraft of the Fuerza Aerea Guatemalteca.

In taking the original decision to buy Tiger Cats to supplement the Regiment's Bofors Triple 'A' squadrons, the MoD had considered their utility against Indonesian P-51 Mustangs during the Confrontation of the mid-sixties. Now the MoD planned to send the Tiger Cats to defend Belize International Airport from the same piston-engined threat.

Hooker dug out the Op Order for Operation OPTIC but quickly realized he was going to have to work around it. While it suggested deploying to British Honduras with oil heaters – average January temperature 84°F – it contained no maps. An atlas soon put him out of his misery.

At RAF Wittering, the CO of 1 (Fighter) Squadron, Wing Commander E. J. E. Smith, had only been in the job for three weeks when his Harrier squadron was brought to readiness to deploy to British Honduras. The unique vertical take-off and landing Hawker Harrier GR1 was the only RAF fast jet able to safely operate from the 5000-foot runway at Belize International – especially given the certainty of heat and rain. The plan was to deploy four of the little attack jets to British Honduras. The issue, though, was getting them there. The only certainty on the 26th was that air-to-air refuelling would have to play a part. Under their new Boss, 1(F)'s pilots and engineers began to plan.

Chapter 33

'What do you think of this, Carl?' John Roberts asked his squadron Boss. 'We've got this signal. There's been a request that we show a presence over here.' And the Captain pointed at the Yucatán Peninsula. Between them, the group studying the charts had decided this was a job for the 809. Wings and Mike Cole, a former fast-jet Observer, had a good handle on the kind of range they could expect from the jets. Load up the Phantoms with drop tanks and there wasn't a lot in it, but the robust Buccaneers still shaded it and, when it boiled down to it, were less likely to go unserviceable just at the wrong moment than the more sophisticated, temperamental supersonic fighters.

'Can we do it?' Roberts asked.

'What, from here? What sort of distances are we talking about?' Carl Davis looked at the map, measuring out the distances involved and making quick mental calculations. Since the initial decision to take the southern route, informal permission had come through from the Americans allowing *Ark*'s aircraft to cut through the Southern ADIZ. Roberts had quickly altered course on to the shorter northern route that would take them through the Florida Straits.

'Off the top of my head, from here' – Davis jabbed at a point in the sea – 'if we fit a belly tank and we've got drop tanks, we can do it there and back with a refuelling, or maybe two refuellings. But we're not going to have much time at low level at the other end. Give me a few minutes and I'll go and check with SOBS and my AEO to see what the sums add up to.'

'Can we say we can do it?' Roberts asked, wanting to confirm his ability to act.

'Of course we can do it!'

As Davis made his way down the ladders and hatches from the bridge in search of Mike Kinch, 809's Air Engineering Officer, the unexpected nature of the request suddenly struck Mike Gretton, *Ark*'s 2nd Navigator. 'What the hell are we doing!' He smiled, drawing everyone's attention to the fact that *Ark* now seemed to be engaged in the business of Buccaneer diplomacy. Like Davis, Gretton was another officer who'd made a good impression on John Roberts through his prowess with a cricket bat. But his initial reaction to being appointed to *Ark Royal* had been disappointment. A Salthorse – a non-specialist – with ambitions to drive ships, he'd wanted to be Navigator aboard a frigate or destroyer rather than number two aboard a huge carrier. But after arriving he realized just what was riding on the job he did.

Before every sortie, aircrews had to sign for the ship's PIM – its Position and Intended Movement. And in the days before global positioning satellites it was an inexact science. The margin of error accepted was twenty miles. When it came to electronic navigation aids there were two and the most accurate of them, Decca, only worked close to shore. The other, Loran Charlie, used signals transmitted from shore-based beacons to provide coverage across the whole Atlantic. It was a useful indicator but could suffer from big errors. That left dead-reckoning, updated by star fixes at dawn and dusk. Every morning and evening, whatever the weather, Gretton would head up and outside on to the roof of the bridge to take an astro-fix using a sextant. And that assumed there was no cloud. Sometimes days might go by without being able to confirm the ship's accurate position and that meant relying on the accuracy – or not – of the Ship's Log, an instrument on the bottom of the ship's hull that recorded the speed through the water. That, along with the ship's direction, was fed into the Admiralty

Research Laboratory table in the chart room which displayed it on the flat surface using a gyroscopically guided spot of light. Without morning stars and night stars, any positional error displayed on the ARL table grew exponentially.

If the Buccaneers were going to be flying to British Honduras and returning low on fuel to *Ark Royal* in the mid-Atlantic with no hope of any possible diversion, making sure that 'Mother' was where he said she was going to be assumed a critical importance.

The AEO of 809 Squadron, Lieutenant Commander Mike Kinch, was the first cadet ever to achieve 100 per cent in his entrance examinations to Dartmouth. Now a card-carrying member of MENSA, he brought his unrivalled brain to bear on any engineering challenge faced by the Buccaneer squadron. Such were his subtlety and academic ability he sometimes left Carl Davis struggling to keep pace with his working, and pleading instead simply for the bottom line. This time, though, it was a relatively straightforward request. In the cramped confines of his cabin on Four X-Ray, Davis explained what they'd been asked to do. Nothing was set in stone.

'Look, Mike, this is what's probably going to happen. We'll need three aircraft with drop tanks and belly tanks, and I'll want two tankers. Can we configure the aeroplanes like that?'

Kinch considered it as his squadron Boss outlined the scenario. 'I think we might just have enough if we take it out—'

'I don't care what you take it out of, Mike, can we do it?'

'Yes, we can. But it'll take time. How soon?'

'Might be quite soon. Look, don't do anything now. Just go find the gear and I'll let you know as soon as I know.'

Kinch gave the squadron Boss a wry smile and left to make his way forward to the lower hangar.

Next, Davis summoned SOBS and SPLOT. Steve Park, his Senior Observer, needed to help him flesh out the planned sortie before he went back to the bridge and he wanted 'Boots' Walkinshaw to organize the squadron. All activity would revolve around British Honduras for the next few days for sure. That in itself needed planning. But, in the back of his mind, Davis knew that the first mission might not be the only flight south. In allocating the tasks, SPLOT needed to keep experience in reserve for the prospect of follow-up sorties.

When Park arrived, Davis had an aviation chart of the western Atlantic spread out on the small desk in his cabin.

'Steve' – he ushered in his Observer and pointed at the Yucatán – 'we're going here. In average weather conditions can we do that?' The two of them went through the sums. In its eight internal fuel tanks, the Buccaneer carried over 12,000lb of fuel. Even supplementing that with another 7000lb plus between slipper tanks fitted under the wings and the big overload tank in the bomb bay, they'd still need to take on significant amounts of further fuel from a tanker on the way out *and* on the way back. But, assuming Mike Kinch gave them the nod, that could be done.

'So we spend ten minutes at low level. And we arrange a top-up here' – Park had marked a spot over the Atlantic, 600 miles south-west of Bermuda – 'and a top-up there' – he gestured towards the Bahamas. The sketched-out flight plan gave them a good safety margin. Assuming *Ark Royal* took them 1200 miles in the right direction over the next forty-eight hours, they could go at lunchtime on the 28th. From Four X-Ray, the ship certainly felt as if she was doing her best to get them to where they needed to be.

'Right, Steve,' Davis concluded, 'I want you to produce a map for all the crews.'

And as far as the strike pair – the four men who'd fly the brace of Buccaneers on the marathon mission – were concerned, the squadron Boss made up his mind quickly. He wasted no time breaking the news to 'Boots' Walkinshaw.

'You and I will go,' Davis told his Senior Pilot. 'Who do you want to drive the tankers?'

Richard Posnett and his wife, Shirley, were packed and ready to leave for the final leg of their journey to Belize City. Their flight out of Jamaica departed at lunchtime. But just before leaving their hotel, Posnett was given a message asking him to stop at the High Commission Office *en route* to the airport. They were sending a car. After the short drive across Kingston, with Shirley holding baby Jonathan, they pulled up at the British mission. The new Governor was handed a FLASH telegram:

```
A FURTHER REPORT TO WHICH WE ATTACH
CONSIDERABLE RELIANCE HAS NOW BEEN RECEIVED
THAT OUTSIDE CONTEXT OF POSSIBLE EARLY
INDEPENDENCE GUATEMALANS ARE SERIOUSLY
CONSIDERING AN EARLY INVASION OF BRITISH
HONDURAS. THE ATTACK MAY EVEN BE IMMINENT.
```

For the first time, Posnett began to take the whole situation a little bit more seriously. He just hadn't given much credence to the Minister's jocular suggestion before Christmas that he might leave early. *Perhaps*, he thought to himself, *I've been rather over-confident*. He showed the signal to Shirley. They looked at each other, not really knowing what to make of it.

'Let's see what happens,' Shirley suggested phlegmatically. Her husband agreed. There didn't seem much else to do except head for the airport and hope for the best.

A Lockheed C-130 Hercules of 36 Squadron RAF had already been airborne for an hour carrying the first twenty-seven Grenadiers on the third leg of their journey from RAF Lyneham. With short hour-and-a-half refuelling stops in the Azores and Bermuda, the journey was a near 24-hour haul to the exhausting accompaniment of the relentless throbbing drone of four Allison turboprop engines.

In November, after the terrible crash of a Hercules in Italy, in which all fifty-two on board had been killed, RAF Air Support Command's mixed bag of Vickers VC-10s, De Havilland Comets, Bristol Britannias, Shorts Belfasts and C-130s had been flat out. They had had to cope with the withdrawal from the Near and Far East, the evacuation of

British subjects from the subcontinent after the outbreak of war between India and Pakistan and, just this week, a secret night flight to deliver the priceless golden funeral mask of Tutankhamun from Cairo to Brize Norton for a landmark exhibition at the British Museum.

Now, an eagerly anticipated VC-10 deployment to California had been cancelled so that 10 Squadron could scatter C-130 slip crews at island airbases around the Atlantic in support of the British Honduras operation. And the 36 Squadron flight inbound from Bermuda to Belize was just the first. Over the next four days, after recalling aircrew from leave, three Hercules squadrons would be flying fourteen sorties, carrying men and materiel, in and out of Belize International.

Chapter 34

News about what was being planned spread throughout *Ark Royal's* crewrooms almost by osmosis before any kind of official announcement was made. But it wasn't until he spoke with Steve Park that Mike Lucas knew he was going. The two Observers immediately set out to plan in more detail. For this one, they'd need to tap CBALS for maps of where they were going. *Ark's* small embarked army unit, 55 CBGLO, bore responsibility for looking after about one and a half million maps kept on board that covered every inch of overland territory across the globe. The thought of being handed an operational tasking couldn't help but get the adrenalin going. *Good to be doing something for real*, Lucas reflected, *as opposed to throwing bombs at big old lumps of rock in the sea.* And it certainly helped put the fun back into a long, dull transatlantic crossing.

After an hour in the hangar, Mike Kinch gave Carl Davis the answer he needed: 'We've got all the gear. We can do it.' Davis made his way back up to the bridge, taking with him the rough plan he'd worked out with Park.

'From 1300 miles, from here,' Davis told Roberts and the gathered heads of department, '809 could get a pair of jets to British Honduras and spend ten minutes overhead making their presence felt.'

'Right, that's it,' Roberts said. 'Thank you, Carl.' He knew he'd been gifted a golden opportunity to show what his ship could do. Within two hours of the FLASH signal arriving on board *Ark*, Roberts confirmed to the MoD that he could have

Buccaneers over Belize City by Friday afternoon. And he requested confirmation of his clearance to overfly US airspace. The two-page signal that had followed the initial order had made it clear that American feelings about a British show of strength in Central America were a little ambivalent, to say the least.

TACA Airlines flight TA751 flew across the Caribbean Sea from Jamaica towards Belize City. Shirley Posnett seemed unruffled at the prospect of what might lie ahead. But then, she had enjoyed more stressful flights than this as an air hostess for BOAC and its predecessors, not least when she flew across the Atlantic with Churchill *en route* to one of his meetings with Roosevelt. As the Vickers Viscount cruised west, Richard Posnett caught the eye of one of the stewardesses and asked quietly if he might go up to the flight deck and have a word with the airliner's Captain. He was ushered forward, introduced himself and pulled the telegram he'd received in Kingston out of his pocket.

'What's this all about?' queried the American pilot as he read the words of Sir Alec Douglas-Home, the British Foreign Secretary.

'Just make sure that the British are in control of the airfield before you land. If there's any doubt, stay clear,' Posnett warned, before adding, 'Don't worry about anything else!' and returning to his family.

As *Ark Royal* leant into the swell, burying her bows deep in a head sea on the starboard bow, green water rolled back along the flight deck while spray was thrown high up into the air, a hundred feet and more above the waves. The seas were getting rougher and, as the 50,000-ton ship pounded forward at 24 knots, the thump and thud of the hull colliding with heavy slabs of water reverberated through the ship. In the aircrew cabins below the quarterdeck, low in the ship's stern, the pitching motion would sometimes be punctuated by the roar of a shaft racing as one of the huge manganese bronze screws found only air to spin against. Those aircraft that couldn't be accommodated in the hangars were ranged aft, lashed to the flight deck away from the bows to enjoy the relative protection afforded by Fly 2, 3 and 4. It was only relative, though. No one would choose to park multimillion-pound jets exposed to the salt, spray and weather of the North Atlantic, but there just wasn't the space in the hangars to shelter the entire air group.

At 2.30 p.m., wearing a lightweight suit with a handkerchief tucked into his breast pocket, the fair-skinned new Governor stepped off his plane into the heat. He was the first passenger to disembark. Waiting to greet him were the Premier, George Price, Rafael Fonseca, who'd been acting-Governor since Sir John Paul's departure, and other local dignitaries, including the Chief Justice, Mayor of Belize City and Commissioner of Police. But only one of the reception committee waiting for him on the Tarmac had any idea of what was developing in the background. As he made his way down the line he reached the blond, uniformed figure of Colonel John Shipster. The two of them shook hands and Posnett leaned towards him.

'I think,' he suggested with a smile, 'we ought to have a talk.'

'Yes, sir,' Shipster replied, knowing there were still hours of formalities to endure before they might get that chance.

After a brief series of press interviews, the whole party embarked on the grinding fifty-mile journey to Belmopan for the swearing-in ceremony. For the first few miles, across Haulover Bridge, and along the river to Belize City, progress was swift. Then they hit the dirt road that took them the rest of the way to the new capital.

It was four hours before the Governor finally got his opportunity to speak to Shipster. Throughout the ceremony at Belize House, he had done his best to behave as though everything was normal, all the time knowing that he not only had to speak with his military commander, but also had to bring George Price into the equation. Conveying the news to the government of British Honduras had been a job saved for Posnett on his arrival.

George Price calmly greeted the revelation that there was intelligence suggesting Guatemala were threatening to invade his country. In fact, he wasn't surprised. Posnett got the impression that the neat, bespectacled Premier had always thought that it was a realistic possibility. It was the new Governor, in country for just a few hours, who was at a disadvantage. 'I'll keep you informed,' he promised Price, 'but things do seem to be getting a little hot . . .'

Then, finally, Posnett got to sit down with his Garrison Commander. And while they spoke a Hercules carrying the first of the Grenadiers deploying to BH disgorged its load of men and supplies at Stanley Field.

After his morning meeting with Sánchez, John Weymes read the telegram telling him *Ark Royal* was on her way. He wasn't at all sure how news of her despatch would break in Guatemala City, whatever hastily cooked-up explanation accompanied her arrival. That afternoon, he was summoned urgently back to the Ministry of External Relations by Sánchez. The mild-mannered Geordie diplomat was immediately struck by the demeanour of his contact in the Belice office. Sánchez seemed caught in the middle: an open, engaging man who now felt his own honour was at stake. Whatever was going on was doing so on his watch and he couldn't help but be anxious about his responsibility for that. Sánchez told Weymes that he'd conveyed their earlier conversation to Arana himself.

'I'm under instructions to assure you that no plan exists at present for the occupation, immediate or otherwise, of Belice by force.' It was what Weymes was expecting, and yet not, given how temperatures seemed to be rising so inexorably, as reassuring as it should have been – especially followed by Sánchez's personal account of his President's mood.

'I sensed,' he said of his meeting with Arana, 'a determination not to accept lying down the independence of Belice . . . no matter what the cost.' And this once more exposed the heart of the crisis. The Guatemalans feared that independence was in the air. They had to demonstrate a willingness to use force in order to ensure that their position was not simply ignored. But if, as it seemed they now feared, that posture was not taken sufficiently seriously to prevent independence being granted, then they had no option but to act. Or lose. The long-planned deployment of the Grenadiers was, Sánchez told Weymes, 'an unfriendly gesture . . . tantamount to the presence of foreign troops on national soil'. News that *Ark Royal* was on her way was not, Weymes reflected, going to be embraced with much enthusiasm.

'Could troop movements in the Petén have possibly led to reports at the frontier?' Weymes pushed, looking for clarification on Guatemalan Army dispositions. But Sánchez again suggested that there were none. Troops had been deployed near the Mexican border to hunt guerrillas, but, he stressed, 'well away from the Petén'. In the climate that existed, it was hard for Weymes not to harbour a measure of doubt about what he was being told, and what, at the highest levels of Arana's government, was being considered.

As background, the MoD's Joint Theatre Plan 60, Operation OPTIC, had noted that an attack on British Honduras could follow a period of rising tension. And that there was every likelihood that that Guatemalan troop movements could be linked to 'preventative action on a small scale against Communist insurgents'.

From Finca Ixabel, deep inside the Petén, Dennis Wheeler watched a heavily armed platoon of soldiers come right through the main gate of his farm. Up and down the road to Flores, khaki-green diesel 6×6s from Poptun barracks were dropping off similar units of a dozen men. Each of the patrols then headed into the Petén jungle.

Chapter 35

As the sun dropped below the horizon off *Ark*'s starboard bow, John Roberts made a broadcast on the ship's CCTV system to explain that the carrier had been ordered to divert to British Honduras in response to reports of possible Guatemalan aggression. He wanted to capture the attention of his Ship's Company. To let them know that whatever job they were doing, it made a difference to *Ark Royal*'s ability to do the job. But in the lower hangar, the home of 809 Squadron's Buccaneers, the engineering team on the graveyard shift missed it all. Eight hours in 'The Hole' was a good way of dodging news from the outside world.

'Welcome to the Mushroom Farm', read the sign on the bulkhead, 'kept in the dark and fed on shit.' The 809 hangar smelt of sweat, hydraulic fluid and Avcat. Facing aft, with wings folded, radomes and airbrakes open at 90 degrees to the fuselage, eight Buccaneers sat storm-lashed to the deck. There was just enough space to make your way between the bombers. But to do so you had to pick your way around hydraulic rigs, air-conditioning rigs and the ninety-six heavy chains that fought to keep the jets rooted to the spot. Around the hangar walls were tanks of liquid oxygen, four spare Spey engines and rails for the underwing slipper tanks. Also squeezed in at deck level were the two Land-Rovers used by CBALS and the Captain's car, a Rover. Just a couple of feet's clearance separated the tops of the Buccaneers' tails from the deep steel beams of the hangar roof. And between the beams more space was eked out for spares like CFDUs, flaps and ailerons, and for the bomb bay tanks, separated and stored in four different cells.

Once Carl Davis had given him the go-ahead, 809's engineering boss got his late-night shift on the case. Ron Sandry, Wiggy Bennett, Jimmy Doyle and Sandy Sanderson were all there.

It's going to be a long night, laughed Sandry, to himself.

The Squadron always kept two of its fourteen Buccaneers set up as maxi-tankers. These aircraft were kept permanently configured with both bomb bay tanks and FR Mk 20 Buddy refuelling pods under the starboard wing. On top of this, a couple more Cabs were assigned the role of mini-tanker. They still had the Buddy pods under the wings but not the overload tanks in the bomb bay. The mini-tankers could be scrambled in a fix, but had far less fuel available to transfer to anyone who needed a top-up. Now, Carl Davis still wanted three maxi-tankers – that meant installing a bomb bay tank into one of the minis – but he was also after something else entirely: a pair of Buccaneers loaded with nothing but as much fuel as they could carry. That meant stripping two jets down to near clean condition before more or less rebuilding them as tankers. But instead of that Buddy pod under the starboard wing, Kinch explained, the squadron Boss wanted a second slipper tank.

For the strike pair, two of the Buccaneers configured to fire Bullpup missiles were chosen. The engineers removed the launchers and pylons before bolting a slipper tank to each of the port inboard weapons stations. The cells of the bomb bay tanks were taken down from the hangar roof, assembled and attached to the door of the Buccaneer's rotating bomb bay. Once the bomb bay door was rolled closed, the only evidence of the 440-gallon tank was the 'donkey plonk' hanging out of the back of the jet's belly to vent excess fuel. The big overload tank then needed to be filled with fuel and pressure-tested.

Here we go, thought Sandry, the Petty Officer with particular responsibility for the Buddy pods, as he and the lads winched the first of them up to the starboard pylon on a

C-type hoist. Shaped like a large bomb, the pod had a small propeller on the nose to generate the power it needed to function and, at the back, ended in the shuttlecock-shaped basket that it trailed on a long hose behind it for thirsty customers. Sandry reminded them to be careful. Act like a bull in a china shop at this point and the frangible glass pillars through which the fuel flowed into the pod would shatter. He attached the 60-pin electrics.

As the banter flew around the hangar through the night, *Ark* pushed on through rolling seas. And as they worked, Sandry and the rest of the 809 engineers almost subconsciously anticipated her movement through the water, riding, not struggling against, her rhythm. And none of them was quite sure yet what this was even all in aid of.

'Boots' Walkinshaw hadn't had cause to think about British Honduras for a decade. After his run ashore there as a young sub-lieutenant in 1959, he'd been dimly aware of the destruction caused by Hurricane Hattie, but since then it had been entirely off the radar. Now, as he planned a long-range mission over the colony, he half remembered conversations from a Governor's drinks party about threatening neighbours. Walkinshaw had to decide who should fly the tankers. For launching a sortie from the middle of the Atlantic he needed experienced, non-diversion-qualified crews, but, equally, he wanted to keep some senior crew in hand, possibly to lead another sortie over British Honduras the day after he and Carl went. At the moment, it was impossible to predict how things would play out.

'Boots' looked at each of the squadron's four divisional leaders. He and the Boss accounted for two of them. Then there were Ian Frenz, the squadron Qualified Flying Instructor, and Neil 'Carbo' Maclean, the squadron's bearded, punchy Air Warfare Instructor. Maclean had been on the squadron longer and Walkinshaw opted for the senior man to lead the tanker section. He'd keep Frenz back to lead the strike pair for the planned sortie on the 29th. Next to 809's AWI, Walkinshaw opted for Pete Lewis and his Observer, George Dammeyer. Walkinshaw put the names against the next day's flying programme that had come down from Ops and got it pinned up on the noticeboard.

John Roberts had insisted that all four aircraft and crews taking part in the mission on Friday get airborne the day before. Not only did they need to prove the integrity of the refuelling systems now being worked on in the Mushroom Farm, but they had to get some deck landing practice. The Captain was conscious of the fact that other than when they re-embarked five days ago, none of his squadrons had flown the deck since the first week of December. Each of the pilots would have been through a series of MADDLs – Mirror Assisted Dummy Deck Landings – using the runways at their respective shore stations, but that had been it in the seven weeks since they'd disembarked before Christmas. Skills had a habit of degrading fast and Roberts wanted to minimize the possibility of any of the four Buccaneers he was launching on an urgent, high-profile mission failing to recover safely on board. As well as checking that some deck landing practice had been built into the sortie, he was also intrigued to see George Dammeyer's name on the flying programme. And he made a mental note to inform the MoD of the fact that 809's American exchange officer would be involved. *We don't*, he thought, *want to be party to another international incident while we're already dealing with one.*

After reporting the detail of his second conversation with Sánchez, Weymes sent a FLASH signal to the FCO alerting them to the effect he feared *Ark*'s arrival off the coast off British Honduras might have in Guatemala. Arana had already reacted badly to the imminent arrival of 200 light infantrymen. Now, as well as *Ark*, the guided-missile destroyer HMS *London*, frigates HMS *Phoebe* and HMS *Dido*, and an RAF Regiment Tiger Cat missile squadron were on their way too. 'They are likely,' he wrote, 'to regard the appearance of a task force as lack of faith in their word and a smack in the face.'

The British Consul worried that the reaction to a strike carrier might be extreme, strengthening the hand of hardliners against those who favoured negotiation. The trouble was that anything Arana and the Army might have planned – or even be teeing up – was entirely deniable. The only way the British government could be sure of dealing with it was indeed by showing sufficient lack of faith to make clear their resolve to defend British Honduras. If lack of faith worked, then a smack in the face wouldn't be necessary. Regardless of how much it might upset the generals, the British had to crush any vestigial hope they had of successful military action against their neighbour – however tenuous or unlikely it might be. And shoring up the defence of the airfield at Belize City appeared to be the best way of doing this.

The trouble was that nearly all of Britain's planning assumptions were wrong. Neither the Joint Intelligence Committee assessment nor the plans for Operation OPTIC had entertained any real doubt about how and where a Guatemalan attack might come. No one had given much thought to the possibility that the Guatemalans would try to do anything other than secure the airfield. Except, that is, the Guatemalan planners.

Chapter 36

Only the overflight of Punta Gorda by a single Fuerza Aerea Guatemalteca F-51 Mustang and the paratroop exercise near the southern British Honduras border at Puerto Modesto Méndez had provided any real clue. But the Guatemalans hoped, if possible, to avoid the British altogether.

Mounting an opposed invasion down the Western Highway was a logistical nightmare. Even against the relatively modest defence offered by a company of British soldiers, it was a long way to take the Guatemalans' motley collection of Second World War-vintage surplus American armour. Just trying to use the unreliable old tanks, armoured cars and APCs probably posed a greater barrier to success than any potential British military resistance.

Instead, Guatemalan planners focused their attention on Toledo District in the south. Not only was this region at the heart of Guatemala's historical claim on her neighbour's territory, but it also offered a greater chance of success. Toledo district was isolated, undeveloped and inaccessible. The 2000 inhabitants of Punta Gorda, the only town in the region of any conceivable significance, were connected to the rest of the country by a nine-hour drive along nearly 200 miles of dirt road and an unpaved 2500-foot airstrip that practically ran through the centre of the town just a couple of hundred yards further inland than the main street. Or by sea.

And the closest major city to Punta Gorda by sea was the deepwater port of Puerto Barrios on Guatemala's Caribbean coast. Unlike its neighbour twenty miles across the Bahia de Amatique, Puerto Barrios benefited not just from the excellent Atlantic Highway, but also from a railway line and an airport with a long Tarmac runway built by PanAm.

In terms of conquest Toledo District didn't offer much: low-lying swamps criss-crossed by tidal rivers lined with mangrove swamps. No resources, no industry. And, despite the best efforts of nineteenth-century Confederate settlers to try to re-create their antebellum plantations after defeat in the American Civil War, precious little agriculture either. But for Guatemala it wasn't about riches – it was about justice.

It was also a formidably difficult place to take and hold ground, but it did play to Guatemala's strengths. For years her Army had been fighting in the jungle against the guerrillas, supported by a small but skilled and experienced force of FAG helicopters. And whatever challenges Toledo District presented to a Guatemalan force trying to take and hold ground it also dealt in spades to a British force trying to dislodge them. Unlike the route down the Western Highway, where an invading Guatemalan column had to expose its flanks and place the logistics chain under greater strain with every mile closer it got to its prize, the land between Punta Gorda and the Sarstoon River border was back-stopped by Guatemala itself, just twelve miles away to the south and twenty to the west.

All that stood between Punta Gorda and Guatemalan occupation was a small police station. And even that was pretty low key, given that the Chief of Police claimed that 'there is no crime in Punta Gorda, only marijuana'. Using 300 paratroopers, supported by Air Cavalry in the helicopters and the F-51D Mustangs of the Escuadrón de Caza flying out of either jungle strips or Puerto Barrios, the remote little town could be taken quickly and easily. Then, from Punta Gorda, Guatemala could reinforce the whole region by air and sea before the British, confined to Belize City except by Land-Rover or small boat, would be able to do anything about it. *At all.*

Having secured their parcel of land with what might even

have been a completely bloodless operation, the plan was to stop there and call for negotiations. 'Liberating' the south of British Honduras was a plan – simple, manageable and realistic – that offered every chance of permanent success. And, by luck rather than judgement, *Ark Royal*, with her air group of fast jets and, crucially, helicopters offering troop mobility, was the only component of the British reinforcements converging on the Caribbean that provided the British with any way of stopping it before it was too late to undo. Without *Ark*, if the Guatemalans chose to give their invasion plan the green light, Britain would be dealing with a *fait accompli*. The political price of a military eviction was likely to be too high. Protests, however persistent, would be unlikely to succeed. And General Arana would have for ever secured his place as a hero at home and throughout Central America.

Chapter 37

'THREAT TO B. HONDURAS – ARK ROYAL SAILS', announced the headline in the *Financial Times*. On Thursday morning, as *The Times* and the *Daily Telegraph* both carried pictures of a forlorn-looking HMS *Eagle* in Portsmouth Harbour, the Pink 'Un broke the story. There were reports, the article continued, 'of Guatemalan troops concentrating on the border.' The MoD was caught on the hop. *Ark Royal's* despatch had been leaked, not announced, and now they were pedalling furiously to seize control of the story. By lunchtime, the *Evening Standard* was reporting the 'Caribbean Alert' too. In an effort to try to keep a lid on speculation, the MoD sent out a press release explaining that *Ark Royal* was simply taking part in Exercise CADNAM. And that her visit to the colony had absolutely nothing to do with Guatemala. Following her long-planned support of the British Honduras garrison, the MoD explained, the carrier would be taking part in multinational exercises with the Americans off Puerto Rico before heading north to New York. 'And,' a Foreign Office spokesman added emolliently, 'there are no reports of troops massing in New York.'

Both the MoD and the FCO were, for understandable reasons, trying to play down the seriousness with which they regarded the situation. But in doing so they were being disingenuous. There had never been any plans to involve *Ark Royal* in Exercise CADNAM. And, in recognizing their own readiness to say one thing while doing another, there was absolutely no reason for them to suspect that Guatemala would be any different. Each side's actions and utterances only confirmed in the mind of the other their worst suspicions.

Through the night, the sea state fluctuated between 5 and 6 – between rough and very rough – as *Ark* crashed into the thick swell at a shade off 25 knots. Off the starboard bow, south-westerly winds reaching Force 9 pulled the crests off 20-foot waves and they toppled, tumbled and rolled around the ship as she drove forward at a steady 200 revolutions. *Ark Royal* was paying a price for her determined progress to the south-west. Heavy weather and a relative wind of nearly 70 knots over the deck had taken their toll. And as the sun came up on the 27th John Roberts took stock of the damage to his ship. Two whip aerials and a boom had been ripped off. So too had a number of guardrails, mainly down the starboard side. But the buckled Three Tango boat deck that housed both a 45-foot motor launch and a 35-foot fast motor boat provided the clearest evidence of the power and weight of the sea. Located immediately aft of the Shipwright's workshop, two-thirds of the way down *Ark*'s starboard side, the crumpled steel was a particularly cruel memento to leave right on the doorstep of the department responsible for the physical maintenance and repair of the ship.

As *Ark* ploughed across the Atlantic towards British Honduras, at RAF Wittering 1(F) Squadron's engineers worked to prepare four of their Harriers to make the same journey. With the jump jet's relatively limited range, the job of bolting the prominent refuelling probes to the port intake and fitting the big 330-gallon drop tanks on the inboard wing pylons was non-negotiable. The initial plan was to try to make the journey non-stop with tanker support from the Victor tankers of 55 and 57 Squadrons at RAF Marham, but this evolved into a three-stage journey – still supported by a smaller number of tankers – with stops in the Azores and Bermuda.

At another RAF station in Cambridgeshire, the third

component of the Air Force's contribution to the Caribbean reinforcement was planning a similar route.

Squadron Leader John Morgan got the word on the 26th. It wasn't great timing. He was sure he was sickening for something. He even visited the Doc to see what was up, but it didn't seem serious enough to affect the planned deployment. So it was on for the following day.

'I'm off in the morning,' he'd told his wife Shirley, 'just heard we're going to the West Indies. Don't know when I'll be back.'

'Oh, all right,' she'd answered, used to her husband's peripatetic existence. Like the RAF's transport squadrons, the English Electric Canberra PR7s and PR9s of 39 (Photo Reconnaissance) Squadron, RAF Wyton, enjoyed deployments throughout the world. January had already seen one of the crews fly a 'Lone Ranger' to Hong Kong via Cyprus, the Gulf, Gan in the Indian Ocean, and Singapore. And just the previous year Morgan himself had led a detachment sent to the Far East to conduct a photographic survey of West Borneo immediately after a trip to Kenya. And now, at less than twenty-four hours' notice, the Canberra navigator was to be part of a two-jet deployment in response to a rumoured threat to British Honduras.

Unlike the Harriers, the Canberra PR9 had the legs to stage across the Atlantic without in-flight refuelling support. The hope had been to route via Gander in Newfoundland, but a Canadian Air Traffic Control strike had put paid to that idea. Instead Morgan drew up a flight plan that took them via Lajes in the Azores. From there, they'd hop to Bermuda and then south to Belize International. Once in country, the unarmed reconnaissance jets could provide not only a visible air presence over the colony but also accurate and up-to-date intelligence by surveying the border with Guatemala.

At two o'clock, with their personal kit already packed inside a wooden case suspended in the aircraft's flare bay, Morgan and his Pilot, Flight Lieutenant Jim Moir, left the Ops block to walk out to the two waiting PR9s. In an unusual arrangement, while the Pilot sat high up in a cockpit offset to the left of the fuselage centreline, Morgan, the navigator, sat encased in the nose of the jet with just a periscope and two 7 × 3-inch rectangular windows on either side to see out of. Wearing the pressure jerkin and leggings designed to save him in the event of a high-altitude pressurization failure, Morgan pulled himself into the open nose of the Canberra using a grab-handle, turned and reversed into his ejection seat. He stowed his nav bag, threaded the laces through his leg restraints and clipped into the heavy canvas parachute harness. Once he was in, the ground crewman closed the hinged nose of the jet to shut him into his claustrophobic little capsule and he and Moir began running through their pre-flight checks.

At the runway threshold, Moir advanced the Canberra's throttles forward to 97.5 per cent rpm, released the brakes and accelerated into the air at 1415ZULU. Their jet, XH131, was followed down the runway by a second Canberra flown by the squadron Boss, Wing Commander Terry O'Brien. Just eight minutes later the powerful Rolls-Royce Avon Mk 206 engines had taken the two PR9s past 40,000 feet.

Prior to the planned arrival of the Canberras in British Honduras, Colonel John Shipster had ordered some aerial reconnaissance of his own. The intelligence picture he had was enormously confused. Signals from London told him that there was an imminent invasion threat, while in country he simply had no evidence of it. Using the only resources he could lay his hands on – a former Luftwaffe fighter pilot, a small four-seat Cessna 172 and his own Military Intelligence Officer, Major Ian Bruce – a special observation mission out over the border into Guatemala was launched.

Flown by the German Second World War veteran, the little red, white and blue striped Cessna flew west on a bearing of 240 degrees from Stanley field, cruising at 120 knots just a few thousand feet above the ground. From his seat on the right of the cockpit, Major Bruce could see that the country's best defence lay in its geography. The country seemed to solidify and take shape west of Hattieville. At the unmarked border, the jungle stretched out unbroken north and south of Benque

Viejo. The thick canopy offered no distinctive features by which to navigate until ahead of them the reflective surfaces of Laguna Sacnab and Laguna Yaxhá broke up the impenetrable green. The road north to where these two lakes met ran out of steam at that point, giving in to the jungle to the north. And, as the propeller-engined Cessna cruised along the north side of Laguna Yaxhá, Bruce could just pick out the tops of three or four stepped pyramids broaching the thick forest – the only evidence of the once thriving civilization the Mayans had carved out of such unconducive territory.

Bruce and his unlikely ally put down at the short landing strip at Tikal before taking off and circling back round to the south. To their right, as they flew over La Reforma before heading east for home, was the incredible turquoise blue of Lago Petén Itzá, stretching out north and east of Flores. But Shipster's Special Observation Mission returned to Stanley Field empty-handed. In flying over all the possible centres for a military build-up around the Western Highway into British Honduras they'd found no evidence of any unusual Guatemalan military activity or troop build-up. And they were never going to. Once more, the assumptions being made by the British about where this would take place were wrong. Bruce and his pilot had delivered useful negative intelligence, but it was not a clean bill of health. And, later in the day, reports that reached Shipster from another source confirmed it. At Airport Camp, the Grenadiers were digging in.

Meanwhile, 1500 miles to the north-east, an elegant, white-painted Vickers VC10 of 10 Squadron RAF touched down at Kindley Field, the US Navy Air Station on Bermuda, after a special, unscheduled flight from the UK via Santa Maria in the Azores. On board, VC10 XV104 was carrying a thick pouch of classified documents relating to British Honduras and Guatemala. They were needed aboard *Ark Royal*. The carrier just had to send someone to come and pick them up.

Chapter 38

As well as its complement of four Gannet AEW3s, 849 'B' Flight usually also brought a fifth Gannet known as the COD and, typically enough, the COD had been left behind. Painted black and with its radar and black boxes stripped out, the old Gannet AS4 had morphed into a Gannet COD4, and earned its nickname from the phrase that described its role: Carrier On-board Delivery. But on this Westlant – Western Atlantic – cruise the decision had been taken to leave the COD behind in favour of an extra Sea King for 824. So, without his dedicated Gannet aboard, 'B' Flight's Boss, Guy Holman was flying one of the AEW3s to Bermuda.

An hour before launching the Gannet, John Roberts had to reduce his speed to 14 knots just to give his Aircraft Handlers a chance of working on deck. Steaming at 25 knots into a 32-knot headwind would have made rearranging the deck park for flying uncomfortable and dangerous.

For the flight to Bermuda, Guy Holman had Dick Schuette, his American Senior Observer, in the back. Schuette had to be first choice on a flight of this importance into an unfamiliar US Navy airfield. After being briefed on the flight the two of them walked out on deck to the waiting Gannet, already loaded on to the bow cat. Lacking steering on the ground other than from differential braking, the Gannet was a pain to manoeuvre around the deck as it had to rely on the help of a pair of Handlers and a metal steering arm bolted to the leg of the nosewheel. The two men responsible for making sure that the

Gannet went where the FDO wanted it to go walked just a few feet in front of the threshing machine of the Gannet's contra-rotating propellers. It made more sense, if possible, to load it on to the catapult with a tractor and *then* fire up the Double Mamba engines.

Holman liked to go off the catapult with his canopy open like a Battle of Britain Spitfire pilot. But his preference had nothing to do with style. Gannet crews didn't have ejection seats. If there was a problem on launch and the aircraft ditched, there wasn't the same potential to bang out that the 'Heavies' enjoyed. The pilots did sit on an underwater escape seat that used compressed air to blow them clear of a sinking aircraft, but, after watching his friend drown trying to get out of a Gannet, the 'B' Flight squadron Boss still found the possibility of unhindered escape offered by an open canopy reassuring.

The catapult fired. The Gannet seemed to snatch before accelerating smoothly along the deck, trails of condensation from the tips of her contra-rotating propellers corkscrewing back along her fuselage. From the bridge, John Roberts watched as the ungainly-looking turboprop climbed slowly away from the ship.

At cruising height, Holman switched the Gannet's autopilot to 'standby' and throttled one of the Mamba engines back to flight idle. He switched the HP Cock to 'feather and brake' then pulled the throttle lever to his left back to ground idle. As the rpm dropped below 20 per cent he pressed the relight button and held it down until the propeller was feathered. For the next hour, he flew along at 135 knots on one engine. As he approached the island, he swapped to the other engine in preparation for a single-engine landing into Kindley Field.

HMS *Malabar* was all that was left of the Navy's West Indies Station where Nelson had helped build his towering reputation, and even the little shore establishment's name made it sound grander than it was. In truth, *Malabar* was now just a couple of rooms in Bermuda, across the water from the Old Dockyard, that came under the command of SNOWI – the

Senior Naval Officer West Indies. And when the VC10 arrived, the current SNOWI, Commodore David Roome, was in the Bahamas, where his two West Indies Guardships, HMS *Phoebe* and HMS *Berwick*, were refuelling, so the job of ensuring that the documents were safely transferred to Holman and Schuette fell to his Staff Officer, an Army captain. He jumped into *Malabar*'s Morris Oxford and headed up to Kindley to meet *Ark Royal*'s inbound Gannet.

In the mid-sixties, as Chief Staff Officer to Flag Officer Aircraft Carriers, John Roberts had circulated documents extolling the necessity of maintaining currency and proficiency in air-to-air refuelling. Since its introduction into the Fleet Air Arm it had become indispensable.

Sir Alan Cobham, the British aviation pioneer who'd made his name with epic seaplane journeys to Australia and around Africa, had since the 1930s been a passionate and relentless advocate for air-to-air refuelling. As well as devoting himself to trying to perfect technology and techniques he'd also lobbied for its adoption by Britain's armed forces. In the end his insistence paid off. By the end of the 1950s, the RAF was well advanced in developing an in-flight refuelling capability using Vickers Valiant bombers modified with equipment made by Cobham's own company, Flight Refuelling Ltd.

Cobham had always worked with the idea of using dedicated tanker aircraft, until during a visit to the United States in 1954 he saw work being done on what the US Navy called the 'Buddy-Buddy' concept. He realized then that nearly any aircraft could become a tanker in the sky – and that's the point at which air-to-air refuelling became something the Fleet Air Arm could use. If a self-contained podded refuelling system could be hung under the wing, the Fleet Air Arm could begin to dispense fuel from its own jets, which, until now, had been forced to rely on RAF tankers.

Since 1960, the Navy's Supermarine Scimitars and De Havilland Sea Vixens used Flight Refuelling's new Buddy system. And, in 1964, 800 'B' Flight was created as a specialist on-board tanker unit using Scimitars permanently configured as tankers. But the unit had been short-lived, lasting only until 1966. Since then, the Navy was learning to live without dedicated tanker flights aboard *Ark* and *Eagle*. In their place, the Buccaneers carrying the same FR Mk 20A pods assumed the role.

'It is essential,' Roberts urged, 'that the art is not allowed to slip back into being considered excellent for an occasional gimmick, but too unreliable to be worth the effort of regular use.' And there was the rub. The refuelling pods had been unreliable. Dedicated to the job, 800 'B' Flight had, eventually, managed to achieve a success rate of nearly 90 per cent. But if a jet returning to the carrier low on fuel had nowhere else to go it *had* to be able to take on fuel. And this was going to be the situation facing a pair of Buccaneers as they passed their PNR – point of no return – inbound to 'Mother' from British Honduras. Any failure of 809's air-to-air refuelling equipment was a showstopper.

Good to get the adrenalin flowing again, thought 'Boots' Walkinshaw as he and Mike Lucas left the catapult 200 miles north-east of Bermuda. Carl Davis and Steve Park had launched three-quarters of an hour earlier behind Guy Holman's Gannet. While the two Buccaneers' time in the air overlapped, Davis and Walkinshaw practised flying in Battle Drill. Then, when the squadron Boss returned to *Ark* for deck landing practice, Walkinshaw and Lucas, under radar control from *Ark*'s ADR – the Air Direction Room – rendezvous'd with the tanker, ready to prove the work done by the engineering team in the Mushroom Farm the night before.

Flying in a steady 250-knot orbit, the tanker banked at 30 degrees, streaming its hose as 'Boots' formed up off its port wing.

Cleared line astern.

With the instruction from the tanker, Walkinshaw throttled back a touch and dropped in behind the other Buccaneer.

Cleared wet.

The Senior Pilot of 809 had had prodding practice ashore

less than two weeks earlier. And if it had just been about pilot
training, a dry prod – a connection between the Buccaneer's
probe and the basket streaming behind the tanker that passed
no fuel – would have sufficed. But this was about making sure
that there were no snags and snafus with the newly re-
configured jets.

Approaching, 'Boots' confirmed over the RT, nudging the
throttles forward to overtake slowly up the line of the hose
that hung heavily from underneath the tanker's starboard
wing. Ahead of him, in the back of the pod itself, a pair of
amber lights shone, confirming that he was cleared to tank.
With a solid thunk, the probe connected, sending a lazy ripple
through the 50-foot hose.

In, reported Walkinshaw as he continued to gain on the
tanker, pushing the hose back into the pod until its retraction
triggered the flow of fuel. The amber lights blinked off,
replaced by green as gallons of Avcat began pumping through
the hose into the Buccaneer's tanks. No problems.

Withdrawing.

After a token transfer of fuel, 809's senior pilot pulled back
on the throttles again, dropping back and away from the
tanker. A small puff of white fuel spray flashed and disappeared as the connection was severed.

Clear.

Mike Kinch's engineering team had done their job. Now it
was down to the aircrew. Walkinshaw rolled away and down
towards a holding point a few miles astern of 'Mother', ready
for a pair of radar-controlled CCAs. One roller landing,
followed by a trap.

For much of the afternoon *Ark Royal*'s progress had been disrupted by flying. But she'd still managed to shave fifty minutes
off the Gannet's return journey from Bermuda. Guy Holman
and Dick Schuette recovered on board at six o'clock, just after
sundown. From the deck, they signed in their aircraft, then
immediately handed over the documents to Mike Cole. With
the last aircraft on board, John Roberts altered course to 248

degrees and increased revolutions to 200. And, in calming seas, *Ark Royal*'s speed through the water rose to over 27 knots.

The information brought on board by the Gannet was a goldmine. The haul included political information about both Guatemala and British Honduras. And Cuba – essential given the route 809 had planned. Maps, photographs and detailed information on Guatemalan airfields and military installations. There were also details of British military capability and resources in British Honduras – of troop dispositions already in theatre and of those to come. As well as *Phoebe*, *London* and *Dido*, there were also further soldiers, a Tiger Cat missile unit and a pair of RAF Canberras on their way, all expected to arrive over the next few days. But not there yet. Of most interest was the JIC threat assessment. Here, for the first time, was substantial detail on Guatemalan military strength. The Guatemalan Army, over 10,000-strong and trained at the United States Jungle Warfare School, it said, 'was probably the best in Central America'. Then there was the Fuerza Aerea Guatemalteca – the Air Force. The JIC assessment listed the FAG order of battle: as well as squadrons of troop transports and helicopters, there were eight Mustangs, eight Cessna A-37s and eight T-33s. British Intelligence had been unable to take account of unserviceability and recent aircraft losses, but it was in the right ballpark. Efficient and battle-hardened by the ongoing counter-insurgency campaigns, the FAG, like the Army, and despite the relatively limited performance of its aircraft, was no pushover. Rules of Engagement specific to the current crisis were included too. For the time being, they said, *Ark Royal*'s air group were employed, 'to demonstrate HMG's capability of resisting Guatemalan aggression'. In the event of hostilities, however, they were to take 'the necessary action against hostile incursions of British Honduras territory'. For Nick Kerr and 892's Phantom crews, that amounted to a blank cheque. Except that the job of dealing with the Mustangs was not quite as straightforward as it appeared.

*

Commander Robert Irving was finally on his way. The Captain of HMS *Phoebe*, one of SNOWI's two West Indies Guardships, was diverted to British Honduras at the same time as *Ark Royal*. But the 3200-ton 'Leander' class frigate's tanks were half-empty when the signal came through. She had to fill up before she could go anywhere. After reaching Freeport in the Bahamas at dawn on the 27th, Irving fuelled from the jetty and was on his way south around the Florida panhandle again by mid-afternoon. By seven o'clock *Phoebe* was making a steady 24 knots towards Belize City. Until reinforcements arrived, British forces in BH had no radar, no surface-to-air missile defence of the airfield and no aerial reconnaissance capability of their own. Irving's instructions were to provide all three. *Phoebe* had her own air defence radar and a trained aircraft controller on board, optically guided Seacat GWS-20 SAMs and a small Westland Wasp HAS1 shipboard helicopter.

She could also, if it came to it, provide naval gunfire support from nearly ten miles offshore with 55lb high-explosive shells fired at a sustained rate of up to 24 rounds per minute from her twin 4.5-inch guns.

At 23.45 that night, the RAF Regiment recce party, just Martin Hooker and Wing Commander Ron Hardy, flew out of RAF Lyneham aboard a C-130 Hercules bound for the British Honduras via the Azores, Bermuda and Nassau. Hooker hoped to be able to use the long, slow journey west as an opportunity to bone up on how to position the Tiger Cat observation posts using the various aide-memoires and notes he'd cadged from the Obs flights before leaving Catterick. The first of the missile systems was due to follow twenty-four hours behind him.

Chapter 39

News of the Guatemalan F-51 Mustangs was greeted with a good deal of interest in the 892 Squadron Ready Room. The Boss, Nick Kerr, was practically banging the desks in his eagerness to get involved. He'd pushed hard for the chance to launch alongside the strike pair to provide a fighter escort – even if it was just through the Florida Straits before leaving them to fly on to British Honduras alone. He'd been denied. It made no sense to John Roberts to add an unnecessary layer of complication to such a crucial and fine-margined mission. But that didn't mean that the fighter crews' chance wouldn't come over the days that followed. And the Mustangs provided them with an interesting challenge. Just how did a supersonic jet interceptor designed to combat regiments of high-flying Soviet bombers mix it with a low, slow, hard-turning, piston-engined Second World War veteran?

Ironically enough, the man who knew the answer was now working in the MoD as Personal Staff Officer to Admiral Sir Peter Hill-Norton, the Chief of the Defence Staff.

While on exchange with the USAF 335th Fighter Interceptor Squadron during the Korean War, Group Captain John Nicholl became the first RAF pilot to shoot down a MiG. By 1963, after being seconded to English Electric as the RAF Liaison Officer during test-flying of the new Lightning fighter, he was CO of the Air Fighting Development Squadron at RAF Binbrook. Much of his unit's time was spent developing tactics for use against high-flying targets, but the prospect of

Lightnings being deployed to the Far East during the Indonesian Confrontation prompted an unusual demand: to develop tactics to defeat P-51s in a dogfight. To simulate the Mustangs they were lucky to have an old Spitfire to hand. A Griffon-engined Supermarine Spitfire PR Mk XIX, withdrawn in 1957, was parked by Binbrook's main entrance, on display as a Gate Guardian. Maintained in an airworthy condition on the orders of the base commander, PS853 was dusted down and fuelled up ready for the fight.

After a short series of air combat trials, Nicholl established that the supersonic jet's best chance of success was to approach from behind and below, out of sight of the piston-engined fighter's pilot, then rake past in a high-speed climb. The golden rule was never, ever to get suckered into a turning fight. Doing all this would certainly keep the faster jets out of harm's way, but for a Phantom given the job of splashing a Mustang it was virtually useless. The problem was that the F-4, unlike the Lightning, had no guns.

The medium-range radar-guided AIM-7 Sparrow was likely to be useless. John Froggatt and Dougal Macdonald had recently flown acquisition trials against fast-moving power-boats in the Mediterranean. The Scots AWI had been so driven to fly *just one more* of the 45-degree dive attacks that Froggatt, in real discomfort from the pressure changes as they swooped again and again into the thick low-level air, haemorrhaged his sinuses. When he'd removed his mask after recovering aboard *Ark* it was dripping with blood. But their persistence and success against the surface of the sea meant nothing. Over land, the big AWG-11 radar wouldn't pick up the Mustangs against the ground clutter.

None of them thought the heatseeking AIM-9 Sidewinders were going to do the trick either. Without the heat of a jet pipe to lock on to, the odds of hearing the infrared missiles' tell-tale acquisition tone in your ears were long – especially as, from behind and below, the F-51's wing would effectively mask the rows of engine exhausts that ran along either side of the Merlin engine's cowling.

The only thing we can do, thought 'Toobs' Charles, *is fly in as close as we can and just try to knock them out of the sky.* And it probably would have worked too. Flying into strong wake turbulence regularly killed pilots. But he knew that the only real answer would be to knock them out on the ground. Trouble was, even in the event of an all-out shooting war, the Rules of Engagement they'd just received made it clear that 'Interdiction against enemy airfields and/or lines of communication outside British Honduras may only be carried out with the express permission of HE The Governor.' So that was out.

But during the Indonesian Confrontation, the Fleet Air Arm's Sea Vixen squadrons were faced with a similar problem. And their solution, flying the missile-armed Vixen, was necessarily a little different to what the RAF had come up with. In 1964, Vixen crews aboard HMS *Centaur* were briefed by their squadron AWI on how to shoot down a P-51 using unguided 2-inch rockets. And, eight years later, it was with this hugely unsophisticated weapon, Nick Kerr realized, that the Phantom's only real attacking option lay. Every one of his crews regularly practised using the 2-inch rocket projectiles in the air-to-ground role. Each RP pod carried 36 rounds which could be fired in any number of combinations or just rippled off in one go.

'You'd never hit anything with those things!' John Froggatt laughed. He was right – to a point. Using them against an enemy aeroplane would be hit and hope at best. And if the Phantom was pulling any sort of 'g' as they pickled their rockets they'd just be spraying them around the sky. But it might, Kerr figured, at least keep an opponent honest; might persuade him, whether he got tagged or not, to abandon any attack against ground targets in search of safer sky. And *that* was definitely worth it. 'Toobs' Charles couldn't help looking on the bright side. *Might make their eyes water if you get a lucky shot!*, he smiled, imagining the scene.

George Dammeyer, 809's US Navy Observer, was wrestling with a problem of his own. Scheduled to fly one of the tankers with Pete Lewis, he tried to unravel where, on this occasion, his loyalties lay. Although a serving US Navy officer, the next day he was due to fly with the Royal Navy in support of an operation against a close ally of the United States in defence of a colony that his own country, officially at any rate, didn't want in its own backyard. The lean, fair-haired American gave up on trying to unpick it all.

'I can't,' he announced in mock exasperation, 'give fuel to these guys!'

As Dammeyer had been running through the various different loyalties involved, official written approval to overfly US airspace came through via the British Embassy in Washington. Despite being denied staging rights through Florida to the RAF transport fleet, the Buccaneers, provided they put calls in to Miami Center, and Homestead Air Force Base and Naval Air Station Key West as they flew through their zones, could transit through the Southern ADIZ on the way to British Honduras.

Before sitting down for dinner, 'Boots' Walkinshaw, dressed in the short sleeves and cummerbund of Red Sea Rig, visited the quarterdeck. At the stern of the ship and open to the elements at the sides and back, it usually gave him a chance to spend a little time by himself, lost in his own thoughts. In just a week's time he'd come to the end of his two years with 809 and, with it, the end of his time in the Fleet Air Arm. As a General List Officer he had a career in the Navy to look forward to but it wasn't necessarily going to be in the air. And tomorrow, with just a couple of weeks until his flying days might draw to a close, he was taking part in one of the most ambitious sorties aircraft from *Ark Royal* had ever mounted. Thoughts about the future churned around his head, but tonight the quarterdeck was no place to think. With the ship trembling from exertion as she cut through the long Atlantic roll at over 26 knots, the noise of the wash was deafening. *Practically need ear defenders!*, he thought, and made his way down two decks to the Wardroom on Six Victor to join the rest of the squadron to eat.

*

Lines of communication between Belmopan and Belize City struggled to cope. While Richard Posnett was installed in Belize House in the new inland capital, his Office of External Affairs remained in Government House in Belize City, where too were the Army Signals unit, at Airport Camp, that handled all telecommunications with the UK. Connecting him with Belize City was a single radio telephone line – or a 2½-hour journey by Land-Rover. On top of this, diplomatic signals and telephone calls competed for space with heavy military traffic on shared MoD off-line cipher and telegraph circuits. But despite the difficulties, the press, alerted by the headline in the *Financial Times*, managed to get through.

Reporters from London, New York, Mexico and even Australia had their persistence rewarded by conversations with Posnett himself. Over crackling and fading telephone lines, the new Governor tried to answer their questions. His concern about the possibility of invasion was soon matched by a worry that the fevered press interest itself would exacerbate an already delicate, uncertain situation. Like his counterparts in London, Posnett did his best to play down British fears.

'Well,' he told one journalist, who'd asked about advancing armoured columns, 'I'm looking out my window towards Guatemala now, but I can't see anything!'

In any case, when it came to explaining Britain's reaction, Posnett's hands were tied. Because it had all come through intermediary governments, he couldn't reveal the sources of British intelligence, and in doing so make public the real reason for Britain's reinforcement of the colony. Instead, he was forced to suggest that the *FT* had got the wrong end of the stick – that they'd put two and two together and made five.

But with *Ark Royal* on her way he realized that he needed to make sure that George Price and his government were singing the same tune in public. Having persuaded the Premier the day before of the reality of the threat from Guatemala, Posnett now had to ask him to make no mention of it at all. Price, ever shrewd, saw an opportunity to tell the BBC that the current situation only strengthened the case for a post-independence defence guarantee from the UK.

Despite having to admit that he'd had no knowledge of *Ark*'s involvement until the previous evening, Posnett's official line was that her deployment was long-planned and entirely unconnected with Guatemala. The Governor issued a press release announcing that 'In connection with the current British Army military training exercise, aircraft from the aircraft carrier "Ark Royal" are expected to fly over some coastal areas.' Better late than never. Posnett knew even as he issued it that it was a little loose with the facts. But news that *Ark Royal*'s strike jets were actually within range wouldn't be well known until the next morning's newspapers were on the stands. And until they were, British Honduras remained a walkover.

Dr Herrera held a press conference of his own. The Guatemalan Foreign Minister began by reiterating Article 1 of the constitution: Belice is part of the territory of Guatemala. Arana's government was *obliged*, it stated, to 'take all measures' to prevent Belizean independence.

'*For the moment*,' Herrera told the expectant reporters, 'Guatemala has no invasion plan re the territory of Belice.' And he expressed surprise that Britain saw the need to despatch such substantial forces to the 'Guatemalan territory of Belice'. Once again, he wondered whether the British military build-up might be attributable to a misinterpretation of Guatemalan security forces in the north and north-west of the country to combat dissident groups. But, like Posnett, as he spoke he knew there was more going on behind the scenes than he cared to admit publicly. As John Weymes was about to discover.

Chapter 40

The British Consul's trawl for information had produced scant reward so far. His enquiries at the US Embassy produced little that illuminated Guatemalan intentions, but, instead, only what they wanted to be known. 'Is it possible,' he'd asked John Dreyfus, the Counsellor, and Colonel Connolly, the Military Attaché, 'that the Guatemalans were thinking about an invasion?' They didn't think so. Guatemala was, the Americans told him, planning manoeuvres throughout the country to test her army's mobility and gauge its ability to reach 'flashpoints' quickly in the event of emergencies. These exercises, however, wouldn't involve 'any unusual concentration of troops in the areas in question'.

But nearly 1,000 soldiers had already been poured into the army base at Poptun.

Then one of Weymes's archaeological contacts told him that he'd been driving through the Petén when, stopping at a crossroads, he was shocked to be confronted by a tank pointing in his direction. This, Weymes worried, just couldn't be explained away as part of an anti-guerrilla operation. At the Ministry of External Relations, Sánchez had always appeared to go to great lengths to be open and honest, but this was definitely at odds with what he'd both said and implied. Weymes suspected that whatever line Sánchez was being told to take, it didn't represent the whole truth. Weymes knew that men like Sánchez and even Herrera were in the minority. The big question was what the Army – working hand in glove with the government hardliners – had in mind.

*

On the same day, John Shipster received reports back from Flores of the huge troop concentration at Poptun. And that tanks and artillery had just arrived at the base as part of that reinforcement.

Still awake at four in the morning, Carl Davis made his way for'd along Four Deck to the lower hangar to talk to the squadron's engineers. In the Mushroom Farm, Ron Sandry was on the nightshift again, four hours into his birthday. The rhythm of the ship powering onward had an almost hypnotic effect. Nearly flat out like this, *Ark Royal* had a very particular movement through the water. Following a kind of 'D' shape, her bow would ascend vertically before falling forward and down and back along the curve of the 'D'. The 809 Squadron Boss greeted them all. Dressed in dark-blue overalls, Sandry and the rest of the Buddy tank team had customized their brown surcoats with embroidered patches from oil companies like Esso, BP and Total, finishing it off with the legend: 'CARL'S GARAGE – 809 TAKE IT UP THE BACK'. Up the back – UTB – had become an unofficial motto for the Buccaneer squadron. Profane, exuberant or world-weary, its meaning depended on its context. UTB had become a useful catch-all. Davis appreciated the solidarity shown by the engineering team. And they, in turn, rated him. He was easy to talk to and, as now, took a conspicuous interest in what they were doing. He was a regular and welcome visitor to the hangar. They'd all come across COs who didn't take the time.

'Well, today's the day,' he announced and explained in more detail the mission that the squadron was mounting to British Honduras – the task their burning of the midnight oil was making possible.

'Thanks very much indeed for all your hard work.' Davis left them to it and returned to his cabin at the back of the ship to get some sleep.

An hour after Davis had come down, Sandry wished everyone good luck and headed back up to the Petty Officers' mess on Two Juliet, directly underneath the waist cat track, to get his head down. Another mission was planned for the following day and he knew that if things didn't work out – if the first sortie over Belize failed to strengthen the hand of the politicians and diplomats – then he might be spending the next night stripping down the jets again, reattaching weapons pylons and configuring them to carry 2-inch RP pods and 500lb bombs. And that would be another very long night. He grabbed himself a can of Courage Special Bitter from the stash they kept hidden in the catapult inspection hatch in the roof of the mess, knocked it back and climbed into his bunk. Hell of a birthday.

Chapter 41

The rest of Fleet Street caught up on Friday morning. The front pages of all the national dailies carried stories about *Ark Royal* and British Honduras. And most had swallowed the line being put out by the FCO that it was all a figment of people's imagination. There were no reports, they maintained, of a threat from Guatemala and *Ark*'s despatch to the region was not in the least bit noteworthy. Only a single MoD spokesman seemed to swim against the tide at all – and, in doing so, came closest to admitting publicly what was *really* going on.

'The added attack power of the Phantoms and Buccaneers,' he said, 'will serve as a much more powerful brake against any Guatemalan attempt to put into practice her old claim to British territory.' The trick the British Government wanted to try to pull off was to make their point absolutely clear while still allowing Arana room for manoeuvre. By forcing the General into a corner, there was the danger of provoking the very thing they were trying to prevent – especially given the view of some with the FCO that the Guatemalan President and his circle were 'odd and unpredictable people'.

At 11 a.m., Sir Peter Hill-Norton met with Lord Balniel, the Minister of State for Defence, to review the situation in British Honduras and agree in advance on the line to take in answering a question in Parliament that afternoon. Balniel cast his mind back to his own exhilarating flight in the back seat of an 809 Buccaneer, little knowing that, in discussing *Ark Royal*'s mission over British Honduras, he was talking about the fate of the pilot he'd flown with just a few months earlier: 'Boots' Walkinshaw. Hill-Norton and Balniel agreed that the key point to emphasize was that, whatever her bombers might be up to, *Ark Royal* herself was going to be over 1000 miles away from British Honduras. For those worried that Arana was being pressured into rash action, it could be safely argued that *Ark*'s long-distance intervention hardly amounted to seeing the whites of his eyes.

The Admiral moved straight on to a meeting of the Defence Operations Executive. Above and beyond the missions already scheduled, *Ark Royal*, it was decided, needed to remain available for the defence of the colony until the RAF Regiment's Tiger Cat missiles were operational. For the first time the possibility of despatching an MI6 officer to British Honduras in an effort to try to improve the quality of intelligence on the ground was raised. And, over a week since he'd first asked for it, 20 tons of Wombat ammunition for Richard Corkran's anti-tank platoon was signed off. It was due to be flown out on the 29th.

Overnight, the strong south-westerly wind off *Ark Royal*'s starboard bow had dropped and changed direction. But even a 10-knot southerly wind, added to *Ark*'s 26.5-knot speed through the water, made the roof of the bridge pretty blowy. But it was a bright clear day with perfect visibility of over 27 miles. And that was what Mike Gretton needed to take morning stars at sunrise. At 0729Q he climbed on to the roof of the bridge to check 'A' gyro and confirmed it was correct. It was a good start: 700 miles out to sea, the stars were the only way to guarantee their position. One element of the complex chain of events that needed to go without a hitch this day had gone their way.

Davis, Park, Walkinshaw and Lucas were already working on their contribution. The first and most uncomfortable part of the equation was starving themselves of tea, coffee and even decent amounts of water. The prospect of six hours in a Buccaneer cockpit without a loo made dehydration the preferred option for all four men. To keep himself going, Davis planned to crack open his survival pack and stash the tin of boiled sweets in the pocket of his flight suit.

The crews got changed early. Over the warm waters of the Caribbean there was no need for the felt-like insulating under-garments or thick rubber immersion suits that were essential when flying over the North Sea. Instead, they just pulled their olive-green flight suits over light shirts. Criss-crossed with zips and each bearing its owner's name on the left breast, the loose-fitting suits had a map pocket covered with transparent plastic on the top of the right thigh and, behind it, sheathed, a survival knife on a lanyard. Epaulettes bore their ranks in gold braid. As well as the colourfully embroidered phoenix of the 809 Squadron crest stitched on to their arms, Steve Park and Mike Lucas also wore crossed swords, winged tridents and yellow and black hornets on crests from previous squadrons. The mottoes alone offered a clear statement of intent: 'Never Unprepared', 'We'll Get Them', 'Beware of the Sting' and – 809's own – 'Immortal'.

The Buccaneer's Operating Procedures manual warned that 'most pilots leave their brains behind in the briefing room'. Fortunately, Davis and Walkinshaw, the two Pilots, had their Observers to make sure they were covered on that front. With up-to-date Met information and the ship's latest position, and already briefed by CBALS and Mike Cole on political and military intelligence relevant to the mission, Park and Lucas planned their flight in relative quiet away from the Crew Room. Lucas was unusual in having flown a Buccaneer sortie that even approached the kind of duration they were now planning. In 1968, while flying as a junior Observer with 803 NAS, the Buccaneer Weapons Trials unit at Lossiemouth, he'd been part of Exercise BOBBIN PLUS, a showcase deployment from Morayshire, via Cyprus and Gan, to HMS *Hermes*, steaming in the Andaman Sea. But even on that epic none of the three legs matched the length of today's mission.

Park and Lucas filled out log cards, breaking the long flight up into its component parts: launch, top of climb, refuelling, outbound cruise, top of descent, bottom of descent, low level and then the same in reverse. Each speed, course or height change had a bearing on their fuel burn and range. Only by working section by section could they accurately plan the flight. Using basic Dalton computers – a type of circular slide rule familiar to any student working towards a private pilot's licence – they calculated the effect of wind speed and direction on their track over the ground. Every known error needed to be accounted for and corrected, from the basic compass magnetic variations to the Coriolis effect. And with pencils and 2½-mil maps they plotted their dead-reckoning plan, marking the route, way points, the RVs with the tankers and landfall and making a note of visual cues along the way. Blessed with good weather on this sortie they would be able to use the distinctive shapes of coasts and islands to fix their position using navigation charts all the way to Belize City and back. They wouldn't need to rely on the Buccaneer's own twin-gyro compasses and Blue Jacket ARI 5880 Doppler navigation radar. Over long distances, like the ship's own gyros, the old fifties technology became progressively more inaccurate. Over their 2600-mile flight its expected 95 per cent level of accuracy could only be relied on to bring them within 130 miles of the ship on their return – and that was on top of any errors in *Ark*'s Position and Intended Movement. Without care it would be too easy to end up nearly half an hour's flying time away from 'Mother'. Even in a relatively sedate cruise, that distance burnt 1500lb of Avcat. On graph paper laid out in squares of inches and eighths, with fuel up the 'X' axis and range along the 'Y', they plotted their fuel burn for the six-hour sortie. To make it work they needed 4000lb from the tanker on the way out and another 4000lb on the way home.

As well as collecting the Terminal Air information – radio frequencies, airfield layouts and circuit procedures – for any possible diversions, Park and Lucas made sure they knew the locations of Cuban airfields and SAM sites *en route*. Batteries of SA-2 Guideline and SA-3 Goa missiles faced north and the Cuban Fuerza Aerea Revolucionaria – FAR – also had a squadron of MiG-21 Fishbed interceptors stationed at San

Antonio de los Banos, near Havana in the west of the island. Alongside the MiGs was a semi-permanent detachment of Soviet Tupolev Tu-95 Bears. San Antonio was barely forty miles south of the strike pair's intended track.

Park and Lucas passed their finished flight plan to Ops. From there it was filed with the US authorities in advance of the Buccaneers' transit through the American Southern ADIZ. And, with an hour to go until launch, the crews made their way to the briefing room in the island.

In London, as *Ark Royal* prepared to enter the fray, Mr John Gilbert, the Labour member for Dudley, rose to his feet in the ornately carved bearpit of the House of Commons debating chamber.

'Will the Minister of State for Defence,' he asked, 'make a statement about the current movement of Her Majesty's Ships and Service Personnel in the Caribbean area.' Following the line agreed with the Chief of the Defence Staff earlier in the day, Lord Balniel got up to answer. In the manner recommended by Teddy Roosevelt the Minister spoke softly, but – as he hoped there was no doubt – carried a big stick. But what was interesting about the Conservative member for Hertford's reply was that, in describing longstanding exercises in the Caribbean and outlining *Ark*'s programme, he implied that the carrier's involvement in British Honduras was long-planned and unremarkable but never actually quite said so. Further enquiries about the nature of a Guatemalan threat were simply deflected in the direction of the Foreign and Commonwealth Office. Then came an unexpected supplementary question.

'Is my Right Honourable friend surprised,' Balniel was asked, 'to see this further illustration of how handy it is to have an aircraft carrier around occasionally?'

Chapter 42

Hands to Flying Stations.

The order, tinny and distorted by the speakers of the ship's main broadcast, brought the flight deck to life. From their Ready Room at the back of the island the Aircraft Handling party, dressed in their different-coloured surcoats, streamed out into a 36-knot wind over the deck to muster. Two Flight Deck Officers, the Captain of the Flight Deck, two Petty Officers, six Leading Airmen and twenty-eight Naval Airmen all had their own discrete list of tasks to contribute to the DIs – Daily Inspections – that needed to be completed before any aircraft were launched.

Firemen, running in flameproof white overalls, circum-navigated the walkways around the edge of the flight deck, checking the drums of foam in the firelockers and the water pressure on each of the twenty-seven firepoints. Whip aerials port aft were lowered to horizontal and, from the armoured glass howdah of the DA2 control position alongside 2 Wire, a thumbs-up signalled all-clear to test-raise the yellow and black striped crash barrier arm.

While Naval Airmen, their overalls flapping in the brisk wind over the deck, checked the batteries, oil and hydraulic fluid of the tractors, forklifts and cranes, the Landing Safety Officer clambered down on to his platform next to the waist cat. He lowered the heavy projector sight to check both the red Perspex side-to-side sight through which he'd judge the accuracy of an approach along the centreline, then jumped back on deck to check the red, green and white lights of the projector sight itself.

Ahead of the round-down, ranged in a herringbone pattern, their noses pointing forward and their wings folded, were the five Buccaneers that had been chosen for the sortie. The strike pair and a spare jet were lashed down in Fly 4 on the port side; the two tankers faced them at Fly 3. Spotted at Fly 2 next to the island were Phantoms and one of the grey and crimson Wessex SAR helicopters, and at Fly 1, on the starboard side of the ship's bow, just beyond the reach of the slashing wingtips of a bow cat launch, were two more Phantoms, another Buccaneer and a Gannet. Each was in the place allocated to it by the ACRO – Aircraft Control Room Officer – in the island.

After Comms links between the deck, the ACRO and Flyco were tested, the Flight Deck Crew made their way mob-handed to the bow for the FOD plod. From there they walked the length of the deck checking for any detritus, no matter how small – discarded screws, pieces of wire, even flakes of paint – that might, if ingested by one of the jet engines, have catastrophic consequences. Any offending articles were thrown off the round-down into the sea.

Half an hour before the first launch was scheduled, the ACRO reported to Flyco that the deck was ready.

On the other side of the island, as the Handling Party worked, the aircrews were finishing their own preparations. But they weren't alone. Sitting in rows along vinyl-covered benches under bright artificial light, the world and his wife were crammed into the narrow 809 Crew Room for the briefing. There were the eight aircrew taking part – the strike pair and the two tankers – but other interested members of 809, not least those who'd been scheduled to fly the sortie the next day, had joined them. As well as the Met Officer and CBALS, they'd also been joined by the Ops Officer, Mike Cole, and Wings had come down from Flyco too. And sitting in the front row was the Captain, John Roberts. Under the low roof, there was a definite sense of occasion.

At the front of the crowded room, the blackboards showed

details of the mission. Davis and Park were going in Buccaneer 030, call sign Red Leader, Walkinshaw and Lucas had 021, call sign Red Two. The Comms channels, fuel calls and times were all laid out. The first refuelling would be at 30,000 feet, forty minutes into the sortie, before the strike pair cruise-climbed to thinner air at altitude. The return RV with the tankers would be overhead Grand Bahama at 25,000 feet. 'Boots' Walkinshaw scribbled notes on the thighpad of his flightsuit.

Against the hum of the air-conditioning and the relentless vibration of the old carrier's engines, the Met Officer began proceedings. There was nothing that Park and Lucas hadn't already factored into their flight plans. The only thing they might need to keep an eye out for was a building weather system in the Gulf of Mexico. CBALS followed. He gave details of the British military presence in British Honduras and laid out the threat posed to British Honduras by Guatemala as he already had in private with the crews. If there was any appearance by the FAG, the Buccaneer crews knew what to do. But, while intelligence from the region was uncertain, he said, they didn't expect Guatemalan forces in the air or on the ground to be an issue. At this stage *Ark Royal*'s task was just to show a presence over the territory. Cuba, on the other hand, might have its nose put out of joint.

Mike Cole briefed them on Cuba's recent history, political outlook, relations with the US and their military capability.

'You may find,' the Ops Officer told them, 'that they send something up to look at you. Keep your eyes peeled and don't give them any reason to send anyone up.' Davis, Walkinshaw, Park and Lucas acknowledged the point and nodded their assent. Cole also highlighted the sensitivities surrounding the US's acquiescence over the British mission.

Then Carl Davis briefed the sortie itself. Systematically, the eager-faced squadron Boss ran through the details on the briefing boards. After the refuelling they'd continue south-west past the Florida Keys, putting in calls with Miami Center, Homestead AFB and Naval Air Station Key West as required by the Americans. For the external Comms, their call signs were Navjet 030 and Navjet 021. Once out over the Gulf of Mexico, search-and-rescue coverage would be provided by HMS *Phoebe*. As they flew overhead they'd check in with her too. And he reminded them that over Belize City they were not to drop below a minimum height of 1000 feet. He asked all four crews to synchronize their watches. It was just after 1130QUEBEC. As the Captain got up to speak, Carl Davis was eager to get started.

As soon as he'd first received the signal from the MoD, John Roberts had known that this was his opportunity to show the reach and flexibility of a strike carrier – a weapon to which he'd been connected in some capacity for nearly his entire career. He believed passionately in the mission his aircrews were about to embark on. And he wanted to make that clear to them. He kept it short.

'We don't often get a request directly from the government. This is a classic demonstration of carrier air power,' he told the assembled strike crews as they sat facing him in their flying suits. 'The world is watching, but we're *Ark Royal* and you are 809. I know you'll do a good job.' As welcome as they were, Carl Davis didn't need the Captain's words for motivation. The 809 Boss was now focused on the mission. Like a sportsman before the big game, he just wanted the whistle to blow and get started. But, like Roberts, Davis had felt bruised and let down by the decision to discard the carriers.

We'll bloody show them, he thought, *we'll show them what we can do.*

Chapter 43

Walkinshaw and Davis signed the A700s to take responsibility for the jets and, after a last, hopeful visit to the heads, followed their Observers through the heavy steel door on to the deck to be greeted by the massive gaping jet pipes of a Phantom ranged at Fly 2. With their flightsuits now decorated by leg restraint garters round their calves and yellow Mae West lifejackets, they walked towards the waiting Buccaneers carrying their white Bone Domes in hands covered with soft calfskin gloves. The wind rolling down the rough, graphite-grey flight deck pushed at them from behind.

The aircrew greeted the squadron engineers who still swarmed around the jets. And while the two pilots walked round their aircraft carrying out systematic external checks, their Lookers climbed the red crew access ladders up over the port engine intake. Steve Park didn't need to fold himself into the cockpit like his 6 foot 4 inch colleague in 021. Mike Lucas secured the cumbersome Hasselblad camera he was carrying for the mission and stowed his nav bag. Contained inside, as well as the details of the British Honduras mission, were documents and references designed to cover any contingency, including launch graphs, search-and-rescue plans, flight reference cards with details of aircraft emergency procedures, diversion fuel and recovery fuel figures, and UHF/HF frequencies. The contents of the nav bag were a safety net. Standard Operational Procedures gave Observers what it called the 'Enid Blyton Manual', a checklist to ensure that nothing of any importance got overlooked.

Folding nose – closed, handle and indicator flush. ADD probe – cover removed, undamaged.

Walking and crouching around his jet, Carl Davis ran through external checks that, although second nature, needed to be systematic.

Mainwheel doors, auxiliary air intakes, jet pipes, pressure heads and static vents.

Satisfied that all on 030 was as it should be, the CO climbed up to the front cockpit and, gripping the frame of the canopy, lowered himself into his Martin-Baker 6MSA Mk 1 ejection seat. With the help of the Pilot's Mate standing on the ladder outside, he clipped himself into the straps of the harness and threaded the leg restraint cords through the D-rings of his garters. Davis pulled on his Bone Dome and clipped the end of the PEC that delivered his oxygen and RT link through his mask into the right of the seat.

Front and back, the safety pins were removed and stowed in specially allocated slots around the cockpit. It was failsafe. A pin in each slot meant that the zero-zero seats – loaded with rockets capable of firing their occupants, from a parked aircraft, high enough for a parachute to save them – were live. After double-checking that the 'Jettison', 'Weapon' and 'Attack' selectors behind the throttles read 'Off', Davis switched on the Battery Master Switch. Dials flickered and lights blinked on all around him as the big strike jet came to life. He glanced at the voltmeter, then he and Park, the intercom now crackling in their ears, began running through eight pages of call-and-response checks they had to complete before starting the engines. From outside, their white helmets could be seen bobbing around the cockpits above red ejection seat warning triangles painted below the canopy glass. Inside, their hands moved around, resting on and gesturing towards switches and panels in a familiar, well-tuned routine.

The Buccaneer cockpit was an ergonomic practical joke. Mounted on black or copper-coloured panels screwed and riveted to grey-painted metal, apparently random clusters of different shaped switches, knobs, tabs, dials, lights, doll's-eyes and displays surrounded them. Clear white capital letters describing the purpose or function of each lent a necessary veneer of order to an otherwise dauntingly complex environment. Heads down, Davis and Park worked their way around the cockpit from left to right: from the engine master switches and fuel cocks and the back of the port console by Davis's left leg, across the main instrument panel and round to the switch panel on the starboard cockpit wall. After completing that sweep there were a page and a half of Observer's checks to run through. To their right, Walkinshaw and Lucas ran through a parallel set of pre-start checks. Call and response echoed between them.

Oxygen on, 100 per cent.

In the event of a soft-shot – a failed catapult launch that despatched them no further than the Atlantic swell ahead of the carrier – anything less than 100 per cent and the two of them would drown trying to breath an oxygen and water mix.

Oxygen on, 100 per cent, Lucas confirmed.

Radar master switch on?

Lucas checked that the radar was on standby and flicked on the bomber's Blue Parrot radar to protect it during the violence of the catapult launch. On his instrument panel, an amber light blinked on, confirming that the system was warming up.

Overload fuel switch on.

Compass variation to zero east/zero west.

Turn to flying course.

At 1156QUEBEC, John Roberts gave the order to bring *Ark Royal*'s bows into wind ready for the launch. The Officer of the Watch reached for his microphone: *Port Five Zero. Steer Two Zero Zero.*

Still maintaining 200 revolutions, the massive 50,000-ton ship heeled to starboard like a speedboat as the huge twin rudders bit into the water at a speed of 24 knots. On her new heading of 200 degrees, a 35-knot wind equivalent to a Force 7 near-gale blew over the deck. There was already competition for space among the army of goofers who were gathering to watch the show from the island's outside spaces.

In front of them, the SAR was the opening act. Spotted on the angled deck just port of Flyco, the pilot of the planeguard Wessex engaged the helo's main rotor and the four blades slowly began to turn above him, flashing as their speed increased. As the old rescue helicopter lifted off the deck and peeled off to port, Little F spoke into the tannoy.

Stand by to start the Buccaneers. Stand clear of intakes and jet pipes. Start up.

Wearing a brown waistcoat and ear defenders, one of the flight deck engineers raised his hand above his head and whirled it round in a vigorous royal wave. Carl Davis returned the gesture through the closed canopy of the Buccaneer then reached back with his left hand to press the port engine starter button. The Low Pressure light flickered on and he nudged the black port throttle lever forward to 'Ground Start'. Over the next ten seconds the powerful Rolls-Royce Spey engine – driven by air from a Palouste that sat on the deck alongside the jet – wound up to nearly 55 per cent power. Suppressed in the cockpit, on deck the rising whine of the jet joined the clatter of the SAR helo and the rush of the wind and sea. As the engine stabilized, Davis notched it back to 50 per cent power and checked the temperatures and pressures. He cycled the big clamshell airbrake at the back of the jet then repeated the start-up procedure for the starboard engine. With both engines idling, he ran through the pre-take-off functional checks, testing every element of the airframe: flight controls, flaps, aileron droop and the Boundary Layer blowing system. No snags.

Davis reached to the switch panel on the starboard wall of the cockpit and flicked on the tab switch for the rendezvous lights. On the spine and underneath the belly of the Buccaneer, two red lights began to flash. Red Leader's Cab was up and running. A brief radio confirmation arrived in Flyco over the intercom: *Zero Three Zero on deck.* It never failed to have a galvanizing effect on the crew transmitting.

We're ready.

Off either side of the stern of the carrier, heat haze from the eight Spey engines clouded the view as rippling jet wash blasted the air sixty feet above the waves. The harsh, unremitting whine of the engines dominated the scene as the four strike bombers waited for the order to taxi forward to the catapults. Whatever illusion of safety and space the flight deck might have once given off was gone. All four of the jets sat expectantly, their RV lights flashing lazily. *Ark Royal* was now more airfield than ship.

High on Flyco, two sets of traffic lights changed from red to amber. The Flight Deck Party were clear to start marshalling the Buccaneers on to the catapults. The yellow-jacketed Range Director signalled 'On brakes' and 'Away chocks'. Carl Davis pushed at the foot pedals to apply the brakes as, underneath him, chocks were removed from in front of the jet's undercarriage wheels. Ahead of him he watched the first of the tankers nod heavily on its nosewheel as it checked the brakes before taxiing slowly up to the bow cat. Davis and Park were next. Using expansive, unmistakeable gestures, the Range Director beckoned 030 forward using both arms. Davis released the wheel brakes then nudged the power. As soon as the aircraft began moving forward, he dipped at the pedals again to test his own brakes. With the nosewheel steering engaged, he turned left and began rolling forward up the deck at walking pace, relayed up the flight deck from the Range Director to the Aft 'Y' Director and on to the Base Loading Director waiting at the catapult. At the direction of the latter, Davis reached down to his right to depress and lock the chunky metal lever that unfolded the Buccaneer's wings. As the dark-grey bomber taxied forward into the wind, the wings spread, unfurling down into the horizontal, ready to cut into the air.

Davis and Park felt the nose bobble as it rolled over the catapult shuttle that protruded just a few inches from the deck. Like the tip of an iceberg, the shuttle gave little hint of what was below – or of the power it harnessed. Beneath the flight deck, high-pressure steam bled from the ship's engines drove heavy pistons along 70-yard-long cylinders. They were capable of dragging a Buccaneer weighing up to 30 tons into the air with explosive force. As 030 came to a standstill, held in place by chocks that rose up out of the flight deck, the water-cooled jet blast deflectors, blackened and scarred by the roasting they were subjected to by the Phantom's reheats, rose up out of the deck below. Davis released his brakes and throttled back to idle.

Then the Badgers, in black and white, swarmed around in their headsets and goggles, scampering and crouching under the Buccaneer's belly. During a multi-aircraft launch like this the precise theatre they performed was slick and assured, each action making a crucial contribution to the successful out-come. First, a single Badger, hemmed in on either side by turbulent columns of 500-degree heat pouring out of the two jet pipes, attached the steel holdback to the rear of the jet. Designed to fail under the combined force of the catapult shot and the engines at full power, the steel holdback would keep 030 secured to the deck until she was launched. Two engineers plugged a lead into the starboard wheel well to update the jet's navigation systems from the ship's most up-to-date position. When the compass light in the cockpit glowed amber, Steve Park held a thumb up against the glass to confirm the alignment.

And at the back of the jet, inhaling lungfuls of sea air laced with the warm tang of burnt jet fuel, one of 809's engineers, dressed in white overalls, recorded the angle of the all-flying tailplane before confirming his observation with Carl Davis to check against the tailplane trim indicator in the cockpit – and the setting calculated for him by Park based on 030's centre of gravity, all-up weight and catapult end-speed.

Wind over the deck was an obsession. During flying oper-ations, John Roberts found it hard to tear himself away from the wind meter installed near his 'Father's Chair'. It occupied the same crucial significance in Flyco. They *depended* on the wind. Wind speed was recorded by an anemometer mounted on a pylon off the starboard bow and it was the single most important variable during launch. Everything except the wind was in the hands of *Ark* and her crew. But the wind could change and, today, conditions were marginal. Full of fuel, with overload bomb bay tankers and slipper tanks under the wings, 030 and 021 were being launched at the limits, just a shade off their maximum catapult launch weight of 54,000lb. Even with 34 knots of wind over the deck, the waist cat would still need to rip them from a standstill to 106 knots to reach their MLS – Minimum Launch Speed – of 140 knots. But they were already pushing the limits of what was possible in the warm air of midday. They were lucky that, even between Bermuda and the Bahamas, it was winter. Even so, they'd be leaving the deck about 15 knots slower than they'd have rotated from a runway ashore. Or even from the deck of one of the bigger American carriers, where MLS +25 was deemed more comfortable – they were lucky they had that luxury.

With a steady 34 knots of wind over the deck, Wings signalled that he was ready to start the launch. Above the Flyco bridge extension, the traffic lights changed from amber to green. A heavy 2-inch gauge wire bridle was immediately dropped around the catapult shuttle in readiness for it to be attached to the Buccaneer. After a thumbs-up from Holdback Badger, No. 1 Badger, crouching ahead of the nose of 030, signalled 'Down chocks' by bringing his arms down ahead of him like a believer prostrating himself at the altar. With the chocks lowered, the Base Loading Director signalled 'Off brakes' to Carl Davis – a necessary step before the catapult was tensioned – before No. 1 Badger threw his clenched left fist forward in a convincing straight right. On that signal, two more Catapult Crew Badgers lifted the bridle and hooked the eyes at either end over heavy lugs each side of the bomb bay doors. Then, like Pete Townshend on rewind, No. 1 Badger wheeled his arm backwards to signal 'Tension'.

Slowly, the catapult shuttle moved forward a few inches, stretching and tightening the steel bridle. As the shuttle tensioned, the nose of the Buccaneer lifted from the deck, until the rear of the big jet was resting on a small metal skid under the tail. At this attitude it would accelerate down the catapult track at exactly the right angle of attack. The careful setting up of the tailplane trim would enable it to launch hands-free, flying itself off the front of the ship without any assistance from the pilot for up to five seconds. The Badgers pulled at it to check its tautness before turning and giving a clear thumbs-up with outstretched arms to No. 1 Badger. With 030 locked and loaded, the No. 1 Badger, still on one knee ahead of the aircraft, dismissed his Catapult Crew by raising both arms up and stretching them horizontally from his sides. The Badgers scurried out from underneath the Buccaneer and ran for safety. Behind the protection of the jet blast deflectors – the JBDs – 'Boots' Walkinshaw and Mike Lucas sat in 021, waiting to taxi forward as soon as the Boss was gone.

No. 1 Badger turned to face the yellow-jacketed Flight Deck Officer and raised both thumbs aloft. With his job done, he joined his crew lined up, their heads down, along the broken red centreline of the angled deck. It was now in the hands of the FDO. Leaning backwards against the fierce wind that snatched at his overalls and flattened them against the backs of his legs, he raised a small, tattered green flag above his head and began to stir vicious little circles in the air.

Wind her up to full power.

Inside 030, Carl Davis pushed both throttle levers forward against the stops to the take-off position. On the right-hand side of the instrument panel, the needles on the two engine-rpm dials spun up to 97.5 per cent. He made a final check of Boundary Layer Control, and the three yellow cheeses of the flap indicators – 45 degrees on the mainplane, 25 on the aileron droop and 25 on the tailplane – his trim settings, and checked he had full and free control movement. Satisfied, he held a gloved hand up to the glass of the cockpit to the FDO to signal that he was ready to go and dropped it smartly from view. Ahead and to his right, he watched clouds of thick condensation billow into the air along the catapult track as the first tanker left the bow of the ship and accelerated away from the carrier. It was 1200Q. To his left, hovering fifty yards from the flight deck, the winchman and rescue diver aboard the SAR helo sat on the sill of the open side door making their own checks for anything that might affect the launch of the Buccaneer.

On deck, the noise from the 030's two Spey engines, unloading over 22,000lb of dry thrust, had grown from an incessant turbine whine into a full-throated, urgent roar. Davis's Buccaneer was visibly shaking, straining to free herself from the holdback, in a tug of war to get airborne. Inside the Buccaneer's cockpit, Davis and Park leaned back against the headrests of their ejection seats in anticipation of the whiplashing effect of the cat shot.

Balanced against the wind, the FDO looked over his shoulder to make sure the Flyco traffic light was still green, made a last check down the track of the catapult, then dropped to a squat, bringing his green flag down to touch the deck alongside him. In the armoured glass howdah beyond the bellowing, struggling Buccaneer, the catapult operator took his cue, dropping his hands from full view of the FDO for the first time. Then he pressed the red 'Fire' button on the console ahead of him. Less than three seconds later, the two half-ton pistons exploded down their cylinders, driven by an irresistible force of around 350lb per square inch of steam. And 030, Carl Davis and Steve Park were dragged from zero to flying speed over less than seventy yards in under two seconds.

As soon as they were gone, the JBDs flattened against the deck, allowing 'Boots' Walkinshaw to be marshalled forward on to the waist cat. Alongside the carrier, clouds of condensation churned out from the catapult spiralled in the air, spun by vicious vortices stirred up by 030's wingtips as she accelerated. The catapult shuttle drew back along the cat track to the loading base like the hare at a greyhound race, ready to launch 021. As the Badgers moved in, Walkinshaw and Lucas kept their hands high and out of harm's way.

Nine minutes after the first tanker left the deck they were airborne. 'Boots' Walkinshaw, his senses returned after the violent initial acceleration of the catapult, gently gathered in the big strike jet and took control. With his right hand around the stick, he reached forward with his left to raise the undercarriage and flaps, then swapped hands to set the autostabilizers to 'High Speed'. Behind him, Mike Lucas turned his oxygen regulator to 'Normal' and switched the radio from Flyco, on Channel 2, to Channel 6 and Harry O'Grady in the ADR. As the senior Controller on board, direction of the mission had been placed in O'Grady's hands. For this one, in every department, they'd gone for experience. Walkinshaw let the jet gather speed then, at 400 knots – Mach 0.82 – he trimmed her into full-power climb. Temperatures and pressures all looked good.

Starboard fifty-five degrees. Set course Two Five Five.

As he watched the dark smoke trail of 021 as she climbed away, John Roberts ordered a turn away from the wind to bring *Ark Royal* back on her course towards the Florida straits. As he issued his instruction, the ship still resonated from the impact of the two catapult pistons being brought to a halt from over 100 knots in just 6 feet by the waterbrake cylinders.

There they go, he thought, *fingers crossed*. The Captain could only wish them Godspeed and hope to follow their progress via the Ops Room. The bridge felt different. After the hell-for-leather transit to the launch position the ship had done what she could. With the Buccaneers airborne there was nothing anyone could do now until the recovery of the tanker pair. But everyone knew that this mission was special – that there was something riding on it beyond the safe return of the crews. Mike Gretton, the 2nd Navigator, could feel it. He'd checked their position on the ship's Loran Charlie direction-finding system fifteen minutes before launch. South-west of Bermuda, they were on the fringe of coverage from the aerials in Florida, Alabama, Virginia and New York. But, even putting aside his fervent hope that it wouldn't be his contribution that let the side down, he thought, *It's a risky operation*. As well as good planning and determination *we'll need a certain amount of good luck*. With the jets gone, *Ark Royal* powered onwards across the Hatteras Abyssal Plain, thick, oily black smoke pouring from her funnel.

Nineteen years old, Roberto Palermo had left school in Guatemala City and was looking forward to university. The last thing he'd considered was the possibility of going to war. But that was the prospect he and his fellow students believed they faced. It seemed ridiculous, but exposed to the long-standing aggressive nationalism of Arana's government over Belice and a media commentary that constantly demanded results, they took seriously the prospect of mobilizing against the British. And it terrified them. Most of all, the young students feared the prospect of being drafted as back-up to the regular forces. It wasn't just excitable speculation either. The Army was trying to set up military camps to train young Guatemalans to fight. In the mood of anxiety that pervaded the capital, Palermo and his friends could talk about little else.

The Foreign Affairs Commission of Guatemala's Congress had prepared a draft resolution. In it they called on their Central American neighbours to reject the British 'affront to Guatemalan sovereignty'. And they urged President Arana and the generals to act in defence of Belice: 'The patience used,' they declared, 'in maintaining a peaceful claim based on international law has come to an end . . . Congress may consider compliance with Section 6 of Article 170 of the Constitution (Declaration of War).' It would be put to the vote on 1 February.

In the Petén, troops from Poptun Army base had been ordered to register and check all foreigners in the region. At Finca Ixabel, it was made clear to Dennis and Luisa Wheeler that, near the border, they were living on the edge of a dangerous situation.

The British have landed, the soldiers told them, *and are about to attack. There might be war.*

As the crisis deepened, the Guatemalan government forward deployed armed Mustangs to Puerto Barrios on Guatemala's Caribbean coast. Proven in combat during a long counter-insurgency campaign, the Guatemalan Air Force was one of Central America's most capable.

Above: In the shadow of the volcanoes that surround Guatemala City, F-51 Mustangs depart their base at La Aurora. Although of WWII vintage, the old piston-engined fighter-bombers remained extremely effective in support of troops on the ground.

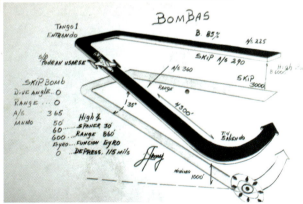

Above: Standard Operating Procedures. This previously unseen illustration reveals some of the Guatemalan Air Force bombing techniques. The Central American Air Arm's pilots were well-trained, experienced and professional.

Above: As *Ark Royal* steamed south the 809 squadron engineers worked in the lower hangar to prepare four Buccaneers for a long-range operation – two to fly the mission and two to provide tanker support.

Left: A Buccaneer with a Mk 20 refuelling pod under the starboard wing. After work had gone on through the night to install it, the refuelling equipment needed to be test-flown. Note the Gannet ready to launch from the bow cat.

Right: As *Ark Royal* steamed towards the Caribbean, a Gannet flew from the ship to Bermuda and back to pick up classified documents relating to the crisis in Central America.

Above: While the Bermuda mission fell to the CO and Senior Observer, it didn't stop the rest of 849 'B' Flight dreaming about what might lie ahead.

Below: The Phantoms of 892 were similarly keen to test themselves against Guatemalan opposition. In the end, it was believed that 2-inch rocket pods were likely to be the gunless interceptors' only effective weapon against the WWII vintage Mustangs. And even that was a long shot, given their inaccuracy in an air-to-air role.

Left: As *Ark*'s squadrons planned ahead, the Grenadier Guards in British Honduras dug in. This poor-quality picture shows guardsmen armed with SLR assault rifles behind a wall of sandbags.

Right: This privately owned Cessna – flown by an ex-Luftwaffe pilot – provided the British garrison with their only aerial asset. A handful of reconnaissance missions were flown.

Left: While the company of Grenadiers in country made the most of their limited resources in an effort to hold up any invasion, reinforcements were being loaded onboard Royal Air Force C-130 transports for the long, noisy and slow transatlantic journey from RAF Lyneham.

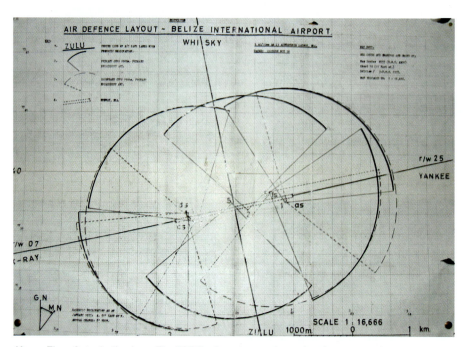

Above: Tiger Cat missile plans. The RAF Regiment were also ordered to prepare for an immediate deployment to Belize International. An advance party left early to establish the position of lookout posts that were necessary to use the missile system effectively.

Below: Although the easily air-portable Tiger Cats were eventually replaced by the Bofors guns shown in the picture, it wouldn't have been possible to deploy the heavy guns and their ammunition so quickly without completely tying up the RAF's fleet of transport aircraft.

Left: While troops were flown into British Honduras, the RAF despatched a pair of Canberra PR9 reconnaissance aircraft from 39 Squadron to provide an air presence over the colony.

Above: As well as the Canberras to the Caribbean, the RAF also stood up 1(F) Squadron at RAF Wittering. In preparation to fly to British Honduras a flight of Harrier GR1s was fitted with long-range ferry tanks and in-flight refuelling probes.

Above: Midday, 28 January. With steam caught in the vortex spinning off the port wingtip, one of the 'strike pair', 021, flown by Colin Walkinshaw and Mike Lucas, accelerates down the waist cat at the beginning of their vital mission to Belize City.

Left: As the catapult bridle falls away, a Buccaneer is pictured at the moment she becomes airborne.

Above: At the top of the climb, the strike pair refuelled from the two tankers that had launched with them. Their job done, the tankers recovered to 'Mother' to prepare, all being well, to meet the two Buccaneers on their return from British Honduras.

Left: Carl Davis and Steve Park approach the Belize International overhead. Airport Camp – home to the British Garrison – can be seen under the nose.

Right: 030 over Belize city. The arrival in theatre of British strike jets – and the suggestion that a strike carrier was nearby – dramatically changed the military odds in Britain's favour.

Left: On alert. A Convair F-102 Delta Dagger waits on the apron at Homestead Air Force Base. The Florida Air National Guard F-102 alert detachment at the base was the busiest in the United States. In 1972, following a serious breach of southern air defences in New Orleans the previous year, the Florida Air National Guard were determined to meet and stop any inbound unidentified radar return.

The Buccaneers return. Nearly six hours after launching from the carrier, the strike pair, escorted by the tankers, flew past *Ark Royal*'s bridge as they joined the carrier's circuit.

Left: Her arrestor hook trailing, ready to catch a wire, 021 recovers aboard 'Mother'.

XN977

Above: Immediately following their return, the two Buccaneer crews were congratulated on the flight deck by *Ark*'s Captain John Roberts and presented with framed pictures of the launch. From left to right, Steve Park, Carl Davis, John Roberts, Colin Walkinshaw and Mike Lucas.

Above: For their successful mission, the crews were awarded the Boyd Trophy. Presented annually, the trophy recognized the year's outstanding feat of naval aviation. Steve Park, Carl Davis and Colin Walkinshaw pose with the trophy. Mike Lucas had already taken up an exchange posting flying A-6 Intruders with the US Navy.

Above: *Ark Royal* soldiered on throughout the seventies as the Royal Navy's only remaining strike carrier. This rare colour picture of her alongside the USS *Nimitz*, the first of a new generation of nuclear-powered US supercarriers, graphically demonstrates how hard she had to work to keep pace.

Above: *Ark* finally paid off in 1978. Following the fly-on-the-wall documentary *Sailor*, broadcast in 1976, she was without doubt the most well-known and well-loved ship in the Navy. Her demise was felt keenly.

Chapter 44

'It's a bit bloody wobbly up here!' Carl Davis told his Looker over the intercom. The Buccaneer was designed with one thing in mind and it wasn't cruising at high altitude. As he formated on the port wing of the tanker at 30,000 feet, forty minutes after he'd been shot from the deck of the carrier, he could feel the mushiness in the flight controls. The ailerons weren't biting the air like they could down low. It made precise flying more difficult – demanded greater anticipation. Davis flew with his right hand on the stick and his left on the two throttles, trying to keep the number of control inputs to a minimum. To help compensate for the greater difficulty he'd have in making contact, Davis set the autostabilizers to 'Approach'. Behind him, Steve Park switched the HF to silent and checked the Blue Parrot control panel ahead of him to make sure that the radar was switched to 'Standby'. No one was going to thank him for microwaving Pete Lewis and George Dammeyer inside the tanker.

While Lewis flew the tanker at a steady 250 knots, in the back Dammeyer reached to bottom left of the Mk 20 control panel and flicked the master switch up and selected 'Trail'. The blue brake-on light blinked out, and the hose-in light next to it began to flash. At full trail the red signal light changed to amber. Ready. Dammeyer looked up at Davis and gave him a thumbs-up to tell him he was cleared to drop into line astern to take on fuel. Davis pulled a few revs off the engines and dropped back and down before nudging on the power again to climb towards the shuttlecock-shaped basket trailing from the Buddy pod under the tanker's starboard wing. Rising slowly through the air, he closed in at no more than two or three knots. The refuelling probe on 030's nose seemed to be reaching forward for the succour of the drogue. Like circling heavyweights, the relative movement of the two big strike jets through three dimensions was languid and unhurried. Davis concentrated on the shape of the Buccaneer's distinctive plan form, rather than the tiny, distracting bobbling movement of the basket as it was pulled through the sky. The vital thing was not to snatch at it in a last-second lunge for a connection. Too much yaw especially and the end of the probe would sheer off like a lizard's tail to protect both the tanker and the receiver from worse injury.

In nearby sky, Walkinshaw and Lucas were conducting a similar aerial ballet behind Neil Maclean's tanker.

Lewis and Dammeyer felt a hint of a bunt forward as 030 made contact then continued to push forward another six or seven feet to trigger the flow of fuel through the 2-inch steel-reinforced hose. On the refuelling pod control panel the amber light was replaced by the green light to the right. Fuel flows. Dammeyer watched the numbers spin up as fuel flowed at just over 1100lb per minute into the Buccaneer's tanks.

In the cockpit of 030, Steve Park watched the three fuel dials to his left revolve clockwise as the jet filled its boots. Four minutes after they'd made contact and 4000lb of fuel to the good, all three recorded full tanks. Ahead of him, Carl Davis watched the lights in the back of the refuelling pod switch to amber. They'd had their fill. He slowly throttled back, careful to try to fly below the trailing line of the hose to avoid being hit by it at the moment of disengagement. As they dropped back, the probe pulled the basket with it, until the hose had unspooled to its full 50-foot extent, then tugged free with the familiar puff of fuel spray.

Well done, Boss, Park volunteered over the intercom.

Gently rolling away, Davis nudged open the throttles again to join the tanker on its starboard wing. Dammeyer gave him a thumbs-up and selected 'Wind'. Fifteen seconds later, Davis confirmed that the hose was fully stowed.

The two tanker crews gave a wave and peeled away for the fifty-minute return flight to 'Mother' leaving the strike pair flying on alone. Walkinshaw and Lucas moved into battle formation a few hundred yards to starboard of Red Leader. Below them, they could see the Bahamas archipelago stretching out to the south, ground features flattened by altitude and high early-afternoon sun. Each island was cocooned by an outline of shallow turquoise that highlighted it against the deep-blue/grey Atlantic beyond. They could see white water lapping at the beaches. The 20,000lb of fuel in their tanks were needed to take them from here to Central America and back again for their next RV with the tanker. For the next four hours they were on their own. Davis and Walkinshaw trimmed the Buccaneers to cruise-climb. As they burnt fuel and became lighter, the two jets would rise gently to an altitude of 39,000 feet. They were a long way from Buccaneer's comfort zone, but, Park and Lucas calculated, in the best place to eke out the precious contents of their tanks.

From the Ops Room, John Roberts heard news of the successful refuelling reported back by Neil Maclean to Harry O'Grady. The 892 Fighter Controller could see both tankers as inbound orange blips on the big CRT display of his Type 965 two-dimensional search radar. No problems so far, but it was in making sure that they made the RV over Grand Bahama with the returning strike pair that he'd really earn his crust.

Keen that the whole Ship's Company were aware of the job they were doing, John Roberts got on to the main broadcast. Wall-mounted speakers throughout the carrier hummed, before Roberts's voice came through.

'This is the Captain. The Buccaneers have refuelled successfully and are now safely on their way to British Honduras.'

Sailing so close to Cuba, Commander Robert Irving had ordered radio silence. HMS *Phoebe* was steaming at 24 knots towards Belize City. Four hours earlier she'd altered course on to a heading of 203 degrees to take her south between the western tip of Cuba and the Yucatán. During the next four hours she would be providing SAR cover for *Ark Royal*'s strike pair. At 1055SIERRA, just five minutes after the two Buccaneers had completed their first refuelling north-west of the Bahamas, *Phoebe*'s Aircraft Controller picked up two contacts on a spoke of 028 degrees which he assumed to be the Buccaneers. When he logged the contact, the Buccaneers were still east of Florida flying in on a heading of 240 degrees. From *Phoebe*'s position she could expect to see them approaching from 060 degrees. Whatever it was he'd picked up on the frigate's Type 903 radar, it wasn't 030 and 021.

Miami Center, this is Navjet Zero Three Zero, do you read?

As the strike pair streamed in at 420 knots towards Florida, Steve Park wasn't having much luck raising the Americans from the back seat of the lead Buccaneer.

Miami Center, this is Navjet Zero Three Zero, do you read?

Carl Davis listened with mounting frustration to his Looker's efforts to obtain clearance to fly through US airspace. The two British jets had diplomatic clearance, but they still needed to inform Air Traffic of their progress.

Miami Center, this is Navjet Zero Three Zero, do you read?

Inside Red Two, Walkinshaw and Lucas listened in, waiting for some sign of life. Davis had had enough. It was time for an executive decision.

'Right,' he declared to Park over the intercom, 'we're clear to go. Whether we speak to them or not, we're going.' Then a Southern accent crackled through the static.

Navjet Zero Three Zero, this is Miami Center, pass your message.

At last.

Miami Center, this is Navjet Zero Three Zero, Park expanded, *we are two Buccaneers en route from Golf Kilo Yankee Sierra to Belize, Flight Level Three Nine Zero, requesting clearance to overfly your airspace.*

There was too long a pause before the reply came.

Ah, Navjet Zero Three Zero, we do not have your flight plan.

Something wasn't right. Their flight plan had been sent by Ops to the US authorities. The crews had double-checked on that before manning their aircraft. Park tried explaining.

Miami Center, a flight plan was filed by Golf Kilo Yankee Sierra. Navjet Zero Three Zero.

The repetition of *Ark Royal*'s unique four-letter international identifier – which should have made it clear that they were flying from a British aircraft carrier – seemed to spark no kind of recognition from the controllers.

We do not have clearance for you.

And that was the last the strike pair heard from Miami Center.

As the Florida coast loomed below them, Davis considered his options. *They didn't*, he figured, *actually tell us to turn back*. And the transit across the tip of the panhandle and the Keys wouldn't take long. *Only five or six minutes*, he thought. *Oh, what the hell*. He quickly decided to simply get on with the job he'd been ordered to do.

The Buccaneers pushed on to the south-west on a heading that pointed them directly at the north-west tip of the Yucatán Peninsula. As they flew out over the Keys, Park put in routine calls to Homestead AFB and Naval Air Station Key West. Below them, the Keys curled out to sea like a length of chain. Linked by causeways, the islands had the appearance of a giant harbour wall protecting the mainland within. The earthy shallows between were a riveting patchwork of rust- and brown-coloured banks and mottled with submarine flora visible just below the blues and greens of water criss-crossed with the white wakes of speedboats. As they cruised overhead the Naval Air Station at the southernmost tip of the archipelago, a magnificent sweep of vivid turquoise seemed to mark the transition to open water. And to the south, they could see Cuba. At altitude they could see both sides of the front line, the two belligerents' proximity to each other clearly apparent. For the men of the Southern ADIZ Control Center at Fort Leigh, Virginia, the Florida Straits were, since the unscheduled arrival of Cubana 877 just three months earlier, practically hostile airspace.

And the intrusion by two Limey strike jets who didn't appear to have filed a flight plan provoked a flurry of activity that was already working its way up the chain of command. And back down again.

Chapter 45

The sky outside was a lot less forgiving than at the heights the Buccaneers usually operated at. Above 10,000 feet, without oxygen, aircrews begin to suffer from hypoxia, or oxygen starvation. Up near 40,000 feet, a point just below where the tropopause marks the transition to the stratosphere, the air temperature could drop below minus 60 degrees Fahrenheit. And, above that, gases inside the body expand dangerously. In 1959 an American fighter pilot bailed out from 50,000 feet. He survived. Just. But when he reached the ground he was bleeding from every orifice.

The altitude flown by the two 809 Squadron jets was dictated solely by the need for economy. Other than giving them the legs for the long mission, it complicated everything else. The autopilot was practically useless. Buccaneer crews could normally set it to follow either a speed or a height along with a heading. But not above 35,000 feet. Davis and Walkinshaw were hand-flying all six hours of this sortie. And if it had been bloody wobbly at 30,000 feet, it was worse at 39,000.

The autostabilizers, three gyros connected by computer to the powered flight controls, helped limit the effects of dutch roll – a tendency of swept-wing aircraft to roll from side to side – and the diminished stability that the Buccaneer, rock-solid at low level, suffered at altitude. Flying straight and level the two pilots were OK, but any manoeuvres at all needed to be gentle – carried out with the kid gloves both were wearing.

Only the engines really seemed settled at 39,000 feet. The Rolls-Royce Spey Mk 101 bypass turbojets, originally designed for the Hawker-Siddeley Trident airliner, were spinning happily, burning frugal sips of Avcat with compressed air in ten combustion chambers before expelling the hot gas through two-stage turbines and out of the jet pipes. But even the Speys demanded a constant vigil from the two pilots. At altitude, the usually comfortable margin between cruising speed and stall speed was greatly reduced. And as unlikely as an engine flame-out might be, it could strike without warning. It wasn't that long ago that, on a similarly long-range, high-altitude flight, it happened, with disastrous effects, to a Buccaneer crew Carl Davis knew well.

No. 24 Squadron of the South African Air Force was re-formed at RNAS Lossiemouth in May 1965. While the sixteen Buccaneers ordered by South Africa were built, their crews were trained in Scotland by 736 Naval Air Squadron. Davis was one of the flying instructors. On 27 October, the first batch of eight South African Buccaneer S Mk 50s took off from Lossiemouth for the long delivery flight to their final destination, AFB Waterkloof near Pretoria. The six-day, 6000-mile journey was broken up into stages and the eight Buccaneers were followed by an SAAF Lockheed C-130B Hercules carrying the squadron's support crew.

On the penultimate leg, flying at high altitude between Cape Verde and Ascension Island, one of a pair of jets suffered a double-engine flame-out and stalled. With their aircraft in an unrecoverable spin, the Buccaneer's Pilot and Navigator, Captain Matin Jooste and Lieutenant Anton de Klerk, ejected, leaving the Buccaneer to tumble out of the sky and crash into the Atlantic. After a brief search carried out by his wingman revealed nothing but a patch of oil on the sea's surface, two of the SAAF's long-range Avro Shackleton MR3 maritime patrol aircraft were scrambled from Portuguese Guinea and Ascension. The two air-crew were eventually found alive, floating inside their small yellow inflatable raft in thousands of miles of empty, grey sea.

And, after two nights at sea, injured, cold and seasick, they were safely picked up by the MS *Randfontein*, a Dutch liner *en route* from the UK to Cape Town.

In the cockpits of 021 and 030, Carl Davis and 'Boots' Walkinshaw coaxed the big low-level bombers on through the thin air, their eyes continually darting to the bottom right of the instrument panel to watch the engine temperatures and pressures. In the back seats, the two Lookers, Park and Lucas, marked their progress against the flight plan on their log cards, making sure that they were exactly where they expected to be. And that the fuel gauges revealed no unpleasant surprises. If there were, each of them had a SARBE beacon, attached to his waistband, that would broadcast his position to a distance of sixty miles on contact with water, flares, dye, markers, a small dinghy and a whistle. And inside the survival pack attached to their Mae West lifejackets, along with ground/air emergency codes, a razor blade and a heliograph, was shark-repellent, rumoured to be as good at attracting barracudas as it was at keeping sharks at bay.

The scratchy metallic amplification of the ship's main broadcast rang out again, ordering *Hands to Recovery Stations*. As the strike pair passed north of Havana, *Ark Royal* turned into wind to bring the two tankers back on board. After an hour and three-quarters in the air, Maclean and Lewis arrived back on deck and were marshalled to the deck park. There was less than two hours before they'd have to strap into their seats and remove the safety pins and spool up the engines ready to launch again.

Officer of the Watch, come back to our course.

As the handlers lashed the two Buccaneers to the flight deck, just six minutes after coming off it, John Roberts was already bringing his ship back on to its intended course.

Steer course Two Five Five.

The wind over the deck dropped a little as the Flight Deck Engineers got to work on the two tankers. With firesuit men standing by, they locked pressure refuelling hoses on to the couplings on the starboard side of the jets' noses to refill their tanks.

With her oiler, *Olmeda*, trailing many hundreds of miles behind, *Ark Royal* didn't enjoy the opportunity to do the same. Still steaming at over 24 knots, she was burning prodigious quantities of FFO, around 1000 tons a day, well over twice the normal rate. Tanks that might normally keep her cruising for over ten days were, after forty-eight hours, nearly half empty. Concerned about just how much longer they could keep hammering along like this, Commander Ewan Maclean, the head of the carrier's Marine Engineering Department, began to plan ahead and marshal his resources.

At school, Maclean's geography teacher had insisted that the class use their fingers to walk their way round a globe naming all the pink bits. It had served him well during his Admiralty Interview Board. After being asked if he could tie a reef knot, Maclean was asked where British Guiana was. He didn't hesitate. So when John Roberts had told him they'd be belting towards British Honduras, Maclean was able to place the little colony instantly. And he jumped at the challenge of being able to deliver *Ark*'s flat steel top to wherever her Captain and Air Department needed it. As far as he was concerned, doing so was the beginning and end of his job and that of the 850-strong department he was responsible for. He was happy to leave cocktail parties to the ship's Salthorses.

Below *Ark Royal*'s waterline, fuel tanks seemed to fill every available space. From the twenty tanks in the double-bottom compartments to long rows of tanks that encircled the central machinery spaces on Eight Deck and inside the watertight compartments of the carrier's double hull, there was room for around 6000 tons of FFO. But many of the smaller tanks never really needed to be drawn on. With regular liquid replenishment from the Royal Fleet Auxiliaries, Maclean could normally limit himself to using the contents of the biggest, easiest tanks. But as *Ark* steamed towards the Caribbean, he tried pumping FFO from the small, bottom tanks early on. Rather than get caught out when it came to the crunch, he wanted to know he could access their contents before being forced to rely on them.

Where there weren't tanks carrying the dark, viscous FFO, there were others holding the Avcat and diesel. Maclean had wondered if he might keep *Ark* steaming a little longer by burning diesel and, as a last resort, the thin aviation fuel. Both would burn, but both, he knew, would also leak out of the joints and glands of the ship's plumbing. The diesel, at least though, was worth a go. As they steamed south, Maclean tried burning a small quantity of FFO diluted with diesel to satisfy himself it was an option. It seemed to do the trick. If it came to Avcat, though, the worst really would have come to the worst.

I'd rather, he thought, *ask some passing Guatemalan for oil.*

In another day or so, Maclean knew he needed to start pumping seawater into the empty fuel tanks to maintain the ballast. It would take months to clean that out of the system. But, in the end, it wasn't fuel that would turn out to be the Engineering Officer's biggest headache.

As Maclean worked to keep *Ark* steaming south, the RAF were enduring problems of their own. Wyton's Canberra PR9s had already been forced to abandon plans to stand by at Palisadoes in Jamaica because of post-colonial sensitivities. Instead they were on their way to Nassau, 300 miles further away from British Honduras. On top of that, a strike by Canadian Air Traffic Controllers forced them to abandon plans to route via Gander in Newfoundland. Instead they'd been forced to opt for the longer, southerly route via the Azores. Now, John Morgan and his colleagues were stuck there. Since Morgan and his CO had flight-planned their next leg, stronger than anticipated headwinds meant that even the long-ranged PR9s couldn't safely make the distance to Bermuda. While it would still be possible to ferry the seventy personnel supporting the detachment on board transport aircraft, 39 Squadron's Canberras were, for the time being, stranded mid-Atlantic. For John Morgan it was almost a blessing. Because he was definitely coming down with flu.

The RAF reconnaissance crews weren't the only ones having difficulties in the Azores. The Portuguese authorities were complaining bitterly to the British government about everything. By flying armed aircraft through Lajes without prior permission, they said, Britain had broken the terms of its agreement to use the island airbase as a staging post. The substance of their contention was open to interpretation, however. Although unarmed C-130s and VC10s had carried armed soldiers in and out of Lajes, not a single armed aircraft had been anywhere near it. But the detail of the argument didn't matter. Britain was issued with an ultimatum threatening to deny RAF Air Support Command vital access to Lajes. On the bright side, there were reports that Gander would soon be open for business again.

And there was progress at RAF Wittering too, where 1(F) Squadron's engineers had successfully fitted the big 330-gallon finned overload tanks under the wings of the Harriers. It looked like each was carrying a pair of Zeppelins. All four now needed to be test-flown by the pilots chosen to fly them as the heavy tanks played havoc with the little jet's centre of gravity and low-speed handling.

'Boss, I think I've got something . . .' There was urgency in the Scottish Observer's voice. Steve Park strained to hear the signal from the Radar Warning Receiver. In fairings under each wing, the Buccaneer carried antennas for its ARI 18218 Wideband Homer – a basic radar warning receiver capable of picking up X and S band radar transmissions. And, through his headset, Park believed he'd picked up a ghost of a tone representing the PRF – Pulse Repetition Frequency – of a search radar. As they flew west, broadly parallel to the north-Cuban coast, they were flying across the face of a heavy concentration of Cuban SAM sites. Park leaned forward into the CRT scope to the left of the cockpit to look for the bright orange spoke that would confirm the direction of the aural warning. He turned up the brilliance control and audio volume, but there was nothing more. Amid the electronic clatter on the airwaves, there were always random clicks and whistles. And sometimes there were phantom returns that sent a surge of adrenalin through the veins of the Looker on sentry duty. They were in the clear, but the scare was a reminder that the Cubans had the potential to be trouble. And, real or not, it was a cue to stay on their guard. One thousand yards off 030's starboard wing, the dark shape of the second Buccaneer flew in battle formation. Inside, Walkinshaw and Lucas watched their Flight Leader's tail.

In Guatemala City, President Arana ordered his Army Chief of Staff, General Laugerud, to place the Army on alert.

Across town at La Aurora airbase, on the apron in front of the Fuerza Aerea Guatemalteca's splendid art deco hangars, a pair of muddily camouflaged North American F-51D Mustangs coughed into life. Watched over by a Crew Chief standing alongside, each of them spat clouds of thick smoke from exhausts on the nose ahead of the cockpit. As their pains-takingly maintained old piston engines warmed up and settled down, the veteran fighter bombers strained at the yellow chocks holding them back, looking skittish as the blast from their big yellow-tipped, four-bladed propellers coursed back over the wings and fuselage. Their canopies open, the pilots pushed forward the throttle levers for their power checks, shutting down each magneto in turn. And two supercharged V-12 Packard Merlin engines, each throwing out nearly 1700 horsepower, let out an angry, thoroughbred roar. The two Mustangs bounced urgently on their little tailwheels. Both were armed with .50 calibre bullets, a pair of 500lb bombs and ten 5-inch rockets. Major Consenza's Escuadrón de Caza was being forward-deployed to the airfield at Puerto Barrios on Guatemala's Caribbean Coast. Just thirty miles from Punta Gorda, the capital of British Honduras's Toledo District.

Five minutes later they were airborne, tucking up their undercarriage as they stayed low along the runway, gathering speed against a spectacular backdrop of perfect volcanic peaks to the south-west.

*

At Finca Ixabel, faced with the escalating Guatemalan army presence and uncertain of what would happen next, the young Americans took refuge in humour. What they needed, they thought, was to make a special flag with the Guatemalan colours on one side and the Union Jack on the other. They'd be ready then for whoever came down the driveway.

Chapter 46

In ten years of flying, much of it in the typhoon-afflicted skies of the Far East, Carl Davis had never seen thunderheads like it. Vast pillars of cumulo-nimbus clouds towered above the two Buccaneers as they crossed the Tropic of Cancer. Layer heaped upon layer like giant white limestone stalactites, but rolling skywards with explosive force, blocking their way. To try to go through them would be madness. They were stormclouds. And their overwhelming power was evident.

The energy contained inside a building cumulo-nimbus formation could power a small town. It was a turbulent, indiscriminate monster of violent wind shear, electricity, rain and hail that could break an aircraft like an ogre toying with a matchstick cathedral.

They're spectacular, thought Carl Davis, transfixed by the massive clouds. But they made the two Buccaneers, as robust as the big naval bombers were, seem very small and very fragile.

'I hope to hell we haven't got one of those over Belize,' he said to Park over the intercom. That really would scupper their plans. There was no option but to come off their heading, to cut the corner and fly round it.

Turn port Three Zero, Boss, Park instructed, *on to Two One Five degrees*. Gingerly, Davis dipped the wing into the turn, careful not to unsettle 030's efforts to cope with the high altitude. Off the starboard nose, he and Park could see the baked, brown coastline of Mexico below them. In the other jet,

Mike Lucas was taking the lens cap off his camera to get those awe-inspiring cunims on film. And as they headed south-west, Steve Park noted Isla Cozumel, shaped like a mini mirror-image of Cyprus, passing below between them and Cancún on the mainland. The outline of her palm-fringed beaches was visible even from seven miles up. They were a long way from the mid-Atlantic.

Ark Royal was losing boiler feed water. And Ewan Maclean knew she couldn't afford to. Fresh water for the boilers was the blood in the veins of a steam ship. But *Ark*'s elderly distillers only produced about 500 tons a day and that was close to what the boilers were consuming daily. Maclean knew that they were the ship's Achilles heel. Even *Eagle* had produced so much that two hosepipes hung off the quarterdeck pumping the excess back into the sea. He thought of the millions that had been spent on refitting *Ark Royal* to operate the Phantoms. *Why*, he wondered, *hadn't they managed to sneak in a spanking-new distilling plant?* He wished the Navy spent a little more time and money trying to get the best out of the kit it had, rather than spending all its time worrying about the shiny new stuff it wanted. He was fed up with the constant anxiety of having enough to keep the boilers going. *This isn't going to bloody well happen again*, he decided. *Time to go and see John Oliver Roberts*. Maclean wasn't going to let the kingdom be lost for the sake of a nail.

'Hello, Chief, what's wrong?' Whenever Maclean appeared on the bridge, Roberts greeted him the same way. The head of the Marine Engineering Department usually took great pleasure in simply announcing: 'Steam in eight boilers, sir.' But not this time.

'Sir,' he told the Captain, 'I think it would be wise to be prepared to anchor because unless we can stop this haemorrhaging of water – and we don't know where it's going – we're going to have to start taking off boilers to try to isolate the problem.' Roberts took it in before replying.

'I've got good news for you, Chief,' he told the engineer,

confident in Maclean's ability to come up with a solution. 'We're heading for the Cayman Deep and I haven't got the cable.' At its deepest point, the Cayman trench, which scarred the ocean floor of the Caribbean Sea between British Honduras and the south coast of Cuba, was nearly five miles below the surface.

Maclean already had a glimmer of an idea. He left the bridge for the Ops Room. He wanted to ask Mike Cole if he could appropriate something from the WAFUs.

Ark Royal's engine rooms and machinery spaces were like a scene from the Industrial Revolution. Claustrophobic walkways, hemmed in by metal bulkheads and low ceilings, threaded around boilers, evaporators, turbines and tanks. On every surface there were exposed pipes of every gauge, dials, wheels, handles and hanging lamps with dented metal shades. As well as iron and steel there were also items furnished in copper and brass. And there was the heat. Seldom seeing the light of day, the 'Steamies' worked in salt-stained overalls undone to the waist, keeping themselves hydrated on a mixture of water and oatmeal. They were a breed apart.

When Ewan Maclean's Senior Engineer, Chris Furse, had acknowledged his appointment, his letter, scrawled in pencil on a sheet of loo paper, arrived from Elephant Island in the South Shetlands. Serving aboard the Navy's Ice Patrol ship, HMS *Endurance*, Furse had apologized, explaining that ink froze and paper was hard to come by. Maclean knew immediately that he'd fit right in.

Maclean and his number two discussed the best way to tackle the problem. They considered the possibility of using one of the empty tanks in the double hull, but dismissed it because of the difficulty of feeding water in and out. They'd have had to use firehoses. In the end, they went for something rather more substantial – and permanent. They were going to take one of the Avcat tanks. As Mike Cole had confirmed, the ship was carrying more aviation fuel than the air group could possibly use.

Furse got to work on rerouting the pipework from the

requisitioned tank into 'A' Boiler Room. Where they didn't have components they needed, they manufactured them. The Navy had a tradition of self-sufficiency that had meant blacksmiths, engine smiths, pattern makers, coppersmiths, boilermakers, fitters and turners were all part of the Ship's Company. But whatever resourcefulness they displayed, the crucial thing was not to contaminate the aviation fuel. Get water in that and the 'Heavies' would start falling out of the sky. Maclean impressed it upon one of his young officers.

'You are to look at every single nut, bolt, screw, split pin, washer, you name it and make quite certain that there's no connection with what we're trying to do and the rest of the ship's system.'

It appeared to be a Heath Robinson solution to a serious shortcoming, but the cleaned-out, re-plumbed ex-Avcat tank worked. Maclean had never doubted it would. *Simple stuff*, he thought, *like moving the garden hose from tulips to daffs*. But, at a stroke, the new tank had doubled *Ark*'s capacity for storing boiler feed water.

Chris Furse christened it the 'Mac Tank'. And Maclean, working on the WOB – Worry the Other Bastard – principle of management, sent a letter, designed to reach the Admiralty as slowly as possible, informing them that he'd made a significant 'Alteration and Amendment' to their only aircraft carrier. He doubted anyone would muster the courage to query his decision if they had any doubts at all about the effect it might have on *Ark Royal*'s ability to do her job.

'Sod it!' Carl Davis hissed, 'I've just dropped my lunch . . .' Before leading the strike pair into their descent towards Belize City, the 809 Boss had hoped to enjoy one of the boiled sweets he'd carefully stashed away in his flightsuit pocket. They'd been strapped inside the cramped confines of the Buccaneer cockpit for over two and half hours now. With oxygen masks clamped tightly to their faces, breathing dry oxygen mix against the almost imperceptible resistance of a valve and with the incessant hiss of static and hum of the aircraft's systems, it was beginning to get a little uncomfortable for both crews. And now, just as he'd tried to pull the sweets out they'd all spilled out on to the metal floor of the cockpit and were rolling around the rudder pedals. And it would be difficult, Davis figured, to jam anything so badly with a boiled sweet that a bit of brute force wouldn't quickly sort it out.

As he looked up, the first thing he saw was the barrier reef – a vivid turquoise echo of the coastline sitting ten to fifteen miles out to sea along its entire length.

'Incredible,' he said to Park over the intercom, 'it's like a camera shot of what we've been looking at over the last two days. What's the range?'

Sixty-five miles, Boss, Park confirmed, *commence range descent now*. Davis scanned his instruments and checked his fuel.

'God, we're spot on here,' he congratulated his Looker as he reached forward with his left hand to pull the two throttle levers back until he had 73 per cent rpm. The tone from the engines that had been a constant since they were east of Florida dropped. And as the two Speys spooled down, Davis maintained a gentle back pressure on the stick, sacrificing speed for height. As the air speed indicator wound down, he kept pulling, raising the nose high until, at the Buccaneer's maximum comfortable angle of attack, he let her go, allowing her to settle into a 320-knot cruise-descent that would save them gallons of precious Avcat. Over 65 miles they'd burn less than 250lb of fuel. And, Park assured him, they'd arrive over the beach in under ten minutes' time at the required 1000-feet minimum altitude. Davis wouldn't have to touch the power until Belize City. With 030 established in the descent he retrimmed her and just let her fly herself. He looked forward to getting some snap back into the flight controls.

Passing 10,000 feet.

In the rear cockpit of 021, Mike Lucas read off the heights from the little altimeter on his port console while 'Boots' Walkinshaw tucked in a hundred yards off the lead jet's starboard rear quarter. The Fleet Air Arm was determined to make an entrance.

Check radio altimeter, called the two Observers as the strike pair descended through 5000 feet.

4000 . . . 3000 . . . 2000 . . .

Chapter 47

Seventeen-year-old David Gibson had only lasted a year at the strict, Catholic St John's College before jumping ship to study for his A-levels at the more accommodating Wessex House. A teenage radical, he found expression in the Black Power movement and Belize's own UBAD party and its leader, Evan X Hyde. It had been Gibson's godfather who'd turned back the Guatemalan President the day in 1958 that he'd arrived at the border demanding to see the Governor. His parents remained immensely proud of the story. But whatever misgivings the seventeen-year-old might have had about the Guatemalans, his strongest feelings were reserved for the British imperialists. And yet, today, he couldn't help but feel conflicting loyalties. The front page of the morning newspaper had carried the news that aircraft from HMS *Ark Royal* would be flying over Belize City.

And Gibson's growing consciousness had never quite pushed aside a boyhood interest in aeroplanes. Charles Lindbergh was the first person to fly into Belize City, when, in December 1927, he brought the *Spirit of St Louis* to town. The landing by the 'Lone Eagle' was, of course, long before Gibson's time, but he vividly remembered his excitement over more-recent visitors like the RAF's elegant white-painted Vickers Valiant V-bombers that had surveyed the country in the wake of the Hurricane Hattie disaster, or the Griffon-engined Avro Shackletons of Coastal Command that occasionally flew in from British bases in the Caribbean. By lunchtime there was a rumour that *Ark Royal* was steaming just beyond English Caye.

*

The view ahead of the Buccaneer's nose was stunning. After his concern over what kind of weather would greet them, Carl Davis was looking at brilliant afternoon sun streaming in from the west through scattered clouds. It had just rained and pools of water on the ground caught and reflected the sun as they turned inland. At 1000 feet, Davis pulled back on the stick to level off and fed in power. If he kept the airspeed above 300 knots they wouldn't need flaps, aileron droop and blowing. That would have meant more drag. Instead, a clean airframe meant lower fuel burn and, this far from home, economy was the name of the game. The squadron Boss thumbed the RT button on the nearside throttle lever.

'Right,' he announced enthusiastically, 'we'd better get around here . . .'

First there was barely a murmur in the air. But just after one o'clock Gibson heard an engine note take shape as the four Rolls-Royce Speys, on Davis and Walkinshaw's command, roared into life to herald the Buccaneers' arrival. Along with his schoolmates, he went running outside to watch the pair of dark, potent-looking naval bombers sweep over the city. They looked fantastic, he thought. And, despite himself, he couldn't help but be impressed by the great power on display. In the rumour and speculation over Guatemalan intentions that had, for the last day and half, dominated conversation in Belize City, it felt better to know that the British were on their side.

With one eye on 030, 'Boots' Walkinshaw could only afford to glance over the City, but it was recognizably the same place he'd seen at ground level in 1959. He picked out the distinctive shape of the mouth of Haulover Creek, where the muddy-brown freshwater flowed out into the clean sea; and, beneath the belly of the other Buccaneer, the big white-painted old Governor's House on the waterfront, where he'd first heard half-forgotten stories about belligerent neighbours. In the back of 021, Mike Lucas snapped away with the big Hasselblad, taking pictures of 030 orbiting the city. One or two buildings stood out, like St John's Cathedral or the big courthouse by the river mouth, but even they, Lucas noticed, were capped by the ubiquitous brown and green corrugated tin roofs that made the most obvious visual impression. All were still wet from the rain, their angles glinting in the high early-afternoon sun behind them. The two Fleet Air Arm jets flew up the southern seafront and out over boats tied up in the creek before they cruised heavily over Fort George, the peninsula pointing down from the north of the city.

From the manicured tropical gardens of the Fort George Hotel, Carl Faulkner watched 030 and 021 cross noisily overhead, leaving faint smoke trails against blue sky. From the ground the threatening-looking shapes of the two bombers seemed locked in grim formation. He picked out the red, white and blue roundels under wings curved like a pair of cutlasses and enjoyed a surge of happy recognition. He'd felt an affinity with the Brits since his life had depended on their guns in Korea. And with the arrival of the Buccaneers he knew that all this worrying talk of a threat from Guatemala would come to nothing. *There are*, he thought, rolling over in his mind a long-held belief, *only three warrior races, America, Israel and Great Britain*. And the sight of *Ark Royal*'s strike pair just underlined it. They were an inspiring presence. The rule of law, he felt pretty sure, would continue in British Honduras for a while yet.

Carl Davis switched VHF frequencies to 118.1 and pressed the RT button.

Belize Tower, this is Navjet Zero Three Zero.

Air Traffic answered quickly and Davis asked for permission to fly through their overhead. It was more of a courtesy call than a request. The civilian controllers in the tower above the small, whitewashed terminal building were expecting the Buccaneers and gave their immediate assent.

OK, Zero Three Zero. Roger.

Davis banked to port and levelled off on a heading of 288

degrees for the two-minute flight along the coast to Stanley Field. Below them, the black strip of the Corozal road led the way.

The inevitable rumour mill on board *Ark* had given rise to talk of incursions on to the airfield, guerrillas in the jungle and small-arms fire. As ridiculous as that Wardroom chat seemed now, it made no sense not at least to be on the look-out. And as Carl Davis saw the long line of the Runway 07/25 heave into view ahead, ringed by the meandering brown loops of the Belize River and bordered by Airport Camp to the north, he looked carefully for anything that seemed amiss. The two Buccaneers crossed the overhead at 1000 feet.

'Steve, do you see anything strange?' Davis asked his Observer.

'Anything on the edge of the jungle?' Park could see nothing.

Maybe they heard us coming. The CO smiled to himself.

The single platoon of Grenadiers dug in around the perimeter to defend the airfield were weapons-tight in anticipation of the Fleet Air Arm's show of force. As the jets' shadows tracked along the ground, the handful of young Guardsmen looked up from their old Browning guns to watch as the formation growled belligerently across the sky, ugly against light, cotton wool clouds. Whatever happened next, the soldiers knew they were no longer on their own.

From inside 021, Mike Lucas strained to get a good view of the airfield, but sitting deep inside the fuselage, with the big circular air intakes on either side of him, the one thing he had absolutely no sight of was what was directly below. Once past the airport, the Observer watched 030 dip a wing and roll into a lazy left-hand turn to bring them back into the overhead. Walkinshaw followed Red Leader a beat later. And as they banked round, bisecting the runway from north to south, Lucas was able to get pictures of the scene below to take back aboard *Ark* for the Intelligence Officers to pore over.

'Time to go home, Boss,' Park told his Pilot. He'd been keeping a close eye on the fuel. They'd only ever had ten minutes over Belize City and it was now up. But there was an opportunity for one final flourish. The whole sortie was about showing a presence. Before they turned for home, Davis wanted to let them know there was a presence. *No good*, he thought, *flying over the airfield at 1000 feet, is there?*

They needed 400 knots on the clock before entering the climb in any case – it made sense to use gravity to help them on their way. Davis turned again and, with 021 a hundred yards off his starboard quarter, raised his right hand, then, holding it flat, palm-down, inclined it forward to tell his Senior Pilot that he was descending. Davis lowered the nose and poured on the coals. As both pilots pushed the twin throttles forward to the stops, the two bombers swooped down towards the airfield, gathering speed as they went down the hill. Park and Lucas called the heights.

900 . . . 800 . . . 700 . . . 600 . . .

Pulling up.

As the strike pair flashed over the terminal building, descending through 500 feet at 400 knots, Davis pulled back on the stick. The nose came up as the all-flying tailplane bit into the thick low-level air. Momentum carried the heavy bomber down through another 100 feet until, 400 feet above the airfield, he and his wingman began to climb away to the north-west, leaving behind thick black trails of smoke, an unholy racket and an indelible impression.

Richard Corkran missed it all. The Commanding Officer of the Inkerman Company was up-country with the troops blocking the Western Highway. But he received news quickly over the radio from the Signals detachment at Airport Camp. *A good thing too*, he thought, reassured that the Grenadiers were no longer the only line of defence.

Nearly 5000 miles away, as the Royal Navy's show of force receded to a low rumble carried on the breeze over a distant outpost, British viewers settled into their armchairs at the end of the working week. After the news, millions of them tuned their sets to ITV to watch Hughie Green host a game show called *The Sky's the Limit*, followed by Roger Moore and Tony Curtis starring in the latest episode of *The Persuaders*.

And in the little two-room Guatemalan Consulate in Belize City, Secretary Tulio Martinez was managing the office while his boss, the Consul, Colonel Dubois, made his way back from a visit home. He picked up the telephone and, overlooked by the official portrait of President Arana that hung on the wall, dialled the number for the Ministry of External Relations in Guatemala City.

Chapter 48

Going to SSB, Steve Park told his Pilot and, with a click, Carl Davis lost the Observer while he tried to send a message to *Ark* on the low-frequency single sideband radio. They'd overflown British Honduras and were now on their way home to 'Mother'. But Park's main concern was fuel. As they climbed up over the long finger of Ambergris Caye, the most northerly and largest of the colony's offshore islands, Park, without acknowledgement of his message from the ship, rejoined Davis on the intercom. Walkinshaw and Lucas, aboard 021, had now drifted back into battle formation a couple of thousand yards to starboard of the lead Buccaneer.

The Senior Pilot heard a beat through the static in his headset followed by Carl Davis's voice asking for a fuel check.

Red Two, Bingo.

Davis checked the fuel gauges before replying.

Bingo minus two.

Walkinshaw was a couple of hundred pounds down on the flight plan.

Christ, that's good, thought Davis in the other jet. He'd known 'Boots' would be down a little just because he'd have needed to work his throttles harder to stay on his Leader's wing, but just 200lb down was better than he'd expected. With over two hours to go, though, until the RV with the tankers over Grand Bahama they needed to be careful. In the back of 030, Steve Park looked at the route he'd marked on his charts and started to think about the possibility of shaving a few miles off the journey home.

Clamped under low cloud at sunrise HMS *Phoebe's* Navigating Officer hadn't been able to check the ship's position. And beyond an uncertain radar contact the Fighter Controller had no luck establishing radio contact with the Buccaneers on the outbound leg either. But, still acting as an SAR picket for the two jets, the West Indies Guardship made no mistake on their return. At 1330SIERRA, as the strike pair climbed to their cruising altitude, the little frigate, steaming south between Cancún and the western tip of Cuba, made a positive ID on radar and radio as 030 and 021 flew past fifty miles off her bow. She'd be arriving off Belize City herself soon after dawn the next morning, carrying the Navy baton until the planned return of 809's Buccaneers to the skies above Belize City at lunchtime. Once they'd got the first pair safely home.

The first priority of any aviator is the safety of their aircraft and the souls on board. And Steve Park was conscious that, beyond the Bahamas, their return to *Ark Royal* was non-diversion. There was nowhere else to go. If, after passing Florida, they were down on fuel before they reached their point of no return, they'd have to turn back and divert into the closest American airfield. And the buggeration that would involve was definitely not on his agenda. It was a calculated risk, but nibbling into Cuban air space looked like a better option. If they got away with it, fine, if the Fuerza Aerea Revolucionaria scrambled anything, the two Buccaneers could duck out quickly and be no worse off than if they'd never tried. They had to do it.

'Let's cut the corner, Boss,' Park recommended. Davis agreed. It was definitely the lesser of two evils.

OK, Park directed, *starboard One Five on to Zero Five Five degrees.*

The squadron Boss gently banked early on to the new heading, a track that would take them inside Cuba's twelve-mile limit. Walkinshaw and Lucas followed them on to the new bearing, and inside the cockpit of 021 the Senior Pilot couldn't help but cast his mind back to the intelligence briefing aboard *Ark*. There was definitely a possibility of starting something. And, flying in battle formation 2000 yards off 030's starboard wing, he and Lucas were over a mile closer to trouble if they did. Steve Park, still wondering how his suggestion might go down with the Cubans, tried to raise American Air Traffic to warn them that they were on their way back. But, as he listened for a reply, keeping a sharp eye to starboard for any signs of the thick white smoke trails from SA-2 Guideline or SA-3 Goa SAMs launched by trigger-happy Cuban missile crews, all he could hear was a lot of background chatter. He kept trying.

Miami Center, this is Navjet Zero Three Zero . . .

In the other Buccaneer, Mike Lucas maintained his own, fascinated lookout over the hazy brown island below them.

Command and control of the US Southern ADIZ was located at Fort Lee, Virginia. From that garrison town, information collected from radar sites lining the perimeter of the continental United States from Texas to New Jersey was processed and coordinated. The limits of the Air Division's area of responsibility extended out from Florida and over Cuba. And anything airborne in their zone was a potential threat that had to be accounted for and, if necessary, dealt with.

When two high-altitude contacts, inbound from the north-west tip of Cuba, appeared on radar screens as a pair of glowing dots, news reached Fort Lee fast. Flying at over 400 knots and 39,000 feet, the two unidentified aircraft would be over Florida in less than half an hour.

At Homestead AFB, the telephone rang in the Combat Alert Center of the 159th Fighter Interception Squadron. The operator, on one of the shifts that had kept the phones manned in an unbroken run stretching back to the fifties, picked up.

I've got a pair of unknowns, he was told by the voice from

Sector at Fort Lee, *I want you to scramble your guys*. Fifteen seconds later a klaxon kicked the two Alert pilots and their crew chiefs into action.

Wearing olive-green flightsuits with colourful unit patches stitched on their shoulders, the pilots ran across the fifty yards of hard-standing from the Operations building to the aircraft shelters where the grey interceptors were parked, their low, sharp, black noses pointing towards the runway. The Air National Guard pilots climbed the ladders into the cockpits of their F-102 Delta Daggers, picked up their helmets and pulled them on. Seated, they slipped straps around their legs and shoulders to fasten themselves tight into their parachute harnesses and ejection seats. Groundcrewmen leaned in, removing and stowing the ejection seat pins. Outside, the Crew Chiefs removed the tags and warning signs that had protected the two alert aircraft from carelessness and curiosity. The pilots flicked the master switches and the two jets immediately came alive. Ahead of them, on the instrument panel, dials flickered and lights came on. Although they could be started independently, the two Alert 'Deuces' used an external starter to preserve as much of their onboard air for the mission as possible. Cleared by their Crew Chiefs, the pilots pressed the starter button on top of the throttle and threw the lever round the horn to idle. Then the compressor blades and turbines of each fighter's single Pratt and Whitney J57-P-23A turbojet engine began to turn, increasing in speed with each revolution. As the jets cranked up, the Crew Chiefs cast a last eye over them for any leaks. At 30 per cent power the J57s were up and running. The pilots released their starter buttons and allowed the powerful jet engines to wind up to 60 per cent rpm and settle.

The Flight Leader thumbed the RT button on the F-102's distinctive double-gripped control column.

Ground Control, this is Echo Hotel. Ready to scramble.

The reply was immediate: *You're cleared for Runway Two Three. Clear for take-off.*

The Flight Leader released his brakes and rolled forward, his hands on throttle and stick. After checking his brakes, he allowed the jet to accelerate towards the end of the runway, a hundred yards ahead of the Alert shelter. As the F-102 gathered speed, Ground Control passed further instructions:

Echo Hotel, you're clear for heading Two Three Five. Angels Three Nine. Buster. Go to tower.

They were being sent south-west, to 39,000 feet, and being ordered to climb out at full military power.

Roger.

As the first Deuce crossed the threshold of the long 11,200-foot runway, the pilot pushed the throttle forward through the gate. A glowing spear of orange flame ignited from the tail of the big interceptor as fuel sprayed into the afterburner: 16,000lb of thrust drove the jet forward. And with a weapons bay carrying a mix of heat-seeking and radar-homing AIM-4 Falcon missiles, and a pair of 215-gallon drop tanks under the wings, the Delta Dagger roared down the runway. At 220 knots – just three minutes after the phone call from Fort Lee – the first F-102 rotated, tucking up her undercarriage as soon as she was airborne.

Barely ten seconds later the second Deuce followed and the pair climbed away at maximum dry thrust, their pilots switching frequencies quickly from Tower through Departure Control then to Sector – to the Controllers at Fort Lee who would direct the mission. Their aim was to vector the big interceptors on to a curve of pursuit that would bring them in behind the two unidentified bogies. Four minutes later, travelling at 325 knots, the two Air National Guard fighters passed through 35,000 feet. Still climbing.

Hands to Flying Stations. The ship's main broadcast once again heralded the next vital stage of the long British Honduras mission. The flight deck burst into carefully orchestrated life. After a break of under an hour and a half, Neil Maclean and Pete Lewis, their Buccaneers once again filled to the gunwhales with Avcat, were going to be launched to bring home the squadron Boss and Senior Pilot. And according to the mission planning, the margins were going to be exceptionally tight. If there were any hiccups in getting them airborne – even a five-minute delay – they'd kill any hope of being able to recover the strike pair back aboard *Ark*. And Carl Davis would have to make swift alternative arrangements to keep his men and aircraft safe.

At 1522Q, the SAR helo, the beat of her main rotor chugging above the howl of her engine, pulled herself into the air once more before John Roberts altered course into wind and increased speed. As Neil Maclean and Pete Lewis ran through their pre-take-off checks with their Observers, *Ark*'s bows swung round on to a heading of 225 degrees. But, unlike the noon launch, the wind had now dropped. With the south-westerly now down to barely 8 knots, the carrier had to do more of the work herself to get the two heavy Buccaneers safely into the air. Roberts increased revolutions. And with the first of the two tankers tensioned on the longer waist cat, *Ark Royal* was driving through the swell at 26.5 knots. An angry white mass of displaced water pushed up and ahead of the bow before being forced aside and down along the flanks of the hull.

Sitting at his console in the ADR, Harry O'Grady felt the heavy thud of the catapult shuttle as it slammed into the water-brake at the end of its track. A little over a minute later it was followed by a second bang resonating through the ship's steel. Both Buccs were away. The noise in the ADR returned to the normal background whine/whirr of the air-conditioning and cooling systems built into the Ops Room's powerful electronics. O'Grady watched the image of the two tankers climb away and vectored them towards the RV over Grand Bahama. Just two bright orange blips on a big CRT display, dependent on his instructions and the power of the two 965 search radars that revolved tirelessly above the carrier's island.

It was impossible to keep concern about their dwindling fuel state entirely at bay. Regardless of whether or not they were still on plan, Steve Park had rarely been in a Buccaneer this far from home with so little in the tanks. And his efforts to communicate with US Air Traffic offered little comfort. Park had been trying without success to raise Miami Center over the RT. If understanding between the Royal Navy Buccaneers and US Controllers had been lacking on the outward leg, it now seemed entirely absent. Until, out of the background chatter, all four British airmen at last heard a message that was broadcast specifically for their benefit. It wasn't exactly what any of them had been hoping or expecting to hear. An American accent, dry and sibilant through the static, announced:

You are about to be intercepted . . .

Chapter 49

Mike Lucas saw it first – just a flash of movement to the right in his peripheral vision. He thumbed the RT.

'We've got company,' he announced. Use of a discrete frequency meant he could talk without being heard by anyone but the other Buccaneer.

'Where?' Davis asked him, already turning his head and scanning the skies.

'In your five o'clock,' Lucas replied. From 021's vantage point a thousand yards off the Leader's port wing Lucas tracked the progress of a big needle-nosed delta. 'Closing fast,' he warned them.

Steve Park refused to be impressed as the interceptor took up station less than a hundred yards off their starboard wing – its proximity was designed to intimidate.

'Ah, it's a Delta Dagger,' he observed over the intercom. 'That's nice . . .'

The Looker cast an eye over the distinctive-looking jet. It was painted light grey with bold red, white and blue American national insignia on the intakes and, in case there was any doubt, 'U.S. AIR FORCE' painted in tall, black capital letters down the fuselage. The look was finished off with lightning bolts on the triangular tail. Carl Davis was struck by how mean and purposeful the Deuce looked.

Spectacular, thought the 809 Squadron Boss, hoping the American pilot was similarly taken with the appearance of his two Buccaneers. But as well as a sneaking admiration for the old Convair fighter's good looks, he was concerned about what its appearance might mean for the success of his own mission.

Is this sinister?, he asked himself. *Is it just a fighter pilot doing what any fighter pilot does when presented with an opportunity to bounce someone?*

In 021, Walkinshaw and Lucas looked over in amusement at their Boss's misfortune. Lucas was sporting a wide grin, visible only in his eyes above the oxygen mask clamped to his face. Then as they looked across at the pair of mismatched jets, a second Delta Dagger, climbed into position between them and 030, just fifty yards off their Buccaneer's starboard wing. That wiped the smile off the young Observer's face.

'Oh bloody hell!' exclaimed Walkinshaw. 'We've got somebody with us too.' He could see the pilot of the American fighter, the black visor of his helmet folded down over his face, looking the Buccaneer up and down.

Steve Park glanced across at the pilot of the Dagger on their wing. He seemed to be signalling for them to go descend. The little Scot just proffered a cheery wave. Carl Davis, determined not to give any suggestion that they might follow, kept his eyes front. He'd made his mind up. Unless one of the Daggers was practically sitting on top of him waggling its wings he was going to pretend they weren't even there.

'Just look straight ahead,' he ordered over the discrete channel. 'Don't change course. Keep going – we haven't seen them . . .'

In any case, Park couldn't help feeling the Daggers were struggling. It seemed unlikely, but they might have been. State of the art in its day, the F-102's design could be traced back to the late 1940s and she was beginning to feel her age a little. The Deuce enjoyed a fraction of the performance available to a fighter like the Phantom. And altitude sapped the performance of any jet fighter. Above 40,000 feet there was barely a fifth of the thrust available at sea level. And the Buccaneers – as uncomfortable as they themselves found it – were cruising at 39,000 feet. Carrying the drop tanks under the wings also limited the F-102 to a top speed of just a shade over Mach 0.95

– no faster than the very definitely subsonic Buccaneers. But however hard their pilots might have been working to keep them there, the Daggers were still hanging off the wings of the British jets; and they were still more than capable of imposing themselves if they chose to.

The men of the 159th FIS held formation a little longer – long enough, thought Walkinshaw, to read the words 'ROYAL NAVY' written on the tail of his jet – before concluding that the British strike pair were harmless – even if they were carrying on as if they owned the place. Then the two Air National Guard interceptors peeled away into a steep descent. 'They're going . . .' Davis confirmed over the intercom, his relief turning to laughter, 'and they can get stuffed!'

The two Buccaneers continued north-east, straight across the Southern Air Defence Interception Zone, without any further contact or trouble from the Americans.

It was as if there'd been no prior knowledge whatsoever of the strike pair's route through the Florida Straits – as if a flight plan had never been filed. And while the 809 NAS Buccaneers had, despite unexpected attention, made it through, the Americans were not taking kindly to what appeared to be an unannounced intrusion through some of their most sensitive, dangerous airspace. Soon after 030 and 021 passed overhead the Keys, the diplomatic mess landed at the feet of Commander Bob Browning, one of a small number of Navy staff attached to the British Embassy in Washington. As Duty Officer he was deemed to be closely enough involved to carry the can. For the next two days he relayed transatlantic signals, trying to pour oil on troubled waters and unruffle diplomatic feathers. It was exactly the kind of pointless headache he could do without. A non-aviator himself, the chaos caused by the flyboys did nothing to further endear them to him. He resolved that if he ever met any of the aircrew responsible he'd make his feelings abundantly clear. And then boot them out of the room. Or wring their necks.

*

After crossing the Florida panhandle, the two Buccaneers flew out over the sea towards the scattered islands of the Bahamas. The crews aboard 030 and 021 kept a careful eye on their fuel gauges. Although still conforming to their finely tuned flight plan, they were, by any yardstick, extremely low on gas. And they wouldn't have been the first military aircraft to be lost over the Western Atlantic after their tanks had been sucked dry.

If you join the dots between Miami, Bermuda and Puerto Rico, you enclose an area of water that has become infamous as the Bermuda Triangle. A number of coincidences, suppositions, half-truths and lies gave birth to the popular mystery, but none have been more central to the legend than the strange and tragic disappearance of a flight of five US Navy torpedo-bombers.

Just after lunch on 5 December 1945, Flight 19 took off from Fort Lauderdale–Hollywood Naval Air Station on a navigation exercise. The five piston-engined TBM Avengers were due to fly east towards Great Abaco Island, then north-west 73 miles, then left on to a heading of 240 degrees for a final 120-mile leg back to the air station. Simple. Except that the last person to see Flight 19 was the skipper of a fishing boat sailing in the Northwest Providence Channel, between Grand Bahama and Andros Island. From 15.40 there was a series of increasingly confused radio exchanges until, at 19.04, a final, faint transmission was picked up: 'FT . . . FT . . .' Part of Flight 19's call sign. As well as the fifteen crewmen lost aboard the TBMs, a further thirteen airmen were lost when a PBM Mariner, conducting a search for the missing Avengers, exploded twenty-three minutes after take-off.

It seems unlikely that there was any great mystery in the disappearance of the five barrel-fuselaged TBMs: no doorway to another dimension, nor an inexplicable magnetic anomaly in the 'Triangle'. They just got lost, disorientated, and failed to follow tried and tested procedures that might have returned them to safety. And when their tanks ran dry – and by 20.00, six hours after they'd taken off, they would have done – they were forced to ditch. That's what happened when you ran out of fuel over the Atlantic. And then you were either found, or you weren't.

In the cockpit of 030, Carl Davis was tapping the fuel dials to make sure they hadn't stuck. Their fuel state was critical. Their RV with the tankers was over Grand Bahama, still over a hundred miles away. On board the lead Buccaneer, Carl Davis and Steve Park were down to 1200lb of fuel. But around 500lb of that was deemed to be unusable, because of the readability and accuracy of the gauges. Some of it might take them a little further, but it couldn't be relied upon in their calculations. Burning around 40lb of fuel a minute, 030 had seventeen and a half minutes of flying left. In the other Buccaneer, 'Boots' Walkinshaw and Mike Lucas had just less than thirteen minutes. They had sufficient fuel to make the RV, but there was absolutely no fat in their calculations. Unless they established a positive contact with the tankers before reaching their PNR – their point of no return – they'd have to turn back towards Florida. And they were going to hit PNR – the last point from which they could safely recover to Miami or Fort Lauderdale – in about eight minutes' time. Eight minutes to be *sure* they'd found the tankers. And, still hundreds of miles beyond the range of the search radars aboard *Ark Royal*, they had only their own resources to rely on.

'How are you going to find the buggers?' Davis asked his Looker. Steve Park had already raised the dark sun-visor on his Bone Dome and was leaning forward into the hooded CRT display of the Blue Parrot radar. Using the joystick by his right knee he raised the dish in the nose to scan the skies ahead of them. Designed to find Soviet capital ships at ranges of up to 240 miles, the old Ferranti radar was a powerful unit but in no way configured to find other aircraft. But it could be done. Park set up the radar to maximize his chances, altering the range scale to scan and display a sector sixty miles ahead.

'Don't worry, Boss,' he reassured Davis, 'the radar's working splendidly.' It might have been, but as they flew on towards the PNR, there was no sign of the tankers.

'News of the carrier force,' John Weymes told London, 'has broken awkwardly.' For all the posturing and denial by both governments over the previous two weeks, the overflight by the Buccaneers was the point at which the British Consul felt the crisis reached its crossroads. It marked an escalation in terms of potential force in the region and, he felt, created the possibility of provoking a rash reaction from an angry, suddenly impotent General Arana. Weymes normally kept the Guatemalans informed of military developments, but the arrival of the 809 NAS had, to all intents and purposes, come out of the blue. But without firing a bullet or dropping a bomb, the British had made their point. *Ark Royal*'s intervention suggested they were now capable of defending British Honduras against *any* Guatemalan military adventure – not just along the Western Highway to the airport, but also, crucially, against Toledo District in the south. Until he saw which way they'd jump, Weymes remained worried. He only hoped that in discussing the news from the consulate in Belize City, the generals were concluding, however reluctantly: *We're not going to take on an aircraft carrier . . .*

'I've got them on radar, Boss,' Steve Park announced, his eyes fixed on a pair of bright-green spots on the lined CRT display. 809's Senior Observer had picked up the tankers at a range of about forty miles. Right over Grand Bahama.

That's bloody good, thought Davis, grateful for the Scotsman's skill with the radar set. Davis pulled back on the power a touch to establish 030 in a descent to 25,000 feet ready for the rendezvous: 5000 feet lower than the refuelling on the outbound leg, both tankers and receivers would have significantly more power and control. With the sun behind him, he looked ahead for the first glimpse of the tankers. With a closing speed of over 700 knots they'd be on top of each other in just a little over three minutes. And past the PNR. In the back, Steve Park placed his target marker over the contacts on the radar display and selected track. Against a clear sky the Blue Parrot should lock on to the return from the tankers.

From the pilot's seat of 021, as he followed the lead Buccaneer down from 39,000 feet, 'Boots' Walkinshaw strained to catch sight of the tankers ahead. Below, he could see the hazy shape of Grand Bahama, fringed with beaches and powder-blue water.

While ejecting from a Buccaneer after a mid-air collision, Steve Park had received a crack on the head so severe that it had fractured the hard shell of his Bone Dome. Strangely, the impact had also permanently improved his eyesight. But it was still 'Boots' Walkinshaw in the other Buccaneer who saw the tankers first. At the limits of his vision, the Senior Pilot saw two black specks moving against the pale sky. He pressed the transmit button on the control column.

'Two bogies left. Eleven o'clock.'

His search now focused, Carl Davis quickly spotted them too. But, ever competitive, he was unable to suppress a twinge of mild annoyance that his wingman had picked them up first. The squadron Boss thumbed the RT.

'Contact,' he told Maclean and Lewis in the tankers. 'Turn back to the north-east.' With the tankers in visual, Steve Park switched the radar to 'Standby' and the HF radio to 'Silence'. In 021, Walkinshaw and Davis were doing the same as they watched the two tankers arc round in a 180-degree turn that should bring them out right in front of the strike pair, flying straight and level at 260 knots, and trailing their hoses.

Cleared line astern, came word from the tankers. *Cleared wet – 4000lb*. Enough fuel to keep them flying over the last 400 miles to 'Mother' with at least 1500lb in reserve when they reached the circuit. The lights in the back of the FR Mk 20 Buddy pod blinked from red to amber.

As the faster strike pair overhauled the tankers, Davis and Walkinshaw, one hand on the throttles, the other on the control column, gently pulled back the power to settle in behind the tankers. They switched the autostabilizers to

'Approach', and then gently edged their probes towards the baskets. At this distance, the effects of gentle disturbances in the air were apparent as the two jets, just yards apart, flew through them: the lazy, fluid weave of the shuttlecock-shaped basket or the gentle rise and fall of the tanker relative to the framework of the receiver's canopy.

This was the bit Mike Lucas didn't like. He'd never been 100 per cent comfortable during in-flight refuelling. Having the huge dark-grey plan form of another Buccaneer looming so close – filling the view ahead – just seemed unnatural. Especially when, as part of a Buccaneer crew, he spent most of his time trying to stay as far away from other aircraft as he possibly could. As they closed, the red anti-collision beacon at the back of the tanker's belly flashed lazily on and off.

He listened to the sound of Walkinshaw's breathing as the Pilot coaxed 021 into a smooth 3- or 4-knot overtake.

Approaching, 'Boots' informed the tanker crew over the RT. Ahead and above him, he watched the familiar shape of the Buccaneer appear to be sliding gently back over his canopy as he closed on the drogue. Lucas looked over his Pilot's right shoulder as they edged ahead. Yards, feet, inches. And then, agonizingly out of reach, the cranked probe on 021's nose seemed to stretch for the basket and miss. Lucas flinched and kept his mouth shut. It was probably nothing more than a small eddy in the airflow that unsettled the smooth flight of the drogue, but of all the occasions not to make contact first time, this one – with less than 500lb of usable fuel in the tanks and 400 miles from the flight deck – really took the biscuit. Irritated with himself, Walkinshaw pressed the transmit button.

Missed, he told the tanker crew and dropped back and down for a fresh approach. He forced himself to stay relaxed, nudged the throttles forward a touch and again pushed 021's nose in underneath the belly of the tanker.

Approaching. Walkinshaw made no mistake second time round. With a dull clunk, the refuelling probe mated with the basket, sending a gentle ripple along the length of the hose.

In, he called and maintained his speed advantage for a second or two longer to trigger the flow of fuel. Under the starboard wing of the tanker, the lights changed from amber to green. And, for the first time since they'd turned into Cuban airspace to save fuel, Walkinshaw and Lucas could afford to breathe out a little. Now they just had to land on the deck of a ship steaming in the middle of the Atlantic. And, of course, they did that every day.

Chapter 50

Escorted by the two tankers, the strike pair were finally on their way back to 'Mother' after their record-breaking long-range mission. Aboard the ship, the announcement of *Recovery Stations* echoed throughout the corridors and out over the flight deck.

Twenty miles out and descending at 6000 feet per minute, Carl Davis called Harry O'Grady.

This is Red Leader. We'll be with you in three minutes.

Roger Red Leader. Charlie time is 1750.

Making sure that the wheels of the first aircraft in a formation hit the deck at the stroke of Charlie time was more than simply a point of honour for the Fleet Air Arm. Anything else wasn't just sloppy – it could cause chaos to carefully worked-out recovery cycles. As the four Buccaneers descended through 10,000 feet in close echelon formation, Steve Park called the height.

On the bridge of *Ark Royal*, John Roberts was already anticipating the successful conclusion of the mission. He ordered his ship into wind.

Starboard Two Five, the Officer of the Watch responded. *Steer Two Seven Five degrees.*

With the jets now a good six tons lighter than when they were launched and a brisk 12-knot south-westerly, Roberts had been able to stop hammering the engines at 200 revolutions. As the old carrier heeled to port through the turn, she was steaming at just 17 knots for the first time in over two days. From the deck, the FDO confirmed to Flyco that the deck was ready to recover the jets. And behind John Roberts, facing back towards the stern of the ship, Little F leaned into his microphone and pressed transmit. His voice was amplified over the flight deck: *Man the SAR. Stand by to recover four Buccaneers.*

The orange sun was just beginning to set in the west. With the ship's long wake visible to their left, Carl Davis led the formation of Buccaneers into the slot down the starboard side of the ship at 650 feet and 300 knots as she steamed along the Designated Flying Course. The four jets were practically past her before John Roberts first caught sight of them snarling through in formation from his chair on the other side of the bridge. It was impossible not to feel stirred by their slick return. The heavy rumble from their eight Rolls-Royce Speys trailed the bombers, enveloping the ship. As they quickly over-hauled the carrier, in the cockpit of each of the Buccaneers, the crews ran through their joining checks.

ADD . . . On

Radio Altimeter . . . On

Harnesses . . . Locked and Tight

Carl Davis continued upwind of the ship before breaking left across her bows. He checked the Blow selector was on auto and, as the speed dropped below 280 knots, took his left hand off the throttle levers, reached forward and selected 15 degrees of flap and 10 degrees of aileron droop and tailplane flap. He glanced at the cheeses – the yellow flap and aileron droop indicators on the instrument panel – to check all three lift devices had deployed in synch: all increased the amount of lift generated by the big jet to enable it to stay safely airborne at slow speeds.

Blow's on, Davis confirmed. They'd got Boundary Layer Control. The hot air bled from the engines would allow the speed to drop further, to 127 knots on approach.

At the limit of the crosswind leg, Davis turned downwind, pushing a switch on the right of the throttle lever with his thumb to extend the airbrakes. At the back of the jet, the huge clamshell was forced open against the direction of travel by a powerful hydraulic jack. Inside the cockpit, Davis and Park could feel it bite, dragging speed from the jet as surely as the anchor of a ship. As they slowed through 225 knots, Davis reached forward and lowered the arrestor hook and the under-carriage. They heard them cycle and felt them clunk reassuringly into place beneath them.

Gear's down: Four Greens – three wheels and the hook. At 200 knots Davis lowered the flaps and aileron droop another stage and their airspeed dropped to 160 knots.

Walkinshaw and Lucas followed them in 021. And behind them were the two tankers. As they flew the length of the car-rier from bow to stern, the day-glo red of the ever-present SAR Wessex caught their eye as she hovered, on station between them and the deck. Even at 200 knots it took them just three seconds to travel the entire length of the deck they were about to land on. Ahead, running parallel to the ship's long white wake, 030 flew on past the round-down for ten seconds before banking and carving round in a slow, gentle 180-degree turn on to finals. Walkinshaw extended, continuing downwind for another fifteen seconds beyond where 030 had turned, to ensure a 45-second separation between his squadron Boss recovering on deck and their own arrival. 45 seconds to clear the deck and reset the wires. Behind him, the two tankers would do the same. And from every inch of outside space on the island, the packed audience of goofers watched their cir-cuit, enjoying the spectacle of the Buccaneers' return. Sea King Observer Ed Featherstone had made a point of claiming a spot up there. He wanted to feel part of it.

Full flap, Davis confirmed over the intercom and checked he had the necessary 20lb per square inch of blow over the wings. The big grey bomber had now lost any semblance of stream-lining, her curved lines broken by all manner of inelegant protrusions. Beneath the high T-tail, the huge airbrakes jutted out at right angles to the fuselage. The flaps and ailerons, rectangular metal slabs, hung off the entire length of the wing's trailing edge. Below her, hanging limp like the legs of a bumble bee, was the undercarriage. And from the back of the fuselage the arrestor hook dangled beneath it all, looking scarcely substantial enough to bring the heavy aircraft to its imminent and violent standstill on deck.

With a gentle twist of his wrist to the right, Davis levelled 030's wings into wind and settled on to finals, losing a last 10 knots of excess speed to fly down the 4-degree glidepath at datum speed of 127 knots. With her nose high, airbrakes out and engines turning at near 85 per cent rpm – fast enough to deliver thick dollops of power quickly enough to get out of trouble – 030 sat comfortably at the back of the drag curve, stable and descending through the last three-quarters of a mile towards the 3 Wire. Davis kept his eyes locked on the meatball shining from the projector sight to the left of the wires. The white light meant he was within a few arc-seconds of the required 4-degree glideslope.

One Two Seven . . . One Two Eight . . . One Two Seven. Over the intercom, Steve Park called the speeds in his warm Scottish burr. No more than one knot either side of the 127 knots was good enough. The familiar electronic tone of the ADD provided an even more insistent reminder of his speed and angle of attack. The picture ahead looked good. *Ark Royal's* deck was stable. With the wind travelling down the angled deck, the black smoke from the funnel was streaming out to starboard and away from his flight path. His gloved hands rested on the throttles and stick ready to make any necessary corrections. But the big jet was settled and trimmed. Nearly flying herself. From the side of the flight deck, the LSO, focused on the approaching Buccaneer through the cross-hairs of his red Perspex sight, confirmed the approach was good over the RT.

Roger. Centreline.

Alongside the LSO, the four 2-inch-thick arrestor cables were tensioned, raised on bowsprings three inches above the steel of the deck. The Flight Deck Party stood safely behind the Wing Tip Safety Line that marked the outer limit of the angle, all eyes on 030's insect shape. Behind the thick armoured glass in Flyco, Wings followed her approach, his hand hovering near the red wave-off button. When things went wrong they did so late and quickly. After what appeared to be a slow, gentle descent, the grey bomber seemed to balloon in size as she streaked over the round down, her speed relative to the deck suddenly strikingly evident.

Within seconds of 1750QUEBEC – Charlie time – the tip of 030's arrestor hook scraped into the deck a couple of yards behind 3 Wire. And as it grasped the thick cable, the tyres of the Buccaneer's main gear smacked into the steel ahead of it, the powerful hydraulic oleos soaking up and absorbing half a million foot-pounds of energy to check and halt the bomber's descent. A moment later, the nosewheel crashed into the deck. The arrestor gear screamed as the wire rope was pulled out from below deck behind the big aircraft. And Davis and Park were thrown forward against their straps, their massive momentum and energy fighting to keep them moving forward even as 030 slowed from over 120 knots to a standstill underneath them. It took a blink over a second. But the moment Davis felt the retardation bite, he pulled the throttles back to idle. Applause rippled across goofers.

The green-waistcoated Hook Men ran forward from behind the safety line to take control. Below decks, the arrestor gear pistons, forced against the limit of their travel, relaxed, pulling the Buccaneer backwards a few feet to release 3 Wire from the grip of her hook. In the cockpit, Davis pulled the yellow and black hook toggle to retract it. Then, reaching just below it, he flicked the flap and aileron levers to zero to clean up the wings.

Outside, the Hook Men signalled to the Wires Director ahead that 030 was ready to taxi and, to the Flight Deck Engineer Officer astern, to reset 3 Wire. While Steve Park switched off his systems in the back of the cockpit, Davis reached down to his right to fold the wings, before, with a touch of power, he taxied forward, marshalled towards Fly 1 over the bow of the carrier. Behind them, 3 Wire slithered back along the deck to take its place parallel with the others, ready for the arrival of the next aircraft.

On sight, called 'Boots' Walkinshaw over the RT as 021 settled into her approach.

Roger. Centreline, came the acknowledgement.

Seven minutes later, all four Buccaneers were safely on deck. Wings got up, put his head through from Flyco to the bridge and informed John Roberts.

Recovery complete, sir.

Thank you, Wings.

They'd done it. Smiling broadly, Roberts got up from his chair and handed control of the ship to his Executive Officer, Willie Gueterbock. *Ark*'s Captain had a surprise in store for the crews who'd just completed the longest mission ever launched from the deck of a British aircraft carrier

In Belmopan, news of the 809 NAS overflight reached Richard Posnett in the early afternoon. Before joining the colonial service, the new Governor had served in the Royal Air Force. Without knowing the details, he had some understanding of the kind of effort that must have been involved in putting jets over Belize City from such a long distance away. Writing a few lines in recognition of that, he thought, might not be a bad idea. In any case, drafting them would provide welcome relief from the incessant press enquiries he'd endured since arriving in country just two days earlier.

And in Cambridgeshire that evening, just off the A1 dual-carriageway, the four Harriers of No. 1 (Fighter) Squadron at RAF Wittering declared themselves to be operationally ready to deploy across the Atlantic.

Chapter 51

'How was it, sir?' asked the naval airman helping Mike Lucas extricate himself from the jet. 'What did you do?'

The tall Observer wasn't used to such solicitousness, but the groundcrews were all smiles as they swarmed round the jets, lashing them to deck, attaching the crew ladders and making the ejection seats and canopy safe. And with goofers packed to the rafters, the level of interest in the marathon sortie started to become apparent. It wasn't at all unwelcome, but a pee, a glass of water, a bite to eat, a cigarette – in no particular order – were the only things on the minds of the crews of 030 and 021. After six hours cooped up inside the cockpits of their Buccaneers they were in urgent need of even a chance to stretch their legs. Yet, for the time being, after wobbling down the ladders on stiff legs, Davis, Park, Walkinshaw and Lucas were asked to stay on deck. The Captain was on his way. As heat shimmered off the four Buccaneers' jet pipes and the smell of burnt Avcat lingered in the wind, Roberts clambered down from the bridge along the narrow metal corridors and companionways of the island to the flight deck.

As they'd launched at the beginning of the mission, the Buccaneers had been photographed from the side door of the SAR Wessex. Over the hours that followed, the ship's Photographic Department had developed the film, made four black-and-white prints of 021 accelerating down the waist cat, and had them framed. Each bore the caption '809 SQDN BELIZE & BACK 28 JAN 1972'.

Hemmed in by the number of spectators, Ed Featherstone watched from the island as John Roberts walked out on deck wearing a beret – a piece of uniform exclusive to those serving on carriers after it was realized that the traditional peaked cap didn't last five minutes in the wind over the flight deck. Roberts shook Carl Davis's hand and presented him with the first of the photographs. As the Captain greeted each of the aircrew in turn, Featherstone spotted Steve Park trying to get the blood circulating around his legs again. 'Boots' Walkinshaw couldn't help feeling slightly sheepish as the four of them posed with Roberts for more photographs in front of a Buccaneer, their hair still matted to their heads after six hours inside a helmet.

Stood here like a row of lemons, he thought as goofers watched on, but despite his discomfort he appreciated Roberts's thoughtfulness. All four of them followed the Captain back across the flight deck and into the island.

'Look at that, Steve.' Davis pointed to where he'd signed the jet back in. 'Five hours and fifty. That's better than an hour and twenty, isn't it!' He enjoyed recording such an exceptional statistic in 030's A700 – especially as there wasn't a single fault to report. They passed their yellow Mae Wests and survival equipment back over the counter. Davis told his Observer he'd catch up with him later. And, while Park made his way down – via the heads – to the Aircrew Refreshment Bar on Two Deck with Walkinshaw, Lucas and the two tanker crews, the 809 Boss climbed up the ladders to the bridge to talk to John Roberts in a little more privacy than had been possible on deck.

Well done, Carl! seemed to greet him from all quarters as he emerged into the grey paint and wood of the Compass Platform. And hearty verbal congratulations were soon joined by slaps on the back and vigorous handshakes. While Davis and the aircrew who'd flown the mission were the most conspicuous part of it, all of the men on the bridge knew it was an achievement they shared in. John Roberts ushered him through to his sea cabin behind the bridge and let the curtain fall across the door behind them. As the two men sat down, Roberts couldn't hide his pleasure at the outcome of the record-breaking sortie.

'It really couldn't have gone better, could it?' Roberts began with a smile. And he was right. For the first time since the possibility of the mission had been mooted, Davis allowed himself to relax a little, he was suddenly acutely aware that he'd just been at the tip of the spear. He stressed, in case there was any doubt, that it had been the engineers who'd made it possible. The Captain agreed, promising that they'd get proper credit. And as the success of his squadron's efforts began to sink in, the fatigue that the 809 Boss had kept at bay for the last forty-eight hours began to take hold. Dehydrated, hungry and worn out after six hours cajoling an ill-at-ease Buccaneer through the high, thin air, he'd earned a rest.

As Carl Davis returned to his cabin anticipating a long, hot bath, the Captain prepared a short signal for CINCFLEET – Commander-in-Chief Fleet – at Northwood HQ in Middlesex. He told them that two Buccaneers had successfully flown to British Honduras, spent ten minutes at low level over Belize City and the airfield and that they'd been recovered safely on board. 'MISSION ACCOMPLISHED', he told them.

He was satisfied that they'd done all that had been asked of them so far. Within forty-eight hours of an alert, he'd shown that *Ark*'s tentacles could reach out 2500 miles. As he considered their achievement, he wondered what lay ahead and finished the signal: 'WE AWAIT FURTHER INSTRUCTIONS'.

There was no shortage of drinks on offer to Davis and his colleagues in the Wardroom that night. Everybody, it seemed, was eager to hear a little more about what the crews had done. Not least those men who were scheduled to be flying to Belize City the following day. Under the pipes that lined the low ceiling, Mike Lucas shared a drink with Paul Meredith, one of the other 809 Observers. Meredith was keen to know what to expect. And Ed Featherstone, never shy about bridging the gap between the Sea Kings and the 'Heavies', pumped Steve Park for information as 809's Senior Observer enjoyed a cigarette. Carl Davis, meanwhile, was starting to get used to being the centre of attention. But he'd barely raised his first drink to his mouth when he was hauled off to be interviewed about the sortie on the ship's closed-circuit TV.

Reluctantly, he left the noise and high-spirited camaraderie of the Wardroom and dropped down a deck to *Ark*'s on-board TV studio. Outside, he was handed a note from the Captain.

'Only say what you have to say . . .' Roberts warned him, obviously concerned about some of the more-sensitive details of the mission and the reasons for it. Davis was more concerned about just trying to strike the right note. He didn't want to sound like he was shooting a line. Nor did he want to sound blasé. He needn't have worried. The questions were being asked by the Ship's Padre and, like all good sermons, the interview outstayed its welcome – at least it did from where Davis was sitting. Soon thirst became his only preoccupation. As it drew to a close the Padre asked, 'Would you go again?'

'Of course I'd go again!' he answered quickly, wondering what grounds he could possibly have to refuse. The Padre finally let him go. And he bounded up the ladder back to Six Deck.

Davis returned to the throng in the Wardroom, happy to be reunited with his drink. He was quickly joined by his counterpart from the Phantom squadron, 892's Boss, Nick Kerr. Kerr was still sore that the Phantoms had been excluded from making any contribution. And, like their two squadrons, Davis and Kerr themselves shared a friendly rivalry. Kerr acknowledged 809's achievement with a nod and paused.

'*We* could have done that,' he added, unable to resist, then smiled.

'Yes. Maybe you could,' Davis conceded with a twinkle in his eye, knowing that it didn't matter a fig what might or might not have been possible. Only what had happened. He raised his glass, smiled and enjoyed a long pull on his drink.

Alone in his day cabin, excluded by his position from the

celebrations in the Wardroom, John Roberts was about to eat his dinner when he was handed a signal. He read it, then wrote and attached a brief covering note and asked for it to be taken straight down to Six Deck and passed to Carl Davis in the Wardroom. He knew it would be well received. The rakish, supersonic Phantoms tended to get more than their fair share of the attention, and 809's Buccaneers were always, he felt, a little unfairly in their shadow. He was pleased to see Carl and his squadron enjoying a piece of the limelight for a change.

Just before he left the Wardroom for dinner, Davis was handed the signal from the Captain. Surely he was going to be allowed now to enjoy a good meal, a couple of glasses of wine and the rest of his evening. 'I thought you'd like to see this,' said a note from John Roberts. Curious, Davis looked at the signal below. It was from the Governor of British Honduras. It read:

```
FOR THE CO OF 809 SQUADRON. MANY THANKS AND
CONGRATULATIONS. WE WERE DELIGHTED TO SEE
YOU. YOUR SORTIES WERE BOTH SATISFACTORY AND
SUFFICIENT. POSNETT.
```

Chapter 52

The sorties planned for the following day were cancelled. The news came through as four new Buccaneer crews planned for the squadron's next sortie. And with anticipation running high, it was a disappointment to many on board the British carrier. Not least John Roberts. *Ark Royal*'s Captain couldn't help feeling a twinge of regret that, after just one sortie over Belize, there would be no further opportunity for *Ark* and her air group to demonstrate what they could do. *The setting*, he thought with regret, *would have provided a classic example of carrier capability*. Steaming a hundred miles off the coast, with the Phantoms and Buccaneers unconstrained by distance, they would really have been able to deliver the good news. But, in the end, 809's long-range intervention had been enough. Any lingering enthusiasm for a tilt against the Toledo District of British Honduras among hardliners within the Guatemalan Army evaporated – for the immediate future, at least – when *Ark Royal* joined the fray.

But whatever John Roberts's private disappointment – and he wasn't the only one aboard to feel that way – the fact remained: just forty-eight hours after being asked, the big British aircraft carrier had introduced a pair of what were arguably the best low-level strike aircraft in the world into a situation that, until that point, was believed to be in the balance.

If there was anyone who was relieved at the curtailment of subsequent operations, it was perhaps Ewan Maclean, *Ark*'s

Chief Engineer. As much as he'd enjoyed the sense of purpose involved in their high-speed charge south, by the time the ship finally replenished her fuel tanks from RFA *Regent*, they were down to just 40 per cent. And he didn't view the prospect of purging seawater ballast from empty FFO tanks with any enthusiasm at all.

HMS *Phoebe* arrived, as planned, off Belize City at dawn the following morning and her presence was welcomed by Colonel Shipster, the commander of British Forces in the colony. He was especially relieved to have access to her little Westland Wasp HAS1 helicopter, which, at a stroke, removed the need for his near daily round trips to Belmopan along unpaved roads. Although an obstruction in the commercial fuel lines at Belize City meant that the frigate soon had to retire to Key West to refuel – a brief absence before returning that was presented by General Arana as a great victory for Guatemalan fierceness – the little Wasp remained in theatre.

Britain continued to reinforce the army garrison. But by the time Martin Hooker was joined in Belize by the rest of 48 Squadron and their Tiger Cat missiles, the Rock Apes' hopes were dashed. After a miserable 23-hour journey by C-130 Hercules from RAF Leeming, they approached Belize airport ready to come out fighting. The soldiers clipped loaded magazines on to their SLRs. But as the ramp came down by the terminal it was clear they hadn't landed in the middle of the firefight they'd been expecting. They were told to make their weapons safe and hand them all in to the armoury.

Another bloody war missed, they lamented.

The RAF had been unlucky. Diplomatic wrangling over their potentially antagonizing effect on the now ultra-sensitive Guatemalans delayed the RAF Regiment Tiger Cats further. At least a settlement of the Canadian ATC strike finally allowed John Morgan and the two 39 Squadron Canberras to complete their transatlantic crossing via Gander on 29 January. They eventually reached their operating base in Nassau the following day, by which time Morgan, who'd shivered and sweated through the final three legs of the journey, was practically bed-ridden with a crippling dose of flu.

The Navy, by contrast, *was* fortunate. When the crisis broke, its single aircraft carrier, *Ark Royal*, happened to be in more or less the right place at the right time: at sea, steaming west across the Atlantic. The combative and partisan Chief of the Defence Staff, Peter Hill-Norton, saw an opportunity, and on board *Ark Royal* her Captain and her air group were prepared, in the finest traditions of the Senior Service, to take a view on what were deemed to be acceptable safety margins in order to grasp it with ambition and boldness. In doing so they gave a striking demonstration of a carrier's ability to offer – unhindered by the actions and influence of potentially unsympathetic third parties – possibilities that, for whatever reason, were simply beyond the reach of their land-based counterparts. And on this occasion, as Britain soon scaled down the size and speed of her reinforcement, *Ark Royal* offered a further, unforeseen bonus – her distance *from* British Honduras. The long reach of her Buccaneer squadron meant that politicians and diplomats could carefully point out that Britain's most powerful warship had at no time come any closer to British Honduras – or Belice – than east of the Bahamas. How could a ship sailing well over a thousand miles away possibly be considered to be provocative? The point soon became an important one.

The brakes were being applied from Guatemala City and Belmopan. In the Central American capitals, John Weymes and Richard Posnett both became increasingly preoccupied with trying to defuse a dangerous and unpredictable situation. What had quickly become an extremely confrontational war of words carried within it the potential to crystallize into something more violent. Weymes, particularly, feared that irreparable damage would be done to Anglo-Guatemalan relations – which, of course, he, as the man on the ground, would be forced to contend with. But his concern was shared by Posnett in Belmopan. Knowing that any hopes of trouble-free independence for British Honduras would depend on

Guatemalan acquiescence, he signalled the FCO, making his support for Weymes clear. And his list of demands was pretty comprehensive:

(A) NONE OF THE SHIPS SHOULD APPEAR OFF BELIZE.

(B) NO FURTHER AIR SORTIES SHOULD BE FLOWN FROM HM SHIPS OVER THE TERRITORY.

(C) LARGE AMOUNTS OF VISIBLE MILITARY MATERIAL, AND IN PARTICULAR THE TIGER CAT SQN, SHOULD NOT BE FLOWN IN.

(D) THE TWO CANBERRAS SHOULD NOT OPERATE FROM BELIZE AIRPORT.

In country for just two days, and with no visible sign of any Guatemalan designs against British Honduras, the new Governor just couldn't credit the possibility that his neighbour would be belligerent and foolish enough to launch a military adventure. But his telegram provoked a contemptuous reaction from the Prime Minister.

'The Governor,' Edward Heath declared, 'is very smug. He would be the first to complain if the Guatemalans had acted.' The PM was in absolutely no doubt that being ready and able to prevent an invasion was of 'the highest importance'. And it was Heath, as Posnett would later discover, who, despite his distance and long list of other urgent preoccupations, had displayed the greatest instinctive understanding of the potential threat.

In the autumn of 1975, towards the end of his tenure as Governor, Posnett and his wife Shirley took their young family on holiday to Guatemala. During the trip, they'd been struck by the scale and mystery of the stunning Mayan ruins at Tikal and enjoyed the faded grandeur and beautiful mountainous setting of the country's ancient capital city, Antigua. But after ten days' trouble-free motoring, on the long drive back home they suffered a puncture at the point the road entered the Petén jungle. As Posnett laboured over changing the wheel a Guatemalan army truck, full of soldiers and towing a heavy trailer, roared past, kicking up clouds of dust behind it. Posnett thought little of it. But when another puncture, just thirty miles from the border, forced him to flag down a truck to take him back to Flores in search of new tyres, his family realized it hadn't simply been a one-off. While he'd been away, his children counted a further six heavily loaded Guatemalan army lorries bellowing along the road towards the colony – officially renamed Belize in 1973 despite continuing reservations in London about how the move might be interpreted in Guatemala.

On returning to Belmopan, the Governor immediately reported the news to his new Garrison Commander, Colonel Duncan Green. But he was startled to hear that the Colonel had similarly alarming news to report. In Toledo District, from a hilltop observation post at the head of the Sarstoon River, ten armoured personnel carriers had been seen rumbling up the road in the direction of Belize and there were reports that a pair of Guatemalan Navy patrol boats, armed with .50 calibre and 20mm cannon, had deployed through the Panama Canal to Puerto Barrios. And, from Israel, deliveries had just begun to the Fuerza Aerea Guatemalteca of a fleet of ten IAI 201 Arava tactical transports that would nearly double their paratroop capability. The FAG armed them with rockets. Near the border, Green had already posted a radio-equipped soldier at the high apex of the Mayan stepped pyramid at Xunantunich ruins to watch for incursions.

In 1972, hard intelligence had been hopelessly sketchy. Neither Britain nor America appeared to have real access to Guatemalan decision-making. And while, by 1975, the situation was greatly improved, the British still didn't regard information from US Military Advisors in Guatemala as wholly reliable – or, at least, reliably comprehensive, But American intelligence *had* unearthed a real nugget that served to reinforce the conclusions drawn by Posnett and Green. An agent run by the Americans had seen and revealed details of Guatemalan plans to invade the Toledo District. Their source, who had access to government and military documents, confirmed that a two-pronged attack was planned: a combined air and sea assault on Punta Gorda and a land incursion across the western border north of Cadenas.

Reluctantly, Posnett drafted a signal to London. After discussing various scenarios and alternatives, he and Green could see no reasonable explanation for their neighbour's military build-up other than to threaten or invade Belize.

The effect of Posnett's signal shocked him. After the lessons learnt in 1972, it was swift and sure-footed. The first troops, he was told, would leave the UK within forty-eight hours. This time, though, the Navy's contribution didn't extend beyond the despatch of the West Indies Guardship, the 'Tribal' class frigate HMS *Zulu*. In the first half of November 1975, *Ark Royal*, the Navy's sole remaining aircraft carrier, was inextricably engaged in her primary role: the defence of NATO's Northern Flank. As, four years earlier, *Ark* had been a vital component of Exercise ROYAL KNIGHT, she was now operating in mountainous seas that saw her bows rising and falling through 130 feet, as part of Exercise OCEAN SAFARI, off the north Norwegian coast. While, ten years earlier, one of four other carriers might have deputized, post-1972, with *Ark* committed to NATO, the Navy had nowhere else to turn. When it came to delivering fixed-wing air power, the Fleet Air Arm's options had been exhausted.

Troop reinforcements arrived in Belize throughout October, supported by three Westland Puma HC1 helicopters flown in aboard 53 Squadron's big Shorts Belfast C1 transports. Then, on 5 November, a C-130 Hercules loaded with engineers, groundcrew and equipment taxied past the RAF Wittering Guy Fawkes night bonfire before taking off *en route* to Belize. A number on board couldn't help regretting that they were going to miss the evening's festivities.

Three days later – a month after he'd first signalled London – Posnett was working in his office in Government House when his peace was interrupted by the sudden thunder of low-flying jets – a noise completely alien to the little colony. He ran outside to see the dark-green and grey shapes of a pair of

RAF Harrier GR1As roar overhead Belmopan. Following a transatlantic flight, staged over two days via Goose Bay and Nassau, No. 1 (Fighter) Squadron had, following its alert and stand-down in 1972, finally made it to Belize. *It feels*, thought Posnett, as British forces responded to the emergency, *like our own miniature version of the Cuban Missile Crisis.*

But on 4 February 1976 the immediate threat to Belize from Guatemala came to a juddering, catastrophic halt. At two minutes past three in the morning, a 45-second earthquake measuring 7.6 on the Richter Scale killed as many as 25,000 Guatemalans, injuring a further 80,000 and leaving nearly 1.5 million people homeless. With this overwhelming tragedy, any immediate prospect of an attack on Belize evaporated as General Kjell Laugerud, Army Chief of Staff during Arana's government and his replacement as President, devoted himself to dealing with the quake's appalling aftermath. In April 1976, the Harriers were flown home, but the fiercely nationalistic General hadn't given up his designs on his little neighbour.

A year later, even as Guatemalan diplomats negotiated with their British counterparts in talks held in Washington DC, he again ordered the mobilization of the Guatemalan army. This time, *Ark Royal* was conducting post-refit trials. So the task fell once again to the RAF's Harriers. Six jets from No. 1(F) Squadron returned to Central America in an epic, non-stop flight direct across the Atlantic from Wittering to Belize airport, refuelled by Victor K2 tankers. The potent little vertical take-off attack jets didn't leave again for *sixteen years*. In 1972, *Ark Royal*'s long reach had acted as a powerful deterrent. But no longer able to rely on the availability of an aircraft carrier, Britain had little choice but to establish a permanent RAF fast-jet detachment in Belize.

Following the failure of the Guatemalan military to force the issue in 1975, Britain, armed with photographic proof of the threat, felt more confident of support from other Latin American countries and successfully pursued Belizean independence through the UN. The Union Flag came down in Belize on 21 September 1981 when she at last became an independent member of the British Commonwealth. Supported by Harriers of No. 1417 Flight, Britain maintained a permanent military garrison there until 1993. Throughout its long existence, 1417 Flight was one of the most popular fast-jet postings in the RAF.

For *Ark Royal*, it was all over by the end of 1978. And she couldn't have gone on any longer. Near the end of the great ship's life, a colleague of John Roberts who'd recently been aboard her asked him, 'I expect you'd like to know about your old ship?' The carrier's former Captain did – very much – but the news he heard saddened him: her old machinery was shot. Roberts was surprised by his emotional reaction to *Ark*'s condition. But then he always knew she was special.

'*Ark* had something,' he told people, 'she was almost human.'

Roberts retired from the Navy as a Rear Admiral. As FONAC – Flag Officer Naval Air Command – he'd risen to the very pinnacle of the Fleet Air Arm. And after a long career that took him from Midshipman in the battleship *Renown* during the early days of the Second World War, and through the bitter Arctic Convoys, to the top of his profession forty years later, his time in *Ark Royal* and, in particular, that mid-Atlantic dash towards British Honduras with its ambitious, effective, long-range Buccaneer mission remained a high point.

At eleven minutes past three on 27 November 1978, Phantom 012 was catapulted from the waist catapult. And with her last, ear-splitting, fiery launch, the Fleet Air Arm's proud tradition of conventional fixed-wing flying came to end, leaving nothing behind but a scorched, cooling deck. *Ark Royal* rang off her main engines for the last time a week later in Devonport on 4 December. And on 22 September 1980, after the failure of an enthusiastic campaign to preserve her as a museum, she was towed out of Plymouth bound for Cairnryan, between Stranraer and Ayr on the west coast of Scotland. And she was scrapped. She'd taken twelve years to build, then, in a 33-year naval career, had steamed the best part of one billion miles, launched and recovered tens of thousands of aircraft and, despite all the limitations imposed by her age and size, had distinguished herself in the company of a new generation of American supercarriers throughout the penultimate decade of the Cold War. But, unlike all of her sixties contemporaries, *Eagle*, *Victorious*, *Hermes* and *Centaur*, she never raised a hand in anger. *Ark* never went to war, but in the epic, post-colonial stand-off between East and West she helped prevent one. And, in the end, she was more famous, regarded with more affection, and more fondly remembered than all the others. For many – perhaps even a majority – of the British public, *Ark Royal* wasn't just a name synonymous with British aircraft carriers – she was *the* British aircraft carrier.

When the last pieces of steel were shipped from Cairnryan to a smelter in Spain, *Ark Royal* was gone, but fixed-wing flying in the Fleet Air Arm wasn't quite dead. Through the skill and experience of her last fixed-wing aircrews there was still a flicker of a flame burning.

In January 1972, while *Ark Royal* had been steaming at 27 knots towards British Honduras, it was reported that Vickers Shipbuilding were being funded by the MoD to work on designs for a new 'through-deck cruiser'. This new ship, the report noted, might be capable of carrying the Harrier. HMS *Invincible*, the first of this new class of 20,000-ton anti-submarine carriers, was laid down in 1974 and launched in May 1977. Three months later, wearing only a coat of yellow primer paint, the Fleet Air Arm's new jet fighter, the Sea Harrier, made her maiden flight from the British Aerospace factory at Dunsfold in Surrey. Each of the Navy's three planned new light carriers would carry a small squadron of five Sea Harrier FRS1s, embarked to provide a limited air defence, reconnaissance and strike capability. And it was, on the face of it, limited.

If, from the same position in the mid-Atlantic, *Invincible* had been asked to provide an air presence over British Honduras, she'd have found the job a great deal more challenging. First of all, her own range was just two-thirds that of *Ark Royal*'s. Her maximum speed only just eclipsed that which *Ark* had maintained for over two days. Her four powerful Olympus gas turbine engines – marine versions of the engines used by Concorde – also burnt fuel at a prodigious rate. And at the same time as facing far greater obstacles in just reaching the position from where *Ark Royal* was able to launch the Buccaneer mission, *Invincible* also had to contend with the limitations of the Sea Harriers as well. The little SHARS – as they were affectionately known to their pilots – just didn't have the legs of the Buccaneers. Without refuelling, the Buccaneer had a radius of action about twice that of the Sea Harrier. But, in 1972, 809's Buccaneers also had the ability to refuel each other in flight using the Buddy tankers. The Sea Harriers did not. For all the little jump jet's willingness, the bottom line is that, even assuming she had the fuel to do so, *Invincible* would have had to steam towards Central America at 25 knots for nearly two days longer than *Ark Royal* to bring her Sea Harriers within range of Belize City.

The capability offered by the tiny Sea Harrier squadrons that would be embarked on *Invincible* and her sister-ships was always going to suffer in any paper comparison to the twenty-six Phantoms and Buccaneers carried by *Ark Royal*. But it was something. And, for a handful of Fleet Air Arm fighter pilots, the Sea Harriers provided a lifeline.

But not for the Buccaneer crews who flew to British Honduras and back. The single seat V/STOL fighters offered nothing for the Observers and neither Carl Davis nor 'Boots' Walkinshaw was still flying fast jets when the SHARs entered service. They were, though, rewarded with the 1972 Boyd Trophy. Named after Admiral Sir Denis Boyd, the Captain of HMS *Illustrious* at Taranto, the trophy was awarded annually for the year's finest feat of naval aviation. The citation described 'their demonstration of the long-range effectiveness of carrier-borne air power'. Davis, Walkinshaw and Steve Park all carried swords as they were presented with the trophy, a mounted silver model of a Swordfish torpedo-bomber above the fish from which it took its name, in a formal ceremony at

RNAS Yeovilton. They accepted it from Vice Admiral John Treacher while standing alongside the imposing dark-grey presence of a Buccaneer. Walkinshaw's Observer, Mike Lucas, had been unable to join them. Having won a place on the exchange programme with the US Navy, he was already in America flying Grumman A-6 Intruders. The only time he could remember Carl Davis appearing to be at all unhappy with him was when the 809 Boss had to break the news that Lucas had got one of the much-coveted slots.

'You're going to get the trip you want,' he told the young Observer with mock indignation. 'Jammy bastard!'

Following the record-breaking sortie to Belize, 'Boots' Walkinshaw barely flew again. He spent only four more weeks with 809 before leaving the squadron and flying home from the Caribbean at the end of February. He never flew an aeroplane again.

And for Carl Davis, the story came full circle. He retired from the Navy at the end of the decade following his last appointment as Senior Naval Officer at RAF Leuchars – the final home of *Ark Royal*'s Phantom squadron. He returned home to Herefordshire, where he became manager of Shobdon, the friendly little airfield between Leominster and the Welsh hills that, when he was a schoolboy down the road, had inspired his childhood dreams of flying in the first place.

Nick Kerr, Davis's counterpart on *Ark*'s Phantom squadron, never did get to fly a Navy fighter in combat. But, ten years later, a handful of the pilots who'd learnt their trade under his command while he was Boss of 892 did. And the results, Kerr noted with pride, turned out to be very one-sided. In a short, unexpected and brutal war that took the Fleet Air Arm across the Atlantic to the southern seas off Argentina, four of Kerr's ex-Phantom pilots accounted for nearly a third of all the confirmed air-to-air kills. He must have been doing something right.

SECTION FIVE

1982

It would have been nice to have had a few more Harriers but I'd have preferred it if we'd had the Ark Royal, *but then again, if we'd had the old* Ark Royal *and all her aircraft I don't think the Argentines would have invaded in the first place.*

Corporal Stuart Russell, 2nd Battalion The Parachute
Regiment, speaking after the Falklands War

Epilogue

Sir Richard Posnett learnt of the invasion from the BBC. Unconfirmed reports first began to filter through during the morning of 2 April 1982. And amid an intense political, diplomatic and military effort in the UK to respond to Argentina's 1982 invasion of the Falkland Islands, official notification of the Governor of Bermuda somehow got overlooked.

Postings to the South Pacific and Uganda in the aftermath of Idi Amin's downfall had followed Posnett's return from Belize before, in 1979, he was recalled from retirement to serve as Governor of the little mid-Atlantic outpost's twenty square miles of volcanic rock and its 60,000-strong population. And from Government House, the extraordinary, turreted official Governor's residence, Posnett followed the development of Argentina's action against Britain's remote South Atlantic colony with fascination.

Since he'd first arrived in Belize in the middle of an invasion scare, his appreciation of the potential for military-flavoured Latin American governments to act rashly had certainly changed. In 1972 he'd credited them with more common sense, and throughout that first crisis he'd dismissed any possibility that the Guatemalans might act. *Surely*, he'd thought, *they wouldn't do anything so stupid?* But by the time he left Central America in 1975, his view had changed. Credible, detailed intelligence reports from both the Americans and what had become a substantial British Signals Intelligence operation in

Belize – not to mention the evidence of his own eyes – had made certain of that. So while Argentina's invasion may have been dramatic, Posnett was no longer shocked that such rash, flawed decision-making could find expression in radical military adventure.

But Posnett's interest in the invasion was more than just curiosity. He was extremely concerned about the safety of a friend. As a district officer in Uganda, one of Posnett's contemporaries had been Rex Hunt. The two young colonial administrators had played in the same rugby team. By 1982, *Sir* Rex Hunt was Governor of the Falkland Islands. News was fragmentary, and, from the sun, money and pink-sand beaches of Bermuda, Posnett struggled to visualize the situation in the South Atlantic. But it occurred to him that, had the fates been different, it would have been a lot easier for Guatemala to invade Belize than for Argentina to cross 300 miles of water to the Falklands.

Posnett greeted confirmation, just days after the invasion, that Hunt was safe and flying home to the UK via Uruguay with huge relief. He sat down at his office in Government House and, at a desk looking out over the clear, turquoise seas, wrote his friend a letter. *You seem*, he teased, *to have chosen the wrong South American opponents, because Guatemala never did it and your chaps did!*

The First Sea Lord had been waiting in the corridor for fifteen minutes. Admiral Sir Henry Leach usually stalked Whitehall in a business suit, but this time, just back from an official engagement in Portsmouth, he was waiting outside the Prime Minister's office in the House of Commons dressed in full naval uniform. Inside, as the Argentine fleet sailed towards *Las Malvinas*, Margaret Thatcher discussed the impending invasion with a small number of Defence and Foreign Office officials, including the Secretary of State for Defence, John Nott. As they carefully weighed the options available to them they learnt the Admiral was waiting outside. Leach, a straight-talking, forceful personality, was ushered in.

'Admiral,' they asked him, 'what do you think?'

Few sailors in 1982 had a more acute understanding of the dangers of operating ships far from home without air cover than the Naval Chief. Despite his own background as a gunnery officer, Leach had discovered a keen interest in naval aviation. Personal tragedy had left him no choice.

On 10 December 1941, while steaming east of Malaya, the battleship *Prince of Wales* and the battlecruiser *Repulse* were attacked and sunk by just eight Japanese Mitsubishi G3M Naval Type 96 strike aircraft. The two capital ships were at the heart of Force Z, sent by Churchill to reinforce the Far East. As much as Taranto and the Japanese assault on Pearl Harbor the following year, the loss of the two British capital ships confirmed the ascendancy of air power at sea. One bomb and between four and six torpedoes did for the 43,000-ton *Prince of Wales* and her ten 14-inch guns, sixteen 5.25-inch guns and forty-eight anti-aircraft guns. An hour after the emergency signal from Force Z arrived at the Air Operations Room at 12.19, eleven Royal Air Force Brewster Buffalo fighters, scrambled from Sembawang airfield at Singapore, entered the catastrophic fray in time to deter another wave of Japanese attacks. But it was too late for the *Prince of Wales*. At 13.20, she heeled sharply, capsized and sank. Her Captain, John Leach, went down with her.

Now, over forty years after John Leach's death, his son explained to the politicians that, if they chose to despatch a fleet to retake the Falkland Islands, the ships, 8000 miles from home, would be vulnerable to air attack. The safety of a Task Force and the success of any operation would rest almost entirely in the hands of HMS *Invincible*, HMS *Hermes* – in her last incarnation as an anti-submarine carrier – and the two small jump-jet squadrons that made up the rump of the Fleet Air Arm's fixed-wing fighter force.

'We shall be entirely dependent on the Sea Harriers,' he told them. 'And, no, we have not really got enough . . .' The Prime Minister had been a member of Heath's cabinet in 1972 when he'd been forced to deter any prospect of Guatemalan aggression against British Honduras. Perhaps she remembered that occasion when – like all American Presidents faced with a global crisis – the Prime Minister reached instinctively for the security of a big, conventional strike carrier.

'What about *Ark Royal*?' she asked in vain. 'What about the Phantoms and Buccaneers?'

You don't truly value something until it's gone.

POSTSCRIPT

The British gave us the English language, a mixture of Latin, French, Greek, German and Gaelic. They gave us the English dictionary. Ninety-three per cent of Belizeans can read and write because of a British education and I am one. William Wilberforce abolished the slave trade. After the break-up of the British Empire they gave us the British Commonwealth, the industrial revolution, railways, the steam engine and the jet engine, the Harrier jump jet and the hovercraft. And in 1981, after Belizean Independence, they told the world that if you want Belize, you'll have to beat us first.

Harry Kuylen, homeless, Belize City, September 2007

Glossary

A-37 Dragonfly American-built light twin-engined attack jet

A-4 Skyhawk American carrierborne single-engined attack jet

A-6 Intruder American carrierborne twin-engined strike jet

A-7 Corsair American carrierborne single-engined attack jet

ACM Air Combat Manoeuvring

ACR Aircraft Control Room

ADD Airflow Direction Detector

ADIZ Air Defence Interception Zone

ADR Air Direction Room

AEO Air Engineering Officer

AEW Airborne Early Warning

AFCS Automatic Flight Control System

afterburner American term for reheat

AFWR Atlantic Fleet Weapons Range

AIM-4 Falcon American air-to-air missile

AIM-7 Sparrow American radar-guided air-to-air missile

AIM-9 Sidewinder American heat-seeking air-to-air missile

Alpha Strike A large-scale air attack launched from an aircraft carrier

ANG Air National Guard

angled deck landing area offset from the centreline to allow safe recovery of aircraft to the carrier

arrestor hook retractable hook used by landing aircraft to catch arrestor wires on the flight deck

arrestor wire high-tension steel cable suspended low across the deck to retard recovering aircraft

ASI Air Speed Indicator

Avcat high-flashpoint JP5 jet fuel used onboard aircraft carriers

AWI Air Warfare Instructor

B-26 American twin piston-engined attack bomber

Badger Navy slang for a Flight Deck Engineer

battle formation loose defensive formation

BH British Honduras

Bingo Fuel pre-briefed fuel level that will allow a safe return to base

BLC Boundary Layer Control

Blue Parrot Strike radar used in the Buccaneer

BOAC British Overseas Airways Corporation

Bofors 40mm anti-aircraft cannon

Bolter attempted recovery aboard a carrier by an aircraft that fails to catch an arrestor wire; an unintentional roller landing

Bone Dome aviator's flying helmet

Bow Cat catapult situated at the bow

Bridle steel strop used to attach a carrierborne aircraft to the catapult shuttle

Buddy pod air-refuelling pod carried under the wing

Bullpup air-launched guided missile for use against surface targets

BVR Beyond Visual Range

C-1 Trader American carrierborne piston-engined transport aircraft

C-130 Hercules American-built four-engined turboprop military transport aircraft

C-47 American Second World War-vintage twin piston-engined transport aircraft

Cab Navy slang for an aircraft

Canberra British twin-engined jet bomber, developed into a photo-reconnaissance aircraft

CAP Combat Air Patrol

catapult steam-powered device for launching aircraft from a carrier

CBALS (Seaballs) Navy slang for CBGLO, the Ground Liaison Officer supplied by the army to Royal Navy carriers

CBGLO Carrierborne Ground Liaison Officer

CCA Carrier-Controlled Approach

CIA Central Intelligence Agency

CINCFLEET Commander-in-Chief Fleet

CO Commanding Officer

COD Carrier Onboard Delivery

Comet British four-engined jet airliner and military transport

Compass Platform a ship's bridge

Coriolis effect the tendency of moving air to veer to the right in the northern hemisphere or to the left in the southern hemisphere

CRT cathode ray tube

cunims cumulonimbus clouds

CVA military acronym denoting a Strike Carrier

'D' Navy slang for the Fighter Controller

DACT Dissimilar Air Combat Training

DOPS Defence Operations

dry thrust unreheated jet power

Duskers deck landing practice in low light of dusk

E-2 Hawkeye American carrierborne airborne early warning aircraft

Etendard IVM French carrierborne single-engined attack jet

Executive Officer Second in Command

F-102 Delta Dagger American delta-winged single-engined jet fighter

F-104 Starfighter American single-engined jet fighter

F-47 Thunderbolt American Second World War-vintage piston-engined fighter-bomber

F-8 Crusader American carrierborne single-engined jet fighter

FAG Fuerza Aerea Guatemalteca (Guatemalan Air Force)

FAR Fuerzas Armadas Revolucionarias

FCO Foreign and Commonwealth Office

FDO Flight Deck Officer

FFO Furnace Fuel Oil

FIS Fighter Interception Squadron

Fish Head Fleet Air Arm slang for a non-aviator

Fly 1, 2, 3 and 4 discrete areas of the carrier deck used for parking aircraft

Flyco Flying Control

FOCAS Flag Officer Carriers and Amphibious Ships

FOD Foreign Object Damage

FONAC Flag Officer Naval Air Command

Fox Two NATO code to signal the release (or simulated release) of a heat-seeking air-to-air missile

full military power maximum power without reheat

g unit of acceleration

Gannet AEW3 British carrierborne Airborne Early Warning aircraft

Gannet COD4 British carrierborne transport aircraft

Goa SA-3 surface-to-air missile

GPMG General Purpose Machine Gun

Guideline Soviet SA-2 surface-to-air missile

Harrier British vertical/short take-off and landing ground-attack jet

Heavies Navy slang for carrierborne fast jets

Helo helicopter

HF high frequency

HMS *Victory* Nelson's flagship at the Battle of Trafalgar; still in commission with the Royal Navy

Hormone Soviet Navy anti-submarine helicopter

Howdah catapult launch position

HP cock high-pressure cock

HUD head-up display

Hunter British single-engined jet fighter-bomber

ICBM Intercontinental Ballistic Missile

Il-38 May Soviet four-engined maritime patrol aircraft

JARIC Joint Air Reconnaissance Intelligence Centre

JBD jet blast deflector

JIC Joint Intelligence Committee

JPT jet pipe temperature

Kotlin class of Soviet guided-missile destroyer

Lepus Swedish-made air-launched parachute flare

Lightning twin-engined supersonic British jet fighter

Little 'F' Lieutenant Commander (Flying); deputy to Commander (Air), or 'Wings'

Loran Charlie radio-based Long Range Aid to Navigation

LSO Landing Safety Officer

M-4 Bison Soviet four-engined jet heavy bomber

MADDL Mirror Assisted Dummy Deck Landing

Mae West life jacket

Marineflieger German naval air arm

meatball signal light from a carrier's projector landing sight

MI6 British Secret Intelligence Service

MiG-17 Soviet single-engined jet fighter

MiG-21 Fishbed Soviet single-engined jet fighter

mirror landing sight visual aid, mounted on deck to assist pilots recovering on deck

Mother Navy slang for an aircraft carrier

NAS Naval Air Squadron (or, in the US, Naval Air Station)

NATO North Atlantic Treaty Organization

NAVEX Navigation Exercise

P-3 Orion American-built four-engined maritime patrol aircraft

P-51 Mustang piston-engined Second World War-vintage American fighter-bomber (known as the F-51 in the Guatemalan Air Force)

PEC Personal Equipment Connector

PIM Point of Intended Movement

PNR Point of No Return

projector sight development of the mirror landing sight

QFI Qualified Flying Instructor

RA-5 Vigilante American carrierborne twin-engined reconnaissance jet

RAG Replacement Air Group

ramp *see* round-down

RAS Replenishment at Sea

reheat fuel injected into a jet engine's jet pipe to boost thrust

RFA Royal Fleet Auxiliary

roller landing a touch-and-go practice landing onboard a carrier; with no intention to catch a wire, the arrestor hook isn't lowered

rotate moment of take-off

round-down extreme aft of the flight deck, gently curved to provide a measure of safety for aircraft that have recovered badly short

RT radio

RV rendezvous

RWR Radar Warning Receiver

Salthorse Navy slang for a Seaman Officer

SAM surface-to-air missile

SAR Search and Rescue

SARBE Search and Rescue beacon

School of the Americas US Army jungle training school in Panama

Scimitar British carrierborne twin-engined attack jet

Sea Harrier British carrierborne vertical/short take-off and landing fighter-bomber

Sea Vixen British carrierborne twin-engined all-weather jet fighter

Seahawk British carrierborne fighter bomber

Shorts Belfast British four-engined turboprop military transport aircraft

SLR Self-Loading Rifle

SNOWI Senior Naval Officer, West Indies

SOBS Navy slang for a Senior Observer

Sonar acoustic underwater detection device

SOPS Standard Operating Procedures

SPLOT Navy slang for a Senior Pilot

SSB Single Sideband

SSN nuclear-powered attack submarine

Sverdlov class of Soviet cruiser

T-33 American jet trainer and light attack aircraft

Tiger Cat British optically guided surface-to-air missile

Topgun US Navy Fighter Weapons School

Trap American slang for an arrested landing onboard an aircraft carrier

Tu-16 Badger Soviet twin-engined jet bomber

Tu-95 Bear Soviet four-engined turboprop bomber and maritime patrol aircraft

U-2 American high-altitude reconnaissance aircraft

UH-1 Huey US-built utility helicopter

UHF ultra-high frequency

UN United Nations

V/STOL vertical/short take-off and landing

VC10 British four-engined jet airliner, converted for use as a military transport

Vickers Viscount British four-engined turboprop airliner

Victor British four-engined medium bomber, converted for use as an air-to-air refuelling tanker aircraft

VID Visual Identification

WAFU wet and fucking useless. Navy slang for aviators

Waist Cat catapult situated along the angled deck

Wasp British single-engined shipborne helicopter

WE177 British tactical nuclear bomb and depth charge

Wessex British anti-submarine and utility helicopter

Wings Navy slang for the Commander (Air)

Wombat British recoilless anti-tank rifle

zip-lip radio silence

Zulu military term for Greenwich Mean Time; different time zones are assigned different letters of the phonetic alphabet, e.g. Quebec, Sierra, Papa

Bibliography

BOOKS

Aerospace Encyclopaedia of Air Warfare, Volume 2: 1945 to the Present, The (ed. Chris Bishop), Aerospace Publishing, 1997

Airfix Magazine Annual 3 (ed. Bruce Quarrie), Patrick Stephens, 1973

Allen, Patrick, *Wessex*, Airlife, 1988

Allward, Maurice, *Buccaneer*, Ian Allan, 1981

Aloni, Shlomo, *Israeli F-4 Phantom II Aces*, Osprey, 2004

—, *Israeli Mirage and Nesher Aces*, Osprey, 2004

Andrade, John M., *Latin-American Military Aviation*, Midland Counties Publications, 1982

Bain, Chris J., *Cold War, Hot Wings*, Pen and Sword, 2007

Ballantyne, Iain, *Strike from the Sea*, Pen and Sword, 2002

Barker, Dennis, *Guarding the Skies*, Viking, 1989

—, *Ruling the Waves*, Viking, 1986

Barnett, Correlli, *Engage the Enemy More Closely*, Hodder and Stoughton, 1991

Beaver, Paul, *The Encyclopaedia of the Fleet Air Arm since 1945*, Patrick Stephens, 1987

Boot, Roy, *From Spitfire to Eurofighter*, Airlife, 1990

Bostock, Peter, *The Great Atlantic Air Race*, Dent, 1970

Brassey's Annual 1969, William Clowes, 1969

Brassey's Annual 1970, William Clowes, 1970

Brassey's Annual 1972, William Clowes, 1972

Brown, Charles H., *Dark Sky, Black Sea*, Naval Institute Press, 1999

Brown, David, *The Seafire*, Greenhill Books, 1989

Brown, Captain Eric 'Winkle', *Wings on My Sleeve*, Weidenfeld and Nicolson, 2006

Budiansky, Stephen, *Air Power*, Viking, 2003

Burns, Michael, *McDonnell Douglas F-4K and F-4M Phantom II*, Osprey, 1984

Burrows, William E., *By Any Means Necessary*, Plume, 2002

Calvert, Denis J., and Gary Madgwick, *HMS Ark Royal*, Aviation Workshop Publications, 2007

Carver, Michael, *War since 1945*, Putnam, 1981

Castillo, Rudolph I., *Profile of Rt. Hon. George Price, P.C.*, RiC (Belmopan, Belize), 2002

Caygill, Peter, *Phantom from the Cockpit*, Pen and Sword, 2005

Chartres, John, *Westland Sea King*, Ian Allan, 1984

Clancy, Tom, *Carrier*, Berkley, 1999

—, *Red Storm Rising*, Collins, 1987

Coonts, Stephen, *Flight of the Intruder*, Pocket Books, 1987

Coram, Robert, *Boyd*, Little Brown, 2002

Crosley, Commander R. M. 'Mike', *Up in Harm's Way*, Airlife, 1995

Cruddas, Colin, *In Cobham's Company*, Cobham Plc, 1994

Daniels, Anthony, *Sweet Waist of America: Journeys around Guatemala*, Hutchinson, 1992

Darling, Kev, *Blackburn Buccaneer*, Crowood Press, 2006

—, *Tweet and the Dragonfly*, Big Bird Aviation, 2005

Davies, Lieutenant Commander Brian, *Fly No More*, Airlife, 2001

Dewar, Michael, *Brush Fire Wars*, Robert Hale, 1984

Donald, David, and Daniel J. March, *Carrier Aviation Air Power Directory*, Airtime Publishing, 2001

Doust, Michael J., *Buccaneer S.1.*, Ad Hoc Publications, 2007

—, *Phantom Leader*, Ad Hoc Publications, 2005

Eltringham, Peter, *The Rough Guide to Belize*, Rough Guides, 2004

Elward, Brad, and Peter Davies, *US Navy F-4 Phantom II MiG Killers 1965–70*, Osprey, 2002

—, *US Navy F-4 Phantom II MiG Killers 1972–3*, Osprey, 2002

Evans, Andy, *Backseat Flyers*, Arms and Armour Press, 1993

Fleet Air Arm Songbook, The, privately published

Flintham, Victor, *Air Wars and Aircraft*, Arms and Armour Press, 1989

Flying Stations: A Story of Australian Naval Aviation, Allen and Unwin, 1998

Francillon, Rene J., *The United States Air National Guard*, Aerospace Publishing, 1993

Friedman, Norman, *British Carrier Aviation*, Naval Institute Press, 1988

Gandin, Gregg, *The Blood of Guatemala*, Duke University Press, 2000

—, *The Last Colonial Massacre: Latin America in the Cold War*, University of Chicago Press, 2004

Gardner, Richard E., *The Flying Navy*, Almark Publications, 1971

Gill, Lesley, *The School of the Americas: Military Training and Political Violence in the Americas*, Duke University Press, 2004

Gregg, Algar Robert, *British Honduras*, HMSO, 1968

Grove, Eric, with Graham Thompson, *Battle for the Fjords*, Ian Allan, 1991

Grove, Eric, *Vanguard to Trident: British Naval Policy since World War Two*, Naval Institute Press, 1987

Gunston, Bill, *Attack Aircraft of the West*, Ian Allan, 1974

—, *Early Supersonic Fighters of the West*, Ian Allan, 1976

—, *F-4 Phantom*, Ian Allan, 1977

—, *Fighters of the Fifties*, Patrick Stephens, 1981

Gunston, Bill, and Lindsay Peacock, *Fighter Missions*, Salamander, 1988

Gunston, Bill, and Mike Spick, *Modern Air Combat*, Salamander, 1983

Hackett, General Sir John, *The Third World War*, Sidgwick and Jackson, 1978

Hagedorn, Dan, *Latin American Air Wars and Aircraft 1912–1969*, Hikoki Publications, 2006

Hagedorn, Dan, and Leif Hellstrom, *Foreign Invaders*, Midland Publishing, 1994

Hampshire, Cecil, *The Royal Navy since 1945*, William Kimber, 1975

Hawk, Robert, *Florida's Air Force: Air National Guard 1946–1990*, Florida National Guard Historical Foundation, 1990

Hazell, Steve, *McDonnell Douglas F-4K and F-4M Phantom*, Hall Park Books, 2000

Healey, Denis, *The Time of My Life*, Michael Joseph, 1989

Herman, Arthur, *To Rule the Waves*, Hodder and Stoughton, 2005

Hill, Rear Admiral J. R., *Anti-Submarine Warfare*, Ian Allan, 1984

Hunt, Peter, *Angles of Attack: An A-6 Intruder Pilot's War*, Ballantine, 2002

Jackson, Robert, *World Military Aircraft since 1945*, Ian Allan, 1979

—, *Sea Harrier and AV-8B*, Blandford Press, 1989

Jackson, General Sir William, *Withdrawal from Empire*, Batsford, 1986

Johnstone-Bryden, Richard, *Britain's Greatest Warship: HMS Ark Royal IV*, Sutton Publishing, 1999

Knopf, Klaus, *German Starfighters*, Midland Publishing, 2002

Lamb, Charles, *War in a Stringbag*, Arrow, 1978

Laming, Tim, *Buccaneer*, Patrick Stephens, 1998

Langewiesche, William, *Inside the Sky*, Vintage, 1998

—, *The Outlaw Sea*, Granta, 2005

Leach, Admiral of the Fleet Sir Henry, *Endure No Makeshifts*, Leo Cooper, 1993

Lee, Air Chief Marshal Sir David, *Eastward*, HMSO, 1984

List, Friedrich, *Marineflieger Geschwader 2*, Ian Allan, 2005

Lithgow, Mike, *Mach One*, Allan Wingate, 1954

Lord, Dick, *From Tailhooker to Mudmover*, Corporal Publications, 2003

Lunnon-Wood, Mike, *Long Reach*, HarperCollins, 1999

Lygo, Admiral Sir Raymond, *Collision Course*, Book Guild, 2002

Manning, Lieutenant Commander Charles (ed.), *Fly Navy*, Leo Cooper, 2000

McCart, Neil, *HMS Eagle 1942–1978*, FAN Publications, 1996

—, *HMS Victorious 1937–1969*, FAN Publications, 1998

—, *Three Ark Royals 1938–1999*, FAN Publications, 1999

—, *HMS Hermes*, FAN Publications, 2001

Melville, Thomas and Marjorie, *Guatemala – Another Vietnam?*, Penguin Books, 1971

Mersky, Peter, *Vought F-8 Crusader*, Osprey, 1989

Mills, Carl, *Banshees in the Royal Canadian Navy*, Banshee Publications, 1991

Morgan, David, *Hostile Skies*, Weidenfeld and Nicolson, 2006

Murphy, James S., *The Guatemalan Claim to Belize: A Handbook on the Negotiations*, James S. Murphy, 2004

Mutza, Wayne, *Convair F-102 Delta Dagger*, Schiffer Publishing, 1999

Neillands, Robin, *A Fighting Retreat: The British Empire 1947–97*, Hodder and Stoughton, 1996

Newton, Lieutenant Commander James, DFC, *Armed Action*, Headline, 2007

Oliver, David, *British Combat Aircraft in Action since 1945*, Ian Allan, 1987

Paringaux, Alexandre, *Adieu 'Crouze'*, Editions Zephyr, 1999

Paxman, Jeremy, *Through the Volcanoes*, Michael Joseph, 1985

Pitchfork, Air Commodore Graham, *The Buccaneers*, Patrick Stephens, 2002

Polmar, Norman (ed.), *The Modern Soviet Navy*, Arms and Armour Press, 1979

Posnett, Richard, *The Scent of Eucalyptus*, Radcliffe Press, 2001

Prest, Robert, *F4 Phantom: A Pilot's Story*, Corgi, 1981

Reardon, Carol, *Launch the Intruders*, University Press of Kansas, 2005

Reed, Arthur, *F-104 Starfighter*, Ian Allan, 1981

Richardson, Nick, *No Escape Zone*, Little Brown, 2000

Rossiter, Mike, *Ark Royal*, Bantam Press, 2006

Royal Air Force Briefing Book, Directorate of Public Relations (RAF), 1971

Setlowe, Richard, *The Brink*, Pocket Books, 1976

Shaw, Robert L., *Fighter Combat Tactics and Maneuvering*, Naval Institute Press, 1985

Shipster, John, *Mist on the Rice-Fields*, Leo Cooper, 2000

Sontag, Sherry, and Christopher Drew with Annette Lawrence Drew, *Blind Man's Bluff*, Hutchinson, 1999

Spick, Mike, *Jet Fighter Performance: Korea to Vietnam*, Ian Allan, 1986

Spufford, Francis, *Backroom Boys*, Faber and Faber, 2003

Stewart, Iain, *The Rough Guide to Guatemala*, Rough Guides, 2006

Sturtivant, Ray, *The Squadrons of the Fleet Air Arm*, Air Britain, 1984

Sturtivant, Ray, with Mick Burrow and Lee Howard, *Fleet Air Arm Fixed-Wing Aircraft since 1946*, Air-Britain, 2004

Tanner, Richard M., *History of Air-to-Air Refuelling*, Pen and Sword, 2006

Thomas, Andrew, *Royal Navy Aces of World War 2*, Osprey, 2007

Thornborough, Anthony, and Peter E. Davies, *Grumman A-6 Intruder/Prowler*, Ian Allan, 1987

—, *The Phantom Story*, Arms and Armour Press, 1994

Toomey, David, *Stormchasers*, Norton, 2003

Treacher, Sir John, *Life at Full Throttle*, Pen and Sword, 2004

Trotti, John, *Phantom over Vietnam*, Airlife, 1997

20th Century Day by Day, Dorling Kindersley, 1999

Twiss, Peter, *Faster Than the Sun*, Grub Street, 2005

Verier, Mike, *Superbase 22: Yeovilton*, Osprey, 1991

Wakeham, Geoff, *RNAS Culdrose 1947–2007*, Tempus, 2007

Waller, Douglas C., *Air Warriors*, Simon and Schuster, 1998

Ward, Commander 'Sharkey', *Sea Harrier over the Falklands*, Leo Cooper, 1992

Weiner, Tim, *Legacy of Ashes*, Allen Lane, 2007
Westlake, Donald E., *Under an English Heaven*, Hodder and
  Stoughton, 1973
Wilcox, Robert K., *Scream of Eagles*, Pocket Books, 1990
Wilson, Harold, *Labour Government 1964–1970: A Personal
  Record*, Michael Joseph, 1971
Wilson, Stewart, *Spitfire*, Crowood Press, 2004
Wingate, John, *Carrier*, Weidenfeld and Nicolson, 1981
Winton, John, *HMS Leviathan*, Michael Joseph, 1967
Woodward Jr, Ralph Lee, *A Short Guide to Guatemala*,
  Editorial Laura Lee (La Antigua, Guatemala), 2005
Wragg, David, *Swordfish*, Weidenfeld and Nicolson, 2003

MAGAZINES, JOURNALS AND NEWSPAPERS

Aircraft Illustrated, February 1972
All Hands, no. 663, April 1972
Amandla (Belize City)
Ambergris Today
ap Rees, Elfan, 'Eyes of the Fleet', *Air Pictorial*, March 1978
Arthur, Max, 'Obituary: Admiral of the Fleet Sir Michael
  Pollock', *Independent*, October 2006
Belize Times (Belize City)
Bilger, Burkhard, 'Falling', *New Yorker*, August 2007
Calvert, Denis J., 'Blackburn Buccaneer', *Wings of Fame*, vol.
  14 (1999)
Dorr, Robert F., 'Convair F-102 Delta Dagger', *Wings of Fame*,
  vol. 17 (1999)
Dorr, Robert F., 'Navy Phantoms in Vietnam', *Wings of Fame*,
  vol. 1 (1995)
Dorr, Robert F., 'Lockheed C-130 Hercules', *World Air Power
  Journal*, vol. 18 (1994), Autumn
'*Eagle* and Her Brood', *Air Pictorial*, February 1972
Edwards, Ron, 'Five TBM Avenger Bombers Lost in the

Bermuda Triangle', *Aviation History*, July 1999

Ellis, Paul, 'From Ark to Omega', *Flight International*, November 1971

'Farewell to a Grand Old Lady', *Evening Mail*

Frater, Alexander, 'Phantom', *Telegraph Sunday Magazine*, October 1976

Fricker, John, 'Lockheed F-104 Starfighter', *Wings of Fame*, vol. 2 (1996)

Gaines, Mike, 'Faster, Lower, Longer . . .', *Jets*, Winter 2000

Gallagher, Brendan, 'The Ark's Strike Power', *Flight International*, 6 February 1976

Graydon, Air Chief Marshal Sir Michael, 'Air Defence in Cyprus', *Royal Air Force Historical Society Journal*, no. 38

Gunston, Bill, and David Donald, 'Fleet Air Arm 1960–69', *Wings of Fame*, vol. 1 (1995)

Hall, Alan W., 'Sea King Trials', *Air Pictorial*, January 1970

—, 'Strong Express Air Operations', *Aviation News*, 13–26 October 1972

Harnden, Toby, 'Obituary: Admiral of the Fleet Lord Hill-Norton', *Independent*, May 2004

Kilduff, Peter, '*Intrepid* – In Name and Spirit', *Aircraft Illustrated*, March 1973

March, Peter R., 'Sea King – Sub-Killer for the Fleet', *Aircaft Illustrated*, November 1971

Marriott, John, 'Exercise Bersatu Padu – Long Range Reinforcement on Trial', *International Defense Review*, 1971

Mobley, Richard, 'The Beira Patrol: Britain's Broken Blockade against Rhodesia', *Naval War College Review*, Winter 2002

'Obituary: Admiral of the Fleet Lord Hill-Norton', *Daily Telegraph*, May 2004

'Obituary: Air Marshal Sir John Nicholls', *Daily Telegraph*, May 2007

Pringle, Ian, 'Flying the Mighty Buccaneer', *Pilot*, March 2003

Reporter, The (Belize City)

Sainsbury, A. B., 'Obituary: Rear Admiral Dennis Cambell', *Independent*, 21 July 2000

Service, Brian M., 'Back in Business: HMS *Ark Royal*', *Air Pictorial*, July 1970

Simpson, Rear Admiral Mike, 'Naval Helicopter Engines in the Beginning', *Journal of Naval Engineering*, June 1998

'The Jets Roar In', *Time*, May 1980

'The Point of the Arrow', *Flight International,* November 1971

'Tomcat Tribute', *Air and Space Magazine*, September 2006

Van der Vat, Dan, 'Obituary: Admiral of the Fleet Lord Hill-Norton', *Guardian*, May 2004

'When the Blood Began to Run', *Time*, March 1971

DVDS AND VIDEOS

Ark Royal: The Complete History, DD Home Entertainment, 2006

At Sea with the Navy, BBC, 1971

Behind Enemy Lines (dir. John Moore), 20th Century Fox, 2001

Buccaneer: The Last British Bomber, DD Video, 1994

Empire Warriors: The British Empire at War 1946–1967, BBC, 2004

Flight of the Intruder (dir. John Milius), Paramount, 1991

Fly Navy, Royal Navy Videos, 2004

Jets of the Fleet Air Arm, DD Video, 2004

Med Patrol, United Motion Pictures, 1971

Sailor, BBC, 1976

Seapower: Carrier, BBC, 1981

Sixties Navy, Royal Navy Videos, 2002

The Ark Royals, DD Video, 1994

Top Gun (dir. Tony Scott), Paramount, 1986

Warship Eagle, Royal Navy Videos, 2002

WEBSITES

http://freespace.virgin.net/john.dell
    John Dell, 'First Blood'
http://junglefighter.panamanow.net
    Fort Sherman/JOTC history
http://news.bbc.co.uk
    Russian 'killed UK diver' in 1956
www.acig.org
    Air Combat Information Group
    Tom Cooper, 'Guatemala since 1954'
    Tom Cooper and March Coelich, 'El Salvador vs Honduras,
        1969: The 100-Hour War'
www.apollomissionphotos.com
    Panama jungle survival
www.axfordsabode.org.uk
    HMS *Eagle* Commissioning Book
www.belizenet.com
www.ejection-history.org.uk
    Project Get Out and Walk
www.laahs.com
    Lieutenant Colonel Dell Toedt, 'Memories of a Mustang
        Driver, Part III'
    Ruben Urribares, Mike Little and the LAAHS Staff, 'The
        Cuban MiGs'
    Mario E. Overall, 'Air Cavalry, Guatemalan-style'
    —, 'Bay of Pigs: The Guatemalan Connection'
    —, 'Guatemala's Combat Dragons'
    —, 'The 100-Hour War'
    Tulio Soto, 'The US Good Will Flight to Guatemala'
www.nukestrat.com
    USS *Intrepid* Cruise Book 1971
www.pprune.org
    Spitfire vs. Lightning

UNPUBLISHED ACCOUNTS

Davis, Commander Carl, RN, 'The First of Many'
Ford, Commander John, RN, *Ark Royal 1971–1973*
—, 'Closed on Sundays'
—, 'Night Carrier Operations'
—, 'Suez 1956'
Grenade: The Newssheet of the Inkerman Company Group, The
Kerr, Commander Nick, RN, 'I Joined the Navy'
Macdonald, Commander Doug, RN, 'Top Gun and the British'
O'Grady, Lieutenant Commander Harry, 'Autobiography'
Roberts, Rear Admiral John, *Journal for the Use of Midshipmen*
Rowland, Dave, 'Phantom Memories'

ARCHIVES AND OFFICIAL DOCUMENTS

Fleet Air Arm, Royal Air Force, Royal Navy
809 Naval Air Squadron Record Book, 1971/72
824 Naval Air Squadron Line Book, 1971/72
824 Naval Air Squadron Record Book, 1971/72
849 Naval Air Squadron 'B' Flight Line Book, 1971/72
849 Naval Air Squadron 'B' Flight Squadron Record Book, 1971/72
892 Naval Air Squadron Line Book, 1971/72
892 Naval Air Squadron Record Book, 1971/72
Aircrew Log Books:
  Carl Davis
  Ed Featherstone
  John Froggatt
  Jerry Granger-Holcombe
  Guy Holman
  Nick Kerr
  Mike Lucas
  Doug Macdonald

John Morgan
Steve Park
Colin Walkinshaw

Ark Royal SAR Flight Squadron Record Book, 1971/72

Buccaneer Operating Procedures

Buccaneer S Mk 2 Aircrew Notes

Buccaneer S2 Flight Reference Cards

Exercise ROYAL KNIGHT, RN/PR, 1971

Gannet AEW3 Flight Reference Cards

HMS *Ark Royal* Commission Book, 1970–73

HMS *Ark Royal*, Captain's Report on Proceedings, 9 March 1971–9, March 1972

HMS *Ark Royal*, FOCAS Report on Proceedings, 10 June–7 July 1971

HMS *Eagle*, Captain's Standing Orders, 1 September 1970

HMS *Eagle* Commission Book, 1970–72

HMS *Ocelot*, Control Room Log, September 1971

HMS *Phoebe*, Captain's Report on Proceedings, 11 February 1972

Lord, Dick, 'Flying and Fighting the Phantom', Naval Air Station Miramar, June 1970

Military Assistance Program Major Weapons Inventory for Guatemala, 1969

No. 1(F) Squadron, RAF, Operations Record Book, January 1972

No. 10 Squadron, RAF, Operations Record Book, January 1972

No. 24 Squadron, RAF, Operations Record Book, January 1972

No. 36 Squadron, RAF, Operations Record Book, January 1972

No. 39 Squadron, RAF, Operations Record Book, January 1972

No. 43 Squadron, RAF, Operations Record Book, September 1971

No. 47 Squadron, RAF, Operations Record Book, January 1972

No. 48 Squadron, RAF Regiment, Operations Record Book, September 1971–March 1972

No. 543 Squadron, RAF, Operations Record Book, December 1961

Phansops, Phantom Standard Operational Procedures, June 1970

Phantom FG Mk 1 Aircrew Manual

Phantom FG Mk 1 Operating Data Manual

Belize Archives and Records, Belmopan

MC-1786 – Colonel Charles A. Lindbergh, 'To Bogotá and back by Air', *National Geographic*, May 1928

MC-30R – Letters to Governor of British Honduras, November 1970

MC-30S – Guatemalan Incursions into British Honduras 1970

MC-310 – A Brief Résumé of Guatemala's Dispute with Britain over the Belize Territory (1783–1975), Ministry of Foreign Affairs, Guatemala

SP-151 – HMS *Mohawk* and British Honduras

National Archives of the United Kingdom

ADM 335/288 – Air Combat Rules and Safety Regulations for Air Defence Exercises 1970

ADM 335/343 – Low Level Air Defence

ADM 335/382 – Exercise GULFEX/MIDLINK

ADM 335/61 – 'The State of the Art': A Review of Fixed Wing Flying Expertise in the Fleet Air Arm 1968–1970; Part 1

ADM 335/62 – 'The State of the Art': A Review of Fixed Wing Flying Expertise in the Fleet Air Arm 1968–1970; Part 2

ADM 53/17588 – HMS *Phoebe*, Ship's Log, January 1972

ADM 1/20977 – The Belize Incident, 1948

ADM 53/175729 – HMS *London*, Ship's Log, January 1972

AIR 20/11718 – Sparrow/Sidewinder

AIR 20/12677 – Aircraft Carriers: Continuation in Service of HMS *Ark Royal* beyond 1972, RAF Perspective

CAB 141/121/7 – The Threat to British Honduras from Guatemala

CAB 185/10 – Joint Intelligence Committee (A) Meetings

CAB 185/11 – Joint Intelligence Committee (A) Meetings: Codeword; Confidential Annexes

CAB 185/7 – Joint Intelligence Committee (A) Meetings

CAB 185/8 – Joint Intelligence Committee (A) Meetings: Codeword; Confidential Annexes

DEFE 13/803 – Operational Shortcomings of Early Spey Engines

DEFE 24/1485 – British Honduras (Belize): general; dispute and negotiations with Guatemala; policy on British Garrison

DEFE 25/357 – Operational Planning: British Honduras; includes deployment of RAF Regiment (Tiger Cat) Squadron

DEFE 4/260/1 – Chief of Staff Committee Meeting, 14 September 1971

DEFE 4/264 – Chief of Staff Committee Meeting, 18 January 1972

DEFE 4/264 – Chief of Staff Committee Meeting, 25 January 1972

DEFE 4/265 – Chief of Staff Committee Meeting, 8 February 1972

DEFE 5/192/16 – Rules of Engagement for British Honduras

DEFE 5/192/17 – Directive to the Forces Commander British Honduras

DEFE 5/192/4 – Reinforcement of the Army Garrison in British Honduras

DEFE 5/192/9 – British Military Assistance to British Honduras in the event of External Aggression

DEFE 56/44 – Exercise CALIBRATE: Phantom FG1 combat air patrol tactics for maritime air defence

DEFE 56/47 – Buccaneer Tactical Study/Phase 2: Part 1, Overland Penetration

DEFE 56/48 – Buccaneer Tactical Study/Phase 2: Part 2, Overland Attack

DEFE 56/62 – Phantom FG1 Tactical Study, Phase 1: Air Defence of Naval Forces at Sea

DEFE 56/78 – Buccaneer Tactical Study Phase One: The Counter Shipping Role Using Conventional Weapons, 1970–71

DEFE 69/462 – Nuclear Warfare: Employment of Disembarked RN Buccaneers in the Strike Role

FCO 44/552 – Preparations for Independence in British Honduras

FCO 44/554 – Change of Title from British Honduras to Belize

FCO 44/578 – The Governorship of British Honduras

FCO 44/707 – First Despatch from New Governor of British Honduras, R. N. Posnett

FCO 44/729 – Military Personnel in British Honduras

FCO 44/731–740 – Guatemalan Military Threat to British Honduras

FCO 44/746 – Local Intelligence Reports from British Honduras

FCO 46/676 – British Armed Forces Participation in Exercise Bersatu Padu

FCO 46/845 – Reinforcement of British Honduras by Armed Forces of United Kingdom

FCO 7/1961 – Activities of Guatemalan Guerillas in Guatemala

FCO 7/1964 – Foreign Policy of Guatemala

FCO 7/2243 – Guatemala: Annual Review for 1971

FCO 7/2299 – Attitude of Costa Rica to Dispute between British Honduras and Guatemala

FCO 7/2453 – Guatemala: Annual Review for 1972

JIC(A)(71) 21 – Report by the Joint Intelligence Committee, Soviet Maritime Policy

JIC(A)(71) 35 – Report from the Joint Intelligence Committee, Belize (British Honduras): The Threat from Guatemala

Appendix 1

Blackburn (Hawker Siddeley)
Buccaneer S2B cutaway

Blackburn (Hawker Siddeley) Buccaneer S.2B

1 Glass-fibre radome
2 Radome latches
3 Fixed flight refuelling probe
4 Hinged radar equipment module
5 Radar scanner
6 Ventral weapons recorder/camera
7 Ferranti Blue Parrot multi-mode search and fire control radar
8 Pressurised radar housing
9 Ice detector probe
10 AOF antenna
11 Windscreen rain dispersal air duct
12 Front pressure bulkhead
13 Cockpit pressurisation valve
14 Radar module hinge arm
15 VHF homing antennae
16 Landing/taxiing lamp
17 Total pressure head
18 Levered suspension nosewheel axle
19 Steerable nosewheel, aft retracting
20 Nosewheel leg door
21 Leg pivot mounting
22 Rudder pedals
23 Canopy emergency release
24 Control column handgrip
25 Instrument panel shroud
26 Pilot's head-up display
27 Windscreen wiper
28 Windscreen panels
29 Ejection seat headrest and face blind firing handle
30 Pilot's Martin-Baker Mk. 6MSB zero-zero ejection seat
31 Side console panel
32 Engine throttle levers
33 Cockpit internal pressure shell
34 Fuel system electrical equipment bay, cockpit air conditioning pack on starboard side
35 Port engine air intake, thermally de-iced
36 De-icing air spill duct
37 Ventral radar altimeter antenna
38 Hydraulic equipment bay
39 Artificial feel control unit
40 Navigator's instrument consoles
41 Radar display
42 Blast screen
43 Starboard engine air intake
44 AN/CPU-123B Paveway II 1000lb (454kg) laser guided bomb, normally carried on starboard inboard stores station
45 430 Imp gal (1955 lit) slipper tank, carried for LGB designator role
46 Sliding cockpit canopy cover
47 Navigator's Martin Baker Mk. 6MSB ejection seat
48 Circuit breaker panel
49 Cockpit rear pressure bulkhead
50 Fuel system recuperator (2)
51 Forward fuselage integral fuel tanks, total capacity of fuselage tanks 1560 Imp gal (7092 lit)
52 Canopy electric drive motor

53 Canopy centre arch
54 Miniature detonating cord (MDC) canopy breakers
55 Starboard wing blowing air ducts
56 Inboard stores station pylon mounting
57 Wing fold hinge joint
58 Outboard stores pylon
59 AN/SLQ-101(V)-10 ECM pod
60 Martel TV-guidance data-link pod, maritime strike role
61 ARI18228 radar warning receiver and wide-band homing antenna fairing
62 Outer wing panel vortex generators
63 Inboard leading edge blowing duct
64 Outboard leading edge blowing duct
65 Starboard navigation light
66 Wing tip fairing
67 Starboard formation light
68 Aileron hydraulic actuator
69 Starboard 'blown' drooping aileron
70 Wing folded position
71 Trailing edge blowing air duct
72 AN/ALE-40 chaff/flare launcher, also beneath jet pipes or rear fuselage
73 Starboard blown flap
74 Wing fold hydraulic jack
75 UHF antenna
76 Anti-collision strobe light
77 Wing spar attachment fuselage main frames
78 Weapons bay roof structure
79 UHF standby antenna
80 Rear fuselage integral fuel tanks
81 Dorsal spine fairing
82 Cable ducting, fuel vent piping on starboard side
83 Fuel tank bay rear bulkhead
84 Radio and avionics equipment compartment
85 Flush HF antenna

86 HF variable capacitor
87 Rear equipment bay conditioning air intake
88 ILS localiser antenna
89 Fin spar attachment joints
90 Tailplane blowing air duct
91 Three-spar fin box construction
92 Tailplane control rod
93 All-moving tailplane hydraulic actuator
94 Moving tail plane sealing fairing
95 ARI 18228 RWR antenna fairing
96 Tailplane leading edge blowing air duct
97 Starboard tailplane
98 Tailplane flap
99 IFF antenna
100 Tailplane flap dual electric actuators
101 All-moving tailplane pivot mounting
102 Tailplane flap operating linkage
103 Tail navigation light
104 Position light
105 Rear ARI 18228 RWR antenna fairing
106 Tailplane flap rib construction
107 Port tailplane multi-spar and rib structure
108 Tailplane blown leading edge
109 Rudder rib construction

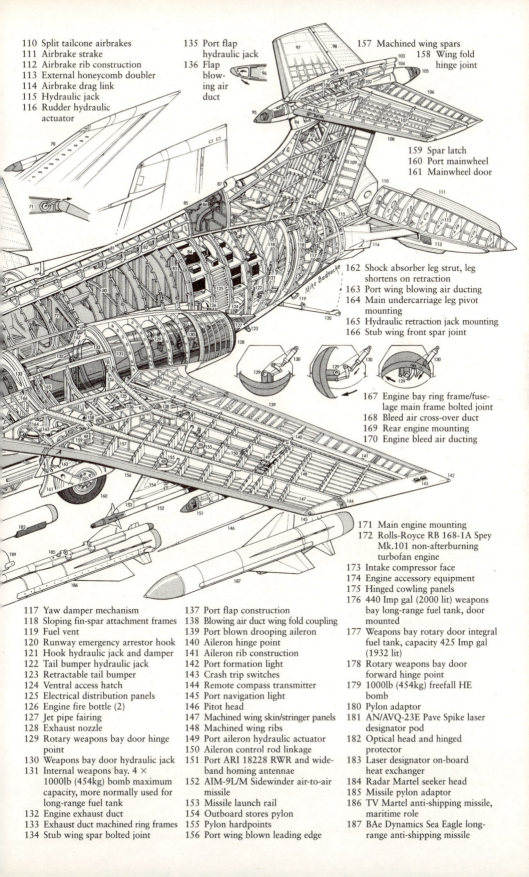

110 Split tailcone airbrakes
111 Airbrake strake
112 Airbrake rib construction
113 External honeycomb doubler
114 Airbrake drag link
115 Hydraulic jack
116 Rudder hydraulic actuator

135 Port flap hydraulic jack
136 Flap blowing air duct

157 Machined wing spars
158 Wing fold hinge joint

159 Spar latch
160 Port mainwheel
161 Mainwheel door

162 Shock absorber leg strut, leg shortens on retraction
163 Port wing blowing air ducting
164 Main undercarriage leg pivot mounting
165 Hydraulic retraction jack mounting
166 Stub wing front spar joint

167 Engine bay ring frame/fuselage main frame bolted joint
168 Bleed air cross-over duct
169 Rear engine mounting
170 Engine bleed air ducting

171 Main engine mounting
172 Rolls-Royce RB 168-1A Spey Mk.101 non-afterburning turbofan engine
173 Intake compressor face
174 Engine accessory equipment
175 Hinged cowling panels
176 440 Imp gal (2000 lit) weapons bay long-range fuel tank, door mounted
177 Weapons bay rotary door integral fuel tank, capacity 425 Imp gal (1932 lit)
178 Rotary weapons bay door forward hinge point
179 1000lb (454kg) freefall HE bomb
180 Pylon adaptor
181 AN/AVQ-23E Pave Spike laser designator pod
182 Optical head and hinged protector
183 Laser designator on-board heat exchanger
184 Radar Martel seeker head
185 Missile pylon adaptor
186 TV Martel anti-shipping missile, maritime role
187 BAe Dynamics Sea Eagle long-range anti-shipping missile

Mike Badrocke

117 Yaw damper mechanism
118 Sloping fin-spar attachment frames
119 Fuel vent
120 Runway emergency arrestor hook
121 Hook hydraulic jack and damper
122 Tail bumper hydraulic jack
123 Retractable tail bumper
124 Ventral access hatch
125 Electrical distribution panels
126 Engine fire bottle (2)
127 Jet pipe fairing
128 Exhaust nozzle
129 Rotary weapons bay door hinge point
130 Weapons bay door hydraulic jack
131 Internal weapons bay. 4 × 1000lb (454kg) bomb maximum capacity, more normally used for long-range fuel tank
132 Exhaust machined duct
133 Exhaust duct machined ring frames
134 Stub wing spar bolted joint

137 Port flap construction
138 Blowing air duct wing fold coupling
139 Port blown drooping aileron
140 Aileron hinge point
141 Aileron rib construction
142 Port formation light
143 Crash trip switches
144 Remote compass transmitter
145 Port navigation light
146 Pitot head
147 Machined wing skin/stringer panels
148 Machined wing ribs
149 Port aileron hydraulic actuator
150 Aileron control rod linkage
151 Port ARI 18228 RWR and wide-band homing antennae
152 AIM-9L/M Sidewinder air-to-air missile
153 Missile launch rail
154 Outboard stores pylon
155 Pylon hardpoints
156 Port wing blown leading edge

Appendix 2

McDonnell Douglas F-4K/F-4M
Phantom II cutaway

McDonnell Douglas F-4K/F-4M Phantom II

1 Glassfibre radome, hinged to starboard
2 Radar scanner
3 Scanner mounting and tracking mechanism
4 Radar mounting bulkhead
5 Nosewheel leg extending pneumatic bottles
6 AWG-11 (F-4M) radar equipment module, AWG-12 (F-4K)
7 Angle of attack transmitter
8 Air conditioning system ram-air heat exchanger intake
9 Temperature probe
10 Deck approach lights (F-4M)
11 Nosewheel leg door
12 Offset torque scissor links
13 Twin nosewheels, aft retracting
14 40in nosewheel leg extension for catapult launch (F-4M)
15 Hydraulic steering unit
16 Nosewheel leg strut
17 Nosewheel bay door
18 Avionics cooling system equipment, cabin conditioning to starboard
19 Cockpit front pressure bulkhead
20 Rudder pedals
21 Control column
22 Instrument panel shroud
23 Windscreen panels
24 Pilot's optical display

25 Disposition of internal fuel tanks, total system capacity 1545 Imp gal (7025 lit, 1855 US gal)

26 Flight refuelling probe, extended
27 Probe actuating arm
28 Forward cockpit canopy, upward hinging
29 Ejection seat face blind firing handle
30 Pilot's Martin-Baker Mk 7A ejection seat
31 Canopy external latch
32 Port side console panel with engine throttle levers
33 Front cockpit floor level
34 Kick-in boarding steps
35 Forward AM-7E Sparrow, air-to-air missile, semi-recessed carriage, F-4K and F-4M
36 Extended boarding ladder
37 Boundary layer splitter plate
38 Boundary layer diverter
39 Avionics equipment racks

40 Intake ramp boundary layer bleed-air perforations
41 Intake front ramp
42 Port engine air intake
43 Intake rear ramp
44 Liquid oxygen converter
45 Variable area intake ramp jack
46 Hydraulic reservoir
47 Intake ramp bleed-air spill louvres
48 Rear canopy external latches
49 Weapons system officer's (WSO) instrument console
50 Fixed centre arch and canopy hinge point
51 Rear cockpit canopy cover, upward hinging
52 Starboard external fuel tank
53 WSO's Martin-Baker ejection seat
54 Gyro unit
55 IFF antenna
56 Rear avionics equipment bay
57 Control cable runs
58 Boundary layer spill duct
59 Intake duct framing
60 No. 1 fuselage fuel tank
61 Engine bleed-air ducting to conditioning system and boundary layer control (BLC) system

62 Position of pressure refuelling connection to starboard
63 Catapult strop support fitting (F-4M)
64 Wing centre section carry-through structure
65 Front spar attachment fuselage main frame
66 Centre-section integral fuel tank
67 Wing panel centreline joint
68 Intake duct overpressure rotary spill duct
69 Engine compressor intake

70 Centre spar attachment fuselage main frame
71 No. 2 fuselage fuel tank
72 Fuel system feed and vent piping
73 Starboard main undercarriage pivot mounting
74 Starboard wing integral fuel tank
75 BLC air slot
76 Inboard 'blown' drooped leading edge flap segment

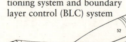

77 Outboard stores pylon mounting
78 Outer wing panel hinge joint
79 Wing fold hydraulic jack and downlock actuator
80 Outer wing panel BLC air ducting
81 Outboard 'blown' drooped leading edge flap segment
82 Starboard navigation light
83 Rear position light
84 Dihedral outer wing panel
85 Outer wing panel folded position
86 Wing tank vent jettison
87 Starboard drooping aileron, down position
88 Aileron flutter damper
89 Starboard spoiler panels, open
90 Spoiler hydraulic actuators

91 Fuel jettison and vent valves
92 Aileron hydraulic actuator
93 Starboard ventral airbrake panel
94 Inboard 'blown' flap, maximim deflection 60 deg
95 TACAN antenna
96 Upper fuselage light
97 Fuel tank access panels
98 No. 3 fuselage fuel tank
99 Emergency ram-air turbine
100 Turbine doors
101 Rolls-Royce Spey202 (F-4K), Spey 203 (F-4M), afterburning turbofan engine
102 Engine oil tank
103 Accessory equipment gearbox
104 Forward outboard engine mounting
105 Rear spar attachment fuselage main frame

106 Emergency generator
107 Engine bay heat shroud
108 No. 4 fuselage fuel tank
109 Auxiliary intake hydraulic actuator
110 Auxiliary intake door
111 No. 5 fuselage fuel tank
112 Fuel system piping
113 Dorsal access panels
114 Tank access panels
115 Immersed fuel pumps
116 No. 6 fuselage fuel tank
117 No. 7 fuselage fuel tank
118 Fuselage tailcone venting ram air intake
119 Tailcone joint frame
120 Three-spar fin torsion box structure
121 Fin ribs
122 Flush HF antenna (F-4M)
123 Anti-collision beacon
124 Stabiliser feel system pressure head
125 Pitot head
126 Forward hemisphere RWR antennae

127 Fin tip antenna fairing, Phantom FG.1 (F-4M) and FGR.2 (F-4K)
128 ILS localiser antenna
129 UHF antenna
130 Rear hemisphere RWR antennae
131 Rudder
132 Rudder horn balance

133 Honeycomb trailing edge structure
134 Fuel jettison
135 Tail navigation light
136 Hinged parachute door
137 Brake parachute housing
138 Tailplane honeycomb trailing edge structure
139 Port all-moving tailplane/stabilator
140 Stabilator mass-balance weight
141 Stabilator fixed leading edge slat

142 Multi-spar torsion box structure
143 Pivot sealing plate
144 Stabilator hinge mounting
145 Rudder hydraulic actuator
146 Stabilator centre-section and hinge arm
147 Stabilator hydraulic actuator
148 Fin spar mounting bulkheads
149 Heat-resistant titanium blast shield
150 Arrestor hook, lowered
151 Stabilator feel system balance mechanism
152 Feel system pneumatic bellows unit
153 Arrestor hook hydraulic jack and damper
154 Variable area afterburner nozzle shroud
155 Engine bay venting air exit louvres
156 Nozzle fueldraulic actuators
157 Afterburner duct
158 Hinged engine bay access doors
159 Aft semi-recessed missile carriage
160 Frazer-Nash missile carrier/cartridge ejector unit
161 Port 'blown' flap
162 Flap blowing slot

163 Flap emergency actuating pneumatic cylinder
164 Lateral autopilot servo
165 Wing rear spar
166 Ventral airbrake jack
167 Flap hydraulic jack
168 Port spoiler actuator
169 Aileron hydraulic actuator
170 Flutter damper
171 Port spoiler housing
172 Aileron rib structure
173 Port drooping aileron
174 Wing tank venting air jettison
175 Honeycomb trailing edge panels
176 Port dihedral outer wing panel
177 Fixed outboard trailing edge
178 Rear position light
179 Outer wing panel multi-spar structure
180 Port navigation light
181 Outboard 'blown' leading edge flap
182 Flap blowing slot
183 Engine bleed-air BLC ducting
184 Leading edge flap hydraulic jack
185 Wing fold hydraulic jack
186 Outer wing panel hinge joint
187 Port mainwheel
188 Wheel hub multi-plate disc brake
189 Mainwheel leg door
190 Port external fuel tank, capacity 308 Imp gal (1402 lit, 370 US gal)
191 Outboard tank pylon
192 Inboard 'blown' drooped leading edge flap segment
193 Flap hydraulic actuator
194 Flap blowing slot
195 Main undercarriage leg strut
196 Pylon mounting hardpoint
197 Mainwheel leg pivot mounting
198 Hydraulic retraction jack
199 Port ventral airbrake panel, open
200 Mainwheel leg uplock
201 Mainwheel bay and inboard wheel door
202 Hydraulic reservoir
203 Hydraulic accumulator
204 Intermediate wing spar
205 Port wing integral fuel tank
206 Skin support posts
207 Front spar
208 Inboard pylon mounting hardpoint
209 Fixed inboard leading edge panel
210 Leading edge BLC air duct
211 Inboard wing pylon
212 Missile launch rails
213 AIM-9G Sidewinder close-range air-to-air missile F-4K and F-4M
214 Fuselage centreline external fuel tank, capacity 500 Imp gal (2273 lit, 600 US gal)
215 AIM-9L Sidewinder, Phantom FG.1 and FGR.2
216 BAe Dynamics SkyFlash intermediate-range air-to-air missile, Phantom FG.l and FGR.2
217 SUU-23A cannon pod with 1200 20mm rounds, carried on aircraft centreline
218 M61-A Vulcan six-barrel rotary cannon

Picture
Acknowledgements

First section

Ark Royal, Merseyside: © Chambre Hardman Trust; *Ark Royal* in 1970: © Isaac Newton; Tupolev Tu-95 Bear: © Isaac Newton; Blackburn NA39 Buccaneer prototype: courtesy Terry Waddington

Captain John Roberts: courtesy John Roberts; Lt Cdr Carl Davis: courtesy Colin Walkinshaw; 809 NAS crest, 809 Squadron in front of Buccaneer, F-4 Phantom FG1: all © Crown Copyright/MoD. Reproduced with the permission of the Controller of her Majesty's Stationery Office; Lt Cdr Nick Kerr: courtesy Nick Kerr; *Ark Royal* in Florida: © Imperial War Museum

Royal Navy F-4, cartoon from squadron Line Book, Phantom firing AIM-7 Sparrow radar-guided missile (x4): all © Crown Copyright/ MoD. Reproduced with the permission of the Controller of her Majesty's Stationery Office; Buccaneer with 500lb bombs: courtesy Lionel Smith; Buccaneer flying low: courtesy Mike Lucas

Buccaneer over AFWR bombing range: courtesy Mike Lucas; 892 with Phantoms: courtesy Lionel Smith; F-4: © Crown Copyright/MoD. Reproduced with the permission of the Controller of her Majesty's Stationery Office; T-33 jet, reconnaissance pictures of Belize City (x2): all © Guatemalan Air Force Photo Archive

Guatemalan pilot in T-33, paratroop drop, F-51 Mustang squadron: all © Guatemalan Air Force Photo Archive; John Weymes: courtesy John Weymes

Second section

Haulover Creek: author's own; Stanley Field: courtesy Harry Norton; Airport Camp, Grenadier Guards, Land Rover: all © Grenadier Guards

Ark Royal and USS *Independence*, 892 cockpit, Fairey Gannet: all © Crown

Third section

Index

Acevado Castellanos, Azilcar 77
AIM-4 Falcon missiles 313
AIM-7 Sparrow missiles 109, 255
AIM-9 Sidewinder missiles 60,
    66, 157–8, 255
air speed records *see* records
air-to-air refuelling 249–51,
    283–5, 321–4
Air Warfare Instructors *see under*
    Royal Navy
Albion, HMS 13
Ambergris Caye, British
    Honduras 23, 309
America, USS 190
Anatina (Norwegian bulk-carrier):
    rescue 146–51
Anguilla (1969) 26
anti-submarine defence 126–9,
    130–31
Apollo XV moon landings 112,
    191
Arana Osorio, Carlos, President
    of Guatemala 28, 29, 84, 113,
    342
    enlists support for invasion of
        Belize 205, 215

meetings with Salvadoreans 82,
    151, 192, 232
and military action by Britain
    209, 218, 237, 238, 241,
    263, 264, 282, 295, 321,
    337
Arbenz, Jacobo, President of
    Guatemala 55, 112
Argentina 202–3
    invasion of Falkland Islands
        348, 349–50
Argos, island of 66
Ark Royal (flagship) 10, 45–6
Ark Royal, HMS (2) 46
Ark Royal, HMS (3) 33, 46, 86,
    94, 132, 168
    sinking of 11–12
Ark Royal, HMS (4) 12, 13,
    14–15, 31
    Air Direction Room (ADR)
        104–5, 106, 250, 314
    aircraft squadrons *see*
        Buccaneer, Fairey Gannet,
        Phantom *and* Sea King
        helicopter squadrons
    Aircraft Control Room Officer

Ark Royal, HMS (4) (*cont.*)
  (ACRO) 269
  Aircrew Refreshment Bar 124–5
  anti-submarine defence 126–9,
    130–31
  army unit (55 CBGLO) 134–5,
    229
  Badgers 4, 277, 278
  boilers 298–300
  catapults and arresting gear 45,
    93–5, 96, 103, 277, 278–81,
    314
  collision with Soviet destroyer
    6–7
  death of crewman 165–6
  defensive tactics 126–7
  dimensions 18
  displacement 18
  engine rooms 299
  and Exercise ROYAL KNIGHT
    87–8, 99–100, *see* Exercise
    ROYAL KNIGHT
  Flyco 92, 135, 275, 276, 277,
    281, *see also* Ford,
    Commander John
  food consumption 71
  fuel and fuel consumption 71,
    208, 217, 219, 220, 292–3,
    337
  Hands to Flying Stations
    (order) 268–71
  Hands to Recovery Stations
    (order) 291, 325–30
  leaving harbour ritual 164–5,
    208
  leisure activities 72–3
  Log 224
  mail 72
  'Mushroom Farm' 131–2,
    234–6, 261

  navigation aids 224–5, 281
  Nuclear Bomb Room 88
  and OCEAN SAFARI (1975)
    341
  Ops Room 105
  Petty Officers' mess 261–2
  Position and Intended
    Movement (PIM) 224
  refit (1969) 15–16, 45
  scrapped (1980) 343–4
  speeds 71, 190, 230, 243, 252,
    257, 274, 314, 325, 345
  Standing Orders 208–9
  Strike Planning Room 88–9
  Taranto Night celebrations
    170–71
  Wardroom 73–4
Auld, Lt Commander Andy 103,
  185–9
Australian Air Force, Royal:
  Dassault Mirage IIIOs 16
Australian Navy, Royal 16–17

Bahamas 141
Balniel, Lord 263–4, 267
Barber, Captain Robin (CBALS)
  134–5, 229, 234, 265, 269,
  270
Baymen 23, 24
BBC 258
bears 135
Beaulier, Lt Jerry 60
Beira Patrol 13
Belize *see* British Honduras
Belize City 21, 22, 67, 166–7, 173
  Airport Camp 68, 69–70, 74–5,
    78, 80, 140, 173, 214, 246,
    258, 306, 307

Battle of St George's Caye Day (1971) 77, 80, 81
British sorties over (1972) 271, 304–5, 307, 310, 336
Fort George Hotel 182, 305
Governor's House 21, 258
HMS *Phoebe*'s arrival 310, 337
HMS *Ulster*'s visit (1959) 37–8
Hurricane Edith 80–82
Hurricane Hattie 22, 79–80, 303
Lindbergh's visit (1927) 303
National Day celebrations (1971) 77, 80, 81
Palotti Convent 82
population 21
rioting at US draft treaty (1968) 83
Stanley Field airport 22, 70, 232, 238, 306
Belize River 23, 24, 70, 306
Belize Times 112, 166, 191, 192, 200, 303
Bell UH-1 Huey helicopters 51, 113
Belmopan, British Honduras 22, 26, 42, 182, 231, 258, 330, 337, 338, 340
RAF Harrier overflight (1975) 341–2
Benecke, Dr Walter 151
Bennett, Wiggy 235
Benque Viejo, British Honduras 39, 68, 76–7, 195, 213, 245–6
Bermuda 190, 243, 244, 349
HMS *Malabar* 248–9
Kindley Field US Navy Air Station 246, 248, 249
Bermuda Triangle 319–20
Berwick, HMS 213, 249

Besly, Lt Colonel Richard 205–6, 212, 215
Binbrook, RAF 254–5
Blackbeard (Edward Teach) 23
Blackburn Aircraft Ltd 35, 95–6
Blackburn Buccaneers 13, 34, 35–6, 44, 45, 95–6, 121, 180, 223, 273–4, 283, 289–90, 356–7
see also Buccaneer squadron
Blackburn Skua IIs 33
Bond, Brigadier Mark 200, 201
Borneo (1960s) 13
Boyd, Admiral Sir Denis 345
Boyd, Major John 59
Brawdy, RNAS 37
British Aerospace factory, Surrey 344
British Guiana 12, 84, 111
British Honduras
Battle of St George's Caye (1798) 24
Blue River Creek 174
and British–Guatemala treaty (1859) 40
governors *see* Paul, Sir John; Posnett, Sir Richard
grenade attack at Benque Viejo 76–7
Guatemalan claim on 20–21, 27, 39–41, 84, *see also under* Guatemala
history 22–5, 28, 40
independence 25, 26, 77, 81, 84, 101–2, 200, 338–9, 342–3
place names 79
population 21, 151
wildlife 69–70
see also Belize City

British Hovercraft Corporation 191

Browning, Commander Bob 318

Bruce, Major Ian 245–6

Buccaneer squadron (809 Naval Air Squadron) 30, 31, 36, 46, 65–6, 86–7, 88

air-to-air refuelling 250–51, 283–5, 321–4

on Exercise ROYAL KNIGHT 131–7, 138–9

launching from *Ark Royal* 275–81

at Lossiemouth 141–4, 155, 156, 195

mounts ship strikes against USS *Independence* 175–6

'Mushroom Farm' 131–2, 234–6, 261

and sortie to British Honduras 223–6, 235–6, 256–7, 261–2, 264–7, 269

see also Blackburn Buccaneers; Davis, Lt Commander Carl; Walkinshaw, Colin

Bulwark, HMS 13, 194

Burnaby, Rear-Admiral Sir William 23

Code 23–4

Buschmann, Lt Toby 175

BVR (Beyond Visual Range) 108, 109

Cairnryan, Scotland 343, 344

Caldow, Guardsman 173–4

Campbell, Captain Dennis 94

CAPs *see* Combat Air Patrols

Carlsen, Kapitän Kurt 145

Carnell, Lance Corporal 173–4

Carrier Borne Ground Liaison Section (CBALS) 135, *see* Barber, Captain Robin

Carrington, Peter 17, 210, 215

Cartwright, 2nd Lt 'Killer' 70

Carver, General Sir Michael 203

Castro, Fidel 55, 152

Catterick, RAF 221–2, 253

CBALS *see* Barber, Captain Robin

Cecil Field, Florida: Naval Air Squadrons 51–2, 63

Centaur, HMS 12, 13, 17, 216, 256, 344

Chandler, Lt John 149

Charles, Lt Nigel ('Toobs') 48–51, 179, 180–81, 256

Churchill, Winston 221, 230, 351

CIA 55, 111

Clemenceau (aircraft carrier) 155–6

Cobham, Sir Alan 249

Cold War 18, 108, 141, 153

Cole, Commander Mike 208, 219, 223, 251, 265, 269, 270, 299

Combat Air Patrols (CAPs) 66, 104, 115

Connolly, Colonel 77–8, 260

Consenza, Major Francisco 42, 67, 173, 295

Constellation, USS 60

Convair F-102 Delta Daggers (the 'Deuce') 153–4, 312–13, 315, 316–18

Cook, Captain James 23

Corkran, Major Richard 69

at Airport Camp 68–9, 70, 74–5, 195–6

and arrival of Guatemalan
airforce 78
informs Operation OPTIC
140–41, 151
opens lines of communications
with Mexicans 174
and threat from Guatemala
207–8, 213–15, 264
up-country with troops 307
Costa Rica 199–200, 202
Courageous, HMS 125–6
Crabb, Commander Lionel
'Buster' 34, 35
Crete, evacuation of (1941) 169
Cromwell, Oliver 198
Crusaders *see* Vought F-8
Crusaders
Cruz, Ramón Ernesto, President
of Honduras 215
Cuba 141
Fuerza Aerea Revolucionaria
(FAR) 152–3, 154, 266–7
relations with US 55, 83,
152–3, 154, 155
and sortie to British Honduras
252, 270, 285–6, 294–5,
310–11
Cuban Missile Crisis (1962) 91,
152
Cubana 877 (airliner) 152, 154
Culdrose, RNAS 145, 146, 147,
149, 150
Cunningham, Admiral Andrew
Browne (ABC) 168–9

Dahlgreen, USS 99
Daily Telegraph 242
Dainty, HMS 31

Dammeyer, Lt Commander
George 155, 237, 256–7, 283,
284–5
Davies, Lt Commander Brian 54
Davis, Lt Commander Carl
30–31, 34, 176, 346
as 'Boss' of 809 Squadron 31,
36–7, 63, 64–5, 72, 73, 74,
87, 89, 98, 99, 184–5
briefs for Exercise ROYAL
KNIGHT 132, 133, 134,
135
at Lossiemouth 141, 142–3,
155, 195, 290
plans sortie to British
Honduras 223–4, 225–6,
229, 235
pre-sortie preparations and
briefing 250, 261, 264, 265,
270–71, 272
successful sortie and return to
Ark Royal 275–80, 283–5,
286–90, 291, 297, 300–2,
304–7, 309, 310, 314–15,
316–18, 320–22, 325,
326–9, 331–5
Trophy awarded to (1972)
345–6
Defence Operational Planning
Staff (DOPS) 201, 202, 203,
204, 215
de Havilland, Geoffrey 34
De Havilland Sea Vixens 13, 63,
249, 256
de Klerk, Lt Anton 290–91
Devonport: Her Majesty's
Dockyard 11, 13, 18, 208
Dido, HMS 237, 252
Dissimilar Air Combat Training
(DACT) 158–9

Donaldson, Group Captain 'Teddy' 34
Dönitz, Admiral Karl 126, 127
Doolittle, Lt Jimmy 180
DOPS *see* Defence Operational Planning Staff
Dossett, Petty Officer 148–50
Douglas B-25s 180
Douglas B-26K Counter Invaders 112
Douglas C-47 transports 43, 68, 113, 178, 202
Douglas Skyraider AEW1s 115
Douglas-Home, Sir Alec 165, 215, 216, 218, 230
Doyle, Jimmy 235
Drake, Sir Francis: prayer 162
Drake, HMS 208
Dreyfus, John 111, 260
Dubois, Colonel, Guatemalan Consul 308
Duke, Neville 34
Dulles, Allen 55, 111
Du Poix, Vice-Admiral Vincent 99

Eagle, HMS 12, 13, 17, 45, 46, 76, 146, 176, 194–5, 216, 242, 298, 344
Eddy, Sergeant 214
ejection seats, Martin-Baker 50, 273
Elizabeth II, Queen 77, 165
Elizabeth, the Queen Mother 15
Ellis, Lt Commander John 108
Endurance, HMS 299
Essex, USS 108
European Common Market 210
Evening Standard 242

Excellent, HMS 58
Exercises
BERSATU PADU (1970) 16
BOBBIN PLUS (1968) 265
CADNAM (1972) 141, 203, 205, 206, 210, 242
CLAY (1971) 141
FETTLE (1970) 141
OCEAN SAFARI (1975) 341
OKEAN 70 (1970) 91–2
OPREDEX (Operations Readiness Exercise) 46, 66
ROYAL KNIGHT (1971) 87–9, 92, 99, 100, 103, 106, 110, 115, 131–9, 141
SUN PIRATE (1972) 203

FAA *see* Fleet Air Arm
Facio Segreda, Gonzalo 199–200
FAG *see* Fuerza Aerea Guatamalteca
Fairey Delta 2 jet 33–4
Fairey Gannet AEW3s 44, 114, 158–9
  icing hazards 99, 115–16
  radar 115, 121
Fairey Gannet squadron (849 Naval Air Squadron 'B' Flight) 46, 136, 247–8, 269
  casualties 63–4
  on Exercise ROYAL KNIGHT 114–16, 121–2, 137
Falklands War 346, 348, 349–52
FAR *see* Fuerza Aerea Revolucionaria
Faulkner, Dr Carl 182, 305
FCO *see* Foreign and Commonwealth Office

FDO *see* Flight Deck Officer
Fearless, HMS 195
Featherstone, Lt Ed 127–9, 131,
   166, 327, 332, 333–4
  Anatina rescue 146–7, 148–9,
   150
Fedoseyev, Anatol 112
Financial Times 242, 258
Fleet Air Arm (FAA) 12–13,
   31–2, 33, 136, 177, 344
  accident statistics 63–4, 94
  aircraft 44–5, *see* Blackburn
   Buccaneers; Fairey Gannet
   AEW3s; Phantom F-4s; Sea
   King helicopters
Flight Deck Officer (FDO) 4, 5
Flight International (magazine)
   190–91
Flight Refuelling Ltd 249
Flint, Commander Lawrence 52
Florida Air National Guard
   (FANG) 153–4
Flying Enterprise, MV 145
Foch (aircraft carrier) 155–6
Fonseca, Rafael 231
'Football War' (1969) 41, 151
Ford, Commander John (Wings)
   65, 92, 177, 185
  and death of crewman 166
  and landings and launches
   92–3, 96, 99, 119, 329, 330
  sortie planning 219, 223, 269
  and US aircraft 179–80
Foreign and Commonwealth
   Office (FCO) 26, 27, 77,
   101–2, 140, 193, 199, 200,
   201, 205, 207, 209–10, 218,
   237, 242–3, 263, 267,
Forsmann, Fregattenkapitän
   Heinz 143, 144

Fort Lee, Virginia 311–12
Fort Southwick, Portsdown Hill
   194, 216
France
  aircraft carriers 155–6
  British air combat manoeuvres
   156–8
Frenz, Lt Ian 65, 236
Froggatt, Lt John 157, 158, 255,
   256
Fuergas Armadas Rebeldes (FAR)
   68
Fuerza Aerea Guatemalteca
   (FAG) (Guatemalan Air Force)
   41–3, 67–8, 78, 202, 252,
   295
  Cessna A-37 Alpha attack jets
   195
  Cessna A-37B Dragonflies 68,
   252
  Douglas C-47 transports 43,
   68, 113, 178, 202
  IAI 201 Arava tactical
   transports 340
  La Aurora Air Force base 41,
   42, 43, 68, 78, 195
  Lockheed T-33 jet 67, 252
  Mustang F-51s 41, 42, 43, 67,
   84, 173, 195, 202, 239, 240,
   252, 254, 255–6, 295
Fuerza Aerea Revolucionaria
   (FAR) (Cuban Air Force)
   152–3, 154, 266–7
Furse, Lt Commander Chris
   299–300

Gander, Newfoundland 244, 293,
   294, 337

Gannets *see* Fairey Gannet AEW3s

General Dynamics F-111 bombers 31, 32

George VI, King 14

German Naval Air Arm: Starfighters 141–4

Gibson, David 303, 304

Gilbert, John, MP 267

Godber, Joseph 193–4

Goddard, Lt Commander Pete 54

Goebbels, Joseph 221

Goodhart, Lt Commander Nick 94–5

Gorshkov, Admiral Sergei 91, 92

Granger-Holcombe, Lt Jerry 48, 50–52, 62, 103, 185–9

Green, Colonel Duncan 340, 341

Grenada 37

Grenadier Guards 69, 205–6, 210, 212, 227, 232, 233, 246, 306, 307

see also Inkerman Company

Gretton, Lt Mike 126, 224, 264, 281

Gretton, Commander Peter 126

Grumman A-6 Intruders 125, 346

Grumman C-1 Trader 179–80

Grumman E-2 Hawkeye AEW aircraft 125

Guatemala

Air Force *see* Fuerza Aerea Guatemalteca

American involvement in 54–5, 77–8, 83, 84, 111–13, 205, 215, 260, 340

Army 42, 202, 209, 211, 233, 239–41, 252, 260–61, 282, 295, 296, 336, 339–40

Batallón de Fuerzas Especiales (Parachute Corps) 112–13

British Consul *see* Weymes, John

claim on British Honduras 20–21, 27, 39–41, 67–8, 70, 77, 84, 101–2, 232–3

earthquake (1976) 342

and El Salvador 41–2, 82, 151, 166–7, 192, 200, 201

endemic violence 20, 27, 28–9, 78, 183

invasion threat (1971–2) 75, 140–41, 192–4, 199–200, 202–3, 207, 210, 215–16, 218–19, 239–41, 258, 259, 282, 340–41

Navy 202, 340

Treaty with Britain (1859) 40

see also Arana Osorio, President; Guatemala City

Guatemala City 20, 27, 29, 78

British Consulate shooting (1971) 27–8

Gueterbock, Commander Willie 73–4, 217, 330

Hallett, Lt Commander 146, 147–8, 149–50

Hardy, Wing Commander Ron 253

Harriers *see* Hawker Harrier GR1s

Hattieville, British Honduras 79, 80

Hawker Harrier GR1s/GR1As 222, 243, 294, 330, 341–2, 343

Hawkesworth, Sir Gerald 214

Hawkesworth, Lt John 70, 173–4, 214

Healey, Denis 13
Heath, Edward 16, 210, 339, 351
helicopters
  Bell UH-1 Huey 51, 113
  Kamov KA-25 Hormone 89
  Westland Dragonfly 145
  Westland Puma HC1 341
  Westland Sea King HAS1 44,
    64, 128–9, 189, *see also* Sea
    King squadron
  Westland Wasp HAS1 253, 337
  Westland Wessex HAS1 45,
    119, 136, 145, 269, 275,
    280, 314, 331
Hercules *see* Lockheed C-130
  Hercules
Hermes, HMS 12, 17, 216, 265,
  344, 351
Herrera, Dr Guillermo de Tejada
  84, 101–2, 172–3, 199–200,
  215–16, 218, 259, 260
Hervey-Bruce, 2nd Lt Sir Jamie
  70
High Wycombe: RAF Strike
  Command 89
Hill, Lt Dave 48, 49–52, 62, 185
Hill-Norton, Sir Peter, Admiral of
  the Fleet 76, 200, 201–4, 210,
  254, 263–4, 338
Hird, Allan 207
Hockley, Sub-Lt Freddie 33
Holman, Lt Commander Guy
  63–4, 114–15, 116, 247–8,
  249, 251
Homestead Air Force Base,
  Florida: Alert Detachment
  153–4, 257, 270, 287, 311–12
Honduras 41, 215
Hooker, Pilot Officer 221, 222,
  253, 337

Hornet, USS 180
Howard of Effingham, Lord 10
Hunt, Geoff 57
Hunt, Sir Rex 350
Hurricane Edith (1971) 80–82
Hurricane Hattie (1961) 22,
  79–80, 303
Hussey, Lt Commander Charles
  97, 98
Hyde, Evan X 303

Illustrious, HMS 94, 95, 170,
  345
Inca empire 22, 23
Indefatigable, HMS 33
Independence, USS 86, 99, 104,
  125, 137, 139, 171, 175, 176,
  179–81
'Indonesian Confrontation'
  (1960s) 13, 222, 255, 256
Inkerman Company 68–70, 78,
  80, 173–4, 195–6, 202,
  207–8, 210, 212, 213–15, 307
Intrepid, HMS 194
Intrepid, USS 86, 99–100, 103,
  120, 125, 139
Invincible, HMS 344–5, 351
Irving, Commander Robert 253,
  285
Israel 91, 340
  air force 177
Ixabel, Guatemala 210–11, 233,
  282, 296

Jamaica 12, 204, 213, 226–7,
  293

Joint Air Reconnaissance
  Intelligence Centre,
  Huntingdonshire (JARIC) 107
Joint Intelligence Committee
  (JIC): reports on Guatemalan
  threat to Belize 75, 76, 140,
  202, 210, 238, 252
Jooste, Captain Matin 290–91
Jupiter, HMS 99

Karel Doorman, Hr.Ms 155
Kerr, Lt Commander Nick 72, 73,
  127, 158, 177, 346
  and aborted flight 3–7
  care for his men 184, 185
  on Independence 180, 181
  intercepts Soviet bomber 108,
    109
  and Phantom accidents 62, 63,
    188
  squadron excluded from sortie
    252, 254, 256, 334
Key West, Florida: Naval Air
  Squadrons 257, 270, 287
Khrushchev, Nikita 34–5, 91
Kinch, Lt Gerry 4, 5
Kinch, Lt Commander Mike 224,
  225, 226, 229, 251
Korean War 47, 60, 75, 182, 254,
  305
Kuylen, Harry 354

Laugerud, General Kjell 29, 78,
  295, 342
Leach, Admiral Sir Henry 350–51
Leach, Captain John 351

Leuchars, RAF 103–4, 346
Lewis, Lt Pete 63, 155, 237, 257,
  283, 291, 313–14
Lewty, Harry 199
Lindbergh, Charles 303
Lithgow, Lt Commander Mike
  33
Lockheed C-130 Hercules 227–8,
  232, 253, 337, 341
Lockheed F-104 Starfighters 64,
  141–4
Logan, Lt Commander Mike 120,
  125
London, HMS 237, 252
Lord, Lt Dick 58–9, 60, 61–2, 64,
  143, 176, 194–5
Lossiemouth: Royal Naval Air
  Squadrons 30, 37, 58, 59, 65,
  141, 143–4, 155, 195, 265,
  290
Lucas, Lt Mike 65
  and arrestor wire failure 93, 95,
    96, 97, 98
  at Atlantic Fleet Weapons
    Range 65–6
  and Exercise ROYAL KNIGHT
    88, 89, 133, 134
  at Lossiemouth 195
  a night sortie 116–19, 121–5
  preparations and briefing for
    British Honduras sortie 229,
    250, 264, 265–7, 270, 272,
    274
  successful sortie and return to
    Ark Royal 279, 280–81, 284,
    285, 286, 291, 295, 298,
    301, 304–5, 306, 309, 311,
    316, 317, 320, 323–4, 327,
    331, 332
  wins place with US Navy 346

Lyneham, RAF 227, 253

Macdonald, Lt Commander
  Dougal 48–51, 61–2, 102–8,
  156–9, 179, 255
McDonnell Douglas A-4G
  Skyhawks 16–17
McDonnell Douglas F-4
  Phantoms 44, 45, 48, 49–50,
  52–3, 57, 125, 190, 360–61
  in combat against Mustangs
  252, 254, 255–6
  see also Phantom squadron;
  United States Navy
McDonnell Douglas Phantom
  FG1s 103
McDonnell Douglas Phantom
  YF4H-1 52–3
McIntyre, Lt Commander (USN)
  Dan 59
Maclean, Commander Ewan
  292–3, 298–300, 336–7
Maclean, Lt Neil ('Carbo') 65,
  236, 284, 291, 313–14
Mahratta, HMS 85
Malabar, HMS 248–9
Malaysia 16
Malta 12, 76, 168
Marham, RAF 243
Marshall, Lt Commander Pete
  ('Little F') 92, 98, 99, 119,
  135, 137, 274, 326
Martinez, Tulio 308
Maund, Captain Loben E. 168
Mayan civilization 22–3, 26, 42,
  246, 339, 340
Melbourne, HMAS 16–17
Meredith, Lt Paul 333

Merlin, HMS 24
Mexico 40, 174, 215, 258
Miami Center, Florida 257, 270,
  286–7, 311, 315
Ministry of Defence (MoD)
  and Ark Royal 17, 71, 76
  and British Honduras/
  Guatemalan hostilities 76,
  84, 140–41, 200, 202, 210,
  215, 222, see also Operation
  OPTIC
  and deployment of Ark Royal
  216, 229–30, 242–3, 263–4,
  267
  funds HMS Invincible 344
Miramar, California: Naval Air
  Squadrons 54, 56, 57–61, 108
MoD see Ministry of Defence
Moir, Flight Lt Jim 244, 245
Monroe, James, US President 112
Moody, Lt Commander Dick
  108–9
Morgan, Squadron Leader John
  244–5, 293, 337–8
Muzorewa, Bishop Abel 210

Nación, La (Guatemalan
  newspaper) 77
Nash, Lt (USN) John 60
NATO 17, 76, 92, 107, 109, 204,
  341
  Atlantic Striking Fleet 17, 45,
  87–8, 89, 99, 104
  see also Exercise ROYAL
  KNIGHT
Naval Air Squadrons
  705 145
  764 58, 60, 61–2

Naval Air Squadrons (*cont.*)
800 'B' Flight 249–50
803 33, 65
809 *see* Buccaneer squadron
824 *see* Sea King helicopter
squadron
826 146
849 'B' Flight *see* Fairey Gannet
squadron
887 33
892 *see* Phantom squadron
Nelson, Lord Horatio 164, 169,
248
Newport News, USS 99
Nicaragua 22, 111
Hurricane Edith (1971) 81
see also Somoza Debayle,
Anastasio
Nicholl, Group Captain John
254–5
Noord Brabant, HNLMS 99
Northern Ireland 210, 221
Norway/Norwegians 85, 86, 88,
105, 132, 134–5
see also Anatina
Nott, John 350

O'Brien, Wing Commander Terry
245
Ocelot, HMS (submarine) 120,
125
O'Grady, Lt Harry (the 'D') 50,
51, 52, 104–5, 106, 314, 325
Olmeda, RFA 217, 219, 220, 292
Operation JUDGEMENT (1940)
169–70
Operation MUSKETEER (1956)
92

Operation OPTIC (1971) 141,
151, 202, 203–4, 222, 233,
238
Operation SKY-BURNER (1961)
53
Operation (Operación) TIKAL
(1971) 43, 67
Operation TOP FLIGHT (1959)
52
Oriskany, USS 176
O'Rourke, Captain Gerald G.
139
Osborne, David 27, 28

Palermo, Roberto 282
Panama Canal Zone 54–5, 112
Park, Lt Steve 65, 86–7, 88,
116–17, 118, 119
on Exercise ROYAL KNIGHT
133, 134
at Lossiemouth 141, 143, 195
piano-playing on Taranto Night
170
and planning and preparation
for sortie 225, 226, 229,
250, 264–7, 270
on sortie to Belize City 272,
276–80, 283–7, 291, 294,
297, 298, 301, 306–7,
309–11, 314–15, 316, 317,
320–22, 325, 327, 329,
331–4
Trophy presented to 345–6
Paul, Sir John 26, 41, 42, 81,
140, 182–3, 192
Pederson, Lt Commander Dan 60
Petén, El (Guatemala) 42, 78, 84,
173, 178, 233, 260, 282

Phantom squadron (892 Naval
  Air Squadron) 46, 48, 53–4,
  93, 104, 109, 136, 175–6, 269
  aborted night-launch 3–6
  air combat manoeuvring 48–52,
    156–9
  Combat Air Patrols 66, 102–3,
    104–8
  crash landing on *Ark Royal*
    185–90
  deployed aboard USS
    Independence 179, 180–81
  and Exercise ROYAL KNIGHT
    115, 116, 137
  see also Kerr, Lt Commander
    Nick; McDonnell Douglas
    F-4 Phantoms
Phoebe, HMS 213, 237, 249,
  252, 253, 271, 285–6, 310,
  337
Pitcairn Island 12
Pollock, Admiral Sir Michael 76,
  150, 203, 204
Poptun army base, Guatemala 78,
  178, 199, 210, 211, 233, 260,
  261, 282
Portsmouth 58, 139, 150, 164,
  216
Posnett, Jonathan 213, 227
Posnett, Sir Richard 26–7
  appointed head of FCO West
    Indies department 26, 140
  and Argentinian invasion of
    Falklands (1982) 349, 350
  becomes governor of British
    Honduras 163–4, 165, 167
  and Guatemalan intentions
    193–4
  in Jamaica 213, 226–7
  and possible Guatemalan

invasion 227, 230, 231–2,
    258
  and sortie over Belize 259, 330,
    335
  and subsequent Guatemalan
    threat 338–42, 349–50
Posnett, Shirley 163–4, 213,
  226–7, 230, 339
Potemkin, Battleship 91
Price, George 26, 77, 80, 81, 83,
  101, 113, 200, 231–2, 258–9
Prince of Wales, HMS 351
Prospero (satellite) 191
Pueblo Viejo, British Honduras
  39
Puerto Barrios, Guatemala
  239–40, 295, 340
Puerto Modesto Méndez, British
  Honduras 68, 239
Punta Gorda, British Honduras
  39, 67, 239, 240, 341

Queen Elizabeth II (QE2) 16

radar systems
  AN/APS-20 115, 121
  AN/AWG-11 pulse-Doppler 48,
    53, 108, 255
  Blue Jacket ARI 5880 Doppler
    266
  Blue Parrot 122, 134, 274, 320,
    322
  EKCO AW391 128
  Type 965 14, 314
radar warning receivers 122, 133,
  294

RAF *see* Royal Air Force
Raleigh, Sir Walter 45
Ramsund naval base, Norway
   132
Randfontein, MS 291
RAS *see* Replenishment at Sea
records
  air-speed 33–4, 53
  altitude 52, 142
  closed circuit (speed) 52
  Los Angeles to New York 52
  Transatlantic 53–4
Regent, RFA 217, 337
Renown, HMS 11, 168
Replenishment at Sea (RAS)
  71–2, 217
Reporter, The (British Honduras
  newspaper) 77, 112, 191
Repulse, HMS 351
RFAs *see* Royal Fleet Auxiliaries
Rhodesia 13, 210
Richthofen, Manfred von 61
Roberts, Captain John 11, 12, 46,
  65, 71, 85, 86, 343
  appointed Captain of *Ark
    Royal* 13–14, 15, 17–18
  congratulates 824 Squadron on
    Anatina rescue 150
  and death of crewman 165, 166
  and Exercise ROYAL KNIGHT
    100, 118, 137, 138
  leads warships through English
    Channel 139
  leaves Portsmouth 164
  ordered to proceed with all
    despatch to British Honduras
    217–18, 219–20
  pays respects to former *Ark
    Royal* 168
  plans and prepares for sortie

    223–4, 229–30, 234, 237,
    243, 249, 250, 254, 269,
    271
  and successful sortie and return
    of aircraft 281, 285, 298–9,
    314, 325, 326, 330, 331–3,
    334, 335, 336
Roome, Commodore David 213,
  249
Rouvillois, Lt de Vasseau 155,
  156
Royal Air Force (RAF) 13, 31–2,
  33, 103
  1 (Fighter) Squadron (Hawker
    Harriers) 222, 243, 294,
    330, 341–2
  10 Squadron 228, 246
  36 Squadron 227–8
  39 Squadron 293
  43 Squadron 103, 104
  48 Squadron 221–2, 337
  53 Squadron 341
  Air Support Command 227–8,
    294
  Buccaneers 204
  English Electric Canberra PR7s
    and PR9s 203, 244–5, 252,
    293
  English Electric Lightning
    fighters 16, 103–4, 254
  Handley Page Victor K2 tankers
    204, 243
  No. 1417 Flight (Harriers) 343
  RAF Regiment 221, 237, 253,
    337
  Vickers Valiant V-bombers 303
Royal Fleet Auxiliaries (RFAs) 71,
  72, 217, 337
ROYAL KNIGHT *see under*
  Exercises

Royal Navy 15, 76, 341
  Air Warfare Instructors 54, 57–8, 59, 60, 61–2, 92
  exchange programme with US Navy 54, 58, 108–9
  Search and Rescue (SAR) squadrons *see* Sea King squadron; Westland Wessex helicopters
Russell, Corporal Stuart 348

Sagastume, Francisco 39–40
St George's Caye, Battle of (1798) 24
Salthorses 74, 224
Salvador, El/Salvadoreans 22, 82, 151, 166–7, 192, 200, 201
  'Football War' 41, 151
  see also Sánchez, General Fidel
SAMS *see* sea-to-air missiles
Sánchez, General Fidel, President of El Salvador 82, 102, 172, 218, 232–3, 260
Sanderson, Sandy 235–6
Sandry, Ron 235, 261–2
SAR *see* Search and Rescue squadrons
Saratoga, USS 179
School of the Americas 54, 55, 112
Schuette, Lt Commander (USN) Dick 247, 249, 251
Scott, Commander David 112, 163
Sea Harrier FRS1s (SHARS) 344, 345, 351
Sea King helicopter squadron

(824 Naval Air Squadron) 44–5, 46, 72, 93, 136, 137, 170, 208, 247
  Anatina rescue 146–51
  anti-submarine exercises 66, 127–9, 130–31
  see also Naval Air Squadron, 826; Westland Sea King HAS1 helicopters
sea-to-air missiles (SAMS) 7, 153, 184, 311
Sea Vixens *see* De Havilland Sea Vixens
Search and Rescue (SAR) squadrons *see* Sea King squadron; Westland Wessex helicopters
Serapis, HMS 85
Severomorsk, Russia 89–90
SHARS *see* Sea Harrier FRS1s
Sheffield, HMS 40
Shipster, Colonel John 75, 207–8, 231, 245, 246, 261, 337
Shobdon airfield, Herefordshire 30, 346
Singapore 16
Skipjack, USS 130, 131
Smith, Wing Commander E. J. E. 222
Smith, Aircraft Artificer Lionel ('Smudge') 188–9
Somoza Debayle, Anastasio, President of Nicaragua 205, 209, 215–16
sonar, Plessey Type 195 128, 131
South African Air Force (SAAF) 195, 290–91
Soviet Air Force
  Ilyushin Il-38 reconnaissance aircraft 107–8

Soviet Air Force (*cont.*)
  Kamov KA-25 Hormone
    helicopters 89
  MiG-15 fighter jet 133
  MiG-17 fighter jets 154, 176
  MiG-21 fighter jets 133, 152–3
  Myasishchev M-4 Bison-A
    bombers 106–8
  Tupolev Tu-95 Bears 74, 108,
    109, 154, 267
Soviet Naval Aviation Regiments
  108
Soviet Navy 74, 88, 89, 91–2
  and Exercise ROYAL KNIGHT
    87–8, 92
  'Kashin' guided-missile
    destroyers 89, 92
  'Kotlin' guided-missile
    destroyers 6–7, 89
  'Kresta' cruisers 89
  'Moskva' guided-missile
    cruisers 89
  nuclear submarines 89–90
  'Sverdlov' class cruisers 34–5,
    89
Soviet Union 85, 112, 132–3
  and Cuba 152, 153, 154, 267
  see also Soviet Air Force; Soviet
    Navy
Soyuz 11
spaceship 112
Spotswood, Air Chief Marshal Sir
  Denis 203
Stalin, Joseph 91
Starfighters *see* Lockheed F-104
  Starfighters
Steel Vendor, SS 146
submarines
  American nuclear 130–31
  British nuclear 120

British 'O' boats 120, 125
German U-boats 12, 85, 125–7,
  130, 168
Soviet nuclear 89–90
Suez Crisis (1956) 91, 92
Supermarine Scimitars 13,
  249–50
Supermarine Seafires 33, 47
Supermarine Sea Otter biplane
  flying boats 145
Supermarine Spitfire PR Mk XIX
  255
Supermarine Swift Mk 4 33
Suthers, Lt Commander E. R. 145

Tanganyika/Tanzania 12, 13
Taranto, attack on (1940)
  169–70, 345
Taylor, David, Junior Ordnance
  Mechanic 165–6
Tecunuman GC 651 (patrol boat)
  202
Texas: Hurrican Edith (1971)
  82
Thatcher, Margaret 350, 351–2
Tiger Cat missiles 221–2, 252,
  253, 337
Tikal, Guatemala 42–3, 173, 246,
  339
Times, The 242
Tjerk Hiddes, HNLMS 99
Toledo District, British Honduras
  39, 239, 240, 295, 321, 340,
Topgun programme 58, 60
Trabanino, Dr Guillermo 82
Treacher, Admiral John 46–7, 66,
  194, 216, 346
Trowbridge, HMS 37

Tutankhamun exhibition, British
Museum 228
Twiss, Lt Commander Peter 33–4

U-boats, German 12, 85, 125–7,
130, 168
Ubico, Jorge, President of
Guatemala 112
Ulster, HMS 37–8
United Fruit Company 55
United States Air Force (USAF)
152
159th Fighter Interception
Squadron 153–4, 312–13,
315, 316–18
604th Air Commando
Squadron 68
605th Air Commando
Squadron 112
Southern Air Defense network
(Air Defense Interception
Zone-ADIZ) 151, 152,
153–4, 223, 257, 267,
287–8, 311
United States Navy
Atlantic Fleet Weapons Ranges
(AFWR) 46–7, 65–6, 208
and British instructors at
Miramar 54, 56, 57–61
F-4 Phantom squadrons 59–61,
154, 176, 179
F-8 Crusaders 57, 60, 176
nuclear-powered supercarriers
190, 344
pilots in Vietnam 54, 55–6, 58,
59–60, 109, 176, 177, 184
and ROYAL KNIGHT exercise
99, 109–10, 130–31, 137

and Topgun programme 58, 60
VF-121 (Replacement Air
Group-RAG) 54, 58, 59,176
see also Independence, USS;
Intrepid, USS
United States of America
and Cuba 55, 83, 152–3, 154,
155
and Guatemala/British
Honduras conflict 54–5,
77–8, 83, 84, 111–13, 205,
215, 230, 237, 260, 318,
340
see also United States Air Force;
United States Navy; Vietnam
War

Vanguard, HMS 35
Vassaux Martínez, Leonel 29
Venezuela 40, 84, 199
VF-102 'Diamondbacks' 137,
175, 179
VF-121 (Replacement Air
Group-RAG) 54, 58, 59,
176
VF-33 'Tarsiers' 137, 175, 176
VF-805 (Australian Navy
squadron) 16
Vickers Shipbuilding 344
Vickers VC10s 227–8, 246
Victorious, HMS 12, 13, 17, 31,
216, 344
Victory, HMS 164
VID (Visual Identification) 109
Vieques Island 66
Vietnam War 17, 75, 76, 155
US pilots 54, 55–6, 58, 59–60,
68, 109, 176, 177, 184

Vought A-7 Corsair II attack jets 125, 175
Vought F-4U Corsairs 41
Vought F-8 Crusaders 57, 60, 156–8, 176

Walker, Captain Frederick ('Jonny') 130
Walkinshaw, Lt Commander Colin ('Boots') 37–8, 176
as Buccaneer pilot 65, 66, 88, 89, 346
deck landing with arrestor wire failure 93, 95–9
night sorties 116–19, 121–5
flying practice over Scotland 195
preparation for sortie to British Honduras 225, 226, 236–7, 250–51, 257, 264, 265, 270, 272, 274
successful sortie and return to Ark Royal 279, 280–81, 285, 286, 289–90, 295, 301–2, 304, 306, 309, 317, 318, 320, 322–4, 327, 331, 332
Trophy awarded to (1972) 345–6
Ward, Lt 'Sharkey' 102–3, 104, 105–8
Warsaw Pact 18, 88, 109, 141
Webster, Bethuel M. 83
Westland Dragonfly helicopters 145
Westland Puma HC1 helicopters 341
see also Sea King helicopter squadron

Westland Sea King HAS1 helicopters 44, 64, 128–9, 189
Westland Wasp HAS1 helicopter 253, 337
Westland Wessex HAS1 search-and-rescue helicopters 45, 119, 136, 145, 269, 275, 280, 314, 331
Weymes, John
appointed British Consul in Guatemala 19–20
arrival in Guatemala City 27
assessments of Guatemalan–British Honduras situation 41, 77–8, 192–3, 260, 338
and British Consulate shooting (1971) 27–8, 29, 30
and JIC report 75
meetings with Guatemalan Ministers 101–2, 172–3, 218, 232–3
and relations with US 111, 204–5, 260
and report of Ark Royal's deployment 232, 237–8, 321
Wheeler, Dennis 177–8, 210–11, 233, 282, 296
Wheeler, Luisa 177–8, 282
Wilson, Harold/Wilson government 12, 13, 15, 19
Wings see Ford, Commander John
Wittering, RAF 222, 243, 294, 330, 341, 342
World War, Second
Arctic Convoys 85
Fleet Air Arm successes 33, 168–70

sinking of *Prince of Wales* and *Repulse* 351

U-boats 12, 85, 125–7, 130, 168

US Navy kill ratio 60

see also Ark Royal (3)

Wyman, Lt Commander Richard 176

Wyton, RAF 244, 293

Yamamoto, Admiral Isoroku 170

Ydígoras Fuentes, Miguel, President of Guatemala 39, 83

Yeager, Chuck 142

Yeovilton, RNAS 92, 158, 170

Zulu, HMS 341